COUNTRY WALKS NEAR WASHINGTON

Revised and expanded 2nd edition

by Alan Fisher

RAMBLER BOOKS

Baltimore

COUNTRY WALKS NEAR WASHINGTON, 2nd edition

by Alan Fisher
Maps and photographs by the author

Rambler Books
1430 Park Avenue
Baltimore, MD 21217

Excerpts from "Life on the C. & O. Canal: 1859," edited by Ella E.
Clarke, *Maryland Historical Magazine,* June, 1960, reprinted by
permission of the Maryland Historical Society.

ISBN 0-9614963-5-5

CONTENTS

MAP 1 — Orientation

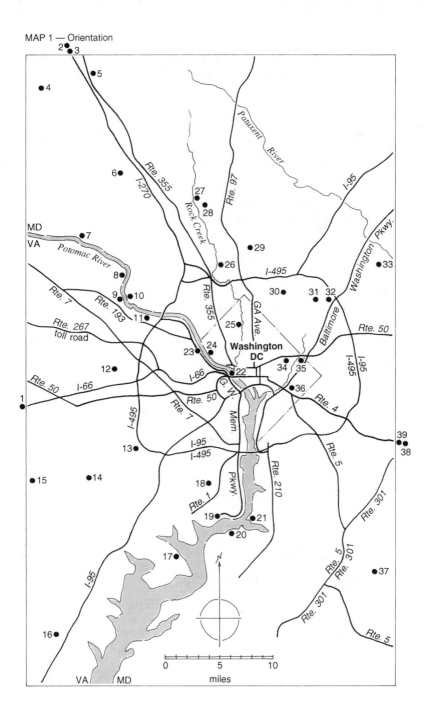

MAP 2 — Hike-bike trails in schematic outline

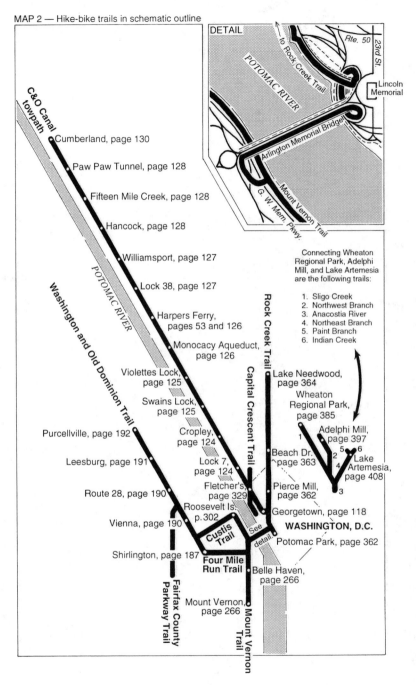

DETAIL

to Rock Creek Trail

Rte. 50

23rd St.

POTOMAC RIVER

Lincoln Memorial

Arlington Memorial Bridge

G. W. Mem. Pkwy.

Mount Vernon Trail

C&O Canal towpath

Cumberland, page 130

Paw Paw Tunnel, page 128

Fifteen Mile Creek, page 128

Hancock, page 128

Williamsport, page 127

Lock 38, page 127

POTOMAC RIVER

Harpers Ferry, pages 53 and 126

Monocacy Aqueduct, page 126

Washington and Old Dominion Trail

Violettes Lock, page 125

Swains Lock, page 125

Purcellville, page 192

Cropley, page 124

Leesburg, page 191

Lock 7, page 124

Route 28, page 190

Fletcher's, page 329

Roosevelt Is, p.302

Vienna, page 190

Custis Trail

Shirlington, page 187

Four Mile Run Trail

Fairfax County Parkway Trail

Mount Vernon, page 266

Rock Creek Trail

Capital Crescent Trail

Connecting Wheaton Regional Park, Adelphi Mill, and Lake Artemesia are the following trails:

1. Sligo Creek
2. Northwest Branch
3. Anacostia River
4. Northeast Branch
5. Paint Branch
6. Indian Creek

Lake Needwood, page 364

Wheaton Regional Park, page 385

Adelphi Mill, page 397

Beach Dr. page 363

Lake Artemesia, page 408

Pierce Mill, page 362

Georgetown, page 118

WASHINGTON, D.C.

Potomac Park, page 362

See detail

Belle Haven, page 266

Mount Vernon Trail

7

PREFACE

THIS BOOK IS FOR PEOPLE who want an outing in a country setting without wasting half the day getting there and back. If you live in the Greater Washington region, the excursions described here are close at hand. The various parks, wildlife refuges, and trail networks cover the gamut of the region's Piedmont and Coastal Plain landscapes, and the routes pass historic houses, mill sites, and ruins along the way. Successive visits during different seasons — to see the changing foliage, views, flowers, and birds — provide an added dimension of enjoyment.

Each chapter of this book includes a brief introduction, a discussion of the area's natural or social history (which you may want to read ahead of time), detailed directions, and one or more maps. Because readers will be driving from different places to reach the sites described here, the automobile directions outline different avenues of approach. Necessarily, there is much repetition, so focus on the set of directions that applies to you and skip the others.

Many of the places described here can be reached by Metrobus or Metrorail, and accordingly there are directions that note the Metro route number or line and the appropriate stop. Telephone (202) 637-7000 for current information on schedules, routes, and connections from your starting point. You may also want to inquire about procedures for taking your bicycle on Metrorail trains.

The following people helped me with this book by reviewing the text for different chapters and making suggestions: Scott Aker, Ted Alexander, Jeannie Allen, Nell P. Baldacchino, Lynn Batdorf, Susan A. Borchardt, Patrick J. Bright, Nancy Brown, Chris Bryce, Kate Bucco, Michael Dwyer, Carolyn J. Gamble, Gordon V. Gay, Dorothy Kengla, Sara Lustbader, Cynthia Salter-Stith, Robert E. Sauer, Jr., Marsha B. Starkey, Richard Steacy, Donald K. Steiner, Russ Whitlock, and Paul Willis. Many, many thanks.

Alan Fisher

COMFORT AND SAFETY

PLEASE READ THIS. It is customary, in guidebooks such as this, to include a catalog of cautions about possible nuisances and hazards. Such matters do not make for scintillating reading, but really, I think that you will be glad to have read here about a few potential problems — so that you can avoid them — rather than learn about them through uncomfortable (or even dangerous) experience. Please also read the introductory matter for each excursion before you go.

For walkers, wear sturdy shoes that you do not mind getting muddy or wet. In winter wear hiking boots that will keep your feet dry and that will provide traction in snow. I usually carry a small knapsack containing a snack, a water bottle or juice carton, insect repellent, and an extra layer of clothing, such as a sweater or rain parka. Bicyclists should wear helmets, yield to pedestrians and horseback riders, pass with care, and keep their speed to a moderate, safe pace.

Some of the trails described in this book traverse steep slopes and follow the tops of cliffs, so control your children closely. Bear in mind that terrain presenting only moderate difficulty when dry can be treacherous when wet, snowy, or icy. And unlike some people I have encountered, don't undertake impromptu rock climbing, only to find yourself perched on a ledge and unable to extricate yourself.

The Potomac Gorge at Great Falls and downstream to Washington requires a warning all of its own. Every year several people die in the vicinity of Great Falls, sometimes by falling off the cliffs but more often by wading or swimming and being swept away by the current. Don't go in the water. The surface may look placid, but the current is, in fact, powerful and turbulent.

During winter, drownings sometimes occur when people fall through the ice after venturing out onto frozen ponds and rivers. I am sure that you have heard this before; everyone has. And yet each winter a few more people die in this manner. So stay off the ice. And tell your kids.

Other sound advice that is ignored with puzzling regularity concerns lightning. If you are in an exposed or elevated area and a storm approaches, return to your car immediately. That is the safest place to be. And if a storm arrives before you get back to your car, hunker down in a low spot. Don't worry about getting wet or feeling stupid as you crouch there with the rain pouring down. Clearly it is better to get

10

wet and yet be safe than to try to stay dry by huddling under an isolated tree or pavilion or some other target for lightning.

Every year the newspapers carry stories about people who pick up a squirrel, a raccoon, or some other animal and get bitten. They then have to undergo a series of painful anti-rabies shots. Don't be one of these people; don't handle *any* wild animals. In somewhat the same vein, remember that poisonous copperhead snakes occur in the Washington region. Be careful where you place your feet and hands, particularly in rocky areas.

Where the trails described here follow roads briefly, walk well off the road on the shoulder to minimize the risk of being hit by a car, and use caution, especially at dusk or after dark, where the routes cross roads. Studies show that in poor light conditions, motorists typically cannot even see pedestrians in time to stop, so your safety depends entirely on you.

Finally, one of the pitfalls of writing guidebooks is that conditions change. Just because this book recommends something does not mean that you should forge ahead in the face of obvious difficulties, hazards, or prohibitions.

In sum, use good judgment and common sense to evaluate the particular circumstances that you find. Heed local regulations and signs, and do not undertake any unusual risks.

TICKS AND LYME DISEASE

I WANT TO DRAW particular attention to the problem presented by ticks, which unlike the hazards discussed in the preceding section, are not so obviously a matter of common sense. Some kinds of ticks (chiefly deer ticks, which actually feed on a wide variety of animals) may carry Lyme disease. If not diagnosed and treated, Lyme disease can cause long-term arthritis and neurological and cardiac disorders. Standard advice about ticks includes how to avoid being bitten, what to do if you are bitten, and what you should know about the symptoms of Lyme disease.

Ticks can be a problem from spring through fall, and especially from May through September, when nymphal deer ticks are so tiny (smaller than the head of a pin) that they are not easily noticed. Although adult ticks are active late into the fall, early in spring, and even during mild weather in winter, they are bigger and so are more easily seen and removed before they bite. It is also thought that adult deer ticks are more discriminating than nymphs and are less likely to bite humans.

The main way to pick up ticks is by walking through tall grass and weeds or along narrow paths where you brush against foliage as you pass. One simple precaution is to walk in the middle of paths. Other standard precautions, especially if bushwhacking or using narrow, overgrown paths, is to wear long pants and a long-sleeved shirt and to tuck your pant legs into your socks and your shirt into your pants in order to keep the ticks on the outside, where you can pick them off. And wear a hat to keep ticks out of your hair. Spray your clothes — especially your shoes, socks, and pant legs — with insect repellent containing DEET (N-diethylmetatoluamide) applied according to the directions on the label. If your clothes are light colored, it will be easier to spot any ticks that may get on you. Inspect yourself from time to time during your outing (have a friend examine your back) and when you return to your car. And when you get home, wash your clothes, take a shower, and examine your body closely. Pay particular attention to your lower legs, the backs of your knees, your groin, back, neck, and armpits, which are all places where ticks are known to bite.

If you are bitten by a tick, remove it immediately. Grasp the tick with sharp-pointed tweezers, as near to your skin as possible, and gently but firmly pull straight out until the tick comes off, then blot the bite with alcohol. Make a note of when and where you were bitten. Some authorities recommend saving the tick in a small jar of alcohol for later identification. If the tick's mouthparts break off and remain in your skin, see your doctor immediately so that he or she can remove them. Research suggests that ticks must feed for two days in order to transmit Lyme disease, so there is a fairly large margin of safety if you remove ticks promptly.

The main early symptom of Lyme disease is a circular, slowly expanding red rash, often with a clear center, that may appear a few days or as long as two months after being bitten by an infected tick. Not all patients, however, will have this rash. Flu-like symptoms are also common, perhaps accompanied by headache, swollen glands, a stiff neck, fever, muscle aches, nausea, and possibly general malaise.

If you develop any of these symptoms after being bitten by a tick, or after visiting an area where you may have been bitten, see your doctor promptly and mention the possibility of Lyme disease so that one of a variety of blood tests can be conducted. Don't put it off, because Lyme disease in its early stages is easily treated with some antibiotics. If allowed to progress untreated, the early symptoms of Lyme disease usually disappear but may eventually be followed by such disorders as swelling in the knees, hips, and ankles, arthritis, severe headaches, numbness, tingling in the extremities, and other problems that are so varied that diagnosis can be difficult.

In short, although the risk of getting Lyme disease is small, there is no good reason not to take simple precautions that will help you to avoid tick bites in the first place or — if you are bitten by an infected tick — that will help you to minimize the consequences.

1

MANASSAS NATIONAL BATTLEFIELD

First Manassas Trail
Second Manassas Trail

Walking and ski touring. This chapter outlines two different excursions, one focusing on the Civil War's first battle of Manassas (or Bull Run) in July 1861 and the other on the second battle of Manassas in August 1862. The **First Manassas Trail**, shown by the bold line on **Map 3** on page 35, is about 5 miles long (8 kilometers). The **Second Manassas Trail**, shown on **Map 4** on page 39, is 7 miles long (11.3 kilometers). The park not only commemorates the two battles but also provides a rare opportunity to walk through an agricultural landscape of hay fields, hedgerows, rail fences, woodlots, and isolated farmhouses that preserve, more or less, the appearance of the mid-nineteenth century.

As an introduction to the first battle of Manassas, I recommend that you start with a short circuit around the plateau at Henry Hill, as shown by the dotted loop on Map 3. Then take the First Manassas Trail, which leads from Henry Hill through rolling countryside to the Stone Bridge at Bull Run and eventually returns via the route of Union advance across Matthews Hill and Buck Hill.

The Second Manassas Trail also starts at Henry Hill and from there loops north through rolling farmland and forest where the battle was fought over a three-day period. In part the trail follows the unfinished railroad where Stonewall Jackson's troops repeatedly repulsed Union attacks. A spur trail leads to Battery Heights, where the battle began. Continue through fields and woods to Chinn Ridge, across which Union troops eventually retreated before making a successful stand at Sudley Road and Henry Hill.

Manassas National Battlefield Park is open daily from dawn until dusk. An admission fee is charged. Dogs must be leashed. The visitor center is open daily, except Christmas, from 8:30

A.M. to 5 P.M. The battlefield is managed by the National Park Service; telephone (703) 361-1339.

FIRST BATTLE OF MANASSAS

ON APRIL 15, 1861, six weeks after his inauguration and two days after the bombardment and surrender of Fort Sumter, President Abraham Lincoln issued a proclamation calling on the states that remained in the Union to contribute 75,000 militia to suppress the rebellion in the deep South. Four months earlier, South Carolina had seceded from the Union, followed in January and February by Georgia and the Gulf states. Exulting over the fall of Fort Sumter and outraged at the Federal summons for troops to quash the South's bid for independence, the states of Virginia, North Carolina, Tennessee, and Arkansas ultimately joined the Confederacy during April and May. At the beginning of June 1861, the Southern capital was moved from Montgomery, Alabama to Richmond in order to cement the loyalty of Virginians and to place the Confederate government where it could respond quickly to the expected Union advance from Washington.

To the Northern populace, the secession of the South and the location of the Southern capital only a hundred miles from Washington seemed a gesture of contempt for the Union's military capacity. According to John G. Nicolay, private secretary to President Lincoln, the North "saw rebellion enthroned in the capital of Virginia; it saw a numerous Union army gathered at Washington; the newspapers raised the cry of 'On to Richmond'; and the popular heart beat in quick and well-nigh unanimous response to the slogan." As time passed without conspicuous Federal action, there arose in the North a "morbid sensitiveness and a bitterness of impatience which seemed almost beyond endurance." Affected by this atmosphere and prodded by Lincoln, the Union army undertook what proved to be a grossly premature thrust southward.

The Union plan was developed by Brigadier General Irvin Mc-Dowell, the Federal commander in northeastern Virginia, where late in May the Union had seized and fortified positions at Alexandria and Arlington. McDowell proposed to attack thirty miles to his immediate front against Manassas. Located on the Orange and Alexandria Railroad connecting Alexandria and Richmond, the town was of strategic importance because of the junction there with the Manassas Gap Railroad, which ran west to the Shenandoah Valley. Defending

Manassas was a Confederate force thought to number about 25,000 men. They were commanded by Brigadier General Pierre G. T. Beauregard, who had directed the siege and capture of Fort Sumter. In the Shenandoah Valley an additional 10,000 Confederates were led by Brigadier General Joseph E. Johnston. To discourage Johnston from reinforcing Beauregard, a Union force at Harpers Ferry was supposed to move south through the Shenandoah Valley at the same time that McDowell made his advance from Alexandria. Presented to President Lincoln, his military advisers, and the Cabinet on June 29, McDowell's plan was approved and the southward march set for July 9.

The plan was opposed by Lieutenant General Winfield Scott, U.S. commander during the Mexican War, and at the outbreak of the Civil War, the North's highest-ranking officer. Scott favored a much more methodical approach to the war and a much longer period of preparation before taking the offensive. He doubted the capacity of the states' militias. Many militia field officers were unequal to their responsibilities, and the militia troops were unused to hard marching and lacked adequate training. In addition, the militia volunteers had enlisted for only ninety days, and their terms would begin to expire in July. Even the militia uniforms announced that the troops were amateurs. In some cases the men wore fancy-dress parade outfits, such as kilts or blazers. Michigan regiments came to the war dressed as lumberjacks. Some Northern units wore gray. Scott proposed to send this motley militia army home. He wanted to assemble, train, and equip a Federal army enlisted for long terms, and then slowly strangle the South by blockade and by conquest of the Mississippi Valley. In broad outline, this is the course that ultimately was taken during 1862 and '63, after Scott's scheduled retirement was pushed forward slightly because of public dissatisfaction with his drawn-out war plan.

McDowell's column of 34,000 men began its march a week late on July 16. On the same day a Union force fought a skirmish near Charles Town in the Shenandoah Valley, but Johnston was not deterred from sending most of his men to Manassas, where it was known that the main Union attack would come. After all, for weeks McDowell's objective had been common knowledge in Washington, where the campaign was discussed with high expectations in the daily newspapers.

The railroad from Alexandria to Manassas had been wrecked by the Confederates, so the Union Army had to march. As the head of the column began to move, the wagon train for supplies at the rear was still being organized. The advance was slow. "They stopped every moment to pick blackberries or get water," McDowell later wrote of his green troops:

[T]hey would not keep in the ranks, order as much as you pleased; when they came where water was fresh, they would pour the old water out of their canteens, and fill them with fresh water; they were not used to denying themselves much; they were not used to journeys on foot.

The first day's march was so exhausting that on the second day the column advanced only six miles. The troops paused to ransack the towns through which they passed, and some men burdened themselves with stolen household items and tools. Aware that their undisciplined troops could not cope with surprise, the commanders warily felt their way forward, with the result that the Union army required three days, and in some cases four, to reach Centreville, three miles northeast of the sluggish stream of Bull Run, behind which Beauregard had placed the Confederate army.

The Confederate line at Bull Run was eight miles long. Most of the troops were massed on the right for a contemplated flanking attack against the Federals. At the center were various fords on roads that ran south across the river from Centreville to Manassas. The Confederate left was posted at the stone bridge on the Warrenton Turnpike (present-day Route 29, or the Lee Highway).

Like the Union army, the Southern troops were high on enthusiasm but short on training, experience, and discipline. They too wore a confusing variety of uniforms. Only the higher-ranking officers were professional soldiers. In addition to Beauregard, there was General Johnston, who had arrived from the Shenandoah Valley by train with some of his men, including a brigade of Virginia troops under Brigadier General Thomas J. Jackson. The rest of Johnston's Shenandoah army, except for a fragment left to fool the Federals at Charles Town, was on its way to Manassas.

In response to the disposition of the Southern troops, McDowell decided to send the bulk of the Union army — 14,000 men — on a wide circle upstream, across Bull Run, and then down from the northwest behind the Confederates. While the Federal army assembled at Centreville on July 19 and 20, Union engineers scouted the river above the enemy's positions and eventually discovered an undefended ford on the Sudley - Manassas Road (now simply Sudley Road) three miles upstream from the end of the Confederate line at the stone bridge. To pin the Southerners where they were while the flanking move was in progress, McDowell directed other units to feign attack opposite the stone bridge and at the fords farther downstream. More than 10,000 Federal troops would remain as a reserve near Centreville, including some units that insisted on being sent to the rear because their ninety-day enlistments had expired.

The Union troops began to move out for battle at 2 A.M. on July 21. One soldier said that in the dark the long column resembled "a bristling monster lifting himself by a slow, wavy motion." Again the march was delayed by confusion and at dawn the Federals were still north of Bull Run. Reaching the Sudley Road ford, the leading troops began to cross at 9 A.M. (two hours late), and the rear units did not cross for yet another two hours. Again there were delays as troops paused to drink and fill their canteens.

Meanwhile, the Union's diversionary attack at the stone bridge had begun with a slow, unconvincing cannonade that went on and on but led to no assault. A Confederate captain of engineers, scouting to the north, saw the sunlight glinting off the muskets and artillery of the Federal column that was approaching the Sudley Road ford. He signaled to the Confederate commander at the stone bridge — a West Point graduate named Colonel Nathan "Shanks" Evans. Evans investigated and confirmed the report, passed on the news to headquarters, and without waiting for orders moved most of his force of 1,100 men to a position behind the brow of Matthews Hill, north of the intersection of the Warrenton Turnpike and Sudley - Manassas Road. When the Union vanguard came into view, Evans' improvised line of defenders opened fire.

Despite their ponderous pace, the Union forces had achieved a large measure of surprise. Nearly half the Federal army was coming in from the north on the weak Confederate left flank. But the attack itself, perhaps unavoidably, never rose above the character of the march that had brought the Northerners to Bull Run. The assault developed in a halting, jerking fashion that lacked cohesion and resolute impetus. The leading Union troops, consisting of four regiments led by Colonel Ambrose E. Burnside, moved slowly from a marching column to a fighting line two ranks deep. Then the men lay down and began shooting ineffectively. Only after two batteries from the regular U.S. Army arrived and began firing from the hilltop (where a row of guns can be seen today) did the Confederates start to suffer significant casualties. Still, the Southerners repulsed two attacks by Burnside's men, who became so disorganized that they withdrew and took no further part in the fighting.

In response to an appeal from Evans, Confederate reinforcements led by Brigadier General Barnard Bee joined the defenders. To the north of the Henry House, a Confederate battery of four fieldpieces began shelling the Federals at a distance. For nearly an hour — from about 11 A.M. until shortly before noon — the Confederates held the line north of the Warrenton Turnpike.

Gradually, however, McDowell pushed more Union troops to the front. He got word to the units facing the stone bridge to cross and join the attack. In response, a brigade led by Brigadier General William T. Sherman waded across Bull Run half a mile above the bridge. As Union pressure increased, the Confederates fell back, pausing for a brief stand behind the stone house at the crossroads. Then they ran southward across the Warrenton Turnpike, splashed across Youngs Branch, and scrambled up Henry Hill, where they formed a new line of defense reinforced by fresh troops. To the north the Federal forces, far superior in numbers, could be seen regrouping for a fresh attack.

By now the Confederate commanders realized that the main Union attack was developing in the vicinity of the Warrenton Turnpike, and Beauregard ordered reserves and newly-arrived troops to go there. Johnston, who after coming from the Shenandoah Valley was the senior Confederate general at Manassas, abruptly rode off with his staff toward Henry Hill, announcing his conviction that "the battle is there." Beauregard soon followed, after ordering the redeployment of troops from the Confederate right, where the planned counterstroke against Centreville had never seriously gotten underway.

The battle was becoming a struggle for Henry Hill. Arriving shortly before Johnston and Beauregard, T. J. Jackson positioned his Confederate infantry and field artillery in a long line well back from the crest of the hill (as shown by the row of guns seen today east of the visitor center). From this position his batteries could rake the broad plateau that forms the top of the hill and his infantry could wait safely in the wooded hollow to the rear.

After a brief lull during the early afternoon, the long Federal battle line began to close in on Henry Hill. About 10,000 Union soldiers pressed the attack against about 6,000 Confederates, but at least half the defenders were disorganized and in retreat. Beauregard had arrived and was trying to rally the men who drifted to the rear. Johnston was farther back attempting to get more units up to the stopgap line. Colonel Francis S. Bartow shouted to his two regiments, "General Beauregard says you must hold this position — Georgians, I appeal to you to hold on!" But then Bartow was killed, and the Confederate troops began to give ground. Only Jackson's brigade at the southeastern edge of the plateau and Wade Hampton's South Carolinians in front of the Robinson House remained in formation. General Barnard Bee, whose field officers had all been hit and whose troops were in disarray, rode to Jackson and reported, "General, they are beating us back." Not visibly perturbed, Jackson is said to have replied, "Sir, we will give them the bayonet." Returning to some of his men in the vicinity of the Robinson House, Bee pointed with his sword to Jackson's artillery. "Look," he shouted. "There is Jackson standing like a stone wall! Rally behind the Virginians!" Soon afterwards, Bee was knocked from his horse, mortally wounded, but at least some of his units reformed along the edge of the woods.

By 2 P.M., the open plateau at the top of Henry Hill had become a no man's land, although some of the Confederates still hid behind the Henry House. The Federals occupied the valley north of the hill, and the Confederates held the southern edge of the plateau and the woods behind, where many troops found time to reorganize. The Confederate right extended to Youngs Branch east of the Robinson House and the left reached almost to Sudley Road south of the Henry House. Describing the battle, John Nicolay wrote:

> Reduced by losses, McDowell's numbers were now little, if any, superior to the enemy . . . a total of fourteen regiments, but several of which were already seriously demoralized; these were massed in sheltered situations in the valley along the turnpike and Young's Branch, mainly west of the intersection of the roads. All the advantages of position during the day had been with McDowell; now they were suddenly turned against him by the very success he had gained. The enemy was on the height, he at the foot of the hill. The enemy needed only to defend a stationary line; he must move forward under prepared fire. They were concealed in chosen positions; he must mount into open view. His men had been under arms since midnight — most of them had made a march of ten miles through the sweltering July heat. They were flushed with victory, but also lulled thereby into the false security of thinking their work accomplished, when in reality its sternest effort was merely about to begin.

There was another pause in the battle while Union batteries were brought to the northern crest of the hill opposite Jackson's guns. At a distance of 300 to 600 yards, an artillery duel began while most of the opposing infantry waited to the rear. As the gunnery continued, a Union battery south of the Henry House was approached on one side by soldiers arrayed in a line of battle. By some accounts they wore blue. The battery's commanding officer held his fire, perhaps thinking that the advancing troops were Northerners coming to support him, but in fact they were Virginians, who leveled their guns and fired from close range. A Federal officer who observed the action from a distance wrote that "it seemed as though every man and horse of the battery just laid right down and died right off." The unmanned artillery became the object of a series of thrusts and counterattacks as each side tried to gain control of the guns.

Again and again Federal infantry advanced up the hill and across the plateau, only to be driven back by artillery and musket fire. As before, the Union effort was spasmodic; each assault was made by a separate regiment at a different point and different time. One Union brigade advanced southward around the Confederate's right flank, but did not attack across Youngs Branch. Burnside's soldiers, who had seen action in the morning, remained well to the rear, and most of the Federal troops posted east of the stone bridge stayed there, despite orders from McDowell to join the battle. Perhaps worst of all, many Union regiments, having made a single charge and been repulsed, "went to pieces like the adjournment of a mass meeting," in the words of Nicolay.

By mid-afternoon the Union attack was losing momentum and the Confederates began to get the upper hand. Reinforcements ordered north from the far end of the Confederate line finally began to reach the scene of fighting, and other units sent by train from the Shenandoah Valley appeared in unexpected places. Federal troops advancing west of Sudley Road against the Confederate left flank were decimated by fresh concentrations of Southerners. "Them Yankees are just marchin' up and bein' shot to hell," a Confederate officer told a friend who had just arrived at the front. Still farther to the west at Chinn Ridge, a Confederate force appeared behind the Union flank and sent it running. At Henry Hill Beauregard organized a counterattack that overran the Federal artillery. Suddenly Union morale collapsed and the Northern forces, without orders, began a general retreat. One Federal captain stated that "at four o'clock, on the 21st, there were more than twelve thousand volunteers on the battle-field of Bull Run who had entirely lost their regimental organization. They could not longer be handled as troops, for the officers and men were not together. Men and officers mingled together promiscuously."

Although disorganized, the retreat was not a first the rout that it later became. The Union forces simply started moving toward the rear, out of range of the enemy's guns. Most of the troops crossed Bull Run by the way they had come. A regiment of regular infantry from the U.S. Army served as a rear guard, and reserves were brought forward to the stone bridge to prevent Confederate pursuit. In any case, the Southern army also was so exhausted and disorganized that orders for pursuit could not be carried out effectively. Confederate President Jefferson Davis, who arrived at Manassas toward the end of the afternoon, saw so many shattered units streaming to the rear that he thought the battle had been lost. There was also apprehension among the Confederate commanders that the Union army was planning another attack with the forces that had remained at Centreville, and so troops were sent back to defend the lower fords.

Gradually, however, the Union retreat got out of hand, generating its own confusion and alarm. The traffic in supply wagons, guns, and caissons began to spill over onto the fields bordering the road. The

mass of vehicles was swelled by the carriages of numerous civilian onlookers who had come out from Washington. The jam of troops and wagons became worse when the men who had retreated north to the Sudley Road ford finally rejoined the column on the Warrenton Turnpike. At Cub Run, a tributary of Bull Run, the road suddenly was blocked when a supply wagon crossing the narrow bridge was hit by Confederate artillery fire. Dismay and then panic gripped the civilians, teamsters, and soldiers who crowded the road and adjoining fields. Now and then shells fired from distant guns fell into the crowd. From the rear cries were heard that Confederate cavalry was coming. Soldiers discarded their muskets, cartridge boxes, packs, and canteens in order to walk faster and at times to run. Teamsters cut loose their horses, scrambled onto their backs, and galloped off. Although the bridge at Cub Run eventually was cleared, artillery, wagons, and even ambulances carrying the wounded to hospitals were left abandoned on the road, obstructing the progress of those drivers, such as photographer Mathew Brady, who remained with their vehicles. The formless retreat continued all night, during which one soldier told Brady that he was not going to stop until he reached New York.

McDowell telegraphed to Washington that he had been driven from the field and hoped to hold Centreville with his reserves until the retreating column could get behind the town, but a little later he had to report, "The larger part of the men are a confused mob, entirely demor-alized. It was the opinion of all the commanders that no stand could be made this side of the Potomac."

In Washington the defeat created alarm that the capital itself might be attacked. During the course of the following day, the general aware-ness of defeat, disgrace, and possible disaster was reinforced by the dismaying appearance of the soldiers themselves, who shuffled into the city alone or in irregular squads for hour after hour, continuing into the night and the next day. Walt Whitman, who stood with other onlookers watching in silence, wrote that by noon on the 22nd, Washington was "all over motley with these defeated soldiers — queer-looking objects, strange eyes and faces, drench'd (the steady rain drizzles on all day) and fearfully worn, hungry, haggard, blister'd in the feet." Many of the lookers-on, Whitman said, were Southern sympathizers, grinning triumphantly, while other Washington residents set out food and drink for the broken troops, many of whom simply flopped down on the sidewalks and in vacant lots and fell asleep in the rain.

Steps were taken to secure the city. Each regiment was assigned a location where it could receive rations and reassemble. Fresh troops were rushed to Washington. There was, however, no effort by the Confederates to march on the Federal capital. General Johnston wrote to Jefferson Davis that his army was in disarray: "Everybody, officer &

private, seemed to think that he had fulfilled all his obligations to country — & that before attending to any further call of duty, it was his privilege to look after his friends, procure trophies, or amuse himself. It was several days after you left us before the regiments who really fought could be reassembled." Johnston later enlarged on this theme:

> The Confederate army was more disorganized by victory than that of the United States by defeat. The Southern volunteers believed that the objects of the war had been accomplished by their victory, and that they had achieved all that their country required of them. Many, therefore, in ignorance of their military obligations, left the army, not to return. Some hastened home to exhibit the trophies picked up on the field; others left their regiments without ceremony to attend to wounded friends, frequently accompanying them to hospitals in distant towns. Such were the reports of general and staff officers and railroad officials. Exaggerated ideas of victory prevailing among our troops cost us more men than the Federal army lost by defeat.

The actual casualties suffered by the two armies were not far out of balance: 481 Federals killed and 1,124 wounded, compared to 387 Confederate dead and 1,582 wounded. The South also took about 1,500 prisoners. In concrete terms, the Confederacy's chief gain from the victory was the immense haul of Federal arms abandoned on the battlefield and route of retreat. Beauregard reported capturing twenty-eight artillery pieces, thirty-seven caissons, and huge quantities of muskets, ammunition, blankets, haversacks, and hospital supplies. Also, mercantile firms in Europe concluded that the Confederacy was here to stay and that the self-proclaimed nation offered a credit-worthy opportunity for the sale of essential goods, including munitions, which before the war were supplied to Southern states by the North.

As days and weeks passed, however, the battle quickly lost whatever military significance it might have had. Except for pickets posted toward Washington, the Confederates advanced no farther than Fairfax Courthouse. At Washington the Union army dug in, and during the following months it regained and surpassed its earlier strength.

The illusion on both sides that the war would be a brief affair began to dissipate. Even prior to the defeat at Bull Run, the Federal government had begun to prepare for a protracted war of attrition based on the Union's overwhelming advantage in naval strength, manpower, war industry, and finance. Meeting in emergency session at the beginning of July, Congress approved Lincoln's executive directive for the formation of a Federal army of 500,000 men enlisted for three-year terms, a national expenditure of $250 million, and a strengthened navy to enforce a blockade of Southern ports. For more than half a year after Bull Run the Virginia front was quiet, except for a few incidents, while the North again prepared to march on Richmond.

≈   ≈   ≈   ≈

SECOND BATTLE OF MANASSAS

LATE IN JUNE 1862, Major General John Pope, who had fought well against the Confederates in the Mississippi Valley, was brought east to command various Federal contingents that had been floundering in northern Virginia. Pope's newly-organized force of 50,000 men was termed the Army of Virginia, and in July he set about concentrating his army at Sperryville, south of the Rappahannock River and not far east of the Blue Ridge.

The Confederate army that had crushed the Union advance at Manassas the year before had been pulled south for the defense of Richmond. Even Stonewall Jackson's force of 17,000 men — which throughout the spring had bedeviled the Federals in the Shenandoah Valley and had stymied Union advance from the north — was withdrawn to Richmond late in June to help repel the attack from the east by the Union Army of the Potomac.

Led by Major General George B. McClellan, the Army of the Potomac had landed at Newport News late in March, and during April and May had advanced slowly west toward Richmond along the peninsula between the James and York rivers. On May 31 the Confederate commander, General Joseph E. Johnston, had been severely wounded, and the next day General Robert E. Lee was placed at the head of the army that he was to lead for the rest of the war. During the last week of June, Lee repeatedly attacked and repulsed the Federals near Richmond. After the Army of the Potomac drew back to a fortified camp on the James River, McClellan's peninsular campaign stagnated. He proposed to transfer his army to the south bank of the James and to attack Richmond through the back door at Petersburg (as Ulysses S. Grant did two years later), but the plan was rejected by Henry Halleck, the Union general in chief.

Meanwhile, Lee decided that the time had come to "suppress" (as he put it) Pope's growing army in northern Virginia. He wanted to smash the Federals before Pope and McClellan joined forces, a combination that would total roughly 140,000 Union troops against Lee's army of about 75,000 men in the vicinity of Richmond. Earlier Lee had pointedly renamed the troops under his command the Army of *Northern* Virginia, and in mid-July, when the Army of the Potomac was still only twenty-five miles from Richmond, Lee started moving detachments of his army north. On July 13 he sent Stonewall Jackson with 12,000 men to Gordonsville, a key railroad junction that was closer to Pope's army than to Richmond. Both Pope and McClellan

learned of the move but did nothing. Encouraged by Federal inaction, Lee sent still more troops to join Jackson, who attacked Pope's forward units near Culpeper on August 9. The inconclusive battle again disclosed to the Union leadership that a large part of Lee's army had left Richmond, but McClellan, who was in a position to strike, remained inert. Lee rightly judged that McClellan's campaign was moribund. In fact, on August 3 McClellan had been ordered to ship his army north to ports on the Potomac River, where his troops could march west to join Pope. By mid-August, Lee had reduced the Confederate forces at Richmond to fewer than 25,000 men opposing 90,000 Federals. Then Lee himself left Richmond to take charge of the large Confederate army, now about 55,000 strong, that was in the field. The suppression of John Pope was under way.

In numbers, if not in spirit or experience, Pope's army in mid-August equaled Lee's, and overwhelming Federal reinforcements were expected. Pope had received orders from Halleck directing him to stay where he was until he was joined by 70,000 or more troops from McClellan's army. But McClellan was unable to move quickly. There was a shortage of transports, and even as McClellan prepared to withdraw, he protested unsuccessfully. He and many of his staff were stung by the order to abandon their position east of Richmond and to reinforce Pope, whom they regarded as an upstart. They thought that Pope's army should pull back to Washington or should join them. Among themselves, they predicted disaster. One of McClellan's officers wrote on August 11, "I have one hope left; when that ass Pope shall have lost his army, and when Washington shall again be menaced (say in six days from this time) then and only then will they find out that our little General is not in his right place and then they will call loudly for his aid." Not until August 13, ten days after receiving orders to move north, did McClellan begin to send his troops toward a rendezvous with Pope. While still near Richmond, McClellan wrote to his wife on August 21: "I believe I have triumphed!! Just received a telegram from Halleck stating that Pope and [Major General Ambrose] Burnside are very hard pressed." And two days later he wrote to her that "I take it for granted that my orders will be as disagreeable as it is possible to make them — unless Pope is beaten, in which case they will want me to save Washington again."

Pope was indeed hard pressed. By August 19 he had retreated north of the Rappahannock River, narrowly escaping a move by Lee to cut him off. Guarding the river crossings, Pope continued to wait for reinforcements, which were beginning to arrive. By August 22 he had 70,000 men, and more were on the way.

Unable to attack directly across the Rappahannock, Lee again divided his forces, despite the standard cautions of military theory. He sent 25,000 men under Stonewall Jackson on a long march to the northwest around Pope's position on the river. Lee would linger briefly to delude Pope that the Confederates were still to his south, then follow Jackson for an attack on Pope's rear. Leaving at dawn on August 25, Jackson's "foot-cavalry," as his hard-marching veterans were called, covered more than fifty miles in forty-eight hours. They crossed the Rappahannock far upstream, then swung southeast to intercept the Orange and Alexandria Railroad — Pope's supply line — on the evening of August 26. The next day Jackson's troops moved northeast along the railroad to Manassas Junction, where they rested, gorged themselves on Federal food supplies, and burned warehouses crammed with Union stores. That night they marched off in several directions, then regrouped the next day, August 28, on a wooded ridge overlooking the Warrenton Turnpike, a mile or two northwest of the fields where the first battle of Manassas had been fought.

Jackson was causing serious trouble, but his position was precarious. He risked being caught between Federal reinforcements advancing from Alexandria and Pope's large army to the south. Jackson was supposed to be joined by Lee, who had moved northwest on August 26, but the following day Pope ordered his own army northward to keep Lee and Jackson apart. Pope directed various units to assemble in the vicinity of Gainsville, west of Manassas. Other detachments were told to converge on Manassas to smash Jackson, but by the time the Federals arrived, the Confederates were gone — apparently. Union columns marched back and forth to Centreville and elsewhere, pursuing reports of Jackson's movements. Late in the afternoon, however, Jackson himself announced his position by attacking a division of 6,000 Federals marching east on the Warrenton Turnpike near the crossroads at Groteton. (See Map 4 on page 39.)

The attack came shortly before sunset. A Confederate officer recalled "a hoarse roar like that from cages of wild beasts at the scent of blood" as the Southerners, who had been concealed in the woods below Stony Ridge, fell into ranks. Confederate artillery rolled into the open at the Brawner Farm, unlimbered, and began firing. The infantry paraded out of the trees and down the gentle slope toward the turnpike, took up positions behind a rail fence, and started shooting.

The Federal response was resolute and disciplined. Part of the Federal column on the road formed an opposing line of battle, then advanced into an orchard north of the turnpike and returned the Confederate fire. Recovering from their initial shock, Federals units that had taken shelter in some woods advanced into farm fields facing the Southerners. Union guns were trotted up and put into action where the turnpike crosses a hill now called Battery Heights. At close range the opposing lines fired again and again. The Confederates mounted several unsuccessful charges. The fighting continued even as the fields and woods grew dark and opposing gunflashes provided the only visible targets. At about 9 P.M. the Union column, nearly a third of its men killed or wounded, withdrew to the road and moved off toward Manassas.

Jackson's position was at last known, and Pope ordered the Federal army to mass on the Warrenton Turnpike near Bull Run. Pope told his officers that "we can bag the whole crowd" if the Union forces acted fast enough. Even the Federal units to the west that were blocking Lee's effort to join Jackson were pulled back to head off and attack Jackson — a move that allowed Lee to advance with 30,000 men. As Pope tried to martial his forces, some Federal units had their orders changed for the third or fourth time in twenty-four hours. One Union general, revising his written instructions to his subordinates, asked an aide from Pope's headquarters how to spell "chaos." The aide told him and wrote later in his diary that he considered the question most timely.

Meanwhile, Jackson's troops had occupied a strong position along an unfinished railroad north of the Warrenton Turnpike. The alternating cuts and fills served as a trench and breastwork (as can be seen today). The Confederate line stretched for nearly two miles along the railroad bed, from Bull Run westward. Much of the line was obscured by woods that extended to the front and rear of the unfinished railroad grade.

Pope was anxious to crush Jackson before Lee arrived, and on August 29 he opened the attack before most of the scattered Union divisions were in position. First Pope sent a corps of 11,000 men against Jackson's line east of Featherbed Lane (where now the Unfinished Railroad Loop Trail enables visitors to see the scene of action). The Union guns shelled the woods, then the infantry advanced into thick fire. As the Federals entered the woods and approached the railroad, their ranks disintegrated and the attack lost momentum. Some Union troops reached the embankment and drove the Confederates farther into the woods, but a counterattack pushed the Federals back.

Pope sent more columns into battle as they reached the front. All told, about 20,000 Union soldiers assaulted the eastern end of the Confederate line near Sudley Springs, but their attacks came piecemeal, one after another. Six times various Federal units advanced, but the Confederates hung on and with desperate effort repulsed each of the Union attacks, which continued until dusk.

Pope also ordered an advance against the western end of the Confederate line, but the assault never occurred. Approaching from Manassas, Brigadier General Fitz-John Porter disregarded orders and held back his corps. An officer in McClellan's Army of the Potomac, Porter detested Pope. Large clouds of dust to Porter's front convinced him that he was opposed by a strong enemy force. In fact, the dust was raised by J.E.B. Stuart's cavalry, which had been directed to create a stir until Lee, who had arrived at midday, could get his troops into place. For his disobedience, Porter was later court-martialed and cashiered from the army, but subsequently reinstated. Still other Federal detachments failed to engage the enemy because of confusion. In all, nearly 30,000 soldiers, about half the Federal force, did no fighting on the 29th.

An equal number of Confederates were held out of the battle. During the early afternoon Major General James Longstreet, commander of the Confederate corps that had come with Lee, massed his men to the west, astride and below the Warrenton Turnpike. Lee wanted to attack, but Longstreet recommended waiting until more troops arrived and until he had reconnoitered, and Lee let him have his way.

By the morning of August 30, Pope believed that he was on the verge of victory. His aide noted that on the previous evening that "Pope was firmly of the opinion that Jackson was beaten and would get off during the night." The Confederates near Sudley Springs, after repulsing the Union attacks, had in fact withdrawn after dark, but only a small distance in order to shorten their line. One of Longstreet's divisions had advanced along the Warrenton Turnpike, skirmished briefly, and also withdrawn at dusk, convincing Pope that the Confederates had begun a nighttime retreat. The next morning Pope telegraphed to General Halleck that on the 28th he had fought the combined forces of the enemy, adding, "The news reaches me from the front that the enemy is retreating toward the mountains. I go forward at once to see."

Pope ordered his army to pursue the enemy, but more than half the day passed before his marching columns were organized. At mid-afternoon on the 30th, the Union army started west on the turnpike and in parallel lines to the north and south. The northern column, however, almost immediately encountered resistance, as strong as ever, along the unfinished railroad. Pope again attacked with wave after wave of troops. Union forces along the turnpike and to the south were, in part, sent north against the railroad. "As one line was repulsed another took its place and pressed forward as if determined by force of numbers and fury of assault to drive us from our positions," Jackson reported afterwards.

Five thousand troops under General Fitz-John Porter attacked the railroad in the vicinity of the Deep Cut. Some Union regiments succeeded in reaching the embankment, but there they could do little more than huddle for protection on one side while the Confederates remained ten yards away on the other side. Soldiers held their rifles above their heads and fired blindly over the brow of the railroad grade. In one incident, Southern troops who had run out of ammunition briefly resorted to throwing rocks pried from the embankment. Thrusting with bayonets and swinging their guns like clubs, some men fought hand-to-hand. As more Federal troops pressed forward, Jackson sent word to Lee that he could not hold his ground without help.

Contacted by Lee, Longstreet sent a division to reinforce Jackson. Longstreet also massed eighteen field guns at Battery Heights, where Jackson had opened the battle two days earlier by attacking a passing Union column. Now Longstreet's artillery raked the lines of Union soldiers who were arrayed against Jackson. The Federals fell back in confusion, leaving the troops who were pinned down near the railroad to fend for themselves. Then Lee ordered a counterattack, which in fact Longstreet had already initiated by sending his entire corps of 30,000 infantry crashing eastward below the turnpike. The Union forces there had been stripped of many units to aid the attack on Jackson, and the Federal position crumbled. Two regiments of New York Zouaves tried to stop the Confederates, and although they briefly slowed Longstreet's advance, they suffered some of the heaviest casualties of the war. (Two stone monuments at New York Avenue mark the location of this action.) Jackson's forces joined the attack, pressing forward from the northwest.

Grossly deceived — perhaps self-deceived — about the disposition of enemy troops and the state of the battle, Pope nonetheless managed to salvage his army and to avoid a rout. He moved troops south of the turnpike to grapple with Longstreet's corps during the late afternoon and evening. The Federals tried to hold at Chinn Ridge, but they were pushed back to Sudley Road and Henry Hill, where they made a stand at dusk. The Confederates were stopped, and as darkness fell the fighting died down.

During the night the Union forces retreated across Bull Run to Centreville, where they were joined by troops advancing from Alexandria. The reinforcements were from McClellan's Army of the Potomac, and according to one of Pope's officers, McClellan's men "greeted us with mocking laughter, taunts and jeers on the advantages of the new route to Richmond; while many of them in plain English expressed their joy at the downfall of the braggart rival of the great soldier of the peninsula."

On September 1 another, much smaller battle was fought near the estate of Chantilly a few miles north of Centreville. Two Federal divisions engaged Jackson's troops, who were attempting to advance in a wide circle around the Union camp. After an inconclusive fight in a thunderstorm, the Confederates drew back. The next day the Union army abandoned Centreville and retreated to Washington. Three thousand wounded Federals were evacuated by wagon and by train. All told, the Union had lost 15,500 killed, wounded, and missing during two weeks of fighting in northern Virginia. The Confederates suffered more than 9,000 casualties, but were soon reinforced to an equal extent. Although still outnumbered by the Federal army, Lee's forces had regained control of northern Virginia and now threatened the Federal capital.

To the immense gratification of the officers and troops of the Army of the Potomac, McClellan was placed in command of the defense of Washington. Pope's demoralized army was merged with McClellan's, and Pope himself was sent out of the way to Minnesota. Within the government, many high officials were dissatisfied — even disgusted — with McClellan also. Lincoln himself had complained that McClellan seemed to want Pope to fail. But for at least the time being McClellan was needed. He alone elicited the devotion and enthusiasm of the many officers he had appointed and of the troops whose training he had supervised during the previous year. On September 22 McClellan wrote from Washington to his wife that General Halleck was "begging me to help him out of his scrape and take command here," and that he had had "a pretty plain talk with him & Abe — a still plainer one this evening. The result is that I have reluctantly consented to take command here & try to save the capital."

McClellan was told to prepare the army for a campaign against Lee. "There is every probability that the enemy . . . will cross the Potomac, and make a raid into Maryland or Pennsylvania," Halleck wrote. "A moveable army must be immediately organized to meet him again in the field." Organization was McClellan's forte, and Lincoln reported a few days later that McClellan was "working like a beaver" at consolidating the existing forces, assigning recruits and miscellaneous units, and re-establishing an effective commissary and a coherent command structure. He had little time, for on September 5 the Confederate army forded the Potomac near Leesburg. Less than two weeks later, on September 17, the opposing armies collided again, this time at Antietam Creek near Sharpsburg, where more men died than on any other single day of the Civil War. (For a discussion of the battle of Antietam, see Chapter 3.)

≈   ≈   ≈   ≈

AUTOMOBILE DIRECTIONS: Manassas National Battlefield Park is located in Virginia about 25 miles west of Washington. (See the top panel on **Map 3** on page 35.)

Access is provided by Interstate 66, which extends from the Potomac River's Roosevelt Bridge west through Arlington toward Front Royal.

To Manassas National Battlefield from downtown Washington: From the western end of Constitution Avenue, take the Roosevelt Bridge across the Potomac River and follow Interstate 66 West nearly 28 miles to Exit 47B for Route 234 North. Follow Route 234 North 0.7 mile to the entrance for Manassas National Battlefield visitor center on the right.

To Manassas National Battlefield from Interstate 495 (the Capital Beltway): Leave the Beltway at Exit 9 for Interstate 66 West. Take I-66 West about 17 miles to Exit 47B for Route 234 North. Follow Route 234 North 0.7 mile to the entrance for the Manassas National Battlefield visitor center on the right.

To Manassas National Battlefield from the west on Interstate 66: Leave I-66 at Exit 47 for Route 234. At the bottom of the exit ramp, turn left and follow Route 234 North 0.8 mile to the entrance for the Manassas National Battlefield visitor center on the right.

≈   ≈   ≈   ≈

WALKING: Two routes are described, one dealing with the first battle of Manassas in July 1861 and the other with the second battle of Manassas in August 1862. For the First Manassas Trail, see **Map 3** opposite and the directions starting on this page. For the Second Manassas Trail, see **Map 4** on page 39 and the directions starting on page 38. Both trails begin at the visitor center.

≈   ≈   ≈   ≈

First Manassas Trail: Before you start on the First Manassas Trail, I recommend taking the mile-long **Henry Hill Tour**, which will provide a quick overview of the first battle of Manassas. The Henry Hill Tour is shown on Map 3 by the dotted circuit. It starts behind the visitor center and is marked by a series of signs and interpretive stations. The route proceeds past field guns and the Henry House to the brow of the hill looking north toward distant Matthews Hill, from which the Union troops

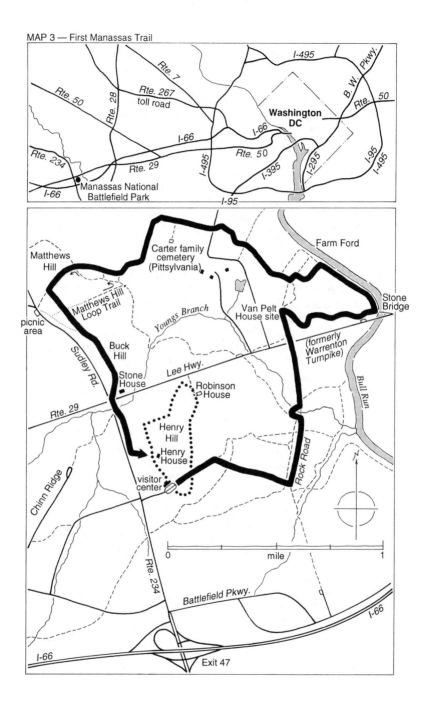

MAP 3 — First Manassas Trail

I-495
Rte. 7
Rte. 267
toll road
Rte. 50
Rte. 28
Rte. 50
B. W. Pkwy.
Rte. 50
Washington
DC
I-66
I-66
I-66
I-495
Rte. 29
Rte. 50
I-395
I-295
I-95
I-495
Rte. 234
Manassas National
Battlefield Park
I-66
I-95

Carter family
cemetery
(Pittsylvania)
Farm Ford
Matthews
Hill
Matthews Hill
Loop Trail
Youngs Branch
Van Pelt
House site
Stone
Bridge
picnic
area
Buck
Hill
(formerly
Warrenton
Turnpike)
Sudley Rd.
Stone
House
Lee Hwy.
Robinson
House
Bull Run
Rte. 29
Henry
Hill
Henry
House
Rock Road
visitor
center
Chinn Ridge
0   mile   1
Rte. 234
Battlefield Pkwy.
I-66
I-66
Exit 47

advanced. Turn right and follow the grassy track to a row of cedars and then to Robinson Lane. Turn right past the site of the Robinson House, then continue past a row of field guns where Stonewall Jackson established his line of defense. Continue around the loop, then return to the parking lot in front of the visitor center.

For the 5.3-mile **First Manassas Trail**, start at the parking lot in front of the visitor center. Facing the visitor center, turn right and follow a grassy track across a level field about a hundred yards to the right (or rear) of an equestrian statue of General Jackson. After passing through a row of artillery, pick up the First Manassas Trail (also called the Stone Bridge Trail), which is marked by occasional blue blazes.

Follow the First Manassas Trail downhill through a row of redcedars, across a small meadow, and into the woods. Fork right to continue through the woods on the blue-blazed trail. Cross a yellow-blazed horse trail and continue downhill along the route used by Confederate troops (including Jackson's brigade) to reach the fighting at Henry Hill. Pass a field on the left and cross a rivulet on a footbridge. Immediately after crossing another yellow-blazed horse trail, turn left on Rock Road, an old lane used by the Confederates to bring up troops from their initial positions farther south along Bull Run.

Follow the blue blazes along Rock Road toward the site of the Van Pelt House and the Stone Bridge. At Youngs Branch you can either ford the stream straight ahead or detour slightly to the left across a bridge and then back to Rock Road. Continue on Rock Road straight across a field toward Route 29, now termed the Lee Highway but in 1861 called the Warrenton Turnpike. Where Rock Road curves right near Route 29, descend straight ahead and — with caution — cross the highway and continue straight uphill. At the top of the knoll, turn sharply right to the site of the Van Pelt House, then right again. Along this ridge Confederate troops were positioned at the beginning of the First Battle of Manassas to block Union advance along the Warrenton Turnpike where it crosses Bull Run at the Stone Bridge. The high ground near the Van Pelt House was the extreme northern end of the Confederate line.

Follow the blue blazes along the top of the ridge back toward the highway, then downhill to the left and along a boardwalk. Pass a parking lot for the Stone Bridge, then descend along a path to the Stone Bridge itself. The bridge was built about

36

1825, destroyed in 1862 when the Confederates withdrew south to defend Richmond, and rebuilt about 1870.

At the Stone Bridge, turn left upstream and go to a trail intersecting from the left near Farm Ford, where Sherman's brigade of Union infantry crossed Bull Run to join the battle as the Federals pushed south from Matthews Hill to Henry Hill. Turn left away from the river and follow the blue-blazed trail toward Pittsylvania Cemetery. Climb right uphill, then turn left at a T-intersection. Climb to the edge of a field, then fork right. With woods on the right, follow the trail along the edge of the field, then straight across the field somewhat to the right of a house, then again along the edge of the field and across a gravel road and into the woods. This was the route taken by Confederate troops as they were shifted north from the vicinity of the Stone Bridge to block the Federals' flanking attack from the ford at Sudley Springs.

Continue straight through the woods and past a clearing that marks the site of Pittsylvania, a mansion built by Landon Carter in the late 1760s. A spur trail leads left to the Carter family cemetery. At the time of the battle, the Carter house stood in open fields. Confederate troops from the Stone Bridge took up positions here before moving farther west once it was apparent that the Federals were advancing down Sudley Road.

Continue through the woods on the blue-blazed trail, which at one point abruptly bends left. Pass several trails intersecting from the left; continue toward Matthews Hill. At one point, pass straight through a four-way intersection with the yellow-blazed horse trail. Eventually, emerge from the woods and continue straight across a field to a row of guns atop Matthews Hill. Here Union troops advancing from the north along Sudley Road first encountered resistance from Confederate troops who had marched from the vicinity of the Stone Bridge. The Confederates formed a stop-gap line a few hundred yards south of the hilltop (or that is, in the direction toward the present-day visitor center, visible in the distance). As shown by the guns, the Federals brought up artillery, and eventually the Confederates, vastly outnumbered, were forced to retreat toward Henry Hill.

With Sudley Road on the right, follow a faint track across the fields toward Henry House and the visitor center in the distance. This is the route of Union advance. Cross Buck Hill and descend to the Stone House, which was used as a Union field hospital. With caution, cross Lee Highway at the intersection, then follow the shoulder of Sudley Road 75 yards across a bridge. Bear left to follow a grassy track uphill along a rail fence, then to the left uphill to the Henry House and visitor center. For hours the opposing armies fought for control of the broad plateau at Henry Hill before the Federals were finally forced to retreat.

≈ ≈ ≈ ≈

Second Manassas Trail: Map 4 opposite shows this 7-mile route, which some park signs refer to as the Deep Cut Trail. In any case, the trail is blazed with green X marks, but these blazes are often very faint or altogether worn away. For the first mile — or that is, as far as Matthews Hill — the trail is congruent with the blue-blazed First Manassas Trail.

From the rear of the visitor center, follow the grassy track to the Henry House. Within a few dozen yards of the house, turn left downhill on an old gravel lane. In front of a gate, fork half-right onto a grassy path next to a rail fence and Route 234 (Sudley Road). Descend to the junction of Route 234 and Route 29 (Lee Highway). Although the roadbeds have in places been straightened and shifted slightly, both roads existed at the time of the Civil War, when the Lee Highway was called the Warrenton Turnpike.

With caution, cross Route 29 to the Stone House, which served as a Union hospital during the second battle of Manassas (as it had also during the first battle of Manassas). With Route 234 toward the left, climb Buck Hill, at the top of which the Union commander, Major General John Pope, had his headquarters on August 29 and 30, 1862. With Route 234 in the distance on the left, follow the grassy track north to Matthews Hill, where today there is a row of guns commemorating action during the first battle of Manassas. At the guns, turn left and — with caution — cross Route 234 to the picnic area at Dogan Ridge, along which Pope arrayed more than thirty guns to support the Union attack on the unfinished railroad on August 30.

From the upper parking lot for the Dogan Ridge picnic area, follow the edge of a road downhill to a lower parking lot, then continue straight across a field on the green X trail. Follow a narrow lane bordered by hedgerows and fields. Continue straight through the woods to a point where the unfinished railroad grade crosses a road (Featherbed Lane). Protected

MAP 4 — Second Manassas Trail

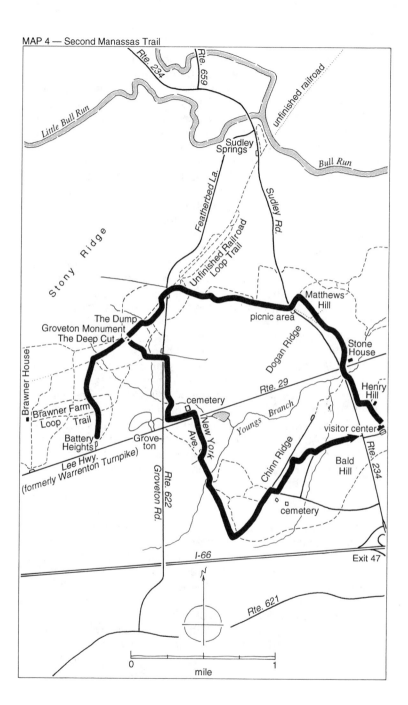

by the cuts and fills of the railroad, Stonewall Jackson's troops repelled repeated Union attacks on August 29 and 30.

The green-blazed Second Manassas Trail crosses the road and continues along the unfinished railroad to the Deep Cut, but first you may want to follow the Unfinished Railroad Loop Trail in the opposite direction to Sudley Springs and back (see Map 4). Most of the fighting on August 29 occurred along the line toward Sudley Springs.

To continue from Featherbed Lane on the green-blazed Second Manassas Trail, cross the road, climb some steps, and follow the green X blazes though the woods next to the unfinished railroad grade. The trail follows the railroad to the Groveton Monument at the Deep Cut.

At the monument in front of the Deep Cut, a spur of the Second Manassas Trail leads 0.8 mile to Battery Heights. To follow the spur trail, continue straight along the railroad bed. Cross a stream and continue on the raised roadbed for about 130 yards, then turn left to follow the green X trail toward Battery Heights. Descend from the railroad embankment and immediately fork right. Follow the path along the edge of a meadow and through the woods. When the trail emerges from the woods at the corner of a large hayfield, continue diagonally downhill across the field and up to Battery Heights. On the way to Battery Heights, the green X trail twice crosses the Brawner Farm Loop Trail, as shown on Map 4. Brawner Farm and Battery Heights are where the Second Battle of Manassas began on August 28, when Jackson ordered an attack against a Union column marching east on the Warrenton Turnpike. From Battery Heights return to the battle monument at the Deep Cut by the way you came.

To continue on the main circuit from the monument at the Deep Cut, follow the green X blazes away from the railroad bed and downhill along a broad, grassy swath through the woods. Continue past trails intersecting from left and right before bearing left and climbing to a road. With caution, cross the road and turn right on the green X trail. Follow the path parallel with the road. Cross a small stream on a wooden pedestrian bridge and continue to a crossroads with Lee Highway (the old Warrenton Turnpike).

At Lee Highway, turn left. With the highway toward the right, follow the path downhill, across a small bridge, through a parking lot, and past Groveton Confederate Cemetery. From the cemetery continue about 100 yards downhill along Lee

Highway. With caution, turn right across the highway at an intersection with a park road called New York Avenue. Walking on the left shoulder of the road, follow New York Avenue several hundred yards to a loop near two monuments to the Duryee and National Zouaves, whose regiments suffered heavy casualties in an effort to stop the counterattack by Longstreet's corps late in the afternoon on August 30.

To the right of the National Zouave monument, pick up the green (and yellow and orange) blazes leading downhill into the woods. Cross a pedestrian bridge over Youngs Branch, then turn right upstream past an intersection where the orange-blazed loop trail leads left. Go 40 yards upstream along Youngs Branch, then bear left uphill on the green X trail. After half a mile the trail reaches a gravel and dirt road intersecting from the left. Turn left and follow the gravel and dirt road, eventually reaching a gate by an asphalt road at Chinn Ridge, where Union troops tried to stop the Confederate counterattack.

At the gate, turn right downhill a few dozen yards to a parking bay near the stone foundation of Hazel Plain, as the Benjamin Chinn house was called. Cross the park road and follow a grassy track along the route by which the Confederates eventually advanced and cleared the Federals from off Chinn Ridge. With a road uphill to the left, follow the hillside to a distant cannon. About 80 yards beyond the cannon, turn right to the Webster Memorial. From behind the memorial, follow the green X trail downhill along the edge of a field to the park road. Turn left and — with caution — follow the shoulder of the road to Sudley Road, where Union troops succeeded in stopping the Confederate advance as night fell.

With caution, cross Sudley Road and follow the park road uphill to the visitor center.

2

HARPERS FERRY NATIONAL HISTORICAL PARK, including Maryland Heights and access to the C&O Canal towpath

Walking — 6 miles (9.7 kilometers). This outing combines a visit to the historic town of Harpers Ferry with a hike to the Civil War citadel and mountain battlefield at Maryland Heights. The mountain is part of the long ridge termed the Blue Ridge in Virginia and Elk Ridge in Maryland. At Harpers Ferry the ridge is breached and carved into cliffs by the confluence of the Shenandoah and Potomac rivers.

The route shown by the bold line on **Map 5** on page 55 starts at Harpers Ferry and crosses the Potomac River on a secure pedestrian walkway mounted on a railroad bridge. After briefly using the towpath of the C&O Canal, the route follows a military road steeply uphill. (Abraham Lincoln, on a tour of inspection in 1862, gave up before reaching the top.) A spur trail leads to the clifftop overlook from which the photograph at left was taken. The main loop continues uphill to the crest of the ridge, where Federal defenders were routed in September 1862. When Union forces later regained possession of Harpers Ferry, they built a stone and earthen fort on the mountain top, and today much of these works is still discernible. The view from the clifftop overlook is spectacular at any time of year, but the views from the crest of the ridge are best when leaves are off the trees.

Please note, however, several caveats. In January 1996, a flood tore up the C&O Canal towpath across from Harpers Ferry. Until the damage is repaired, people who want to climb Maryland Heights will have to drive around from Harpers Ferry to the Maryland side of the Potomac River. Also, the excursion up Maryland Heights is not recommended during snowy or icy weather. It is probably wise to stay off the clifftop overlook during wet weather, when the rocks may be slippery.

A pleasant and easy alternative to the climb up Maryland Heights is to walk from Harpers Ferry for as far as you want up and down the Potomac River on the towpath of the C&O Canal.

The towpath, of course, is also good for ski touring and bicycling. Do not, however, under any circumstances swim or wade in the river, where there are strong currents. For a discussion of the C&O Canal, see Chapter 7. For visitors to Harpers Ferry, the first order of business is to find a place to park for the day. By far the largest parking lot is at the national historical park visitor center, from which shuttle buses run at frequent intervals to the old part of Harpers Ferry. Dogs are not permitted on the buses and must be leashed elsewhere in the park. Parking at the visitor center and elsewhere at Harpers Ferry is discussed in greater detail at the beginning of the automobile directions on page 53.

Harpers Ferry National Historical Park is managed by the National Park Service. The various park museums are each devoted to a different theme — Industry, Transportation, John Brown, the Civil War, African-American History, and the Environment — and are open daily from 9 A.M. to 5 P.M. For information telephone (304) 535-6029 or (304) 535-6298.

HARPERS FERRY was named for Robert Harper, who in the mid-1700s operated a ferry for people traveling the frontier road that crossed the Potomac River at its confluence with the Shenandoah River. In response to the recommendation of President George Washington, Congress in 1796 established a U.S. Armory here, harnessing the rivers for power and making use of the region's nascent iron industry. During the second quarter of the nineteenth century, the Potomac River and the water gap at Harpers Ferry provided a corridor for construction of the Chesapeake and Ohio Canal and the Baltimore and Ohio Railroad. From a junction with the B&O at Harpers Ferry, the Winchester and Potomac Railroad followed the Shenandoah Valley southwest. By the late 1850s, Harpers Ferry was a thriving center for transportation, manufacturing, and retailing. The main industry, of course, was the armory, where nearly four hundred men were employed making more than ten thousand muskets and rifles annually. The government works also included an arsenal, where about 100,000 guns were stored.

It was these weapons that the abolitionist John Brown, who was convinced that he had a commission from God to destroy slavery, attempted to seize during his abortive raid on the night of October 16, 1859. Brown intended to distribute the weapons to a revolutionary

44

army of slaves and anti-slavery whites whom, he thought, would swarm to a refuge that he planned to establish in the Virginia mountains. With twenty-one men, including three of his sons, Brown easily captured the arsenal and took forty-two prominent citizens hostage, but the counter-attack next morning by local militia was perhaps far more swift than he anticipated. Soon a contingent of U.S. marines led by Lieutenant Colonel Robert E. Lee arrived, and by midday on the 18th, ten of Brown's men had been killed, five had fled, and the rest, including Brown, had been captured. All the prisoners were soon tried and hanged at nearby Charles Town. But in less than a year and a half, Harpers Ferry was engulfed in the Civil War, fought at first simply on the issue of secession, but which eventually accomplished Brown's purpose to end slavery.

≈   ≈   ≈   ≈

DURING THE COURSE of the Civil War, Harpers Ferry passed from Northern to Southern control and back again four times. Indeed, the Federal fortifications built atop Maryland Heights during the war's middle years were a case of closing the barn door long after the horses had got out — or in this case, after Stonewall Jackson and other Confederate war horses had got in. At the outbreak of the war, the Federal arsenal, the C&O Canal, and the railroad tracks, sidings, depot, and bridge were guarded by only forty-two Union infantrymen. Virginia seceded from the Union on April 17, 1861, and within two days a thousand armed Virginians led by Rebel militia officers forced the small Federal garrison to evacuate Harpers Ferry. Although the Federals burned the government buildings and destroyed 15,000 weapons before they left, the Virginians salvaged machinery for making rifles, as well as several thousand rifle barrels and gun locks, all of which were shipped south.

Soon after seizing Harpers Ferry, the Confederates there were put under the command of Colonel Thomas Jonathan Jackson (later Lieutenant General Stonewall Jackson), who managed to intercept a number of B&O trains, depriving the railroad of 56 locomotives and 386 freight cars. Most of these were wrecked and pushed into the river, but fourteen locomotives were sent to Richmond, a journey that entailed hauling them by horses along roads for much of the way.

The Confederates stayed at Harpers Ferry for two months, then on June 15 abandoned the town, which they regarded as indefensible. When Union troops reoccupied Harpers Ferry in July, they found, according to one diarist, that "charred ruins were all that remain of the splendid public works, arsenals, workshops and railroads," and that "stores, hotels, and dwelling houses [were] all mingled in one common destruction." By building a pontoon bridge over the Potomac, the Federals reopened the B&O Railroad west, and for the remainder of 1861 all was quiet at Harpers Ferry.

Late in February 1862, the Union high command decided to stockpile military supplies at Harpers Ferry in preparation for an advance south toward Winchester. But late in May, Stonewall Jackson took the offensive in the Shenandoah Valley, marching to the outskirts of Harpers Ferry before again withdrawing. By late summer the railroad and depot at Harpers Ferry were guarded by 10,400 soldiers, commanded by Colonel Dixon S. Miles, whom a court of inquiry the year before had found to be drunk while leading a division at the first battle of Manassas. (See Chapter 1 for a discussion of the two Civil War battles at Manassas.) Another 2,500 Union troops were stationed at Martinsburg farther west along the B&O Railroad. Most of these two garrisons had never seen combat, and some units were merely militia; but they and their commander were considered adequate to guard the railroad and canal against Confederate raids.

In September 1862, however, a full-scale Confederate invasion came their way. Following his victory at the second battle of Manassas, General Robert E. Lee led his Army of Northern Virginia into Maryland on September 5, wading across the Potomac at White's Ford, midway between Washington and Harpers Ferry. Encamped near Frederick, Lee decided on September 9 that before marching farther north into Pennsylvania, as he hoped to do, he should clear his lines of communication to the rear by eliminating the Union garrison at Harpers Ferry. To prevent the Federals from escaping, he and Jackson devised a plan to approach the town from all sides at once. One Confederate column of about 3,000 men was directed to retrace the army's invasion route, cross the Potomac back into Virginia, and occupy Loudoun Heights, as the end of the Blue Ridge overlooking the Shenandoah and Potomac from the southeast is called. Another Confederate force of about 9,000 men, commanded by Major General Lafayette McLaws, would seize Maryland Heights, which dominates Harpers Ferry from the northeast side of the Potomac. And a third column of about 13,500 men under Jackson would march west from Frederick along the National Road, then circle south and east to push the Union troops at Martinsburg into Harpers Ferry. Once the Federals were corralled at Harpers Ferry, they and their vast store of supplies could be captured by overrunning Bolivar Heights, where the defenders had their main line of defense west of Harpers Ferry.

The Union high command had been aware of the threat to Harpers Ferry ever since the Confederates first crossed the Potomac into

Maryland. Major General George B. McClellan, commander of the Army of the Potomac, urged that the garrison at Harpers Ferry be withdrawn before it was cut off, but Henry Halleck, at that time the general in chief of all Union forces, ordered that the town be held. On September 5, Colonel Miles at Harpers Ferry received a telegram from his immediate superior in Baltimore: "Be energetic and active, and defend all places to the last extremity. There must be no abandoning of a post, and shoot the first man that thinks of it, whether officer or soldier." Six days later, as the Confederates closed in on Harpers Ferry, Miles telegraphed to Washington, "I expect this will be the last you will hear of me until this affair is over. All are cheerful and hopeful."

By nightfall on September 12, Lafayette McLaws' Confederate column was poised to seize Maryland Heights at the southern end of Elk Ridge. McLaws sent two brigades totaling 3,000 men to scale Elk Ridge four miles north of Maryland Heights and then to advance south along the wooded ridge. With the rest of his troops, McLaws moved south along the foot of the mountain to seal the eastern exit from Harpers Ferry. Also on September 12, the Federal garrison from Martinsburg to the west arrived in Harpers Ferry, retreating before Stonewall Jackson, who was on the last leg of his circuitous approach.

Maryland Heights was the key to the defense of Harpers Ferry. Halfway up the southwestern slope and directly across the Potomac from the town, a powerful gun emplacement called the Naval Battery had been erected the preceding May. The armaments were formidable: two 9-inch naval Dahlgren guns (smoothbores), one 50-pounder Parrott rifle, and four 12-pounder smoothbores. The largest guns were far bigger than anything the Confederates had brought with them. Within range of the Naval Battery were the summit of Loudoun Heights to the south and the crest of Bolivar Heights to the west. If handled well, the battery could break up the deployment of enemy field artillery and the massing of troops for an assault. Little, however, had been done to guard against an attack from the north or east, as now was threatened. Except for a log breastwork and a hundred yards of abatis (a bristly barrier of sharpened and intertangled branches) that had been thrown up facing north at the last moment, the crest of the ridge was unfortified. Both Halleck and McClellan had suggested that the entire garrison at Harpers Ferry withdraw to Maryland Heights, but such a move was not practicable on short notice because there was no water on the mountain, nor had cisterns been built. For the defense of the heights, Colonel Miles assigned only 1,600 troops, some of whom had been in the army only three weeks and were still unpracticed at loading their guns.

The attack on Maryland Heights opened at daybreak on September 13. The Northern recruits were posted in a line of battle about four hundred yards in advance of the makeshift breastwork, and they could hear to their front the Southerners talking and moving in the dim woods and underbrush. Even before the Confederates were seen, their first volley crashed into the defenders. After firing their own rifles into the smoke and woods, the green Federal troops scrambled for the breastwork behind them. There a new line of battle was formed, but when the Confederates advanced and fired another volley, a regiment of raw Union recruits broke and ran. "They were in wild confusion and dismay . . . . Nobody could possibly hold them," a lieutenant of a veteran regiment later testified. As the veterans tried to form a new line, the rookies took shelter to their rear. One officer saw three men trying to hide behind a single tree.

Colonel Thomas H. Ford, the Federal commander at Maryland Heights, sent a dispatch to Colonel Miles in Harpers Ferry saying that one regiment had run, and that his remaining troops were out of ammunition. "I must leave the hill unless you direct otherwise," Ford reported. Miles came up to the heights to see, but when Ford pleaded for reinforcements, Miles told him, "You can't have another damned man. If you can't hold it, leave it." Ford tried to hold on, but his small force was outnumbered. The Union troops were pushed back from the north and east, and soon Ford ordered an evacuation. After spiking their guns at the Naval Battery or pushing them down the mountainside, the Federals crossed the pontoon bridge over the Potomac River and joined the rest of the trapped garrison in Harpers Ferry.

By now the Confederate encirclement of Harpers Ferry was complete. Maryland Heights was in their hands; two Southern brigades occupied Loudoun Heights, which they had found undefended; and Stonewall Jackson's large force was drawn up opposite the Federal positions on Bolivar Heights. During the night of September 13, ten Union cavalry troopers broke out from the besieged town and managed to carry a verbal message from Colonel Miles to General McClellan, who had advanced with the Army of the Potomac from Washington to Frederick. McClellan was told that the Harpers Ferry garrison could hold out for forty-eight hours, but that if the town was not relieved in that time, Miles would have to surrender. McClellan replied with a dispatch saying that help was on the way. "Hold out to the last extremity," he told Miles. "If it is possible, reoccupy the Maryland Heights with your whole force." This message was carried by three separate couriers, but none got through. As for the promised help, the prior afternoon McClellan had, in fact, ordered Major General William B. Franklin, commanding a force of 19,500 men, to break the siege at Harpers Ferry by advancing against the Confederates who were pressing the town from the northeast, but Franklin had not gotten underway until the next morning, September 14.

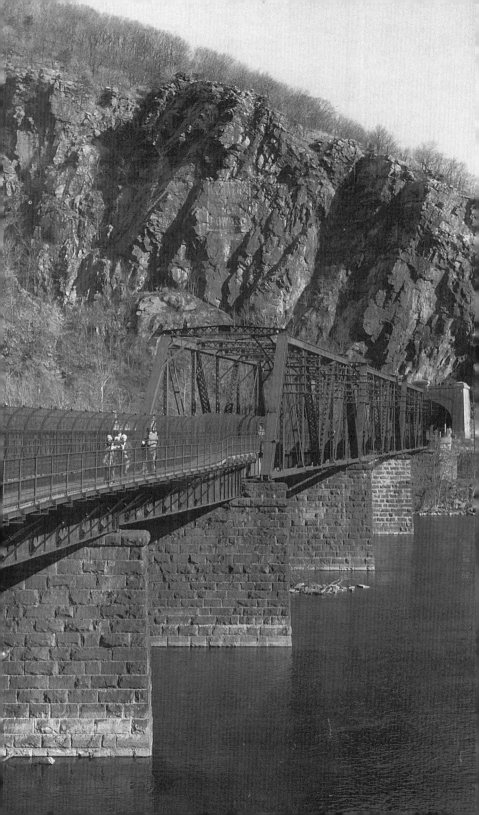

Meanwhile, the Confederates spent the morning of the 14th getting their artillery into position on the high ground surrounding Harpers Ferry. On Loudoun Heights five rifled fieldpieces were in place by noon, with all Harpers Ferry within range. At Maryland Heights the track along the ridge was impassable by artillery, so a shorter path was cut up the mountainside from the east. Ropes were tied to four field-pieces, and with as many as two hundred men on each gun, the artillery was hauled up to the crest. At the same time, Jackson seized positions from which to rake the Union defenses on Bolivar Heights.

Early in the afternoon, the Confederate guns on Loudoun Heights and Maryland Heights opened fire. "Their shells at first fell far wide of the mark and we laughed at them," a Union cavalryman wrote later, "but they soon got the range and plumped shell after shell among us, hitting a few horses and causing a rush for cover." Another man recalled, "*The infernal screech owls* came hissing and singing, then bursting, plowing great holes in the earth, filling our eyes with dust, and tearing many giant trees to atoms." Union gunners tried to reply, but the battery atop Maryland Heights was out of range and the Confederates on Loudoun Heights suffered only four casualties.

The next morning, September 15, the Confederates resumed their bombardment. Jackson's guns to the west joined in the action, and the Federal positions on Bolivar Heights were shelled from several angles. At sunset a division of 3,000 Confederates under A. P. Hill had advanced along the low ground by the Shenandoah River, and by dawn this force occupied a hill that was behind the south end of the Federal line across Bolivar Heights. By 8 A.M., the Union artillery, its ammunition exhausted, had stopped firing, and shortly afterwards, as Jackson's troops prepared to charge and overwhelm the demoralized defenders, the Federals surrendered, sending a horseman forward with a white flag. Even so, several minutes passed before word reached all the Confederates batteries, many of which continued to lob shells into the Union positions. Among the last casualties was Colonel Miles, who received a mortal wound in the leg.

Meanwhile, that same morning, the Union relief column under William Franklin arrived to the east of Elk Ridge, where the Federals encountered 5,000 Confederates. The Southerners appeared to be caught in a vise between the garrison at Harpers Ferry and Franklin's 19,500 troops. But as Franklin pondered whether to attack, cheering was heard from the Confederate lines, and word soon reached the Federals that Harpers Ferry had surrendered. Early in the afternoon, the Confederates withdrew rapidly around the southern end of Maryland Heights and crossed the pontoon bridge to the captured town, joining forces with Jackson's troops.

Except for 1,300 Union cavalrymen who had managed to break out of Harpers Ferry during the previous night, the entire Federal garrison was captured. It was the largest Union surrender of the war, and remained the largest surrender by the U.S. Army until the fall of Bataan and Corregidor during World War II. The prisoner count came to over 12,500 men, a figure so disturbing that when the news was released to the Northern press, censors in the War Department cut the figure in half to reduce the public's outrage. Captured war material included 73 pieces of artillery, 13,000 rifles and other small arms, 200 wagons, and abundant supplies of all kinds. New Springfield rifles were distributed to Southern regiments that previously had old smoothbores, and Confederate recruits who had marched for days with no guns at all were armed.

By evening on the 15th, most of the Confederate troops had left Harpers Ferry, heading upstream along the Potomac to Sharpsburg, where General Lee and the rest of his army were drawn up behind Antietam Creek, awaiting attack by the Army of the Potomac. At Harpers Ferry, only Major General A. P. Hill's Confederate division remained behind to organize the wagon train to carry the booty to Richmond. Even Hill's troops abandoned the town after only two days, leaving early on the morning of the battle of Antietam. Marching seventeen miles in eight hours, they arrived at Antietam in time to turn back an attack that threatened Lee's right flank. (See Chapter 3 for a discussion of the battle of Antietam.)

After the bloody standoff at Antietam Creek, Lee withdrew into Virginia, and Harpers Ferry changed hands for the fourth time of the war as Federal troops returned. In response to what quickly was dubbed the Harpers Ferry fiasco, measures were taken to strengthen the defenses. All trees on the upper third of Maryland Heights were cut down in order to provide a clear field of fire. In October 1862, a substantial earthwork mounting a battery of six 30-pounder Parrott rifles was constructed high up the ridge to sweep Loudoun Heights and Bolivar Heights. During the winter a fort was built spanning the crest of the ridge farther north. The fort consisted of an earthen breastwork nine feet high facing north, with embrasures for five 30-pounder Parrott rifles. Side walls, not as high, faced down the mountain flanks to east and west. Termed the Interior Fort, it was bordered on the west by the Exterior Fort, built during 1863. The Exterior Fort consisted of two long parallel stone walls, each chest-high and fronted with an earthen mantle and a dry moat. These breastworks served as rifle-pits for ranks of infantrymen. Located one behind the other about eighty yards apart, both walls faced north and, together with the Interior Fort, completely blocked advance along the top of the ridge. Yet another work, now

51

called the Stone Fort, was planned for the southeast corner of the Interior Fort, at the very crest of the ridge. It was to consist of a stone blockhouse, forty by one hundred feet, with bastions at two corners — and in fact a massive foundation, on its downhill side taller than a man, was built overlooking the mountain slope to the east. Another impressive military installation entailed pulling a five-ton 100-pounder Parrott rifle to the crest of the ridge, where it was mounted on a carriage that rotated 360 degrees. Also, cisterns to collect rain were prepared for a possible siege. The garrison that manned these fortifications, which are still evident, lived on the mountain year-round in log shelters and tents. All supplies had to be hauled up the steep military road. Thirteen scattered depressions in the ground are the remains of powder magazines, each of which consisted of a bunker with a log superstructure covered with earth.

During Lee's second invasion of the North in June 1863, the Confederate army forded the Potomac twelve miles upstream from Harpers Ferry. The depot's garrison withdrew to Maryland Heights, then was ordered to join the Army of the Potomac as it passed north up the Frederick Valley to intercept Lee's march toward Harrisburg, Pennsylvania. For a brief period Southern troops guarding Lee's lines of communication occupied Harpers Ferry and the abandoned works on the mountain, but after Lee's defeat at Gettysburg early in July, the Confederates retreated into Virginia.

A year later the Federal garrison again evacuated the town and withdrew to Maryland Heights during Major General Jubal Early's sudden march across Maryland and thrust at Washington. This time, however, the Federals waited out the invasion behind their defenses atop the mountain. The Southerners were in a hurry, and after some skirmishes and exchange of artillery fire, Early decided that the defenses were too strong to take quickly or cheaply. Bypassing the Union position, he continued toward Washington via Frederick, reaching the outskirts of the national capital on the same day that Union reinforcements arrived to turn back his attack. Early's raid was the last gasp of Southern offensive effort in the East. As the war continued and the North worked relentlessly to grind down the South, Harpers Ferry became a major supply base for Union operations in the Shenandoah Valley. Never again did the town or its mountain forts come under Confederate attack.

≈　　　≈　　　≈　　　≈

Following the Civil War, Harpers Ferry failed to recover its former prosperity or importance. The Federal armory was not rebuilt. As

American industry turned from water power to steam, Harpers Ferry — subject as it was to periodic flooding — lost its attractiveness as a site for industry. A flour mill built in 1867 was damaged by a flood in 1870. The water-driven Shenandoah Pulp Mill operated from 1887 to 1935 at the former locks of the Shenandoah Canal. Storer College, founded in 1867 primarily for the education of ex-slaves, opened in several former armory buildings. During the latter part of the nineteenth century, tourism became a staple of the local economy as people traveled by train to Harpers Ferry in order to enjoy its history and the dramatic scenery of the rivers, mountains, and water gap — and they have been coming ever since. In 1944 the federal land at Harpers Ferry was declared a National Monument. The authorized size was 1,500 acres, but since then thousands of acres outside the town have been added, and in 1963 the site was redesignated a national historical park.

≈   ≈   ≈   ≈

TRAIN: AMTRAK (telephone 800-872-7245) and MARC (telephone 800-325-7245) both run trains between Union Station in Washington and Harpers Ferry. However, the schedules are such that you have to spend the night — or better still, two nights — in Harpers Ferry. This is a great weekend getaway.

A very enjoyable place to stay in Harpers Ferry is the Hilltop House hotel and restaurant, in business since 1885. Reservations for Friday or Saturday night are required far in advance and cancellations require 24-hour notice; telephone (304) 535-2132 or 1 (800) 338-8319. To reach the Hilltop House from Shenandoah Street at the bottom of the hill in Harpers Ferry, follow High Street (it becomes Washington Street) uphill 0.4 mile, then turn right onto Columbia Street, then right again onto Ridge Street.

There is also a Comfort Inn at Harpers Ferry; telephone (304) 535-6391 or 1-800-221-2222. It is located on Union Street at Route 340 near the Shenandoah River bridge.

≈   ≈   ≈   ≈

AUTOMOBILE DIRECTIONS: Harpers Ferry is located at the confluence of the Potomac and Shenandoah rivers about 60 miles northwest of Washington. (See the corner panel on **Map 6** on page 75.) Access from Washington is provided by

Interstate 270 toward Frederick, then Route 340 toward Charles Town. If you are coming from Virginia, you may prefer to head west past Leesburg on Route 7, then take Route 9 to Route 671 North to Route 340 and Harpers Ferry.

The automobile directions below will guide you to the large parking lot at the Harpers Ferry National Historical Park visitor center, which is open daily except Christmas. An admission fee is charged. From the visitor center, shuttle buses run at intervals of 10 or 15 minutes to the oldest part of town. The buses operate from 8 A.M. to 6 P.M. (or until 7 P.M. during summer). Cars must leave the visitor center parking lot by 7 P.M. (or by 8 P.M. during summer). Dogs are not permitted on the buses and must be leashed elsewhere in the park.

Taking a shuttle bus may seem a strange way to begin a mountain hike or a walk on the C&O Canal towpath, but in fact the arrangement works very well and provides by far the surest way to find a secure and legitimate place to park in the vicinity of Harpers Ferry.

For people interested simply in walking at Maryland Heights or on the C&O Canal towpath, there are a few parking spots on the Maryland side of the Potomac River across from Harpers Ferry. However, by early in the day on weekends, these places are usually taken, and occasionally there have been thefts from cars parked here.

Finally, please do not park in the lot just inside the Harpers Ferry entrance at the west end of the Route 340 bridge over the Shenandoah River. This lot is intended for the use of fishermen, canoeists, rafters, and others at the Shenandoah River.

To Harpers Ferry from Interstate 495 (the Capital Beltway):
Leave the Beltway at Exit 35 (off the Outer Loop) or Exit 38 (off the Inner Loop) in order to take Interstate 270 North toward Frederick. Once you are on I-270 heading north, follow the directions in the next paragraph.

To Harpers Ferry from Interstate 270 past Rockville and Gaithersburg: Follow I-270 North, but before reaching Frederick take the exit for Interstate 70 West toward Hagerstown. After merging with I-70, go only 0.5 mile, then exit onto Route 340 West toward Charles Town. Follow Route 340 for 18.7 miles. Toward the end you will first cross the Potomac River, then the Shenandoah River. After crossing the

MAP 5 — Harpers Ferry and Maryland Heights

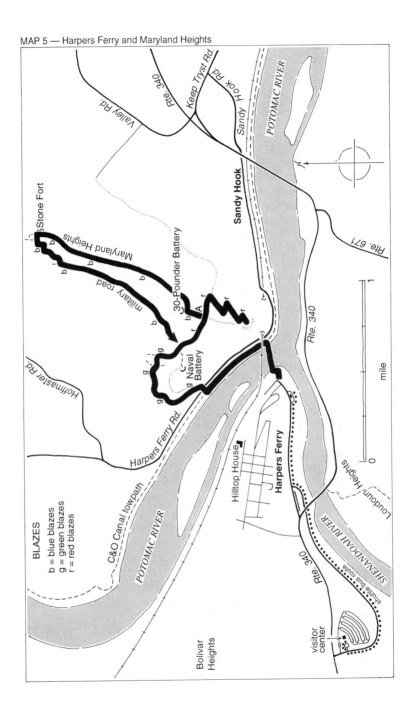

BLAZES

b = blue blazes
g = green blazes
r = red blazes

Shenandoah, continue on Route 340 for 0.9 mile, then turn left at a traffic light into the entrance for Harpers Ferry National Historical Park. Go 0.2 mile, then turn left into the visitor center parking lot.

≈   ≈   ≈   ≈

WALKING: The 6-mile route described below is shown by the bold line on **Map 5** on page 55.

From the Harpers Ferry visitor center, take the shuttle bus to the old lower town.

From the bus pavilion at the lower town, follow the main street (Shenandoah Street) through Harpers Ferry, which features a variety of small museums devoted to different themes of history. If you tour all the museums, you won't have time for the hike described below, but at least stop by two or three. And if you have time after your walk, you can visit a few more. What you don't see in one day can always help to justify a return visit.

At the end of Shenandoah Street just beyond the intersection with Potomac Street, turn right past the John Brown Fort and under a railroad bridge. Take the footbridge across the Potomac River to Maryland Heights and the C&O Canal. (If the bridge is closed, you can drive around to the other side by taking Route 340 downstream, then Keep Tryst Road and Sandy Hook Road back upstream, as shown on Map 5.)

At the far end of the bridge, descend to the canal towpath. With the canal ditch on the right and the Potomac River on the left, follow the towpath past the ruins of lock 33. At the first opportunity, turn right across the canal ditch on a pedestrian bridge. With caution, cross a road and bear left steeply uphill on an old unpaved military road, now called the Maryland Heights Trail. As of 1996, this trail was marked with green blazes on wooden posts.

Follow the trail uphill and around to the right away from the river. After about three-quarters of a mile, pass a blue-blazed trail intersecting from the left. (You will return later by this route.) Continue more or less straight steeply uphill on a red-blazed trail. About 70 yards after the trail levels off, you will reach a trail intersection marked A on Map 5. From here the red-blazed trail continues straight 160 yards, then turns sharply right and zigzags down to the clifftop overlook. Be careful at the overlook and control your children closely.

From the overlook, return to the four-way intersection marked A on Map 5, and from there follow the blue-blazed trail uphill. At the 30-Pounder Battery, turn right. With the dry moat and earth breastwork on the left, continue along the blue-blazed footpath, which soon veers left uphill. The trail is at times obscure, but if you momentarily lose the path, just follow the ridge until you are back on the trail. Pass the pits of old, collapsed powder magazines and the site where a 100-pounder Parrott rifle was mounted. Follow the blue blazes along the rocky ridge to the Stone Fort.

From the Stone Fort, continue along the ridge 25 yards beyond the fort, then turn left on the blue-blazed path. (The Elk Ridge Trail, also marked with blue blazes, continues north.) Go 80 yards to a low stone wall; this and the earth breastwork to the right are the west and north perimeter of the Interior Fort. Turn left and continue to the southwest corner of the Interior Fort. Cross the wall and follow the path downhill on log steps and behind a long stone and earth breastwork on the right. This wall was one of two parallel rifle-pits forming the Exterior Fort. Together, the Interior and Exterior Fort defended against possible attack along the ridge from the north — such as had occurred in 1862 before the fortifications were built.

From the Exterior Fort, follow the path as it winds through a level area where the garrison troops camped. Soon the trail joins the military road. With the slope falling off to the right, follow the dirt road along the plateau and then downhill along the mountainside. At a T-intersection, turn right downhill on the green-blazed trail that you earlier followed uphill. Follow the dirt military road downhill to the paved road and the C&O Canal, and from there return to Harpers Ferry by the way you came.

3

ANTIETAM NATIONAL BATTLEFIELD

Walking and bicycling (or car touring); distances are discussed in the next two paragraphs. This outstanding battlefield park preserves a rolling landscape of fields and woods, scattered farmhouses, and a few famous landmarks: the Dunker Church (reconstructed), Bloody Lane, and the Burnside Bridge. Here, on September 17, 1862, the Union and Confederacy fought the bloodiest one-day battle in U.S. history.

For bicyclists who are experienced at riding in automobile traffic and who are equipped with helmets, the bold line on **Map 6** on page 75 shows a 10-mile (16-kilometer) battlefield tour via paved roads. The route is intended primarily for cars but is also popular with cyclists. About half the route follows one-way roads where most cars are moving fairly slowly. The rest of the route, however, follows two-way roads where traffic is sometimes fast.

Tour the battlefield by automobile or bicycle, stopping along the way at the Burnside Bridge. From this historic bridge, shown in the photograph on page 69, a 2.5-mile (4 kilometer) footpath leads in a loop downstream along Antietam Creek to Snavely's Ford, as shown by the dotted line on Map 6. This trail is closed to bicycles, so cyclists who plan to stop and walk here should bring a lock for their bikes. The trail can be muddy after rain or during periods of thaw, and occasionally it is damaged by floods. Of course, the most "authentic" time for a visit is the dry season during late summer and early fall.

Unfortunately, there are presently no other dedicated hiking trails at Antietam National Battlefield by which visitors can advance across the fields and slog up the slopes *on foot*, as the soldiers did, but several such trails are planned. Inquire at the visitor center or call ahead of time for dates in spring and fall when a park historian leads walks through different sections of the battlefield. Visitors are asked not to hike cross-country through the battlefield because many of the fields are leased by farmers for growing crops or grazing livestock.

Antietam National Battlefield is open daily from dawn until dusk. An admission fee is charged. Dogs must be leashed. The visitor center, which offers a slide program and a movie, is open daily, except Thanksgiving, Christmas, and New Year's Day, from 8:30 A.M. to 5 P.M. — or until 6 P.M. from Memorial Day weekend through Labor Day. The battlefield is managed by the National Park Service; telephone (301) 432-5124.

THE BATTLE OF ANTIETAM (or Sharpsburg, in Southern parlance) was an outgrowth of General Robert E. Lee's success at the second battle of Manassas, fought on August 28, 29, and 30, 1862. (See Chapter 1 for a discussion of Second Manassas.) After pushing the Union army into Washington, Lee decided to carry the war to the North. On September 5 he led his Army of Northern Virginia into Maryland by wading across the Potomac River at White's Ford, midway between Washington and Harpers Ferry. Lee wrote to Jefferson Davis, President of the Confederacy, that by invading Maryland he would at least throw the Federals on the defensive and be able to feed and refit his troops in an area as yet unscathed by the war. He told one of his officers that his goal was Harrisburg, Pennsylvania, where he wanted to burn the Pennsylvania Railroad's bridge over the Susquehanna River. But his ultimate objective was to make a demonstration in Northern territory and thus lure the Union Army of the Potomac, commanded by Major General George B. McClellan, into a showdown. As Lee said after the war, "I went into Maryland to give battle."

Lee already had faced McClellan the prior spring during the Peninsular Campaign, where Lee had learned to exploit the Union general's excessive prudence. Now Lee felt that he could defeat McClellan again and perhaps even destroy a large part of the Federal army, putting the South in a strong position to offer the North an armistice in exchange for independence. He told Davis that the invasion would help convince Northern voters in the impending fall elections to support candidates who favored a settlement accommodating the Confederacy. Also, another victory in the field might provide the occasion for Great Britain and other European powers to recognize the Confederacy as an independent nation and to exert pressure on the North to let the South go its own way. After all, England wanted cotton for its textile industry, which was being hurt badly by the Federal blockade of Southern ports; nor was the prospect of a weaker Union — the Balkanization of the United States — upsetting to English leaders for whom the pre-eminence of the British empire was the paramount consideration.

When Lee entered Maryland, his army numbered somewhat less than

50,000 men. The Southern soldiers were experienced and self-confident, but after three months on the offensive, they were physically run-down, ill-nourished on a diet of apples and unripe corn, and poorly equipped. Many had no shoes. One Confederate veteran later recalled that the troops were a "set of ragamuffins," and that "it seemed as if every cornfield in Maryland had been robbed of its scarecrows." He continued:

> None had any under-clothing. My costume consisted of a ragged pair of trousers, a stained, dirty jacket; an old slouch hat, the brim pinned up with a thorn; a begrimed blanket over my shoulder, a grease-smeared cotton haversack full of apples and corn, a cartridge box full, and a musket. . . . There was no one there who would not have been "run in" by the police had he appeared on the streets of any populous city.

After crossing the Potomac, Lee rested his army for a few days at Frederick while he pondered what to do next. On September 9 he issued marching orders to his top officers. His plan was to move west of South Mountain, which stretches from the Potomac below Harpers Ferry north into Pennsylvania, and to use the long ridge as a shield behind which to march toward Harrisburg. But first, in order to secure his lines of communication through the Shenandoah Valley, he had to capture Martinsburg and Harpers Ferry, held by Union garrisons totaling 13,000 men. Three Confederate columns would approach the towns from separate directions, drive the Federals at Martinsburg into Harpers Ferry, then bag the lot while Lee remained with about a third of the Confederate army west of South Mountain. (For a discussion of the capture of Harpers Ferry, see Chapter 2.)

Lee's plan of dividing his army in the face of a numerically superior army that was known to be advancing from Washington defied conventional military wisdom, but Lee had used similar tactics to confuse and defeat Major General John Pope at the second battle of Manassas. By the time General McClellan realized what was going on and prepared his response, it would be too late to save Harpers Ferry or to stop Lee from reuniting his army. Then Lee expected to deal with McClellan as opportunity afforded.

McClellan, however, benefited from a freak of fortune: the discovery near Frederick on September 13 of a copy of Lee's Special Orders 191 setting forth his entire plan and the route taken by each Confederate column. The document appeared to be genuine — and was. How the order was lost is unknown (it was found wrapped around three cigars) but in any case the paper clarified what until then had been a series of seemingly contradictory reports on the movements and whereabouts of the Southern army. McClellan was exultant. He foresaw the destruction of Lee's forces one piece at a time. In a letter to President Lincoln, the Union general said, "I think Lee has made a gross mistake, and that he will be severely punished for it. . . . I have all the plans of the rebels, and will catch them in their own trap if my men are equal to the emergency. . . . Will send you trophies."

Yet even extraordinary opportunity could not galvanize McClellan into quick action. On the morning of September 14, nearly seventeen hours after he first read the lost orders, he finally moved the Army of the Potomac forward from Frederick. By that evening the Federals had broken enemy resistance at Turner's Gap and at Crampton's Gap on South Mountain, but the Union army halted for the night atop the ridge while the Confederates prepared to withdraw. Lee sent word to the men besieging Harpers Ferry that he planned to retreat into Virginia and that they should do the same. But then he received a message that Harpers Ferry was expected to fall the next morning (as indeed it did), so he issued new orders directing the scattered Confederate army to join forces at Sharpsburg, where he and the 15,000 troops with him took up positions west of Antietam Creek on the morning of September 15. Lee deployed his infantry along a wide front, as though they were far more numerous than they really were, then waited for reinforcements. By mid-afternoon the leading units of the Army of the Potomac confronted the Confederates from across the creek, but McClellan was taken in by Lee's bluff and did not attack.

Accounts of the battle of Antietam are replete with recitations of the opportunities and advantages that McClellan let slip through his fingers. Among the more prominent instances are McClellan's failure to press the attack on the afternoon of the 15th, or even the next day, when he had 60,000 troops on hand, outnumbering the Confederates four to one. But McClellan's chief of intelligence, Allan Pinkerton, consistently overestimated the size of Lee's army, and McClellan gave credence to Pinkerton's figures, unlikely as they were. Four days earlier McClellan had told the Union high command in Washington that the Confederates numbered 120,000 men, thus casting himself as the underdog. So McClellan spent September 16 waiting for still more troops to arrive, while those already on hand took up their assigned positions. Meanwhile, most of the Confederate units that had captured Harpers Ferry reached Sharpsburg, swelling the Southern ranks to 35,000 men, with more coming.

Just as surprising as McClellan's reluctance to fight is Lee's willingness. He, at any rate, knew that he was greatly outnumbered. Although his position was strong — it stretched in a wide, shallow arc along the brow of the plateau north, east, and south of Sharpsburg, with good roads providing interior lines of communication — he had his back to the Potomac, and if the battle went against him, the river would prevent a quick withdrawal. One can only assume that Lee thought he could win, as he had won before, due to the fighting superiority and tenacity of his veterans, the skill and nerve of his officers, and the possibility of Union blundering.

By dawn on September 17, McClellan felt that he was ready. If he had a preconceived plan, he had not told anybody, so that as the attack developed, it took on an ill-coordinated and ponderous momentum of its own. Even in his report afterward, McClellan seems to have been somewhat unsure of just what it was he had attempted to do, saying that he had intended "to make the main attack on the enemy's left — at least to create a diversion in favor of the main attack, with the hope of something more by assailing the enemy's right — and as soon as one or both of the flank movements were fully successful, to attack their center with any reserve that I might then have in hand." But as things turned out, there was no main Union attack. Instead, the Federal assault came piecemeal, as had occurred during the first and second battles of Manassas. The Union blows were heavy, but none was a knock-out punch, delivered with the overwhelming power and resources at McClellan's command. The battle became a series of separate engagements, in which different Federal corps attacked, were used up in desperate fighting, and retired. Even as the day wore on and the Confederates appeared to weaken under the successive blows, McClellan held back his ample reserves, fearful of making an all-out commitment.

The battle began at first light as Union and Confederate artillerists shelled each other north of Sharpsburg. At sunrise Major General Joe Hooker's First Corps of 8,600 Federals advanced south along both sides of the Hagerstown Pike. (See Map 6 on page 75.) Hooker had moved into position astride the turnpike the prior afternoon, in full sight of the Confederates, who had adjusted their lines to face him. Blocking the Union advance was Major General Thomas "Stonewall" Jackson with 7,700 men, some of them drawn up in a line of battle stretching out from each side of the road, facing north, and the rest held in reserve to the rear. Four Confederate batteries occupied a rise near a plain, whitewashed building; it was called the Dunker Church because the congregation of German Baptist Brethren practiced baptism by total immersion. More Confederate artillery was arrayed to the northwest on Nicodemus Hill, where the guns could rake the advancing ranks of Union infantry.

The Federals, however, were supported by their own artillery. From the far side of Antietam Creek, long-range 20-pounder Parrott rifles maintained a steady bombardment. Firing over the heads of the advancing Federals, still more Union artillery occupied a low, wooded ridge called the North Woods farther up the turnpike. (There are no woods there now.) These guns blasted the Confederate infantry waiting in a field of head-high corn just east of the turnpike and less than half a mile north of the Dunker Church. This area, afterward called simply *the* Cornfield, became one of the chief killing-grounds of the battle. To its east were the East Woods, which repeatedly changed hands but were eventually held by the Federals, and to the west, on the far side of the turnpike and behind the Dunker Church, were the West Woods, shielding the Confederate reserves. (Again, the locations and extent of these small patches of forest do not altogether correspond to the woods seen today.)

By 7 A.M. a general melee, half-obscured by smoke, covered the area of the Dunker Church, the Cornfield, and the woods to east and west. In a series of surges, retreats, and renewed assaults, the Union troops pushed southward toward the Dunker Church. The casualties on both sides quickly mounted, and men afterward spoke of the "terrible fire," the "fearful and incessant" gunnery, and wondered how they had got out alive. Hooker's attack appeared to be succeeding, and the general himself was seen riding from one part of the Cornfield to another, urging his men on. But then 2,300 Confederate reinforcements from the division of Brigadier General John Hood poured out of the West Woods, crossed the turnpike, and broke the Federal spearhead with a volley that was "like a scythe running through our line," according to a Union field officer. The Federal formation faltered, then a gradual but general withdrawal began. The Union troops were beaten back along the turnpike to the North Woods, where their artillery, using double charges of canister shot, stopped the Confederate counterattack. In the face of this fire, "whole ranks went down," a Federal officer said, and later the Southern dead were found heaped on top of each other.

The carnage continue unabated. As Hooker's First Corps retreated, the Union Twelfth Corps of Major General Joseph Mansfield advanced from the northeast along the Smoketown Road. The Federals drove the Confederates out of the East Woods. Although Mansfield was mortally wounded, his troops continued to push the Southerners back across the Cornfield and the Hagerstown Pike, where the fences were draped with corpses, and out of sight behind the West Woods. The Confederate line in this sector had been facing north, in the direction of Hooker's earlier attack, but now the Confederates regrouped in ranks facing east, reinforced by troops that Lee shifted from his center near Sharpsburg, where he had his headquarters.

There was a lull in the fighting while the Twelfth Corps waited for support and a third Union attack got underway. At 7:20 A.M. Major General Edwin Summer, commander of the Second Corps, which included three divisions with about 5,000 infantry in each, received orders to cross Antietam Creek and join the troops already in battle. Two divisions, one commanded by Major General John Sedgewick and the other by Brigadier General William French, moved out immediately and waded across Antietam Creek at Pry Ford north of Pry House, where McClellan had his headquarters. But the fighting was two miles to their front, and by the time Sedgewick's division, which took the lead, arrived at the East Woods, the attack of the Twelfth Corps was stalled and French's trailing division was nowhere to be seen, having veered off toward the south. Without waiting to consult with the officers of the Twelfth Corps, Sumner deployed Sedgewick's division in three ranks 500 yards wide, one behind the other, and sent them forward. Setting out shortly after 9 A.M., the Federals were at first unopposed and moved west across the Cornfield, but when the Union ranks reached the turnpike, they were hit by artillery fire from the hills to the west. Still the Federals advanced, entering the West Woods above the Dunker Church. But then 4,400 Confederates, who had been shifted from positions below Sharpsburg, dashed in from the south. In a flanking attack, the Confederates poured volley after volley down the ranks of Union infantry, who broke and retreated north out of the battle after suffering 2,200 casualties. The Confederates pursued, were blasted by the Union artillery at the North Woods, and in turn retreated to the cover of the West Woods.

With that, most of the fighting at the northern end of the battlefield came to an end, after a morning of nearly constant killing. Later in the day, some of McClellan's officers urged him to renew the attack at the north end of the field with reinforcements that had arrived that morning, but McClellan refused. By then he feared that Lee was preparing a counterstroke, and he felt that he needed all the reserves on hand for defense.

Meanwhile, the battle had spread farther south. William French's division from the Second Corps had become separated from Sedgewick's division, so now French decided to direct his attack toward a road (since termed the Sunken Road or Bloody Lane) that was so worn and eroded that it occupied a shallow trough zigzagging across the Confederate center east of the Hagerstown Turnpike. The road served as a trench for about 2,000 Southerners, and as French's division appeared over the rise to their front, the Confederates' first volley brought the Union ranks to a standstill. "The effect was appalling," a Southern officer later reported. "The entire front line, with a few exceptions, went down in the consuming blast." More frontal attacks were tried and failed. A Confederate sergeant described the action as "systematic killing." Recalling the experience of advancing over the brow of the hill, a Union soldier wrote:

> An occasional shell whizzed by or over, reminding us that we were rapidly approaching the "debatable ground" . . . . The compressed lip and set teeth showed that nerve and resolution had been summoned to the discharge of duty. A few temporarily fell out, unable to endure the nervous strain, which was simply awful.

For about two hours the Federals were stymied in front of the Sunken Road. Eventually, another Union division of 5,000 men, commanded by Major General Israel Richardson, arrived on the scene. Although Richardson's division was part of the Second Corps, which had gone into combat hours earlier, McClellan had not allowed Richardson to cross Antietam Creek until 9:30 A.M., when reinforcements had arrived to take the place of Richardson's division among the reserves. Finally, after another futile frontal assault by the Union troops, the Confederates in the road were outflanked by a brigade that approached from the southeast, where the Federals could shoot down the length of the lane, which was crowded with infantry. A Confederate soldier wrote, "The slaughter was terrible! When ordered to retreat I could scarcely extricate myself from the dead and wounded around me." Scores of men were shot as they scrambled up the bank behind the road and ran across the field to the rear.

The Confederates pulled back and the fighting continued as Union troops, advancing from the Sunken Road, tried to break their enemy's final line of resistance in front of the Hagerstown Pike. For the Confederates, the situation was desperate, Their infantry, weakened earlier by the withdrawal of units to bolster positions to the north, had suffered heavy casualties. Those men still fit to fight were in disarray, although they were supported by a line of fieldpieces. The Union commanders on the scene felt that one more push would split the Confederate center wide open. Richardson asked for artillery support, but was told that no guns were available. McClellan wanted them in reserve or massed to the north in case of a Confederate counterattack there. As he tried to organize an attack with the forces on hand, Richardson was killed. And so the Union attack petered out, and the Federals pulled back below the Sunken Road.

As the fighting died down in the central area of the battlefield, it intensified in the south, where a stone bridge (later named the Burnside Bridge) crossed Antietam Creek. Major General Ambrose Burnside and Brigadier General Jacob Cox, his field commander, had spent the early part of the morning waiting for orders to send the Union Ninth

Corps into battle. This force consisted of four divisions totaling 13,000 men, and it was opposed — in the immediate vicinity of the bridge — by only four or five hundred Georgians. But the Confederate position was strong: the Georgians were concealed in the woods atop a bluff that not only overlooked the bridge but also the road that approached it from the southeast along the opposite bank of the creek. Up the hill, on the open slopes south of Sharpsburg, Confederate artillery and 3,000 infantry waited to counter a breakthrough at the bridge. Earlier there had been more infantry south of Sharpsburg, but Lee had shifted them north to repel attacks at the opposite end of the Confederate line.

A few minutes before 10 A.M., while Burnside and Cox watched from a distance the start of General French's attack on the Sunken Road, a courier arrived from McClellan with orders directing Burnside to cross the stone bridge. Almost immediately, the Union artillery opened fire in a preliminary bombardment, and then a regiment of Federals moved forward to form a skirmish line along the east side of the creek. But they made easy targets and fell back after a third had been shot. A larger force, which was supposed to storm down the hillside facing the bridge and cross under cover of fire from the skirmishers, got lost in the woods and eventually reached the creek 350 yards upstream, where they stayed, sniping at Confederates on the opposing hillside.

Meanwhile, a Union division numbering about 3,000 men under Brigadier General Isaac Rodman was supposed to wade across the creek two-thirds of a mile downstream from the bridge at a ford selected earlier by McClellan's engineers, but the place proved to be unusable because the stream banks and bluff were too steep. So Rodman continued marching downstream, looking for a place called Snavely's Ford that had been mentioned by local farmers.

Back at the bridge another attack was mounted and failed. A column of 300 Federals charged down the road next to the creek, but at every step they were blasted by riflemen on the opposite bank and by artillery on the hill still farther back. The column disintegrated after the attackers lost nearly half their men.

Eventually, at about 12:30 P.M., a third attack was organized. From a position upstream, Union artillery raked the opposing bluff with grapeshot. While two Union regiments fired their rifles from the top of the slope facing the bridge, another two regiments, the 51st New York and the 51st Pennsylvania, charged down the hill. The plan was to storm straight across the bridge, but Confederate fire forced the regiments to take cover to either side. Lieutenant George Whitman, brother of the poet Walt Whitman, later wrote, "We were then ordered to halt and commence fireing, and the way we showered the lead across

that creek was noboddys buisness." Soon Confederates were seen leaving their positions and retreating up the hill. As the enemy fire slackened, the two Union regiments followed their color bearers across the bridge in a solid column and fanned out to either side.

It was 1 P.M. by the time the bridge was taken, and another two hours passed while Burnside and Cox brought men and artillery across the creek and organized the troops on the western side. During the interval, General Rodman led 3,200 Union troops across the river at Snavely's Ford, then continued north up a ravine to join the Federals who had crossed the bridge.

At 3 P.M. the Union attack south of Sharpsburg was renewed as more than 8,000 Federals advanced uphill toward the town on a front three-quarters of a mile wide. For the next hour they moved forward by stages, pressing toward Cemetery Hill and reaching the southern edge of Sharpsburg itself. One Virginian described the approach of the Federal line:

> The first thing we saw appear was the gilt eagle that surmounted the pole, then the top of the flag, next the flutter of the stars and stripes itself, slowly mounting, up it rose, then their hats came in sight, still rising the faces emerged, next a range of curious eyes appeared, then such a hurrah as only the Yankee troops could give, broke the stillness, and they surged against us.

Each side fired volley after volley at pointblank range. The Union troops rushed forward, and the lines collided in hand-to-hand combat. Finally the Confederates ran for the rear. "I was afraid of being struck in the *back*," a Southern private recalled, "and I frequently turned half around in running, so as to avoid if possible so disgraceful a wound." As he ran he heard the Yankees cheering in unison, "as if they had gained a game of baseball."

Again, Lee's army seemed to be on the brink of disaster. But then the troops at the left end of the Federal line broke in confusion, suddenly attacked by Confederates who had come up from the southwest via Millers Sawmill Road. Major General A. P. Hill's division had marched seventeen miles from Harpers Ferry in eight hours, and now, swinging off the road into a line of battle, his troops entered the fight without pausing. The shock recoiled down the Union line, and after Hill got his artillery into action, the Federals were forced into a general withdrawal toward the bridge.

The Confederates were not strong enough to pursue the Federals, but they regained sole possession of the slopes immediately south of Sharpsburg. To the north their lines were also intact, reformed a few hundred yards to the rear of their original positions. With the approach of dark the fighting died down, and each side began the task of searching the fields for their wounded. Describing the battlefield, a Southern officer wrote:

> The dead and dying lay as thick . . . as harvest sheaves. The pitiable cries for water with appeals for help were much more horrible to listen to than the deadliest sounds of battle. Silent were the dead, and motionless. But here and there were raised stiffened arms; heads made a last effort to lift themselves from the ground; prayers were mingled with oaths, and oaths with delirium, men were wriggling over the earth; and midnight hid all distinction between the blue and the gray.

The Union and Confederate forces prepared for a resumption of the battle at dawn on the 18th. Even after subtracting its losses, the Army of the Potomac was still powerful, numbering more than 62,000 soldiers, a third of them veterans who had not fought on the 17th. But McClellan continued to be apprehensive about a counterattack, and so he did not renew the fighting. Indicating that he would risk nothing, McClellan reported, "I concluded that the success of an attack was not certain. . . . I should have had a narrow view of the condition of the country had I been willing to hazard another battle with less than an absolute assurance of success."

For his part, Lee had only 28,300 exhausted infantry and 4,500 cavalry; nonetheless, for a period, he *did* contemplate a sweep to the north, but the odds were too great. So as the day passed and Mc-Clellan's inaction showed that the Confederates could retreat in safety, Lee decided to withdraw that night. McClellan made no attempt to interfere, and the entire Army of Northern Virginia, with its artillery, wagon trains of supplies, ambulances and walking wounded, moved out from Sharpsburg in the dark and forded the Potomac at Shepherdstown.

The battle at Antietam Creek is commonly termed a military stalemate by which both sides suffered grievously. Federal losses were 2,108 dead, 9,540 wounded (many died later from their wounds or were maimed for life or at least invalided out of the war), and 753 missing and for the most part probably dead. The total of 12,401 Union casualties was 25 percent of those who went into action. The Confederacy lost at least 1,500 dead, 7,750 wounded, and 1,000 missing. Although Confederate casualties were marginally less than those of the Union, on a percentage basis they were greater. Moreover, Southern losses were more difficult to replace than those of the populous North.

The battle worked to the disadvantage of the Confederacy in other ways also. Although Lee extricated his battered army from a position where a Union commander more aggressive and relentless than McClellan would have tried to crush the Confederates before they could escape across the Potomac, the fact remained that Lee's invasion was turned back. The British government decided that the moment to recognize the Confederacy had not arrived after all. The failure of the invasion also provided Lincoln with an opportunity to issue his Preliminary Emancipation Proclamation on September 22, declaring that, by virtue of his power as commander in chief, he was freeing all slaves in territory in rebellion "as a fit and necessary war measure for suppressing said rebellion." Lincoln had been considering this step for at least two months but had decided to postpone his announcement until the military news was better than it had been all summer. The proclamation was to take effect on January 1, 1863, and although it left slavery untouched in areas where rebellion had never occurred or had already been quashed — and of course did not by itself free any slaves in areas controlled by the Confederates — it nonetheless made clear that the war was being fought not only to restore the Union but also to end slavery. One immediate, practical effect was to reduce still further the possibility that the British government, which had outlawed the slave trade and slavery in its own colonies during the first half of the century, would support the South.

Following the battle, Lee withdrew through the Shenandoah Valley, while McClellan remained at Sharpsburg for more than a month. On October 9 Lincoln arrived at McClellan's camp to view the battlefield, review the troops, and confer with the general. "I incline to think that the real purpose of his visit is to push me into a premature advance into Virginia," McClellan wrote to his wife the next day. As the President and the War Department continued to prod him during the following weeks, McClellan told his wife that he was being bombarded with insults, innuendoes, and accusations "from men whom I know to be greatly my inferior socially, intellectually, & morally! There never was a truer epithet applied to a certain individual than that of the 'Gorilla.'" Nor did McClellan like the President's policies. McClellan had been appalled by the prospect of emancipation, which he regarded as unconstitutional. As far as he was concerned, the proper and limited objective of the war was simply to end the rebellion in the South and to reunite the country, whereas emancipation was itself a revolution.

As days and weeks passed and the Union army remained in camp, Lincoln became increasingly disgusted with McClellan's reluctance to take to the field. He chided McClellan for what he called his "overcautiousness" (Lee had used much the same term in analyzing McClellan's abilities) and even told a friend that so far from being an offensive force, the Army of the Potomac was simply McClellan's bodyguard. Waiting until the army had finally moved into Virginia and until after the fall elections, Lincoln dismissed McClellan on November 7 and replaced him with General Burnside. Two years later McClellan ran for the Presidency against Lincoln but lost by a substantial margin.

As for Burnside, in December 1862, he led the Army of he Potomac to defeat at Fredericksburg, where the Union (but not the Confederacy) suffered losses comparable to the battle of Antietam. General Hooker then took over, but again the Federals were defeated at Chancellorsville in May 1863, ushering in Lee's second invasion of the North, which culminated at Gettysburg.

≈   ≈   ≈   ≈

AUTOMOBILE DIRECTIONS: Antietam National Battlefield is located at Sharpsburg, Maryland, about 55 air miles northwest of Washington. (See the corner panel on **Map 6** on page 75.) From Washington, access is provided by Interstate 270 toward Frederick, then Route 40 Alternate to Boonsboro and Route 34 to Sharpsburg. If you are coming from Virginia, you may prefer to head first past Leesburg and then take Route 9 to Route 480 north to Sharpsburg.

To Antietam National Battlefield from Interstate 495 (the Capital Beltway): Leave the Beltway at Exit 35 (off the Outer Loop) or Exit 38 (off the Inner Loop) in order tó take Interstate 270 North toward Frederick. Once you are on I-270 heading north, follow the directions in the next paragraph.

To Antietam National Battlefield from Interstate 270 past Rockville and Gaithersburg: Follow I-270 North, but before reaching Frederick take the exit for Interstate 70 West toward Hagerstown. Within the space of a few miles, pass the exit for Routes 340 and 15, then take Exit 59 for Route 40 Alternate toward Braddock Heights and Middletown. At the end of the exit ramp, turn left (west) and follow Route 40 Alternate 11.4 miles west to Boonsboro. At a traffic light in Boonsboro, turn left onto Route 34 West and go 6.3 miles to Sharpsburg. In Sharpsburg, turn right onto Route 65 North. Go 0.8 mile, then turn right onto Dunker Church Road. After only a hundred yards, continue straight in order to reach the visitor center.

≈   ≈   ≈   ≈

CAR TOURING and BICYCLING: The 10-mile route described below is shown by the bold line on **Map 6** on page 75. Most of the route follows park roads, but it also makes use of regular automobile roads where traffic can sometimes be heavy. The route examines in sequence the morning, midday, and afternoon phases of the battle. Along the way are frequent battlefield signs and interpretive stations, as well as parking lots at the main landmarks. Even if you assimilate only a general impression of the mass of information set forth on the many signs, they underscore the tumultuous seesaw movement of the opposing armies as units advanced and attacked, were decimated or ran out of ammunition, fell back or were withdrawn, or marched from one defensive position to another.

About two-thirds of the way through the tour route, you will reach the Burnside Bridge, where there is an opportunity to park and walk along Antietam Creek, as discussed on page 76 and shown on Map 6 by the dotted line. There are also other opportunities for short walks, as discussed below.

Tour route: Turn right out the visitor center parking lot and follow Dunker Church Road (formerly the Hagerstown Turnpike) north past the Dunker Church. Go nearly 1.0 mile, then turn right onto Mansfield Avenue in the vicinity of what once was the North Woods, from which Hooker's First Corps of Federal troops attacked southward at the battle's outset — and where twice, later on, the Union artillery repulsed Confederate counterattacks.

At a T-intersection, turn right onto Smoketown Road, along which Mansfield's Twelfth Corps of Federal troops advanced from the northeast — and along which Mansfield himself was carried mortally wounded to the rear. Pass a road intersecting from the left in the vicinity of the East Woods, then turn right onto Cornfield Avenue. Continue across the Cornfield, where so much of the fighting occurred during the battle's morning phase.

At a crossroads, turn left back onto Dunker Church Road. Go only 0.1 mile, then turn right to a monument at Philadelphia Brigade Park, in the vicinity of which Sedgwick's division of the Union Second Corps was repulsed by Jackson's troops.

Turn right back onto Dunker Church Road, go 0.2 mile, then turn left onto Smoketown Road. Go 0.2 mile, then turn right to pass the cemetery and farmstead of the Mumma family, whose buildings the Confederates burned to prevent their use by Union sharpshooters. Turn left at a T-intersection and follow Richardson Avenue parallel with the Sunken Road (or Bloody Lane), which — during the battle's midday phase — Richardson's Federal troops captured, only to be stopped as

MAP 6 — Antietam National Battlefield

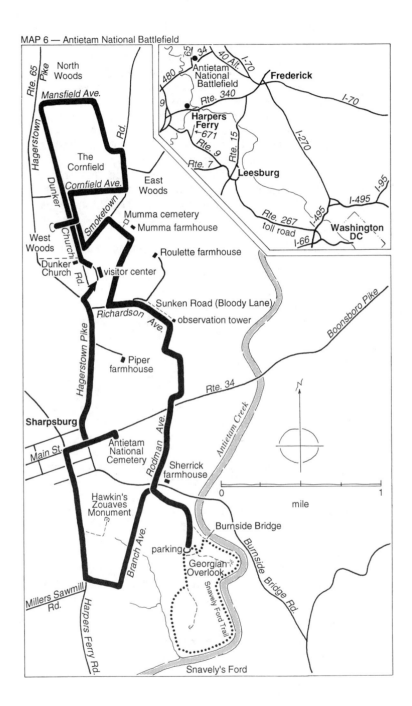

they tried to continue their advance toward the Piper farmhouse and Hagerstown Turnpike on the right. The parking lot at the Sunken Road or at the observation tower is a good place to stop in order to walk up and down the Sunken Road. From the observation tower, continue along the park road. With caution, cross Route 34 and follow Rodman Avenue below Cemetery Hill. At a T-intersection, turn left toward the Burnside Bridge and follow the road all the way to its end, where there is a parking circle above the bridge. After being held off for hours, Burnside's Federal Ninth Corps eventually captured the bridge early in the afternoon. **The 2.5-mile walk described at the bottom of this page starts at the bridge and returns to the parking circle.**

To complete the tour, follow the road away from the Burnside Bridge. Pass the intersection with Rodman Avenue, then curve left uphill on Branch Avenue. Turn right, then turn right again at a T-intersection in order to head north into Sharpsburg. After just 0.3 mile, there is a small parking bay on the right from which a paved path leads a few hundred yards to a monument commemorating the Federal Hawkin's Zouaves. This is a good spot from which to view the heights that Federal troops, after crossing Antietam Creek, eventually succeeded in capturing during the battle's afternoon phase, only to be pushed back again at the end of the day by A. P. Hill's Confederate division that had just arrived from Harpers Ferry.

Continue north into Sharpsburg. Turn right onto Route 34 (East Main Street) and follow it 0.4 mile to Antietam National Cemetery.

To go from the cemetery to the visitor center, turn around (with caution) and follow Route 34 back into Sharpsburg, and there turn right onto Route 65 North. Go 0.8 mile, then turn right onto Dunker Church Road. After only a hundred yards, continue straight to the visitor center.

≈ ≈ ≈ ≈

WALKING ON THE SNAVELY'S FORD TRAIL: This 2.5-mile circuit is shown by the dotted line on at the bottom of **Map 6** on page 75.

From the parking circle above the **Burnside Bridge**, follow the paved walkway as it zigzags downhill to the bridge. (A paved side trail leads to the Georgian Overlook.)

At the near end of the bridge, descend to the Snavely's Ford Trail. With Antietam Creek on the left, follow the path downstream. Eventually, at Snavely's Ford, where Rodman's Union division waded across the stream, follow the path as it curves right uphill away from the creek. Continue as the trail climbs to a plateau, then turn left at a T-intersection. Follow the path to the McKinley Monument at the Burnside Bridge parking circle.

4

SUGARLOAF MOUNTAIN

Walking — 6 miles (9.7 kilometers). The circuit shown on **Map 7**
on page 83 offers sweeping views over the Frederick Valley.
From the highest parking lot, a short climb leads to the Sugarloaf
summit. (Purists who eschew driving up the mountain can start
at the Mountain Entrance and climb up from the south.) From
the summit the loop continues along a ridge of lesser peaks to
the north, then descends to the valley of Bear Branch before
returning up another ridge to the high Sugarloaf parking lot. The
circuit entails a fair amount of hiking up and down and may take
as long as three hours. If you run out of time or steam, the map
shows other trails for a shorter loop.

On weekends in spring and fall, the mountain parking lots and
summit attract large crowds, so try to arrive early in the day.
Sugarloaf Mountain is open daily from sunrise to sunset. The
mountain road opens at 8 A.M. and closes at posted times that
correspond approximately with sunset. The road is also closed
on Christmas and when snow and ice make it impassable.
Motorcycles are prohibited on the mountain road. Dogs must be
leashed. Camping and fires are prohibited.

Sugarloaf Mountain is a privately owned conservation and
recreation area. It is managed by Stronghold, Inc., Dickerson,
Maryland 20842.

SUGARLOAF MOUNTAIN is a monadnock. Rising more than eight
hundred feet above the surrounding Piedmont upland and still farther
above the Frederick Valley to the west, this small but conspicuous
mountain is a remnant of a former, higher landscape. The term *monadnock* is from Mount Monadnock in New Hampshire, left as an isolated
eminence by erosion of the region around it.

Sugarloaf stands high while the surrounding land has been worn to a
much lower level because the mountain is made of particularly resistant

rock. The summit is a massive plate of quartzite composed of grains of quartz sand so solidly cemented together by silica that the rock breaks across the individual grains rather than around them. The quartzite slab that caps the mountain is about two hundred feet thick and is not prone to dissolution, decay, or chemical disintegration. In consequence, cliffs about 150 feet high have formed around the edges. Below the cliffs are slopes of jumbled, angular boulders (called *talus*), split from the quartzite massif by the expansion of water when it freezes in joints and fissures in the rock.

Underlying the thick quartzite capstone are softer layers of impure, mica-rich quartzite, slate, and shale that together are about 170 feet thick. Occurring in beds one on top of another, these materials have eroded more quickly than the rock above. They have been carried away, leaving a level terrace of soil and loose material resting on yet another layer of durable quartzite, similar to the summit slab but not as thick. On the western side of the mountain, part of the terrace is occupied by the West View parking lot at an elevation of about one thousand feet. Occupied by the blue-blazed trail, the terrace extends around the north side of the mountain to an overlook at a slightly higher elevation. Occupied by part of the mountain road, the terrace extends around the south side of the mountain to the East View parking lot at a slightly lower elevation. Again, the layer of quartzite that bolsters the terrace has formed a ring of low cliffs and viewing points.

On a larger scale, Sugarloaf Mountain and the ridge to the north constitute the top of a tight fold of rock strata which, viewed end-on and in cross-section, form an inverted U. Such a downward-opening fold is called an *anticline*. Some geologists assert that the Sugarloaf formation is really the eroded edges of a U-shaped fold opening upward (or *syncline*), but the most recent investigations indicate that whatever synclines occur in the area are lesser folds and minor dimples in the overall anticlinal structure. The top of the anticline peeps above what is now the surface of the earth, and the sides (or *limbs*, as geologists say) plunge beneath the surface to the northwest and southeast, forming a ridge stretching north from the main peak. The rock strata at the north end of the ridge dip beneath the surface, and according to one study, so do the strata at the south end, suggesting that the structure actually consists of an elongated anticlinal dome, now dissected by erosion. Some geologists speculate that the peaks and rock outcrops along the ridge may be areas where the deposits of sand that formed the quartzite were thicker or purer (thus creating a more durable stratum of rock) than in areas that now are gaps and saddles between the peaks. However, a more favored view is that the peaks and outcrops are areas where the strata, originally deposited as horizontal beds of sand, have been crumpled and creased so tightly by pressure exerted from the southeast that the quartzite layers — now folded over upon themselves — are thicker than they were originally and have thus withstood erosion longer.

The sand that formed the quartzite at Sugarloaf Mountain is thought to have been deposited originally as ocean beach (or possibly by rivers) in late Precambrian or early Cambrian time — or that is, about 560 million years ago. The regional compression that transformed the deposits into quartzite and folded the strata occurred perhaps 500 to 450 million years ago during the Taconic Orogeny (*orogeny* being a geologic term for a mountain-building event). In broad terms, the Taconic Orogeny was one of a series of such events that have occurred in the eastern United States, characterized by pressure from the southeast as large sections of the earth's crust have drifted from that direction and collided with the continental margin of North America.

There is no knowing what materials were once deposited or thrust over the Sugarloaf Formation and have since been worn away to expose the mountain, although presumably the sequence and structure of rock strata found at other places in the Piedmont Plateau provide a clue. It is perhaps instructive that at its present level, the floor of the Frederick Valley is formed of soft red sandstone, siltstone, shale, and limestone — all sedimentary rocks that are not particularly resistant to erosion. The Piedmont uplands in the vicinity of Sugarloaf are formed primarily of phyllite, a metamorphic rock intermediate in grade between slate and shist. Phyllite is significantly harder than the sedimentary materials of the Frederick Valley but not as durable as quartzite.

≈   ≈   ≈   ≈

Sugarloaf Mountain's main peak and the surrounding land belong to Stronghold, Incorporated, a nonprofit corporation organized in 1946 by Gordon Strong, who during the first decades of the century acquired the mountain for a vacation retreat and retirement home. Strong and his sister built houses located at the foot of what is now the exit road. In 1925 Strong considered erecting a planetarium designed by Frank Lloyd Wright on the mountain top, but then rejected the idea in favor of keeping the area in a more natural state. At the time of Strong's death in 1954, his holdings at Sugarloaf totaled 2,350 acres, which he left to Stronghold, Inc. to be managed as a natural reservation. Since then, about a thousand acres have been added. If you want to support the work of Stronghold by making a small contribution, write to Stronghold, Incorporated, P.O. Box 55, Dickerson, MD 20842 for a brochure.

≈ ≈ ≈ ≈

AUTOMOBILE DIRECTIONS: Sugarloaf Mountain is located in Maryland about 30 miles northwest of Washington. (See the corner panel on **Map 7** opposite.)

To Sugarloaf Mountain from Interstate 495 (the Capital Beltway): Leave the Beltway at Exit 35 (off the Outer Loop) or Exit 38 (off the Inner Loop) in order to take Interstate 270 North toward Frederick about 22 miles. Once you are on I-270 heading north, follow the directions in the next paragraph.

To Sugarloaf Mountain from Interstate 270 about half-way between Gaithersburg and Frederick: Leave I-270 at Exit 22 for Route 109. From the bottom of the exit ramp, follow Route 109 South 2.9 miles, then turn right onto Route 95 (Comus Road) toward Sugarloaf Mountain. Go 2.4 miles to a wide paved area at the Sugarloaf Mountain Entrance.

Turn right into the mountain entrance and follow the road steeply uphill. Pass the East View parking lot. Continue along a level stretch of road, then fork right uphill for the West View parking lot. Immediately past a small traffic circle, turn right into the West View parking area.

If you want to climb the entire mountain rather than drive most of the way to the top, park at the Sugarloaf Mountain Entrance and use the white-blazed trail that starts a short distance up the entrance road, as shown on Map 7, or take another white-blazed trail that starts near the foot of the exit road. The climb is not difficult. As noted in the introduction, however, if you follow the loop shown on Map 7, you will get plenty of climbing even if you first drive to the parking lot near the summit.

≈ ≈ ≈ ≈

WALKING: The bold line on **Map 7** opposite shows the 6-mile walk described here.

From the circular drive below the West View parking lot, follow a flight of stone steps uphill between massive walls. Continue to the summit on a green-blazed trail that at first consists of flagstones, then a dirt footpath with log steps, and finally stone stairs.

After touring the summit, pick up the red-blazed trail at the edge of the brush to the north, not far from where the main

MAP 7 — Sugarloaf Mountain

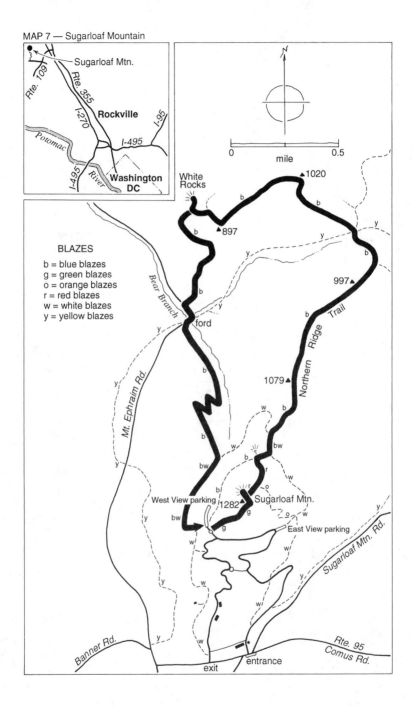

Sugarloaf Mtn.

Rte. 109

Rte. 355

I-270

Rockville

I-95

I-495

I-495

Potomac River

Washington DC

N

0   0.5
mile

White Rocks

▲1020

b

b

b

▲897

y

BLAZES

b = blue blazes
g = green blazes
o = orange blazes
r = red blazes
w = white blazes
y = yellow blazes

Bear Branch

b

b

y

b

997▲

b

Northern Ridge Trail

ford

y

b

1079▲

Mt. Ephraim Rd.

y

w

b

b

bw

w

bw

b

r

w

b

r

o

West View parking

1282▲ Sugarloaf Mtn.

bw

g

o

w

g

East View parking

w

w

y

Sugarloaf Mtn. Rd.

y

w

o

w

y

w

Banner Rd.

y

w

Rte. 95
Comus Rd.

exit   entrance

83

green-blazed trail enters the spacious glade at the top of the mountain. (If you cannot locate the red-blazed trail, return to the rocky high point where the green-blazed trail first reaches the summit, then walk toward the glade 35 yards to where red blazes and a footpath appear on the right.)

Follow the red-blazed path downhill. Pass a junction where the orange-blazed trail intersects from the right. Continue to a T-intersection with the blue-blazed trail. To return to the West View parking lot, turn left; but for the longer hike across the northern peaks as shown on Map 7, turn right and continue as described below.

Follow the blue blazes downhill to an intersection with the white-blazed trail. Turn left and follow the blue and white blazes through level woods. Fork right on the blue trail where the white trail veers left. From now to the end, simply follow the blue trail.

Follow the blue trail through level woods, then uphill to the left. Continue along the side of a ridge, down through a broad saddle, then up along the ridge again before descending to a junction with the yellow-blazed multi-purpose trail.

Cross the trail intersection and continue on the blue trail slightly left uphill, then along the hillside, with the slope falling off to the left. Continue as the trail bears right and climbs steeply to another summit. Bear left across the summit, then downhill and along a broad wooded ridge on the blue-blazed trail. Eventually, descend steeply, then continue along the ridge to a sharp bend in the blue-blazed trail, where a spur trail leads right 100 yards to a cliff of white rocks overlooking the Frederick Valley.

Leaving the rocky escarpment behind you, follow the blue-blazed trail downhill, up again, then downhill through the woods to Mt. Ephraim Road. At the road, turn left and follow the road uphill 100 yards to an intersection. (Walk on the far left in order to minimize the risk of being hit by a car approaching from behind.) At the intersection, follow the road right for 100 yards, then bear half-left into the woods on the blue-blazed footpath, which climbs gradually away from the road and up the side of a broad ravine. Continue as the trail switches back and forth uphill and along a wooded ridge.

At an intersection with the white-blazed trail, bear right. Follow the blue and white blazes along the mountainside, then abruptly left uphill. At an intersection where the white trail diverges to the right, fork left on the blue trail. Cross a boulder field and climb steeply uphill to the West View parking lot.

5

LITTLE BENNETT REGIONAL PARK

Walking and ski touring — The 5-mile (8-kilometer) route shown on **Map 8** on page 93 starts at Hyattstown Mill and from there follows a narrow country road along the valley of Little Bennett Creek. This road is closed to through traffic, but you should be prepared for an occasional car — and also for the shallow ford at Little Bennett Creek. After leaving the road, the trail climbs a wooded ridge and follows the crest back toward Hyattstown Mill.

A longer circuit of 7 miles (11.3 kilometers) is shown on **Map 9** on page 95. This route has more variety than the other; it climbs up and down over several ridges and passes through large meadows as well as woods — but the trails can be very muddy because of their use by horses. Again, the route in part follows a narrow country road used occasionally by cars and that at one point fords Little Bennett Creek.

Little Bennett Regional Park is open daily from dawn until dusk. The park is managed by the Montgomery County Department of Parks (Maryland-National Capital Park and Planning Commission); telephone (301) 972-6581. For information on camping April through October, call (301) 972-2222.

LITTLE BENNETT REGIONAL PARK typifies Maryland's Piedmont region. A branching system of minor streams — in this case Little Bennett Creek and several of its tributaries — has carved the Piedmont upland into a landscape of rolling hills and low, rounded ridges. Although there are no dramatic rapids or falls, the streams have sufficient gradient and volume to have powered a series of mills built during the eighteenth and nineteenth centuries. This walks passes the sites of several of these works, where in one instance water-driven milling continued well into the twentieth century.

The principal operation along Little Bennett Creek was Hyattstown

Mill, which still stands on the south side of Hyattstown Mill Road a few hundred yards east of the intersection with Frederick Road (Route 355). A gristmill and sawmill were first built here sometime between 1783 and 1794 by William Richards on land purchased from Jesse Hyatt, who laid out Hyattstown at the turn of the century. The mill property changed hands frequently during the first half of the nineteenth century. By 1850 George W. Darby, a tenant-miller, was operating the business with the aid of one employee. According to the census of that year, the mill had two pairs of buhrstones and one saw. Annual output was 6,000 bushels of meal and 35,000 feet of lumber. An advertisement of sale that appeared in the Montgomery County *Sentinel* on October 8, 1858 provides a more detailed description of the mill:

> 25 Acres of Land, more or less, improved by one large Frame DWELLING HOUSE, one small Dwelling House, one FLOURING MILL, 2 pairs of 4 feet burs, new, and all the latest improvements for a Merchant Mill, 1 Country Mill, 1 pair of 3 feet, 7 inch burs, all new machinery; 1 SAW MILL, connected with the Merchant and Country Mill.

The terms "merchant mill" and "country mill" do not refer to separate structures but to different machinery for specific tasks; all the apparatus, except for the sawmill, was housed in the same building. The two pairs of buhrstones and other "latest improvements" that constituted the flouring mill or merchant mill produced high quality flour for sale on a commercial basis, while the country mill ground corn or other grain on demand for local farmers. At such country mills — also called custom mills — the miller typically retained part of what he ground as a toll or fee for his services, whereas the grain for merchant milling typically was purchased outright in large quantities by the miller.

The 1858 advertisement did not lead to a sale, but five years later the property changed hands at an auction ordered by the Circuit Court of Montgomery County to pay the owner's debts. In 1868 the mill again was sold by court-appointed trustees, whose handbill described the property as "16 acres of land on Bennett's Creek a little southeast of the village of Hyattstown and 6 miles from the B & 0 RR. Improved by a 1st rate grist and saw mill with an excellent water power capable of driving two sets of burrs." The advertisement also listed a comfortable dwelling house containing eight rooms, a miller's house containing five rooms, a large barn, a carriage house, and a "meat house with a never failing spring of pure water convenient to the buildings."

The high bidder, at $2,901, was George A. Darby, perhaps the son of the tenant-miller in 1850. In any case, Darby owned and operated the mill until 1905. The G. M. Hopkins atlas of Montgomery County, published in 1879, shows Darby's gristmill, sawmill, and residence, and also carries an advertisement for George A. Darby, Miller: "Dealer in Flour, Meal, Buckwheat Flour, Feed and Grain of all kinds & Lumber." The 1880 census valued annual output at Darby's mill at $9,160. Business was divided evenly between commercial flour production and custom milling. A fourteen-foot fall of water drove an overshot wheel five feet wide at five revolutions per minute, enabling the mill to grind up to sixty bushels per day.

After Darby sold the property in 1905, the new proprietor installed a modern steel roller mill. Only one pair of stones was retained for producing cornmeal, stone-ground wheat, and animal feed. Water power was supplemented by a steam engine, housed in a shed next to the mill building. A photograph from the early twentieth century shows a structure very much like that seen today. Only a few trees stand nearby, and open fields are visible in the background. A horse-drawn wagon rests outside the large door fronting the road.

In 1911 the mill again changed owners, and the following year it was purchased by Frank L. Mortimer, a machinist, and Charles A. Luhn, a cabinetmaker. In addition to continuing their own trades on the premises, Mortimer and Luhn operated the mill. According to the recollections of Charles R. Murphy, who started work at the flour mill about 1914, Mortimer & Luhn purchased outright most of the grain that they processed. The mill produced cornmeal, whole wheat flour, and a higher grade of baker's flour from which the bran and other coarse particles had been removed by bolting. The firm had its own truck for distributing its flour and cornmeal to stores throughout the area. Some custom milling of animal feed and flour was still done, either for a cash fee or for 25 percent of the finished product.

In 1918 the mill burned, as reported in the *Sentinel* for September 6:

> Fire, supposed to have originated in the engine room, destroyed the Hyattstown Roller Mills, owned and operated by Mortimer & Luhn, Thursday morning of last week, causing a loss of about $12,000. A barn across the road was also destroyed and a number of horses were endangered. The flames were discovered by a colored woman after such progress had been made that nothing could be done to save the structure or its contents. About 1,000 bushels of wheat and a quantity of corn, flour and a new equipment of machinery were made a total loss. The mill had been operated by its owners for six years . . . . The livestock and other contents of the barn were saved. An insurance of about one-fourth the value of the mill and contents is reported.

Despite the financial loss, Mortimer and Luhn rebuilt the mill. They dismantled a warehouse from Price's Distillery (namesake of Price's

Distillery Road east of the park) and used the lumber to reconstruct their mill on the old foundation. On the outside, at least, the new structure closely resembled the old mill, except that the building was sheathed in corrugated metal siding that formerly covered the warehouse. New mill machinery (now no longer in place) was purchased from a manufacturer in Kentucky. The basement of the mill contained the cog pit or gears; the first floor held the stones and the rollers; and the second and third floors contained storage bins, dryers, sifters, and other machinery. Belt-and-bucket elevators moved the grain through the milling process. According to Mr. Murphy, the Mortimer & Luhn employee mentioned earlier, during periods of persistent rain or high humidity when mold might develop, the corn and wheat on the top floors had to be aired by running the grain up and down the elevators.

For a few years after its reconstruction, the Hyattstown Mill enjoyed moderate prosperity, but business began to decline during the 1920s as larger mills, located on the railroad in Germantown and Rockville, overshadowed the Hyattstown operation. For decades wheat production in Maryland and other Eastern states had been shrinking, and unless mills were located to receive shipments of wheat by rail from the Middle West, they were reduced to grinding out cornmeal or to "corn crushing" for animal feed.

Mortimer and Luhn sold the Hyattstown Mill in 1928. Five years later another sale occurred, for which the advertisement stated, "The mill has been in operation up until this time and has a well established business. It is noted for the fine quality of its water ground corn meal." Operations continued for a period, probably lasting until the late 1930s or early '40s. In 1966 the property was purchased by the Maryland-National Capital Park and Planning Commission for inclusion in Little Bennett Regional Park, and in 1996 the mill was restored to its appearance in the early twentieth century.

Behind the mill is the wheel pit, from which the trench of the tailrace extends toward Hyattstown. The miller's house still stands just up the road, where a millstone is set into the earth in front of the porch. Several hundred yards beyond the miller's house, the ditch and berm of the millrace come into view below Hyattstown Mill Road. The race follows the road for about half a mile to the site of the former millpond. Apparently the dam was located just downstream from the confluence of Dark Branch and Little Bennett Creek. The millpond was ten to twelve feet deep at the dam, and covered five to seven acres of what is now low, swampy woods north of Hyattstown Mill Road where it intersects with Prescott Road.

This road intersection also marks the site of another old mill: David A. Zeigler's Sumac Mill. The 1850 Census listed the mill as employing six hands to produce annually 130 tons of ground bark, which Zeigler used for tanning hides. The mill was powered by a horse and three mules. Zeigler's property included a farm of three hundred acres stretching to the Frederick Road, where his log house, now covered with shingles, still stands near the intersection with Prescott Road. A later Zeigler enterprise was a water-driven saw and a bone mill that ground animal bones for fertilizer. Shown on Simon Martinet's 1865 map of Montgomery County and again in 1879 on the G. M. Hopkins atlas, it was located about a hundred yards east along Hyattstown Mill Road from Sumac Mill, which by then was defunct. Traces of this later mill remain. From the road a shallow ditch (the former tailrace) extends south thirty yards to a stone headwall that was part of the mill foundation. The mill's headrace runs east next to Hyattstown Mill Road, then curves off to the south along the side of the hill to join Little Bennett Creek at the former dam site about 180 yards upstream from the present-day ford.

Finally, the G. M. Hopkins atlas shows still more rural industries farther upstream along Little Bennett Creek. Lee Wilson's sawmill stood just below the intersection of Hyattstown Mill Road and Clarksburg Road. Luther G. King's distillery, sawmill, and "old mill" were located in King's Valley, about two and a half miles above the Wilson sawmill. King placed an advertisement in the Hopkins atlas declaring that he was a "Manufacturer and Dealer in Pure Rye and Common Whiskey." The 1880 census valued King's distillery at $6,000, with two employees and output worth $3,888 over a six-month season. The distillery works were powered by both a waterwheel and a small steam engine. Thirty years earlier the census had said that his gristmill, with two pairs of stones and one employee, produced 1,800 bushels of meal annually and his sawmill 25,000 feet of lumber. By 1880, when the gristmill was not mentioned as a separate enterprise in the census, King presumably was grinding rye and corn exclusively for use in his own distillery, which operated until about 1907.

Another remnant of rural life in the valley of Little Bennett Creek is the one-room Kingsley Schoolhouse, which was used from 1893 to 1935. It stands next to the creek and is passed by the route outlined on Map 9 on page 95. The schoolhouse is shown near the right end of the map.

≈   ≈   ≈   ≈

AUTOMOBILE DIRECTIONS: Little Bennett Regional Park is located in Maryland northwest of Rockville and Washington. (See the corner panels on **Maps 8 and 9** on pages 93 and 95.) Access is provided by Interstate 270 linking the Capital Beltway and Frederick.

To Little Bennett Regional Park from Interstate 495 (the Capital Beltway): Leave the Beltway at Exit 35 (off the Outer Loop) or Exit 38 (off the Inner Loop) in order to take Interstate 270 North toward Frederick about 22 miles, then follow the directions in the next paragraph. In the process, you will pass Exit 18 with its sign for Little Bennett Regional Park; that exit is convenient to the campground but not to Hyattstown Mill, where the walks shown on the maps start.

To Little Bennett Regional Park from Interstate 270 about half-way between Gaithersburg and Frederick: Leave I-270 at Exit 22 for Route 109. From the bottom of the exit ramp, follow Route 109 North 0.4 mile into Hyattstown.

At a T-intersection with Route 355 (Frederick Road), turn right. Follow Route 355 South only a hundred yards, then turn left onto Hyattstown Mill Road just beyond a firehouse. Turn right immediately into a parking lot opposite the end of the firehouse. Although a number of Montgomery County vehicles may be parked in the lot, it is intended also for park users.

There is another small parking area a few hundred yards father up Hyattstown Mill Road opposite the mill itself. That lot, however, is intended for mill visitors and not for hikers who, presumably, will be gone for hours. So on days when the mill is open, don't park there. Yet other small parking areas are located still farther up Hyattstown Mill Road.

≈   ≈   ≈   ≈

WALKING: The two walks shown on **Map 8** opposite and on **Map 9** on page 95 are described in turn below.

Map 8 shows a 5-mile walk. With the firehouse on the left and a children's play lot on the right, follow Hyattstown Mill Road away from Frederick Road. (Walk on the left shoulder in order to minimize the risk of being hit by a car coming from behind; step off the road onto the shoulder as cars approach.) Go 275 yards to Hyattstown Mill.

From the mill, continue on Hyattstown Mill Road past the miller's house and (eventually) above the remains of the millrace that is located on the right. Follow the road across Dark Branch and Little Bennett Creek, near the site of the former milldam.

Continue along the road to a junction where Prescott Road intersects from the right. (This was the site of David A.

MAP 8 — Little Bennett Regional Park: 5-mile loop

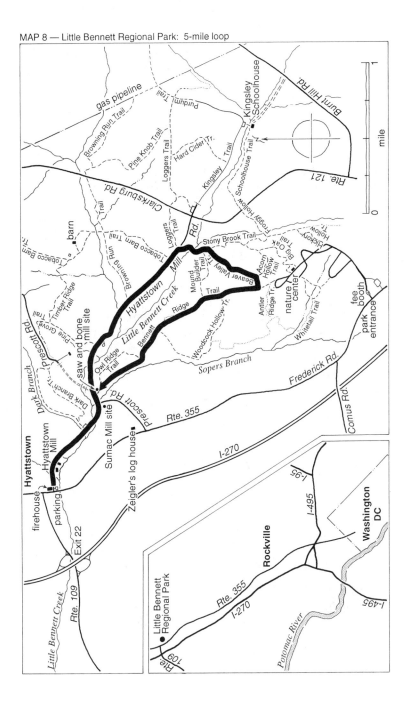

93

Zeigler's Sumac Mill.) Bear half-left to continue on Hyattstown Mill Road. Pass a gate on the right where the Bennett Ridge Trail emerges from the woods; you will return later by this trail.

At a road junction near the tailrace of Zeigler's saw and bone mill, bear right to continue on Hyattstown Mill Road past a barrier. (Notice the berm and ditch of David A. Zeigler's headrace running parallel with the road on the right.) Continue to a ford across Little Bennett Creek. Do not attempt to wade across if the stream is higher than your ankles; if it is, return to the Bennett Ridge Trail and follow it to the campground and back.

After crossing Little Bennett Creek, continue along Hyattstown Mill Road. Pass different trails, a barrier, and a small bridge. Eventually, after the road bends abruptly half-left, bear right off the road onto the Beaver Valley Trail toward the nature center.

Follow the Beaver Valley Trail away from the road and across Little Bennett Creek on a footbridge. At an intersection with the Mound Builder Trail, fork left to remain on the Beaver Valley Trail. At an intersection with the Stony Brook Trail, fork right to remain on the Beaver Valley Trail, which climbs through scrub and pines. As the trail levels off, continue through deciduous woods. At an intersection with the Acorn Hollow Trail, turn right to remain on the Beaver Valley Trail.

At a T-intersection with the Bennett Ridge Trail (a dirt and gravel road), turn right. Follow the Bennett Ridge Trail for a mile along the ridge, straight across a weedy clearing, and through an area of scattered sycamores, new growth, and occasional mounds of Allegheny mound-building ants. At one point, the trail descends abruptly, then bears right along the hillside. With the slope rising toward the right, continue on the grassy track past an intersection with the Owl Ridge Trail on the right.

At a T-intersection with Hyattstown Mill Road, turn left. Walking on the far left for safety, follow Hyattstown Mill Road back to the starting point by the way you came.

Map 9 opposite shows a 7-mile walk. With the firehouse on the left and a children's play lot on the right, follow Hyattstown Mill Road away from Frederick Road. (Walk on the left shoulder in order to minimize the risk of being hit by a car coming from behind; step off the road onto the shoulder as cars approach.) Go 275 yards to Hyattstown Mill.

MAP 9 — Little Bennett Regional Park: 7-mile loop

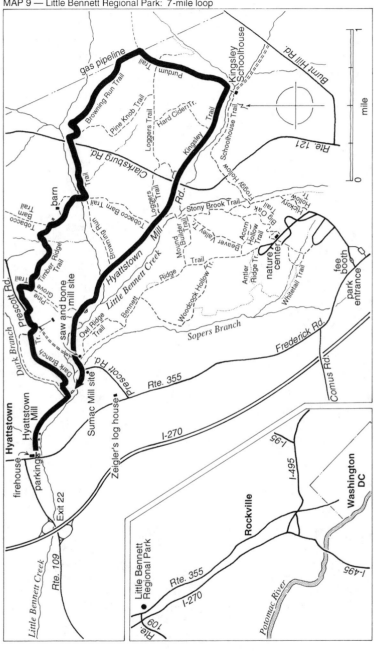

From the mill, continue on Hyattstown Mill Road past the miller's house and (eventually) above the remains of the millrace that is located on the right. In all, follow the road half a mile to Dark Branch, where there is a small parking bay on the left.

Turn left onto the Dark Branch Trail, which soon veers right up the side of the ravine, then winds along a ridge. Turn right at a T-intersection and go to Prescott Road.

Turn left and follow Prescott Road gradually uphill. (If you prefer, you can follow a horse track slightly to the right of the road.) Pass a sign board at a clearing where horse trailers are sometimes parked. Before long, descend to the right on the Pine Grove Trail and follow it as it curves sharply right. Very soon, turn left onto the Timber Ridge Trail and follow it uphill, then around the corner of an overgrown field, and back into the woods. Eventually, cross a small clearing at the top of a ridge, then descend steeply into a ravine. Cross a stream and bear left, then turn right under some overhead wires and go uphill to an intersection with the Tobacco Barn Trail at a large field.

Bear right on the Tobacco Barn Trail and follow it across a rolling field above a barn, then downhill and into the woods. Cross a stream and, after a few dozen yards, turn left onto the Browning Run Trail and follow it to Clarksburg Road.

With caution, cross Clarksburg Road and follow the trail along the lower edge of a field. Fork left into the woods on the Browning Run Trail where the Pine Knob Trail forks right uphill. Zigzag through scrubby woods, then bear right uphill. Climb gradually, then bear half-right at the top of the ridge along a gas pipeline right-of-way. At a four-way intersection with the Purdum Trail, turn right. Pass an intersection with the Logger's Trail, then pass through a camping area as the trail becomes a road that eventually descends steeply into the valley of Little Bennett Creek across from the Kingsley Schoolhouse.

Turn right on the Kingsley Trail (a road) and follow it along the valley, with Little Bennett Creek toward the left. Pass an intersection with the Hard Cider Trail. With caution, cross Clarksburg Road and continue along the valley on Hyattstown Mill Road all the way back to your starting point. Eventually, the road fords Little Bennett Creek. Do not attempt to wade across if the stream is higher than your ankles; if it is, retrace your steps to the Beaver Valley Trail on the right, then (referring to Map 8 on page 93) complete your walk by following that route.

6

SENECA CREEK STATE PARK

Walking and ski touring — 4 or 5 miles (6.4 or 8 kilometers), depending on whether you pass around Clopper Lake at the west end or east end. The route shown on **Map 10** on page 103 starts at the visitor center and follows a series of interconnected blazed trails along Great Seneca Creek, Long Draught Branch, and the shore of Clopper Lake. Farmed for two centuries, most of the area has now reverted to woods, although a few meadows are maintained north of the lake.

Seneca Creek State Park is open daily from 8 A.M. to sunset, with the exception that on weekends from November through March it does not open until 10 A.M. A small admission fee is charged on weekends and holidays. Dogs are prohibited, even on a leash. The park is managed by the Maryland State Forest and Park Service; telephone (301) 924-2127. Call for information about canoe, rowboat, and paddleboat rental at Clopper Lake.

SENECA CREEK STATE PARK, which comprises about six thousand acres in all, extends from the vicinity of Gaithersburg downstream thirteen miles to the Potomac River, but only the northern section around Clopper Lake is developed for walking and other activities. Clopper Lake itself is a recent creation, made in 1975 by damming Long Draught Branch, but the name "Clopper" goes back in this neighborhood to the early nineteenth century, when Francis C. Clopper acquired the land. The tract remained in the ownership of his descendants through four generations until purchased by the state in 1955. Starting at the park's visitor center (site of the former Clopper house), the walk described at the end of this chapter follows streams that used to supply water power to Clopper's various mills, and crosses woods that in many parts of the park have grown up in Clopper's farm fields and pastures during the last half-century.

One enterprise here was Clopper Mill, which actually predates the period of Clopper ownership. According to a patent, or deed, dating from 1777, when Montgomery County was sparsely settled, Nicholas Sybert, "yeoman," conveyed to Benjamin Spyker, also styled yeoman, 222 acres of land "with all and singular the improvements, mills, ways, water and watercourses" on Great Seneca Creek at what is now the present mill site. Sybert had patented the land nine years earlier, and apparently it was he who first built a mill there.

By 1783 the property was owned by William Benson, who contracted to sell the tract "Good Part" to Zachariah Maccubbin (or McKubin), owner of a modest tobacco plantation nearby. Although Maccubbin tore down the old mill and erected a new one sometime between 1792 and '95, he never received title to the land because he failed to complete payment to Benson — who had died in 1790 — or to Benson's heirs. In 1804 Benson's daughter and son-in-law complained that Maccubbin was cutting down timber on the property, and later they filed a suit to eject Maccubbin, who told the court that the Benson clan had "most cruelly swept away all the horses, stock, corn, wheat . . . threatening to turn him and his family out of doors in poverty and distress." After the parties had engaged in legal sparring for several years, a jury was impaneled and ruled that Maccubbin owed the Bensons £3,499 plus 5,254 pounds of tobacco (frequently used as a cash substitute). Maccubbin could not pay, and on September 2, 1807, a court-appointed trustee advertised the property for sale in the *Federal Gazette & Baltimore Daily Advertiser*, where it was described as a plantation of 488 acres "with a large and commodious mill house 38 feet by 42, three stories high, one story of which is stone and two of brick." The mill had two water wheels, three pairs of millstones, and two bolting clothes, one for sifting fine-grade, merchant baker's flour, and the other for sifting coarser flour. The property also included a sawmill, a stable, a smith's shop, a dwelling, and a store house. When the trustee's sale was completed in 1808, the proceeds fell slightly short of the amount of the judgment against Maccubbin, who was ruined and left the vicinity. The purchasers were the Benson heirs, who in 1812 sold the mill and 541 acres for $7,000 to Francis Cassatt Clopper.

Born in Baltimore in 1786, Clopper had already achieved business success as a tobacco merchant in Philadelphia, but he abandoned trade in order to take up the life of a country gentleman and mill owner. Clopper undoubtedly improved the Maccubbin mill, and he may even have rebuilt it; a stone marked "F.C.C. 1834" was set in the wall, and unlike the description in the 1807 advertisement, the surviving ruins of Clopper Mill have two stories of stone and only one of brick. In any case, the operation was run by a series of resident millers, one being Charles Mansfield, who on May 8, 1857, announced in the Rockville *Sentinel* that he was removing from the F. C. Clopper Mill and wished his creditors would settle with him. A year later Richard H. Bennett advertised wool carding at the mill. In 1863 Clopper deeded the mill and Good Part to his married daughter, Mary Augusta Hutton, but retained a life interest for himself and for a spinster daughter, who was to receive half of the "tolls of the mill and mill seat . . . including the tenements now on the right bank of the mill race."

Judging from advertisements, the period of greatest activity at Clopper Mill was between 1850 and 1880. It is not known when the mill stopped operating. An old photograph of the mill shows a stone and brick structure topped by a peaked roof with clapboard gables; four millstones lie on the ground in front, perhaps a sign that the building was no longer used for milling. Although the mill burned in 1947, the gutted ruins still stand. The mill walls, shown in the photograph on page 98, are visible from Clopper Road across from the intersection with Waring Station Road, about half a mile west of the park entrance (see Map 10 on page 103). Part of the millrace still runs along the west bank of Great Seneca Creek for a few hundred yards upstream from the Clopper Road bridge, and the tailrace is discernible below the mill.

In 1814 Francis C. Clopper bought another mill two miles upstream from Clopper Road. Called Middlebrook Mill, it had been built about twenty years earlier by Abraham Faw, who on May 12, 1794, advertised the works in the *Maryland Journal* as a newly-built merchant gristmill with four pairs of stones "on the most powerful and constant stream in the county." At that time, the property of 240 acres also included a sawmill, a tavern, a store, and a blacksmith's shop.

Clopper also owned a small woolen factory, probably located west of Long Draught Road on land that now is submerged under Clopper Lake. Before the reservoir was created, a millrace and mill ruins were visible. The 1850 census listed the Francis C. Clopper Woolen Manufactory as a water-powered operation with seven employees and a monthly payroll of $125. The works included three looms and various carding machines, fulling stocks, pickers, and spinning frames. Clopper's woolen mill reportedly made blankets during the Civil War.

Clearly, F. C. Clopper was a man of considerable means and business enterprise. As a farmer he probably grew some tobacco but mostly wheat for his own merchant mills. Archbishop Ambrose Maréchal of Baltimore met Clopper on October 9, 1823, and described him in his diary as a "rich miller whose wife and children are Catholics." In 1847 Clopper gave the land for construction of St. Rose of Lima Church, located on Clopper Road a short distance east of the park entrance. He designed the Rockville courthouse, built in 1840 and torn down fifty years later. Toward the end of his life, he helped to organize a corporation for building a railroad through Montgomery County; when the company failed in 1857 without making much progress, Clopper interested the Baltimore and Ohio Railroad in the project, leading ultimately to construction of the Metropolitan Branch, linking Hagerstown and Washington via Frederick. The line passed through Clopper's land a short distance upstream from Clopper Mill, and the local station, for which he donated the land, was named for him, as was the surrounding neighborhood. Clopper died in 1868, and he and his wife and many of their descendants are buried in the graveyard behind St. Rose Church.

Clopper's house was called Woodlands. It formerly stood immediately west of the present-day visitor center, where there is now a small log house moved from Germantown. The oldest part of Woodlands, built before 1800, was a two-story log structure covered with stucco, but in 1812 Clopper constructed a brick and stucco addition that was substantially larger and more elegant than the original house. Following Clopper's death, his daughter Mary Augusta Hutton came into possession. Her husband, William Rich Hutton, was an engineer of note, serving from 1869 to 1874 as Chief Engineer of the C&O Canal. During other periods he was involved in canal, bridge, aqueduct, and railroad projects throughout the mid-Atlantic states and New York. It is not clear how much time Hutton spent at Woodlands, but he died there in 1901 and, like his parents-in-law and his wife, is buried in the graveyard at St. Rose Church. Several unmarried Hutton children, including a son who farmed the estate, lived at Woodlands all their lives. Other descendants lived at Woodlands until it was acquired by the state of Maryland. Left vacant, the house was vandalized and burned in part, then torn down.

Nonetheless, traces of the homestead are evident in the immediate vicinity of the visitor center. For example, behind the bulletin board at the end of the parking lot is a large linden tree, and beneath it a millstone, brought up the hill from Clopper Mill by Clopper's grandson, is set into the ground. Behind the millstone are several old, large boxwood bushes, and they and other ornamental shrubs originally from the Clopper era compete with the brush at the edge of the woods. To the left (east) of the visitor center a series of four earth terraces that once were flower and vegetable gardens descend into the woods.

≈   ≈   ≈   ≈

BUS: The Montgomery County Ride-On bus 61 to Germantown originates at the Shady Grove Metrorail station (Red Line) and passes the entrance to Seneca Creek State Park on Clopper Road. Let the driver know that you want to get off at the stop closest to the park. For current schedule information, telephone (301) 217-7433.

≈   ≈   ≈   ≈

MAP 10 — Seneca Creek State Park

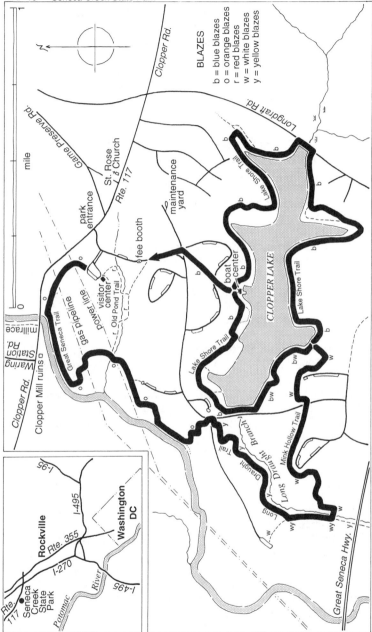

BLAZES

b = blue blazes
o = orange blazes
r = red blazes
w = white blazes
y = yellow blazes

103

AUTOMOBILE DIRECTIONS: Seneca Creek State Park is located in Maryland northwest of Washington and Rockville. (See the corner panel on **Map 10** on page 103.) Access is provided by Interstate 270 linking the Capital Beltway and Frederick. Please note, however, that if you are approaching from the south on I-270, you should use Exit 10; and if you are approaching from the north, use Exit 11B. Both approaches are described below.

To Seneca Creek State Park from Interstate 495 (the Capital Beltway): Leave the Beltway at Exit 35 (off the Outer Loop) or Exit 38 (off the Inner Loop) in order to take Interstate 270 North toward Frederick more than 10 miles. Once you are on I-270 heading north, follow the directions in the next paragraph.

To Seneca Creek State Park from the south on Interstate 270: Leave I-270 at Exit 10 for Route 117 West (Clopper Road). From the bottom of the exit ramp, follow Route 117 West 2.0 miles to the entrance to Seneca Creek State Park on the left. Follow the entrance road only a hundred yards, then turn right to the visitor center parking lot.

To Seneca Creek State Park from the north on Interstate 270: Leave I-270 at Exit 11B for Route 124 West (Quince Orchard Road). From the bottom of the exit ramp, follow Route 124 West only 0.3 mile to an intersection at a traffic light with Route 117 (Clopper Road). Turn right onto Route 117 West and go 1.5 miles to the entrance to Seneca Creek State Park on the left. Follow the entrance road only a hundred yards, then turn right to the visitor center parking lot.

≈   ≈   ≈   ≈

WALKING: The bold line on **Map 10** on page 103 shows the 4- or 5-mile walk described here.

From the end of the visitor center parking lot that is farthest from the visitor center itself, follow the orange-blazed Great Seneca Trail down into the woods. Pass under power lines and across a pipeline right-of-way. At Great Seneca Creek, turn left. With the river on the right, follow the orange blazes downstream. Eventually, follow the path away from the river, then left again. Pass back across the pipeline right-of-way. At the power lines, pass the Old Pond Trail intersecting from the left. Follow the orange blazes steeply uphill and along the edge of the power-line right-of-way. Where the transmission lines cross Great Seneca Creek, veer left into the woods and along the top of the bluff before eventually descending to the river. About 75 yards before a large rock slopes prominently into the creek from the left bank, turn half-left and follow the orange-blazed trail as it zigzags uphill and emerges from the woods at a road intersection.

Cross the road that intersects from the right. Descend into the woods on the yellow-blazed Long Draught Trail, which at first runs parallel with the road toward the right, then zigzags downhill. Near the bottom of the slope, bear right and follow the yellow-blazed trail through the woods, now and again near Long Draught Branch.

Eventually, turn left at a T-intersection. Follow the white-blazed Mink Hollow Trail (which for a few hundred yards is congruent with the yellow-blazed Long Draught Trail) along the side of the valley. At the first opportunity, turn left to follow the white blazes across a pedestrian bridge over Long Draught Branch. Turn left along the foot of the slope, then right up a tributary ravine, then left again near the top of the slope. Continue through the woods, with the slope falling off to the left. Eventually the white-blazed trail reaches a park road.

Cross the road obliquely toward the right and re-enter the woods on the white-blazed path. Follow the trail as it zigzags uphill. Continue on the white-blazed trail through the woods, past shelters and a parking lot on the right, then downhill through the woods to Clopper Lake.

As shown on Map 10, at Clopper Lake you can turn right or left to pass around the east or west end of the lake and, in either case, eventually reach the boat center. The eastern route is about a mile longer than the western route. The trail around the lake's east end is marked all the way by blue blazes. The trail around the lake's west end is marked by both blue and white blazes as far as the dam, then by blue blazes from the far end of the dam to the boat center.

Once you reach the boat center, follow the left shoulder of a road uphill away from the lake. At a T-intersection, continue across a road and a small footbridge over a ditch. Follow a blue-blazed footpath half-right uphill to a crossroads. At the crossroads, turn left toward the park exit, where the fee booth is visible in the distance. Again, walk on the left shoulder, well off the road. Follow the road past the fee booth and a parking lot. Turn left onto a road leading to the visitor center.

7

CHESAPEAKE AND OHIO CANAL

Walking and bicycling. The C&O Canal towpath stretches 184.5 miles (297 kilometers) along the Potomac Valley in Maryland between Cumberland and the Georgetown terminus at Rock Creek in Washington. The entire path is shown on **Map 11** on page 119 and — in greater detail — on the four overlapping **Maps 12-15** on pages 120-123. The dirt towpath is excellent for walking and is also easily passable by fat-tired and hybrid bicycles; it is not suitable for thin-tired roadbikes. Most of the canal itself is empty and overgrown, but for the 22 miles nearest Georgetown, the canal has been restored, more or less, to its appearance during the first quarter of the twentieth century, when it was still an operating commercial waterway. Lift locks and lockkeepers' houses, stop gates and levees to divert floods, dams and feeder canals to bring in water, spillways to drain off the excess, and other intriguing engineering works punctuate a walk or ride along the towpath. At intervals the towpath also provides spectacular views of the Potomac, and some sections border the river for miles at a time. In short, the C&O Canal towpath is one of the nation's great historic and recreational facilities.

Different options for walking or bicycling the canal towpath are discussed starting on page 130. My personal feeling is that the 22 miles of towpath nearest Georgetown are best appreciated on foot, but that beyond Violettes Lock bicycling is the way to go, in part because cycling will reduce monotony in the long sections where there are no views of the Potomac. Accordingly, for the first 22 miles, several access points at intervals of 5 to 7 miles are described in the automobile directions starting on page 117. For the rest of the towpath, access points at intervals of 15 to 30 miles are described. Hikers and even cyclists may want to arrange a car shuttle so that they can walk or ride one-way, as discussed briefly in the automobile directions. Another possibility is to take the bus to Cumberland, as discussed on page 131 under the heading of "Bicycling from Cumberland to Georgetown."

Hikers with dogs must keep their pets on a short leash to avoid accidents with cyclists. Cyclists, in turn, must ride single file, yield to other trail users, and keep their speed to a moderate, safe pace. For cyclists, good weather is essential; if you ride on the dirt towpath during rain, or for a day or two after rain when the towpath is still wet, you will quickly become covered with grit. If you are cycling and plan to bring children, they should be old enough to steer steadily; if they can't and they veer off the path, they could plunge into the canal or down the steep embankment into the Potomac River. In some places, the towpath briefly doubles as an access road to adjacent properties, and between milepost 85 and 88 there is a bicycle detour that follows local roads, as shown by the detail on Map 13. For other closures, see below.

The C&O Canal towpath connects with several other hike-bike trails, as outlined schematically on **Map 2** on page 7. For a 20-mile circuit via the towpath, the Washington Crescent Trail, local streets, and the Rock Creek Trail, see Chapter 24.

The C&O Canal is managed by the National Park Service; telephone (301) 739-4200 for general information, including information about camping along the towpath. **Call also to learn whether any closures are in effect because of damage by floods,** such as that which occurred in January 1996. For information about the 22 miles nearest Georgetown, telephone the visitor center at Great Falls Tavern: (301) 299-3613.

THE CHESAPEAKE AND OHIO CANAL along the Maryland bank of the Potomac River was successor to a project of the Patowmack Company, which between 1785 and 1802 built five short canals that skirted the river's worst falls and rapids. Although the Potomac was thus made navigable to shallow-draft cargo boats between Cumberland and Georgetown, the system worked only during periods of high water. By 1819 the Patowmack Company was bankrupt, and in 1828 it conveyed all its rights and property along the river to the newly-formed Chesapeake and Ohio Canal Company, which set about building a continuous waterway that paralleled the Potomac. (For a discussion of the Patowmack Company, see Chapter 9.)

The practicality of a continuous, man-made waterway between the interior of the country and the Eastern seaboard was demonstrated in

1825 by the completion of the Erie Canal connecting Buffalo and Albany. By linking the Great Lakes and the Hudson River, the Erie project provided cheap transport for heavy loads between what was then called the Northwest (and is now termed the Middle West) and New York City. Alarmed that the potentially vast trade with the nation's interior would be channeled through New York, other Eastern cities and states began building their own canals.

On July 4, 1828 — the same day that construction began on the Baltimore and Ohio Railroad, the nation's first commercial rail venture — President John Quincy Adams broke ground for the C&O Canal. The waterway was to extend 360 miles to the Ohio River at Pittsburgh. The federal government and the city of Washington each subscribed for $1,000,000 in stock; Maryland put up $500,000, Georgetown and Alexandria each contributed $250,000, Shepherdstown $2,000, and individuals $607,400. Navigation between Georgetown and Seneca opened in 1831. Harpers Ferry was reached in 1833 and Hancock in 1839. But by 1850, when the canal reached Cumberland, the cost had mounted to almost three times the original estimate for construction of the entire canal, and many millions of dollars had been paid in interest during a period when the waterway produced only negligible income. Maryland had paid an additional $5 million toward the project, jeopardizing the state's credit; other investors simply refused to advance additional funds. In the meantime the B&O Railroad had reached Cumberland in 1842 and had forged westward across the Allegheny Mountains. By 1852 the railroad stretched to the Ohio River at Wheeling, and plans to extend the canal beyond Cumberland were abandoned.

The slow pace and high cost of constructing the canal reflected a series of logistical, legal, and labor problems — and also a shortage of qualified contractors. Tardy deliveries of building stone, dressed lumber, and lime for cement slowed construction of locks and retaining walls. Excavation often revealed unexpected rock, hardpan, or other difficult materials close to the surface. West of Point of Rocks, where the B&O Railroad also follows the Potomac River, competition for a right-of-way led to high land prices, litigation, and delay. Because of the shortage of manpower in America, laborers, stone cutters, masons, carpenters, and even miners were brought from Ireland, England, Wales, the Netherlands, and Germany, often on an indentured basis. Brawls occurred between antagonistic Irish factions, and more than a few men were beaten to death in pitched battles, culminating in January 1834, when federal troops were summoned to restore order. The episode ended with a formal treaty signed by twenty-eight leaders of the warring groups, but labor unrest flared again at different camps and among different groups as construction dragged on. Dissatisfied with poor food, makeshift barracks and shacks, low and often late pay, and indentured servitude, many workers simply ran away, and still others died in epidemics that swept through the camps. Contractors, too, came and went. Construction contracts were let for half-mile sections on which work was supposed to progress simultaneously, but many contractors were not up to their task, and in some sections work was performed by a series of contractors, each picking up where the prior one had failed.

The canal company eventually completed 184.5 miles of canal that included 74 lift locks compensating for a difference in elevation of 605 feet between Cumberland and tidewater at Georgetown. In addition the company constructed guard locks and levees that were supposed to hold out floods. Eleven aqueducts were built to carry the canal across tributaries of the Potomac River. Seven Potomac dams diverted water from the river into the canal. To bypass the serpentine course of the Potomac at the Paw Paw Bends, the canal passed through a 3,118-foot tunnel that took fourteen years to finish at a cost that was about eighteen times greater than the original estimate.

Even after the canal was completed as far as Cumberland, its upkeep and improvement demanded large expenditures. Floods frequently damaged the waterway and locks (as still occurs), and the Civil War brought further destruction that required extensive repairs. Because of Maryland's huge financial commitment to the canal, the waterway became, in effect, a government operation. The corporation's officers were appointed by the state, and preference for low-level jobs, such as lock tending, was given to Civil War veterans.

The canal's most prosperous period was the 1870s, when more than seven hundred mule-drawn boats were in operation. Eastbound cargo consisted mainly of grain, building stone, lumber, whiskey, and above all else, coal from Cumberland. Westbound boats carried miscellaneous provisions and manufactured goods, but the tonnage going upstream was always much less than that going down.

Even during the canal's peak years, however, profits did little more than pay the interest on the enormous construction debt, which, in fact, was never repaid. After a disastrous flood in 1889 left the waterway in ruins, the bankrupt canal company incurred still more debt to rebuild under the receivership of the Consolidation Coal Company, a subsidiary of the Baltimore and Ohio Railroad. The receiver used both the canal and the railroad to transport coal, but during the first two decades of the twentieth century, tonnage carried by the canal gradually declined as the B&O acquired outright ownership of the waterway by purchasing the canal company's depressed shares and bonds. When a flood in April 1924 tore long gaps in the canal bank, the waterway was abandoned. By then 87 percent of the canal company's stock was owned by the B&O, which had long since demonstrated the superior flexibility and efficiency of the railroad. But the B&O in turn became financially troubled during the Great Depression, and in 1938, at the suggestion of Secretary of the Interior Harold Ickes, the railroad conveyed the canal to the federal government in satisfaction of an unpaid debt of $2 million owed the Reconstruction Finance Corporation, a Depression-era agency that made loans to hard-pressed industries. For a period the Department of the Interior considered using the canal right-of-way for an automobile parkway, but eventually preservationists prevailed. In 1971 Congress established the C&O Canal National Historical Park, combining outstanding scenery and a fascinating glimpse of the past.

≈   ≈   ≈   ≈

AN EXCELLENT DESCRIPTION of life on the Chesapeake and Ohio Canal in 1859 is provided by a manuscript of an unknown author who, as the guest and helper of a boat captain, made the trip from Cumberland to Georgetown, across the Potomac to Alexandria via the Alexandria Aqueduct and Canal, then back to Cumberland. Aside from the author and the captain, the crew consisted of a Negro bow man named Pic and two boys who took turns guiding a team of mules along the towpath. There were four mules, and the usual routine was to work them in shifts of two. Loaded with 120 tons of coal and moving at a steady pace of about two miles per hour, the boat had great momentum, and this made passing through the locks an operation that required considerable skill:

> To enter a lock requires care and experience. The boat had to be steered in a direct line in the center of the canal, for the least deviation would cause a collision with the stone walls that might sink it, for it fitted the lock like a nickel in a slot. The boat must also have sufficient motion to carry it to the end of the lock and at the same time it must not strike the lower gate. The Capt. steered the boat in, Pic stood on the bow and jumped ashore with a line and give it two turns around the snubbing post. At the right moment the Capt. gave the word to the tow boy to stop; Pic tightened the rope on the post and the boat came to a standstill just before the cutwater touched the gate. The friction of the rope around the post has to be carefully governed or the momentum of the boat and its load will break it. This friction and the rubbing of the boat against the side of the lock and the force of the water confined in the end of the lock combined to bring the boat to a stop.

After a boat heading down the canal had floated into the lock, the upstream gates were closed and wickets (i.e., sluices) in the downstream gates were opened, draining the water down to the level of the canal below the lock. Then the downstream gates were opened and the boat towed out. For boats headed up the canal, the procedure was reversed; the water in the lock was raised by opening wickets in the upstream gates after the boat was sealed in the lock. Alerted by the blast of a trumpet carried on each boat, the lockkeeper would have the water at the right level and the appropriate gates open for an approaching boat, whose crew would help operate the gates and wickets as the boat passed through the lock.

In order to maximize capacity, most boats were made to fit the locks closely, with the result that the standard craft was 90 feet long, 14.5 feet wide, and drew 4.5 feet when fully loaded. At each end was a cabin with the roof raised about three feet above the deck. The forward cabin was a stable where the mules rode and rested when they were not in harness. The aft cabin held a galley and a couple of berths. Between the cabins was the hold, covered with hatches, and amidships was a small cabin-like structure holding feed and hay for the mules. Behind the aft cabin was a small tiller deck. The entire arrangement was thus in balance so that the cargo did not depress one end of the long, narrow boat more than the other. According to the anonymous account mentioned earlier, "A hundred or more of these boats were brought from the Erie Canal, when that was enlarged, by the canal companies who now own nearly all the boats, the boatmen furnishing teams and outfit, receiving so much a ton for hauling the coal, paying their own expenses and the toll on the empty boat back to Cumberland."

The days were long and monotonous:

> We were tied up to no regular hours and lived in Arcadian simplicity. We rose with the early morning light, fed the mules, and when they had eaten their breakfast a pair was hitched up and we started on our day's journey driving them about four hours when they were changed for the other pair; at the end of the next four hours they were again changed, and so on making four shifts and sailing from sixteen to eighteen hours a day, the Capt., Pic and myself taking turns at the rudder while the two boys changed off from time to time and occasionally Pic and myself would drive for an hour or two, walking for exercise; the boys usually rode the rear mule.
>
> Some days the four mules were hitched tandem, then we drove about twelve hours, with a short rest at noon, ungearing them to let them roll which seemed to refresh them nearly as much as a half day's rest. These might seem long days to work in the present eight and ten hours times, but as far as the work was concerned, it mattered little whether the boat sailed or not. There were meals to cook, someone must stand at the tiller, and the mules must be driven, and there was about five minutes work for one of the others at each lock, the rest of the time could be spent reading, sleeping, viewing the landscape or telling stories, in which all but the boy driving could take part . . . .

Along the canal at villages, or important agricultural districts, or where valleys break through the mountains, there were warehouses where mule feed and other boat stores including bread could be procured, and where goods could be received and delivered by the boats, and occasionally there were basins where several boats could be stored to turn around, for the canal was not wide enough to turn a loaded boat . . . .

Once in a while the boat would take a quantity of hay or grain on speculation and peddle it out to the other boats. We met one who had oats for sale and we bought a few bushels at a discount but found when we used them that they were so light in weight that we had paid more than they were worth. Every boat carries what might be called ship papers, that is a bill of lading which states what you have carried for freight to the smallest item, and the distance it was carried, as the canal charges toll on all freight and also on the boat itself. These papers have to be subscribed to under oath. The only extra freight we had was two barrels of whiskey sent from one village to another. Pic and the Capt. sampled the whiskey by driving down a hoop and boring a small hole with a gimlet and drawing out a flask-full. After plugging the hole they drove the hoop back and none but the crew were the wiser for it. On the previous trip the Capt. had a boat load of timber from some point up the canal to Cumberland . . . .

The first question asked a boatman is how do you live on board. We had a small cook stove in which we burned the soft coal with which the boat was loaded, a spider, an iron teakettle, plates, knives, forks, and several of the small cooking utensils including a molasses jug. The bread was purchased at the warehouses along the canal and at the village grocery stores. Ham and bread was the standby. Luxuries in the shape of fresh meat and vegetables were occasionally purchased.

It was bread, dried bread, bread and molasses, and bread. Ham, fried ham, and ham that made up the usual variety. By bringing the slices of ham to a boil in one or two changes of water removed much of the salt and smoke and made it much more palatable and tender. Potatoes when we had them were boiled in the teakettle, then the coffee was made and the dish water heated all in the same utensil. I did most of the cooking but shall not brag of any fancy dishes for I lacked that essential for young housekeepers, a cook book . . . .

Boating was a profitable business when they had a lucky season. If I remember rightly they had about one dollar a ton for transporting the coal when you used your own boat and somewhat less in the company's boats. With a good team two round trips could be made in each month from April to December and the expense was for the help, board, team, and seven dollars toll on each return trip. It was easy to figure a profit on this basis especially in the dull times and low prices that followed the panic of 1857, but the "ifs" were so many that the margin for profit was very small. Sometimes they had to wait for their load at Cumberland as you had to take your turn with the other boats, or there might be an accident at the mines or on their railroad as they might be filling a special order by rail and there is always the possibility of a strike. Then the delay at the other end of the canal was often longer for a storm or head wind sometimes prevents the arrival of any schooners sometimes for weeks. You might wait in Georgetown or Alexandria for a chance to unload while your neighbor made two round trips for one of the other lines. Still worse than these were the breaks and washouts on the canal that detained all the boats alike[;] these sometimes caused months' delay . . . . In some seasons these breaks will follow one after the other until the whole season is used up and in the fall the boatmen will not have enough money to pay expenses. There was more or less freight to be carried besides the coal but as Washington was not a commercial city a larger share went to and from Baltimore. Sometimes the boatmen and warehousemen would pick up a boat of fruit or grain to be sold on speculation and after harvest there was considerable wheat and corn delivered to the mills at Georgetown but when all the local freight was divided among the three or four hundred boats it amounted to very little to each. At the end of the season the navigation is closed. It is desirable to keep the canal open as long as possible and not have the boats freeze in or the locks freeze and burst. When freezing weather grows near a day is appointed giving a few weeks' notice when the canal will be drawn off, then there is a hurrying around with their last load and getting their boats home or in some place where they can lay in safety until spring. There would of course be a few who would be belated . . . and find themselves stranded along the canal.

Sometimes on the more northern canals nature will close the canal before the appointed time catching hundreds of boats in transit. On the day appointed the . . . gates are closed and the water drawn off from every canal except the one at Georgetown which supplies the mills and during the winter the canal is cleaned and the many needed repairs made. The next spring soon after the arrival of the bluebird the water is turned in and as the canal is free from ice the navigation is resumed.

For those who navigated the C&O Canal , boating was a unique way of life handed down from father to son. During the declining years of the waterway, few outsiders were drawn to the work, which paid poorly. "The children are brought up on the boat and don't know nothin' else, and that is the only reason they take up boating," one mother told investigators from the Federal Children's Bureau in 1921. She continued, "Boys work for their fathers until they are big enough to get a boat of their own, and it's always easy to get a boat." At the time of the federal survey, most C&O captains carried their wives and children with them, and in consequence the children did not attend school for more than a fraction of the year. Few children finished the elementary grades and many were illiterate.

Aside from doing the cooking, washing, and other "household" chores, the wives at times helped to steer the boats. Except in critical circumstances, the children too took turns steering, and also drove the mules, walking or riding for long hours in all weather. The boats were

kept moving for as much of the day and night as each family could stand; fifteen hours per day was a minimum, eighteen hours typical, and some boats were operated longer or even continuously. "We don't know it's Sunday," said one captain and father, "til we see folks along the way, dressed up a'goin' to Sunday school." And according to another captain, "The women and children are as good as the men. If it weren't for the children the canal wouldn't run a day."

On the standard C&O Canal boat, the aft cabin, where the family lived, was only ten by twelve feet, with two narrow berths, each used by two people. Often children had to sleep in the floor or the deck or in the feed box where hay was stored for the mules. In pleasant weather, the family spent most of their time on deck, but cooking on a coal stove had to be done in the stifling heat of the cabin. Some families lived on their boats year round, even when the craft was on the bottom of the canal during winter, but most had small homes at some point along the canal.

Today a corps of canal enthusiasts is as firmly bound to the C&O Canal as the boatmen ever were. Much canal literature has been written, and some of these books are available at the various canal visitor centers.

≈   ≈   ≈   ≈

METRO: The Metrorail station closest to the canal in Georgetown is Foggy Bottom - GWU (Blue and Orange lines). As you exit from the station, turn left and follow 23rd Street north one block to Washington Circle. Circle left across K Street, then bear left onto Pennsylvania Avenue and follow it a few blocks over Rock Creek to M Street in Georgetown, where the canal is downhill to the left.

Several Metrobus routes, including 32, 34, 35, 36 and 38B, pass through Georgetown on M Street, which is paralleled by the canal one block downhill.

Telephone (202) 637-7000 for current Metro information, including schedules, routes, and connections.

≈   ≈   ≈   ≈

AUTOMOBILE DIRECTIONS: The Chesapeake and Ohio Canal in Maryland more or less follows the Potomac River for 184.5 miles. (See **Maps 11-15** on pages 119-123.) Some access points are described below.

So that you do not have to turn around and retrace your route, you may want to arrange a **car shuttle**. Obviously, a shuttle involves either two cars and two hiker-bikers, or a driver who drops you off at the start (after you have left your car at the end) or who simply meets you at the end.

GEORGETOWN, of course, is the canal's eastern terminus. From M Street in Georgetown, the towpath can be reached by walking downhill on almost any cross street. However, finding a place to park in Georgetown is so difficult that you may be better off going to **Fletcher's Boat House** near milepost 3 on the C&O Canal. (Directions to Fletcher's Boat House start on page 329 in Chapter 24.)

To Georgetown from downtown Washington: M Street in Georgetown can be reached via Pennsylvania Avenue. Alternatively, take K Street and then the Whitehurst Freeway to the T-intersection with M Street, and there turn right into Georgetown.

To Georgetown from Virginia: Cross the Potomac River on the Roosevelt Bridge, which can be reached via Route 50 East or Interstate 66 East. At the Washington end of the bridge, stay in the far left lane for I-66 East and then follow the signs for the Whitehurst Freeway. At the end of the freeway, turn right onto M Street into Georgetown.

Alternatively, cross the Potomac River via the Key Bridge, which can be reached via the southbound lanes of the George Washington Memorial Parkway. (From the parkway's *northbound* lanes, exit for Spout Run; go 0.5 mile uphill, then make a U-turn to the left in the lane provided for that purpose. Once you are back on the GWM Parkway southbound, take the first exit for the Key Bridge.)

At the Georgetown end of the bridge, turn right onto M Street.

To Georgetown from the northwest: Follow the directions below for **Lock 7** from Interstate 495, but then continue as the Clara Barton Parkway turns into Canal Road and then into M Street in Georgetown. (Remember, on weekdays from 2:45 P.M. to 7:15 P.M., Canal Road is westbound only.)

To Georgetown from the north: Take Route 355 South, which is served by Exit 34 off Interstate 495 (the Capital Beltway). Route 355 becomes Wisconsin Avenue, which leads through Bethesda to M Street in the center of Georgetown.

MAP 11— Overview of C&O Canal towpath

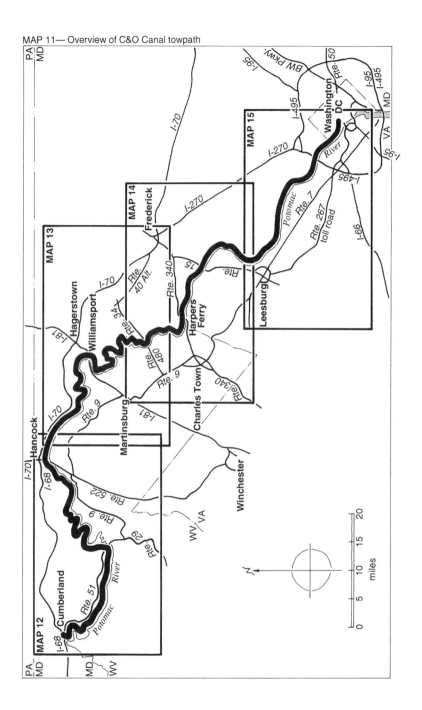

119

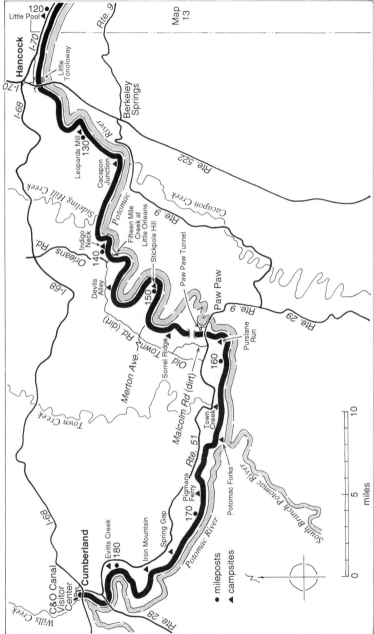

120

MAP 13 — C&O Canal towpath: milepost 70 to milepost 120

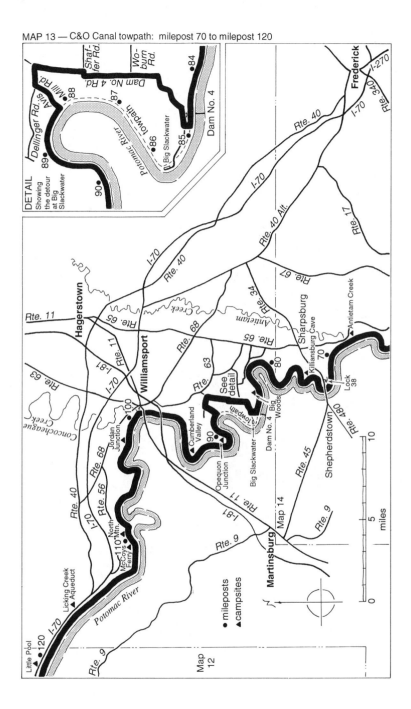

DETAIL
Showing
the detour
at Big
Slackwater

Dam No. 4

121

MAP 14 — C&O Canal towpath: milepost 35 to milepost 70

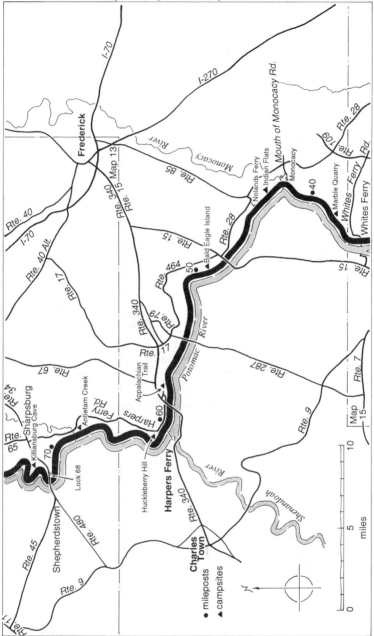

MAP 15 — C&O Canal towpath: Georgetown (point 0) to milepost 35

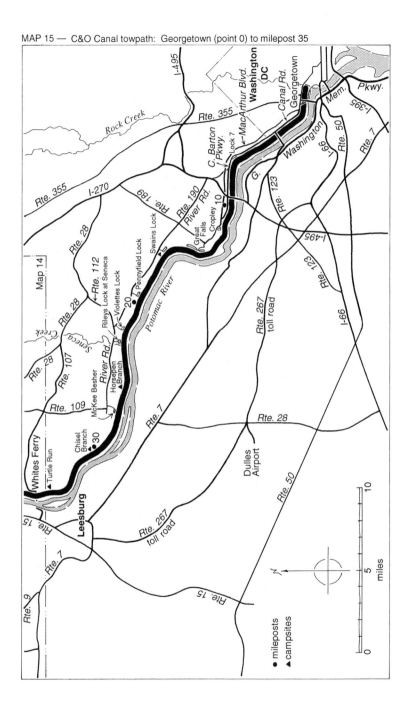

≈   ≈   ≈   ≈

LOCK 7 is at milepost 7 on the C&O Canal towpath. If the parking lot is full, there are other parking areas nearer Washington at Lock 6 and the Chain Bridge.

To Lock 7 from Interstate 495 (the Capital Beltway): From the Beltway's Inner Loop, take Exit 41 immediately after crossing the Potomac River northwest of Washington. As you exit, fork right for Glen Echo, then follow the Clara Barton Parkway 2 miles to the C&O Canal Lock 7 parking area on the right. Or instead, you can pull off the parkway earlier at Lock 10 or Lock 8.

From the Beltway's Outer Loop, take Exit 40 for the Cabin John Parkway, which leads to the Clara Barton Parkway. After merging onto the Clara Barton Parkway, go 0.5 mile to the C&O Canal Lock 7 parking area on the right.

To Lock 7 from Georgetown: Follow Canal Road (which is the westward extension of M Street) 0.5 mile past the **Key Bridge** and the **Whitehurst Freeway**, then bear left to continue on Canal Road. Pass the **Chain Bridge** from Virginia and continue west on the Clara Barton Parkway. After passing exits for MacArthur Boulevard and I-495 North, take the Cabin John exit. Make a U-turn over the parkway, then return 0.8 mile to the C&O Canal Lock 7 parking area on the right.

When you leave the Lock 7 parking area, there is no direct access to the westbound lanes of the Clara Barton Parkway. If you want to return to the Capital Beltway, drive east a few hundred yards to the first exit on the left; bear very sharply left, then left again immediately to reach the parkway westbound.

≈   ≈   ≈   ≈

CROPLEY is near milepost 12 on the C&O Canal towpath. If the parking area at Cropley is full (as it often is), there are other lots at Carderock near milepost 10 and at Great Falls near milepost 14.

To Cropley from Interstate 495 (the Capital Beltway): Leave the Beltway at Exit 41. This exit is northwest of Washington and — if you are approaching on the Outer Loop

— is the last exit in Maryland. The exit signs are for Carderock and Great Falls, MD. If you are approaching from Virginia on the Inner Loop, Exit 41 is the first exit after crossing the Potomac River into Maryland, and in this case, be prepared to fork left (west) for Carderock immediately after exiting from the Beltway.

After leaving the Beltway, follow the Clara Barton Parkway west past Carderock to a T-intersection with MacArthur Boulevard. Turn left onto MacArthur Boulevard and follow it west 1.1 miles to the unmarked parking lot on the left opposite Old Angler's Inn. Join the towpath by walking downhill on the dirt road.

If the parking area at Cropley is full, you can either return to Carderock or continue on MacArthur Boulevard 1.1 miles to an intersection with Falls Road at the entrance for the Chesapeake and Ohio Canal National Historical Park at Great Falls, Maryland.

≈   ≈   ≈   ≈

SWAINS LOCK is about 16.5 miles from Georgetown along the C&O Canal towpath.

To Swains Lock from Interstate 495 (the Capital Beltway):
Leave the Beltway at Exit 39 (Exit 39A from the Inner Loop) for Route 190 West (River Road) toward Potomac. Follow River Road about 3 miles to the crossroads with Route 189 (Falls Road) in the center of **Potomac**, and from there continue west on Route 190 for 2.1 miles to Swains Lock Road, which is on the left and is rather inconspicuous. Turn left onto Swains Lock Road and follow it 0.3 mile to the parking area by the canal.

If there is no room in the parking lot, continue west along Route 190 for 3.1 miles to Pennyfield Lock Road, which leads to a parking lot near milepost 19 on the towpath.

≈   ≈   ≈   ≈

VIOLETTES LOCK is at milepost 22 on the C&O Canal towpath.

To Violettes Lock from Interstate 495 (the (
Leave the Beltway at Exit 39 (Exit 39A from t

Route 190 West (River Road) toward Potomac. Follow River Road about 3 miles to the crossroads with Route 189 (Falls Road) in the center of **Potomac**, and from there continue west on Route 190 for 7.8 miles to Violettes Lock Road. Turn left onto Violettes Lock Road and follow it 0.6 mile to the parking area by the canal.

≈   ≈   ≈   ≈

THE MONOCACY AQUEDUCT is at milepost 42 on the C&O Canal towpath.

To the Monocacy Aqueduct from Interstate 495 (the Capital Beltway): Leave the Beltway at Exit 35 (off the Outer Loop) or Exit 38 (off the Inner Loop) in order to take Interstate 270 North about 6 miles to Exit 6B for Route 28 West. Follow Route 28 West for 20 miles through **Darnestown** and **Dickerson** to a crossroads with Mouth of Monocacy Road, and there turn left. Go 1.3 miles, then fork left to the aqueduct parking area.

≈   ≈   ≈   ≈

HARPERS FERRY is at milepost 61 on the C&O Canal towpath. For directions to Harpers Ferry, see page 53 in Chapter 2. From the visitor center, hikers can take the shuttle bus and cyclists can ride to the historic district by turning left out of the parking lot. At the foot of Shenandoah Street (which is the main street through the historic district), cross the Potomac River on the pedestrian bridge to the C&O Canal towpath.

≈   ≈   ≈   ≈

LOCK 38 (SHEPHERDSTOWN), WILLIAMSPORT, HANCOCK, FIFTEEN MILE RUN (LITTLE ORLEANS) PAW PAW TUNNEL, and CUMBERLAND are other access points described in turn below. In each case the automobile directions start at Interstate 70 near **Frederick**, Maryland.

From **Washington**, you can join I-70 West near Frederick by taking Interstate 270 North from Interstate 495 (the Capital Beltway). To do so, leave the Beltway at Exit 35 (off the Outer Loop) or at Exit 38 (off the Inner Loop), and then — just before Frederick — leave I-270 to join I-70 West toward Hagerstown.

Alternatively, if you are coming from the western suburbs in Virginia well outside the Washington Beltway, it may be faster to go first to **Leesburg** and from there take Route 15 North across the Potomac River to Route 340 East and the junction with I-70 West near Frederick.

≈   ≈   ≈   ≈

LOCK 38 (located near Sharpsburg and across the Potomac River from Shepherdstown) is at milepost 73 on the C&O Canal towpath.

To Lock 38 from Interstate 70 near Frederick: Follow I-70 West only a few miles, then take Exit 59 for Route 40 Alternate toward Braddock Heights and Middletown. At the end of the exit ramp, turn left (west) and follow Route 40 Alternate 11.4 miles west to Boonsboro. At a traffic light in Boonsboro, turn left onto Route 34 West and go 9.5 miles, in the process passing through Sharpsburg. Just before the Potomac River, and across the road from the C&O Canal Headquarters, turn left toward Blackford's Ford. The parking area for Lock 38 is at the bottom of the hill.

If there is no room at this small parking area, you can try Taylors Landing at milepost 81 on the C&O Canal towpath. Return to Sharpsburg and turn left onto Route 65 North. Go 3.1 miles, then turn left onto Taylors Landing Road and follow it 1.2 miles to a bridge across the canal ditch on the left.

Finally, if there is no room at Taylors Landing, you can continue upstream to Dam #4 and Big Slackwater near milepost 85. Turn left out the entrance at Taylors Landing and go 2.0 miles, then turn left onto Woburn Road and follow it 1.3 miles to Dam #4 Road. Turn left and follow Dam #4 Road 1.6 miles to the dam or continue another mile to Big Slackwater.

≈   ≈   ≈   ≈

WILLIAMSPORT is located near milepost 100 on the C&O Canal towpath.

To Williamsport from Interstate 70 near Frederick: Follow I-70 West about 28 miles to Exit 24 for Route 63. At the bottom of the exit ramp, turn left and follow Route 63 South 2.4 miles to an intersection with Route 11 (Potomac Street) in Williamsport. Turn right and follow Route 11 South 0.3 mile and then — where the road curves left — go straight into the C&O Canal access area at Cushwa Basin. After stopping by the visitor center, move your car as far back toward the canal as possible before setting out on the towpath.

≈ ≈ ≈ ≈

HANCOCK is located at milepost 124 on the C&O Canal towpath.

To Hancock from Interstate 70 near Frederick: Follow I-70 West about 49 miles to Exit 3 on the left for Route 144. At the bottom of the exit ramp, bear right and follow Route 144 West 1.5 miles, in the process passing the C&O Canal visitor center on the right, where you may want to stop in. At an intersection at a traffic light with Pennsylvania Avenue, turn left and then — at a T-intersection in front of the canal ditch — turn right then left to the Little Tonoloway access point.

≈ ≈ ≈ ≈

FIFTEEN MILE CREEK is located at Little Orleans near milepost 141 on the C&O Canal towpath.

To Fifteen Mile Creek from Interstate 70 near Frederick: Follow I-70 West about 52 miles to Exit 1A on the left for Interstate 68 West. Go nearly 12 miles, then leave I-68 at Exit 68 for Orleans Road. Turn left onto Orleans Road South and follow it 5.7 miles, then turn left toward the C&O Canal. Pass under the railroad and turn right to the Fifteen Mile Creek access point.

≈ ≈ ≈ ≈

PAW PAW TUNNEL is located near milepost 156 on the C&O Canal towpath.

To Paw Paw Tunnel from Interstate 70 near Frederick: Follow I-70 West about 51 miles to Exit 1B on the left for Route 522 South. Cross the Potomac River and go 6 miles, then turn right in Berkeley Springs onto Route 9 West and follow it 25 miles to and across the Potomac at the town of Paw Paw. After crossing the river, the road changes designations to

Route 51 North. Go 0.5 mile to the Paw Paw Tunnel access point on the right just beyond a railroad bridge.

≈   ≈   ≈   ≈

CUMBERLAND is the western terminus of the canal, which ends at the Western Maryland Railway station half a mile beyond milepost 184.

To Cumberland from Interstate 70 near Frederick: Follow I-70 West about 52 miles to Exit 1A on the left for Interstate 68 West. Go 36.5 miles, then leave I-68 at Exit 43C for the Western Maryland Station Center in downtown Cumberland. At the bottom of the exit ramp, turn left. Cross Mechanic Street and go straight into the Station Square parking area. The C&O Canal visitor center is on the station's second level. The towpath starts to the left.

≈   ≈   ≈   ≈

WALKING and BICYCLING: Maps 11-15 on pages 119-123 show the C&O Canal towpath between Cumberland near milepost 184 and Georgetown at milepost 0. Except at Big Slackwater, where there is a detour between mileposts 85 and 88 (see the detail on Map 13), the route is self-evident. For mile after mile, the dirt path leads the way — although below Great Falls, some bicyclists prefer to use the Berma Road (Map 19, page 167) rather than carry their bikes a few hundred yards.

The most obvious way to use the towpath is to go to one or another access point, walk or ride upstream or down, then turn around and go back to your car. Applied systematically, this approach is an easy way to see the entire trail in the course of a series of excursions. For a one-way trip, there is Amtrak train service to Cumberland (no bikes on train) and also Greyhound bus service (bikes permitted — see page 131).

If you do not want to retrace your route as a part of each outing, a car shuttle is necessary. In particular, I suggest arranging a car shuttle to set up a **22-mile, all-day walk from Violettes Lock to Georgetown**. This section still has water in it, and a day's outing here provides plenty of time to soak in the plodding but pleasant monotony of the canal. Although walking on the level towpath is easy, the long distance brings in an element of work that is altogether appropriate to the old commercial waterway, where eighteen-hour days covering 30 to 40 miles were the norm. As the historic terminus for most cargo carried on the canal, Georgetown provides a strong sense of destination, as well as numerous eateries and watering holes where you can celebrate completion of the trip.

Bicycling from Cumberland to Georgetown: The total distance is 184.5 miles. By way of preparation, a day's trial ride on one or another section of the towpath will let you know beforehand what to expect and how far you can go in a day — and still be in condition to keep going the next day.

One major question is whether to stay in motels along the way or to camp out. The itineraries that are outlined below include a discussion of lodgings. Camping is discussed briefly on page 133.

To get to Cumberland, you will either need someone to drive you there (see the automobile directions on pages 126 and 130) or you can take the bus. Greyhound has an early-morning bus from Washington to Cumberland; telephone 1-800-231-2222. To transport your bike on the bus, you must take off the handlebars, pedals, and wheels and pack the bike in a box that you can buy from Greyhound or get from a bicycle store. After reassembling your bike at the Cumberland bus depot, ride downhill to the railroad, then turn left along the tracks. At a traffic light, turn right across the tracks and go straight downhill on Baltimore Street, which soon becomes a brick-paved mall. At Canal Street just before the Western Maryland Railway, turn left to the Western Maryland Station Center. The C&O Canal visitor center is on the second level. The towpath starts at the station square.

Finally, if you want to leave your car beforehand at Great Falls near milepost 14 and then end your trip there two or three days later, you may do so — at your own risk — if you first let the park staff know your plans. For directions to Great Falls, see page 162 in Chapter 10.

Two-day trip from Cumberland to Georgetown: A two-day trip entails a maximum of physical effort (or at least of butt fatigue) and a minimum of planning as compared to a more leisurely excursion. Two days, of course, fits the weekend. For a two-day trip, all that is required is a good weather forecast, a reservation for a night's accommodation at Williamsport, and a small daypack containing tools, spare tube, patch kit, minimal toiletries, street clothes for the evening, and lunch and snacks for both days. You may also want a flashlight for the 3,118-foot Paw Paw Tunnel.

Williamsport is located at milepost 100 on the towpath. I found the Days Inn entirely satisfactory. It is located on Route 11 across from the McDonalds about 0.7 mile north of the Potomac River bridge; telephone (301) 582-3500 or 1-800-DAYS INN. To reach Route 11 from the towpath, turn away from the Potomac River at the Cushwa Basin, where a large sign painted on the end of the old warehouse — now a canal visitor center — reads "Cushwa's • Coal • Brick." For information on other accommodations at Williamsport, call the Washington County Chamber of Commerce at (301) 739-2015.

Three-day trip from Cumberland to Georgetown: Dividing the trip into three parts, so that you go about 60 miles each day, jibes conveniently with the location of Hancock at milepost 124 and Harpers Ferry at milepost 61. Accommodations at Hancock and at Harpers Ferry are discussed in the next four paragraphs.

If you get off the towpath at the Little Tonoloway access point in **Hancock**, the nearest motel is the Comfort Inn; telephone (301) 678-6101 or 1-800-221-2222. To reach the Comfort Inn, go to Main Street (Route 144). Turn left onto Main Street and follow it west 0.3 mile, and then — just before the Route 522 bridge — turn right uphill onto Limestone Road and go another 0.3 mile to the motel.

Other motels in **Hancock** are the Budget Inn [telephone (301) 678-7351] and the Hancock Motel [telephone (301) 678-6108]. To reach the Budget Inn from the towpath, go to Main Street and follow it right nearly a mile. To reach the Hancock Motel, go to Main Street and follow it left 0.4 mile under a bridge, and then — with caution — turn left up the Route 522 South ramp to the motel. At the Hancock Motel, you may not bring your bicycle into your room, but you can arrange to have it locked in the basement.

Harpers Ferry is reachable from the towpath by a pedestrian walkway mounted on a railroad bridge across the Potomac River. A very enjoyable place to stay in Harpers Ferry is the Hilltop House hotel and restaurant, in business since 1885. Reservations for Friday or Saturday night are required far in advance and cancellations require 24-hour notice; telephone (304) 535-2132 or 1 (800) 338-8319. When you check in, ask that your bicycle be locked in the hotel's storage building for the night. To reach the Hilltop House from Shenandoah Street at the bottom of the hill in Harpers Ferry, follow High Street (it becomes Washington Street) uphill 0.4 mile, then turn right onto Columbia Street, then right again onto Ridge Street. There is also a Comfort Inn at Harpers Ferry; telephone (304) 535-6391 or 1-800-221-2222. It is located on Union Street at Route 340 near the Shenandoah River bridge. For information on other accommodations in Harpers Ferry, including a number of bed-and-breakfast establishments, call the C&O Canal headquarters at (301) 739-4200 and ask to be sent a list of lodgings.

Bicycle trip from Great Falls to Harpers Ferry and back: This two-day excursion links the towpath's two most spectacular areas, and has the further advantage of entailing a minimum of planning and no automobile shuttle. Leave your car at Great Falls and spend the night in Harpers Ferry at the Hilltop House, as discussed in the preceding section. The distance each way is 47 miles, which allows time for sightseeing at Harpers Ferry. If you live near one of the interconnected trails shown on **Map 2** on page 7, you may even be able to ride from your residence out to Harpers Ferry.

A variation is a three-day trip with two nights in Harpers Ferry. On the middle day ride upstream to Dam 4 at milepost 85 and back again to Harpers Ferry along a section of towpath that continuously borders the Potomac River. Another outing at Harpers Ferry is to climb to the Civil War fort atop Maryland Heights, as described in Chapter 2.

Camping: Camping is permitted only in designated areas. **Maps 12-15** show hiker-biker overnight campsites located approximately every five miles along the towpath between milepost 25 and milepost 180. These sites have pumps for water (the handles are removed in winter) and portable toilets. There are also a few drive-in camping areas, equally primitive. Sites are available on a first-come basis; there are no reservations. If you plan to camp, call (301) 739-4200 for information, including whether any of the camp sites have been closed.

8

RIVERBEND PARK

Walking and ski touring — 5 miles (8 kilometers). The route shown by the bold line on **Map 16** on page 137 stretches from the nature center at Riverbend Park downstream along the Potomac River to Great Falls. Return by the way you came or — for part of the distance — by the Upland Trail, shown on the map by a dotted line. After rains or during periods of thaw, the riverside path may be muddy, and occasionally it is even flooded.

Riverbend Park is open daily, except Christmas, from 7 A.M. until dusk, more or less. The precise closing time is posted at the entrance. Dogs must be leashed. The visitor center is open weekdays, except Tuesday, from 9 A.M. to 5 P.M. For information telephone (703) 759-9018. The nature center is open for scheduled programs; telephone (703) 759-3211. The park is managed by the Fairfax County Park Authority.

RIVERBEND PARK typifies the Piedmont landscape along the Potomac River above Great Falls. The Piedmont, of course, is one of several physiographic provinces, including the Coastal Plain to the east and the Blue Ridge to the west, that follow the trend of the Atlantic coast in bands of varying width. Along the Potomac Valley from Seneca to Georgetown — with Great Falls at about the midpoint — the river cuts across that part of the Piedmont that consists of hard crystalline rocks.

Above Great Falls, the Potomac flows within a wide but steep-sided valley. The surrounding countryside remains as rolling upland that slopes abruptly down to the river, at times in high bluffs studded with rocky outcrops. Narrow strips of flood plain form a low, level shelf at the foot of the bluffs, and it is this band of bottomland that is followed along the river by the route shown on Map 16 on page 137. The river is broad and shallow, the current moderate. Rock ledges have been worn down so that they produce occasional riffles and a few mild rapids.

There are many islands, but most are merely low mounds or ribbons of sand and gravel deposited by the river itself and are not much higher than the level of floods that occur about once every two years.

The elevated terrain lying immediately adjacent to the river reflects the hardness of the Piedmont bedrock, which includes schist, quartzite, gneiss, serpentine, gabbro, diabase, and other crystalline metamorphic rocks. These materials are very resistant to erosion. Nonetheless, physical and chemical weathering have produced a thick layer of crumbly "rotten" rock called *saprolite*, particularly in areas underlain by schist, as is the case at Riverbend Park. Judging from records kept when water wells are drilled, the saprolite lying on the uplands near Riverbend Park is 60 to 80 feet thick, and in places extends to depths of 120 feet. This thick, soft mantle has been shaped into a landscape of rounded hills and broad, shallow valleys by many small streams. Slopes are gentle, as would be expected in easily eroded material. But where larger rivers have penetrated to the relatively unweathered bedrock below, valley walls retain a steep profile, as is usual in hard material. The result is a two-tiered landscape, in which the gently rolling terrain characteristic of the soft saprolite remains as an uneven plateau above precipitous valleys cut into the hard bedrock by large rivers. Smaller streams and minor watercourses that flow placidly across the upland ultimately descend through steep ravines to the larger rivers below.

As the region's largest river, the Potomac presents the fullest development of this picture. At Riverbend Park the Potomac has carved a valley about two hundred feet lower than the land along Riverbend Road immediately west of the park, and as much as three hundred feet lower than the land four miles to the west. Generally speaking, the bluffs at first rise steeply from the narrow flood plain, reflecting bedrock at or near the surface. But the upper slopes become more gentle as the bedrock grades into saprolite. This valley profile is easily seen along most of the riverside trail described at the end of the chapter, as well as along the C&O Canal on the Maryland side of the river.

≈   ≈   ≈   ≈   ≈

AUTOMOBILE DIRECTIONS: Riverbend Park is located on the Virginia side of the Potomac River 12 miles northwest of Washington. (See the corner panel on **Map 16** opposite.) Two avenues of approach are described below. Both lead to the park's nature center, which for walking is a better place to start than the visitor center. (The visitor center is reached via a different entrance that you will pass along the way.) Among

MAP 16 — Riverbend Park

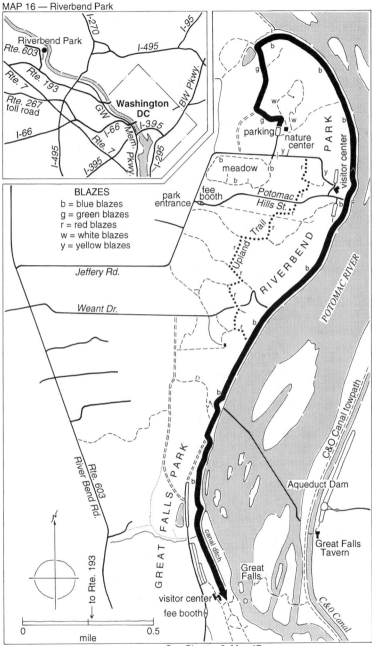

Riverbend Park
Rte. 603

I-270

I-95

I-495

Rte. 193

Rte. 7

Rte. 267
toll road

Washington DC

GW

I-66

Mem. Pkwy.

BW Pkwy.

I-395

Rte. 7

I-66

I-495

I-395

I-295

BLAZES
b = blue blazes
g = green blazes
r = red blazes
w = white blazes
y = yellow blazes

parking

nature center

meadow

park entrance

fee booth

Potomac Hills St.

visitor center

Upland Trail

R I V E R B E N D

Jeffery Rd.

Weant Dr.

POTOMAC RIVER

C&O Canal towpath

Rte. 603
River Bend Rd.

G R E A T   F A L L S   P A R K

to Rte. 193

canal ditch

Aqueduct Dam

Great Falls Tavern

Great Falls

C&O Canal

visitor center

fee booth

0   0.5
mile

See Chapter 9, Map 17.

137

the advantages of parking at the nature center is that no entrance fee is charged.

The riverside trail shown on Map 16 can also be reached by going to Great Falls Park, Virginia (see Chapter 9) and then walking upstream along the river.

To Riverbend Park from Interstate 495 (the Capital Beltway): Leave the Beltway at Exit 13 for Route 193 (Georgetown Pike). From the top of the exit ramp, follow Route 193 West about 4.5 miles, then turn right onto Route 603 or River Bend Road. (This intersection occurs 0.4 mile past the entrance to Great Falls Park.) After 2.2 miles, turn right onto Jeffery Road. Follow Jeffery Road 1.1 miles, in the process passing the main entrance to Riverbend Park at Potomac Hills Street. At the end of Jeffery Road, turn right toward the nature center. Go 0.2 mile, then turn left to reach the nature center itself, where there is a small parking lot that is open even if the nature center building is closed, as it often is.

To Riverbend park from Route 7 (Leesburg Pike) north of Herndon: From the intersection of Route 7 and Route 193 (Georgetown Pike) , follow Route 193 East 4.8 miles to an intersection with Route 603 (River Bend Road). Turn left and follow Route 603 for 2.2 miles, then turn right onto Jeffrey Road. Follow Jeffery Road 1.1 miles, in the process passing the main entrance to Riverbend Park at Potomac Hills Street. At the end of Jeffery Road, turn right toward the nature center. Go 0.2 mile, then turn left to reach the nature center itself, where there is a small parking lot that is open even if the nature center building is closed, as it often is.

≈   ≈   ≈   ≈   ≈

WALKING: The 5-mile walk described below is shown by the bold line on **Map 16** on page 137.

From the lower end of the nature center parking lot, follow a footpath 40 yards uphill into the woods. Just before reaching a paved path (the Duff-n-Stuff Trail), turn left downhill on the unpaved Paw Paw Trail, which is marked with green blazes. Cross a stream on a footbridge, then turn right downhill at a T-intersection. At a pond, turn right toward the Potomac River, then turn right again at the river's edge.

With the Potomac on the left, follow the riverside path downstream. Because of periodic flooding, the path can be rough in places. Pass a boat ramp and parking lot below the visitor center. Continue downstream past the intersection with the Upland Trail, which is shown on Map 16 by dots. Eventually, the riverside trail passes Aqueduct Dam, where water for Washington enters the conduit at the Maryland end of the dam. Continue to Great Falls, which is best seen from several vantage points that are slightly downstream from the national park visitor center.

Return to Riverbend Park by the way you came. For variety, you may want to follow the red-blazed Upland Trail for part of the distance.

9

GREAT FALLS PARK, VIRGINIA

Walking — 4 miles (6.4 kilometers). Located only 10 miles upstream from Washington, the cataracts and gorge at Great Falls are our local Niagara and Grand Canyon. The route shown on **Map 17** on page 149 starts at the falls and at first traces the remains of the old Patowmack Canal, built to implement George Washington's dream of converting the Potomac River into a waterway to the West. Downstream from the canal, the trail continues along the rim of Mather Gorge, then follows the bluff and ridge high above the river. If you want, you can descend to the Potomac where Difficult Run enters the river. Return to Great Falls on an old carriage road. Other trails provide the opportunity to cut short the route described here if it becomes too strenuous.

The excursion is not recommended during wet, snowy, or icy weather, when the rocks can be slippery. Be careful at the tops of the cliffs, and do not under any circumstances swim or wade in the river, where there are very strong currents.

Great Falls Park in Virginia is open daily (except Christmas) from 7 A.M. until dusk. In pleasant weather during spring, summer, and fall, the park is very popular, so arrive early if you want to avoid the crowd. An admission fee is charged; the ticket is good for a week and also covers admission to the C&O Canal park at Great Falls in Maryland (see Chapter 10). Dogs must be leashed. The visitor center is open from 10 A.M. to 5 P.M. The park is managed by the National Park Service; telephone (703) 285-2966.

PRESIDENT THEODORE ROOSEVELT, who often found time for hikes and rides in the vicinity of Washington, called Great Falls "the most beautiful place around here." Weaving its way in several channels through a wide swath of jagged rocks, the Potomac River drops nearly forty feet in two hundred yards, then enters a narrow gorge with vertical walls. Smaller rapids above and below the main cataract create an overall fall of about seventy-five feet in a mile. The entire spectacle can be seen from the Virginia shore at points passed by this walk.

The Virginia shore at Great Falls also features relics of the Patowmack Canal, built late in the eighteenth century before the Chesapeake and Ohio Canal was constructed along the Maryland side of the river in the second quarter of the nineteenth century. As early as 1772 the colonial legislature of Virginia approved a bill, prepared by George Washington and Henry Lee, for improving navigation above tidewater on the Potomac. A similar bill was needed from Maryland because Maryland's territory includes the river itself, but the legislation failed to pass in the face of opposition from Baltimore. Baltimore's merchants feared that the canal project would divert trade from their city, from which a rough wagon road ran west through Frederick and Fort Cumberland to the Ohio Valley, recently wrested from the French and now a magnet for settlers.

Following the Revolutionary War, however, both Virginia and Maryland passed bills, at the urging of George Washington, authorizing the formation of a corporation to make the Potomac navigable from tidewater at Georgetown to the highest point possible on the river's north branch, but at least as far upstream as Fort Cumberland. Where feasible, a channel would be cleared in the river itself, allowing passage by shallow-draft boats, even during the summer dry season. The company was authorized to construct canals and locks around rapids and was granted powers of eminent domain to acquire the necessary land. The legislation specified an elaborate schedule of tolls based on the value of the cargo, with upward adjustments for bulky items. The governments of Virginia and Maryland subscribed for large blocks of stock. Other shares were purchased by many of the region's leading families, who hoped that the project would channel commerce through the ports of Georgetown and Alexandria and, of course, earn a large income in tolls. Some boosters even predicted a 50 percent annual return on the investment. On May 17, 1885, the stockholders met at Alexandria to organize formally the Patowmack Company and to elect George Washington as its president, a position he held for four years until he became President of the United States.

Washington had long been interested in development of the Potomac River, which he called "one of the finest Rivers in the world." As a young man who helped to survey the vast domain of the Fairfax family and later as a frontier soldier and land speculator, Washington had explored the river's upper watershed. In 1785 a visitor to Washington's home at Mount Vernon wrote in his diary, "The General sent the bottle about pretty freely after dinner, and gave success to the navigation of the Potomac for his toast, which he has very much at heart." On a personal level, as part of an award to those who had enlisted early in the Virginia Regiment during the French and Indian War, Washington in 1770 had secured title to thirty thousand acres of wilderness in the Ohio Valley that would increase in value if communication with the seaboard could be improved. More sanguine than some of his fellow veterans, he perfected not only his own claim but also purchased the claims of others. And apart from his speculations, he was convinced that the Potomac was the best route to the West from the mid-Atlantic states. Saying that "there is nothing which binds . . . one State to another but interest," — or that is, mutual commercial interest — he supported a number of canal and road projects that would increase commerce and interdependence among the former colonies and the Ohio Valley, where there was considerable separatist sentiment. West of the Appalachian Mountains, the best water routes for trade were south to the Mississippi and Spanish territory, or north to the Great Lakes and British territory. The western settlers, Washington said, "stand as it were upon a pivot; the touch of a feather, would turn them any way. . . . [A] Commercial connexion is the only tie we can have upon them."

For three decades after its incorporation, the Patowmack Company struggled to bypass a series of major obstacles along the Potomac River and its tributaries. Five canals up to two miles long were built next to the Potomac at Little Falls, Great Falls, Seneca Falls, and above and below Harpers Ferry. Short canals were also cut around rapids on the Shenandoah River and Antietam Creek, and improvements were made on other tributaries as well. The goal of making the river passable even during periods of low water did not prove feasible, but by an expenditure of $730,000, the Patowmack Company opened several hundred miles of river to navigation by small boats during favorable water conditions.

The biggest obstacle along the river was, of course, Great Falls, where the Patowmack Company built the Great Falls Skirting Canal. It had five lift locks and was 1,820 yards long. Above the falls a wing dam 400 yards long projected at an angle upstream into the river, gathering water into the canal. Spillways fed water to a gristmill and a forge midway along the canal. A large holding basin provided a reservoir for operating the lift locks farther down the waterway and also served as a place for boats to load or unload goods or to wait their turn to descend through the locks. Finally, a series of locks, the last two occupying a deep cleft blasted through the rock, conveyed boats to and from the gorge below. Although in an advanced state of ruin, many features of the canal are still visible, and some have even been partially restored.

Begun in 1786, most of the Great Falls Skirting Canal was excavated in one year, but the section containing the lift locks was not finished until 1802. Experienced engineers were hard to find, and a series of five men supervised the project. One route for the locks was abandoned, on the advice of an English consultant, after much time and money had been wasted. As late as 1797, when Leonard Harbaugh took over as chief engineer and superintendent, none of the locks had been completed. Harbaugh already had finished construction of the skirting canal around Little Falls, and he also carried the work at Great Falls through to completion, but not until after the company's funds were temporarily exhausted and work interrupted for two years. In 1798 the company obtained loans to finish the project, pledging shares of its own stock and even its future tolls as collateral. Of the five Potomac canals, the Great Falls project was the last to be finished, and for several years the area was a bottleneck where boats had to be unloaded and their cargo carried by wagon around the cataract. For a period barrels of flour and other commodities were rolled down an inclined plane to boats below.

Because of the shortage of workmen in eighteenth-century America, the Patowmack Company contracted for slaves and indentured laborers (termed *servants*) to dig the various skirting canals and to clear the river. Virginia slaveowners hired out their slaves for a yearly sum; clothes and rations were the obligation of the company, which also had to reimburse the owner if one of his slaves died. Indentured immigrants, who had agreed to work for a specified number of years for the person or company that paid their way to America, were hired from ships arriving in Baltimore and Philadelphia. Most of these men were Irish or German, and occasionally some attempted to avoid their obligations by running away. For example, on February 22, 1786, the *Maryland Chronicle* stated:

> From the *Alexandria Gazette* of the 1st of January we hear that several servants who had purchased to work on the Patowmack Navigation lately ran away, but soon after being apprehended, were sentenced to have their heads and eyebrows shaved, which operation was immediately executed, and is to be continued every week during the time of their servitude, or until their behavior evinces that they are brought to a sense of their duty. This notice, it is expected, will sufficiently apprize the country should they again make a similar attempt.

Nonetheless, four months later the superintendent at Great Falls advertised that eight indentured servants, two of them shaved, had run off, and he offered a reward for their return.

During the summer of 1786, the Patowmack Company employed more than two hundred men, most of them at Great Falls. Some of the workers were skilled artisans, such as blacksmiths, wheelwrights, carpenters, and stone masons, paid by their output. Masons, for example, cut individualized marks like brands into their stones in order to identify work for which they were entitled to be paid. Most of the men, however, were laborers engaged in digging, hauling, and drilling. A few of the men were assigned the task of filling drill holes with black powder, to which fuses were set to blast the rock apart — at that time a novel (and dangerous) technique. Apparently the laborers were a rowdy lot, not above swarming over and plundering the company wagons that brought in supplies. Work quotas were enforced by withholding the daily ration of rum (three-quarters pint for whites, less for slaves) from those who fell short of their assigned tasks. Working from seven in the morning until six in the evening and living in crude cabins and barracks, the laborers led a rough life. Some of the men had wives who were hired to do cooking, cleaning, and housekeeping for the camp. A report written by the superintendent on the subject of blasting powder reflects the atmosphere that prevailed at the Great Falls project when the canal was first being dug:

> Great Falls, potowmack July 3rd 1786. Sir, We have Been much Imposed upon the past Two weeks in the powder way. (We had our Blowers, One run off, the other Blown up.) We therefore was Obliged to have two new hands put to Blowing and there was much attention given to them least Axedents should happen, yet they used the powder Rathr too Extravagent, But that was not all They have certainly stolen a Considerable Quantity as we have not more by us that will last until tomorrow noon. Our hole troop is Such Villains that we must for the future give the powder into Charge of a person appointed for that purpose to measure it to them on the ground by a Charger.

Construction of the Great Falls Skirting Canal gave rise to other projects. In 1790 the Virginia legislature granted a charter to Henry "Lighthorse Harry" Lee, the Revolutionary War cavalry commander, friend of Washington, and (later) the governor of Virginia, for the development of a town on land that he had acquired along the canal. Lee called the settlement Matildaville after his first wife. It consisted of forty half-acre lots, some of which were purchased by the canal company for construction of a superintendent's residence, offices, a barracks, and houses for clerks and mechanics. Other structures in the vicinity were a few warehouses, a market house, a gristmill, a sawmill, a foundry, a number of huts and boarding houses, a spring house, an ice house, and Meyer's Tavern (later called Dickey's Inn), which survived until 1942. Traces of a few of these structures remain. Please take care not to damage them or relics of the canal itself, which has been declared a National Historic Landmark.

Even before the completion of the Great Falls Skirting Canal, the Patowmack Company obtained permission in 1798 to collect tolls at Great Falls, provided that the company hauled the cargo around the cataract for no additional charge. Between August 1799 and August 1822, nearly 14,000 craft carrying 164,000 tons of cargo paid tolls to the company. The peak year was 1811, when the company received tolls on 16,350 tons. For the trip from Cumberland to Georgetown, transport costs by water were about half or two-thirds those by land. Boats going downstream carried agricultural products, such as flour, wheat, corn, rye, oats, tobacco, hay, hemp, butter, livestock, and meat. Whiskey poured out of the hinterland. Lumber, furs, and pig iron were also sent to the cities at tidewater. Manufactured goods, tools, hardware, firearms, cloth, refined products, and some luxury items made the return trip.

Most of the traffic, however, was one way: downstream. The ability of the inland communities and isolated settlements to produce substantially exceeded their capacity to consume, and in any case the return trip against the river current was difficult. Long rafts of logs, narrow enough to fit through the locks, carried farm products to market and then were broken up for lumber. Even substantial barges called gondolas were dismantled and sold at journey's end, since such craft were too clumsy to row or push back upriver.

Some craft, however, were designed to make the return trip. One such boat was called the *sharper* because it was pointed at each end. Sharpers resembled oversized canoes, 60 to 75 feet long, 5 to 7 feet wide, and drawing only 1.5 feet even when loaded with 20 tons of cargo. Amidships a tarpaulin, like the canvas cover of a Conestoga wagon, was stretched over bent poles or metal hoops to protect the cargo. A crew of three men — required by law to be licensed — guided the boat downriver and laboriously poled it back upstream by pushing against the river bed and walking toward the stern along the boat's running boards. Slightly larger than the sharper was the keelboat, similar in shape but capable of carrying 100 to 125 barrels of flour. For such boats the downstream trip from Cumberland to Georgetown took three to five days, depending on the current, but ten to eighteen days were required for the return trip. Not infrequently, boats and rafts foundered on the river's rocks, and some communities along the Potomac made a good thing of salvaging the cargo that sank or floated down the river.

Navigation on the open river was affected not only by the current but also by annual floods and periods of low water. Despite the charter requirement that the river be made navigable at all seasons, the Patowmack Company never succeeded in clearing a channel for use during summer droughts. The season for river traffic began in February but ceased in May as the river fell and became impassable. Autumn rains brought another brief period when boats could move on the river before ice formed in winter.

Dissatisfaction with river navigation led to agitation for a continuous canal from tidewater to Cumberland and beyond. At first the Patowmack Company successfully opposed inauguration of the new project, but the company gradually lost influence as its finances became deranged. During the entire period of the corporation's existence, annual expenses always exceeded revenues, often by a substantial margin. Except for one dividend paid in 1802, shareholders received no return on their investment. The legislatures of Virginia and Maryland constantly pressed the company to clear the Potomac channel and to make other costly improvements. Maryland provided loans to extend navigation up tributaries of the Potomac, but these projects were never finished and did not pay. The company even sponsored a lottery to raise funds but lost money instead. During the War of 1812, traffic on the river declined because of the curtailment of foreign trade. By 1819 the company was insolvent and struggling merely to keep its canals and locks in working order.

In light of the failure of the Patowmack Company, Virginia and Maryland authorized formation of the Chesapeake and Ohio Canal Company in 1824, and in the following year the Patowmack Company agreed to surrender its charter to the new corporation. (See Chapter 7 for a discussion of the C&O Canal.) On August 15, 1828, a few weeks after construction began on the new waterway, the Patowmack Company conveyed its property to the C&O Canal Company and passed into oblivion. As compensation Patowmack creditors and shareholders received C&O stock. At Great Falls the skirting canal was used until 1830, when the lock gates were removed. For a longer period the canal continued to supply water power to the gristmill and forge that were located near the present-day visitor center.

≈   ≈   ≈   ≈   ≈

AUTOMOBILE DIRECTIONS: Great Falls Park in Virginia is located on the Potomac River 10 miles northwest of Washington. (See the corner panel on **Map 17** on page 149.) Two avenues of approach are described below.

To Great Falls Park from Interstate 495 (the Capital Beltway): Leave the Beltway at Exit 13 for Route 193 (Georgetown Pike). From the top of the exit ramp, follow Route 193 West toward Great Falls a little more than 4 miles. At a crossroads marked by a traffic light, turn right onto Route 738 (Old Dominion Drive) and enter Great Falls Park. Go about a mile to the fee booth. If you can, park near the visitor center.

To Great Falls Park from Route 7 (Leesburg Pike) north of Herndon: From the intersection of Route 7 and Route 193 (Georgetown Pike), follow Route 193 East 5 miles to an intersection with Route 738 (Old Dominion Drive). Turn left into Great Falls Park and go about a mile to the fee booth. If you can, park near the visitor center.

≈   ≈   ≈   ≈   ≈

WALKING: The 4-mile walk described below is shown by the bold line on **Map 17** opposite.

After stopping by the visitor center and viewing Great Falls from some of the nearby overlooks (and, if you want, walking upstream a few hundred yards to see the mouth of the old Patowmack Canal above the falls), follow the former canal ditch "downstream" on a wide path several dozen yards back from the edge of the gorge. With the Potomac River toward the left, pass an old mill site near the visitor center.

A gristmill — later converted to a sawmill — was built here in the 1790s by Samuel Briggs. Water from the canal was carried by a short flume to the waterwheel. Part of the mill's masonry foundation is still visible. Grain ground here could be transported by canal and river downstream to Georgetown.

Cross the canal ditch and continue downstream, with the old canal on the right and the Potomac River toward the left. Pass the site of a forge. Continue on the wide path through a picnic area and straight into the woods. Pass an area on the right that, although now dry, was once a holding basin above the canal locks.

The path here follows the top of the dike that held water in the boat basin where canal craft waited their turn to descend through the locks to the river below Great Falls. Near the far end of the basin, a bridge over a gap in the wall marks the location of the wooden waste weir. As necessary (usually during summer or winter when the canal was not in use), the waste weir was opened in order to drain the basin and canal so that repairs could be made and silt removed.

Near the far end of the basin, fork right across the bridge at the waste weir. Curve right, then turn left past the remains of a canal guard gate on the left. Uphill to the right are the ruins of

MAP 17 — Great Falls Park, Virginia

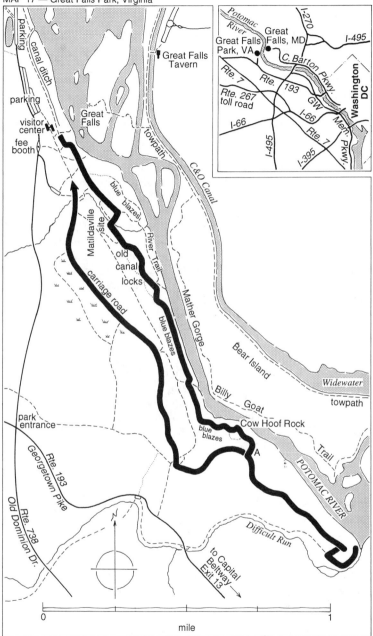

parking

canal ditch

Great Falls Tavern

Potomac River

Great Falls Park, VA

Great Falls, MD

I-270

I-495

C. Barton Pkwy.

Rte. 7

Rte. 193

Rte. 267 toll road

I-66

GW

I-66

Rte. 7

I-395

Mem. Pkwy.

Washington DC

I-495

parking

visitor center

fee booth

Great Falls

towpath

C&O Canal

blue blazes

Matildaville site

old canal locks

River Trail

carriage road

blue blazes

Mather Gorge

Bear Island

Widewater

towpath

Billy Goat

park entrance

blue blazes

Cow Hoof Rock

A

Trail

POTOMAC RIVER

Rte. 193

Georgetown Pike

Rte. 738

Old Dominion Dr.

N

Difficult Run

to Capital Beltway Exit 13

0   1
mile

149

the Company House, where the canal superintendent lived and where the canal's records were maintained. Other Matildaville buildings were nearby.

Located at the downstream end of the holding basin, the guard gate was not a lift lock but simply a single set of swing gates that could be closed in case of flood to protect the locks below. The gate posts pivoted in the concave corners of the quoin stones that are still visible. Another guard gate was located near the upper end of the canal.

Continue along the canal ditch to Lock 1. Note the recesses in the walls for the open lock doors. Continue past Lock 2 to a cleft where the canal turns and joins the Potomac River.

The point where the canal turns was actually within Lock 3. Lock 4 and Lock 5 occupied the deep cut, which was blasted with black powder. Locks 3, 4, and 5 worked in combination, so that the lower gate of Lock 3 was the upper gate of Lock 4, and so on. Flooding has filled the locks with silt and rubble and has destroyed most of the stonework, but the location of the gate separating Locks 4 and 5 can be discerned (when standing in the bottom of the cleft) from three large holes in the wall and a few courses of stone masonry at the top of the rock face on the right.

From the upper end of the canal cleft, continue downstream. At a small plateau above the cleft, turn right and follow a footpath marked with blue blazes uphill a few dozen yards. Turn left at a slightly skewed T-intersection. Follow the blue-blazed River Trail to the rim of Mather Gorge. With the river on the left, continue downstream, sometimes near the rim of the gorge and sometimes behind an escarpment of jagged rocks.

Before the Potomac carved Mather Gorge, the trough behind the escarpment was one of the river's several channels, as indicated by a few potholes that are visible. (See Chapter 10 for a discussion of the geology and formation of Great Falls and Mather Gorge.)

Eventually, the blue-blazed River Trail reaches a road. Cross the road obliquely to the right, then follow the blue-blazed trail down into a small ravine and up the other side. Continue along the edge of a shelf of land above the river. Pass through a notch in a spine of boulders. With the river downhill to the left, follow the blue-blazed path along the slope

and up to Cow Hoof Rock, which juts out above a bend in the Potomac.
From Cow Hoof Rock, follow the blue-blazed path uphill.
Pass a faint trail intersecting from the right. Continue uphill to a T-intersection with the Ridge Trail at a point marked A on Map 17.
Turn left onto the Ridge Trail. With the river downhill to the left, follow the wide path through the woods and along the ridge, which gradually narrows. Eventually the Ridge Trail reaches an intersection with a path that descends to the right toward Difficult Run. If you want, follow this path downhill to a T-intersection, then turn left downhill to the mouth of Difficult Run at the Potomac River.
Return along the Ridge Trail by the way you came. At Point A on Map 17, pass the intersection with the blue-blazed River Trail and continue along the Ridge Trail as it winds through the woods and away from the river. Eventually, merge with a wide, well-graded gravel road (the carriage road) and follow it right. Pass a dirt road intersecting from the right. Follow the carriage road through the forest. (The road and swampy woods to the left occupy a broad trough that was once another channel of the Potomac River.) Continue back to the visitor center and parking lots.

10

C&O Canal National Historical Park at GREAT FALLS, MARYLAND

Olmsted Island
Billy Goat Trail
Berma Road and towpath
Gold Mine Loop

Walking. This chapter outlines four different excursions on the Maryland side of the Potomac River near Great Falls, which is located 10 miles upstream from Washington. The various trails range in length from 1 mile (1.6 kilometers) to a dozen miles (19 kilometers). The last two excursions — the Berma Road and Gold Mine Loop — are suitable also for ski touring.

The detail in the corner of **Map 18** on page 163 shows a 1-mile introductory stroll via towpath, bridge, and boardwalk to the **Olmsted Island overlook** at Great Falls. Even if you intend to take one of the longer walks described below, I suggest that you start by going to the Olmsted Island overlook and back.

Also shown on Map 18 are Sections A , B, and C of the aptly-named **Billy Goat Trail**. Each of the three sections is accessible from the C&O Canal towpath, shown as a dotted line. Section A — the one closest to Great Falls — is the most demanding; it crosses rugged terrain along the rim of Mather Gorge below Great Falls, at times climbing over bare and broken rock and descending into secluded hollows and coves. After completing Section A of the Billy Goat Trail, you can follow the towpath back to Great Falls, for a round-trip of 4 miles. Another option, if you want a longer outing, is to continue downriver on the towpath to Section B and then Section C of the Billy Goat Trail, as discussed starting on page 165. The Billy Goat Trail is not recommended during wet, snowy, or icy weather, when the rocks and mud can be slippery. Be careful at the tops of the cliffs, and do not under any circumstances swim or wade in the river, where there are strong currents.

Map 19 on page 167 shows two easy alternatives to the Billy

Goat Trail. Each is 4 miles long (6.5 kilometers). One route follows the **Berma Road** — a dirt and gravel track closed to motor vehicles — along one side of the C&O Canal to Cropley, then returns via the canal towpath to Great Falls. Directions start on page 168. The other route is the **Gold Mine Loop**, which circles through deep woods for 4 miles. A short spur leads to the ruins of the Maryland Mine, last in a series of gold mines at Great Falls. See page 169 for directions.

The Chesapeake and Ohio Canal National Historical Park at Great Falls is open daily from dawn until dusk. In pleasant weather during spring, summer, and fall, the park is very popular, so arrive early if you want to avoid the crowd. An admission fee is charged; the ticket is good for a week and also covers admission to Great Falls Park in Virginia (see Chapter 9). Dogs must be leashed. The museum and information center at Great Falls Tavern are open daily from 9 A.M. to 5 P.M. The park is managed by the National Park Service; telephone (301) 299-3613 for the Great Falls Tavern office. Before coming to the park, you may want to call to learn whether any **closures are in effect** because of damage by floods, such as that which occurred in January 1996.

For a discussion and maps of the entire C&O Canal, see Chapter 7.

OVERLOOKING THE PRECIPITOUS GORGE of the Potomac River below Great Falls is a bedrock terrace riddled with potholes of the kind that every hiker has seen along rugged riverbeds at low water. Such potholes, of course, are worn by cobbles that are swirled in eddies at the bottom of the river, but at the Potomac gorge — called Mather Gorge after the first director of the National Park Service — the holes are more than sixty feet above the water. The conclusion is clear, even to non-geologists, that the elevated terrace was once part of the riverbed. Other conspicuous features also reflect the existence of earlier, higher channels where the river once flowed before massive erosion created the cataract and gorge we see today.

In broad outline, there is a natural sequence, both in time and place, by which a river dissects an elevated landscape and slowly reduces it to low rolling hills or even a plain. At the upper reaches of the watershed, stormwater runoff carves gullies and steep-sided ravines across the upland. As these streams merge to form a larger watercourse, the river carves a deeper, wider valley, so that the valley floor is occupied not just by the river itself but also by a flood plain of varying width. Joined by still other tributaries, the river eventually reaches the ocean, which constitutes a base level and limit for downward stream erosion. But even where downward erosion has ceased, sideward erosion continues as the stream current is deflected by each curve in the channel. Gradually the river carves a wide valley across which it twists and meanders in an ever-changing course, reducing the bordering terrain to the level of the river. Meanwhile the countless gullies and ravines at the river's headwaters continue to fan outward like the roots of a growing tree, so that the watershed becomes bigger and bigger, perhaps even intercepting and diverting to itself streams that previously took a different course to the sea.

Such, at any rate, is the general model of stream erosion, which is discussed in greater detail in Chapter 15. But the actual appearance of any particular stretch of river and the surrounding countryside is determined largely by the durability and structure of the underlying rocks. For example, the Monocacy River, which flows south through the Frederick Valley and joins the Potomac River twenty-eight miles upstream from Great Falls, is underlain by red sandstone, siltstone, shale, and limestone, all of which are sedimentary rocks that are not particularly resistant to erosion. Consequently, the terrain there has been smoothed into a gently undulating surface by eons of physical and chemical weathering and by the erosive power of the Monocacy River and its tributaries. Flowing past the confluence with the Monocacy, the Potomac River occupies a wide, shallow channel bordered by low, wide terraces.

Farther downstream, however, between Seneca and Washington, the Potomac crosses a region of crystalline, metamorphic rock that forms the bulk of the Piedmont Plateau in Maryland. The metamorphic materials are more resistant to erosion than the sedimentary bedrock upstream. Focusing on the region immediately above Great Falls, the Potomac has carved a wide channel disturbed only by minor rapids and riffles, but the resistant metamorphic bedrock remains as a rolling upland sloping abruptly down to the river in high bluffs along each bank. At the foot of the bluffs narrow strips of flood plain border the river. Except for a gradual increase in width, this stretch of valley has remained essentially unmodified for at least two million years, during a period that has seen major changes occur at Great Falls and farther downstream.

At Great Falls the river encounters a particularly resistant band of rock called *metagraywacke* (pronounced with a long *e* at the end). It is a form of metamorphosed muddy sandstone, somewhat like gneiss, and shows a sugary texture on weathered surfaces. Occurring in a series of vertically tilted strata, some a yard thick, the metagraywacke layers form a barrier that retards erosion above the falls. In effect, these rocks are like the remains of a breached dam, and they constitute a temporary base level below which the river upstream cannot carve until the barrier is worn away.

Below the falls, the metamorphic rocks (primarily mica schist) in the vicinity of the river are hard, but not as hard as the metagraywacke. In consequence, the rocks immediately bordering the river still stand as high cliffs, but the river itself — with its powerful, churning erosive energy that is obvious to any onlooker — has worn a narrow, deep gorge.

Nonetheless, surviving from the period before the gorge was cut, various features downstream from Great Falls indicate that the river here used to resemble the wider valley seen today immediately above the falls — at Riverbend Park, for example, as discussed in Chapter 8. Remnants of the old flood plain and river bottom still exist as terraces perched high above the gorge. MacArthur Boulevard follows one of these terraces downstream from Cropley to Cabin John. The C&O Canal occupies the extension of this terrace upstream. Another terrace on the Virginia side of the river defines the opposing edge of the former flood plain. In many places these flats are now the rim of the gorge. The terraces occupy a plain which, if projected upstream, still corresponds to the level of the valley floor above Great Falls. Even the islands (such as Olmsted Island) immediately below Great Falls have flat tops, representing what once was bottomland and river bed. As noted at the outset, in places the terraces are riddled with potholes.

Based on this and other evidence, the development of the present landscape can be explained. It appears that about two million years ago, when the level of the ocean was higher than at present, the Potomac had carved a broad channel through the Piedmont upland. At the site of Great Falls, outcrops of metagraywacke caused rapids and split the river into several channels. The planet's supply of water included less ice than at present, so sea level was higher and the coast farther west than it is now. But with the onset of the Ice Age — or Pleistocene Epoch — sea level fell as water was amassed in continental ice sheets. (Even now the Ice Age continues at higher latitudes, where enough ice remains to raise the ocean 130 feet from the present level if the ice were to melt.) The drop in sea level caused a renewal (or *rejuvenation*, as geologists say) of downward erosion along the broad course of the Potomac, creating the deep valley that now extends from tidewater upstream to the resistant metagraywacke barrier at Great Falls.

To some extent, formation of the gorge below Great Falls was affected by weaknesses in the rock structure. A zone of closely-spaced fractures and joints just below the falls has caused the river to cut laterally toward the Maryland shore and to split into three channels, of which the two eastern ones are dry during periods of low water. Similarly, the straight chasm of Mather Gorge marks a fault line where erosion along the zone of fracture has been relatively rapid. The existence of the fault is indicated by vertical veins of rock called *dikes*, running more or less at right angles to the gorge; these dikes were intruded into the surrounding bedrock before the fault occurred and so should align if extended across the gorge, but in fact they have been offset more than seventy-five feet by horizontal movement of the opposing faces of the fault.

As the crushed and broken rock along the fault became the site of relatively rapid downward erosion, old channels were left high and dry — or if not dry, as mere sloughs and swamps. One of these abandoned channels is Widewater, now artificially flooded and incorporated into the C&O Canal about a mile downstream from Great Falls. (See Map 19 on page 167.) Another former channel is occupied in part by the carriage road that extends south from the visitor center at Great Falls, Virginia.

The result is the river that we see today, but, of course, it is by no means the final result. Erosion continues, and eventually the barrier of resistant metagraywacke at Great Falls will be worn away so that downward cutting will advance upstream into the valley above the falls. Erosion below the falls will deepen and widen the valley downstream to tidewater. The locus of tidewater will change as the ocean rises and falls with the demise and recurrence of continental glaciation. If large portions of polar and Greenland ice melt, the sea will flood farther up the Potomac valley and may even reach Mather Gorge. Such flooding has already occurred in the "drowned" valleys of Chesapeake Bay and its various tidal rivers. Or erosion and rising sea level may be offset, at least in part, by upward adjustments in the earth's crust, as appears to be occurring along the East Coast. To see what happens, check back in another two million years.

≈   ≈   ≈   ≈

NOW LET'S TALK GOLD — and I don't mean the spectacular autumn colors that bring many people out to Great Falls for a walk along the C&O Canal towpath. The fact is that there is gold in them thar hills at Great Falls. And not just gold but the trenches, pits, and ruins of abandoned mines, one of which ceased operating as recently as 1940.

Gold Mine Loop (see Map 19) passes some of these abandoned works, although for the most part the excursion is just a walk through the woods.

Fantasies, rumors, and reports of gold in the Chesapeake region are as old as the first European settlers. In his *Adventures and Discourses*, Captain John Smith mentions how glad he was when a certain Captain Martin left Jamestown to return to England in 1608, for Martin "was always hankering after finding that gold, which did not exist, thereby creating great disunion amongst us." Smith also relates that the colonists who were sent to Jamestown by the London Company, which sponsored the settlement, included two refiners and two goldsmiths: "And, again, see how the lust of finding gold, was apparent in their sending out refiners and goldsmiths, who never had occasion to exercise their craft." Nonetheless, while exploring the Potomac River, up which he sailed as far as Little Falls above present-day Georgetown, Smith himself showed considerable interest in a place where the sand was "mingled with yellow spangles." He asked Matchqueono, the King of Patawomeke, about the metal, and was conducted by Indian guides to a mine seven or eight miles inland:

> The mine was a great rocky mountain like antimony, in which they had digged a great hole with their shells and hatchets. Hard by ran a fair brook of crystal-like water, in which they washed away the dross and kept the remainder, which they put in little bags and sell all over the country, where it is used to paint their bodies, faces, or their idols; which makes them look like blackamores dusted over with silver. . . .

Smith sent some of the material to England to be assayed. The result was strangely contradictory; he was told later that the dust was half silver but that it "proved of no value." In any case, nothing came of the matter.

The first authentic report of gold in Maryland occurred when traces were found in 1849 on a farm near Brookville in Montgomery County, but no production is recorded. A dozen years later, gold was discovered near Great Falls by a Union soldier whose Pennsylvania regiment camped in the area during the autumn and winter after the first battle of Manassas. According to one account, this man was either Private Alexander McCleary or Private John Carey, both of whom are listed on the regimental rolls at that time. By another account, the soldier (whoever he was) found specks of gold while washing the skillets in a stream near Cropley. Following his discharge from the army, he supposedly organized a group of investors who bought the farm on which the discovery had been made. In any case, prospecting did indeed begin, and in 1867, after considerable investigation, the mining company sank a shaft a hundred feet into a seam of gold-bearing quartz. This shaft was about two hundred feet south of the ruins (still visible today) of the Maryland Mine, an operation that was developed later just downhill from the intersection of Falls Road and MacArthur Boulevard. Production, however, was disappointing and the work was soon abandoned.

In the 1880s a prospector from Georgia found gold about a mile to the north of the earlier mine. By 1890 large pits had been dug in the side of the ravine at Cool Spring Branch, which joins the Potomac about nine hundred yards north of the Great Falls parking lot. A small processing mill operated near the mouth of the stream.

During the following three decades, considerable prospecting and mining were done in the area between Cool Spring Branch and the site of the Maryland Mine. More shafts were sunk in the uplands, and more pits and tunnels were dug in the sides of ravines by a series of companies, including the Great Falls Gold Mining Company, the Maryland Gold Mining Company, and the Empress Gold Mining Company. In May 1901, the *Maryland Journal* reported six gold mines in operation along the Potomac River upstream from Washington. The most systematic effort was made by the Atlantic Development Company, which during World War I undertook extensive trenching, stripping, and drilling on more than 2,100 acres that it had acquired in the Great Falls area. A series of long trenches stretching east and west are still discernible in aerial photographs as parallel lines running through the woods and up and down hills and ravines. Some of the trails shown on Map 19 cross or follow these trenches. In 1917 surface exploration was abandoned and the mines were closed, but the next year the Maryland Mine was reopened, worked for three years, and then closed again.

Gold fever, however, was not long in remission. In 1934 the price of gold rose to $35 dollars an ounce, and the next year the Maryland Mining Company was organized. The Maryland Mine was opened again and a new mill was installed for crushing the quartz into fine ore. A photograph of the mill shows a heavy timber contraption resembling a series of sheds and shanties built on stilts and stuck together at different levels. From the mill, the ore passed through an amalgamator, where the gold particles were chemically extracted by amalgamation with mercury. Later the amalgam was processed to yield pure gold and to recycle the mercury.

In its new (and so far last) incarnation, the Maryland Mine processed about six thousand tons of ore, yielding 2,570 ounces of gold worth more than $1 million at January 1996 prices. The mine closed in 1940.

The mining activities at Great Falls have revealed that the principal vein of gold-bearing quartz occurs as a seam that meets the surface in a curved line extending about two miles from the mouth of Cool Spring Branch in the north to the eastern end of Widewater in the south. Other scattered seams run more or less parallel with the main vein. The gold occurs as grains, wires, or sheets in the quartz, which in turn occupies old faults in the surrounding metamorphic rocks. The distribution of gold in the seams is erratic, and this lack of consistency has been one of the chief obstacles to large-scale development of the deposits, most of which have only marginal gold content. Nonetheless, a few rich pockets have been found. Of the gold recovered from the Maryland Mine between 1936 and 1940, more than 8 percent came from only seventy pounds of ore, or that is, from .0006 percent of the six thousand tons of ore that were processed.

A word of caution: The old mine shaft and tunnels at the Maryland Mine have not been maintained. They are extremely dangerous and should not be entered. Stay out of the fenced enclosure.

≈   ≈   ≈   ≈

AUTOMOBILE DIRECTIONS: Great Falls Park in Maryland (actually part of the Chesapeake and Ohio Canal National Historical Park) is located on the Potomac River 10 miles northwest of Washington. (See the corner panel on **Map 17** on page 149.) Two avenues of approach are described below. Both sets of directions will guide you to the Great Falls entrance at the intersection of MacArthur Boulevard and Route 189 (Falls Road). In the process you will pass Carderock on the Clara Barton Parkway and Cropley on MacArthur Boulevard, which provide closer access to Sections C and B of the Billy Goat Trail, as shown on **Map 18** opposite. Even people going to Great Falls sometimes prefer to park at Carderock or at Cropley (if there is room) and then walk along the canal towpath to the falls. However, the walking directions that start on page 164 are all based on the assumption that you will drive directly to Great Falls and that you will set out for your walk from the handsome and historic Great Falls Tavern, where the visitor center is located.

To Great Falls from downtown Washington: Take the Whitehurst Freeway upriver to Canal Road just west of the Maryland end of the **Key Bridge**. (Alternatively, take Pennsylvania Avenue and then M Street through Georgetown to the point where M Street turns into Canal Road just west of the Key Bridge).

MAP 18 — Great Falls, Maryland: Omsted Island and Billy Goat Trail

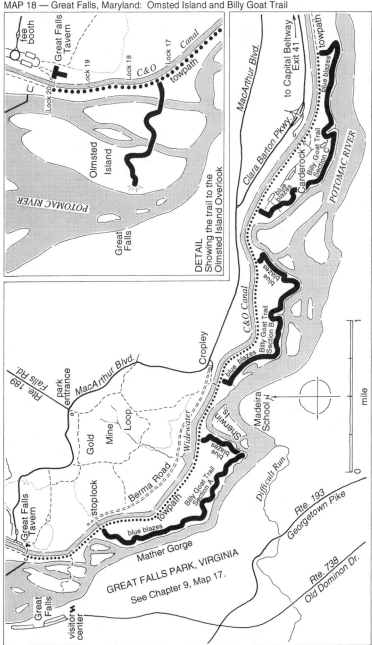

DETAIL
Showing the trail to the
Olmsted Island Overlook

163

With the river and the C&O Canal toward the left, follow Canal Road upriver, passing the **Chain Bridge**. Continue as Canal Road turns into the Clara Barton Parkway. Do not exit for MacArthur Boulevard or Interstate 495 (the Capital Beltway).

Eventually, the Clara Barton Parkway passes under I-495. If you plan to park at Carderock Recreation Area, take the Carderock exit, but for Great Falls continue on the parkway to a T-intersection with MacArthur Boulevard. Turn left onto MacArthur Boulevard and follow it west 2.2 miles to an intersection with Route 189 (Falls Road) at the entrance for the Chesapeake and Ohio Canal National Historical Park at Great Falls, Maryland. Continue straight into the park and downhill along the winding road that leads 1.1 miles to the fee booth and parking lots by the C&O Canal.

To Great Falls from Interstate 495 (the Capital Beltway): Leave the Beltway at Exit 41. This exit is northwest of Washington and — if you are approaching on the Outer Loop — is the last exit in Maryland. The exit signs are for Carderock and Great Falls, MD. If you are approaching from Virginia on the Inner Loop, Exit 41 is the first exit after crossing the Potomac River into Maryland, and in this case, be prepared to fork left (west) immediately after exiting from the Beltway.

After exiting from the Beltway, follow the Clara Barton Parkway West. If you plan to park at Carderock Recreation Area, take the Carderock exit, but for Great Falls stay on the parkway to a T-intersection with MacArthur Boulevard. Turn left onto MacArthur Boulevard and follow it west 2.2 miles to an intersection with Route 189 (Falls Road) at the entrance for the Chesapeake and Ohio Canal National Historical Park at Great Falls Park. Continue straight into the park and downhill along the winding road that leads 1.1 miles to the fee booth and parking lots by the C&O Canal.

≈   ≈   ≈   ≈

WALKING: Four routes are described below. Each starts at the Great Falls Tavern, where the visitor center is located.

≈   ≈   ≈   ≈

Olmsted Island Overlook: The corner panel of **Map 18** on page 163 shows the route to the overlook. A walk to the overlook — the round-trip distance is less than a mile — is recommended as a prelude to any other, longer hikes that you may choose to take at Great Falls.

From the tavern visitor center, cross the canal on the footbridge at lock 20. With the canal on the left, head downstream along the towpath. Pass locks 19 and 18, and then — before reaching lock 17 — turn right and follow the pedestrian bridges and boardwalk to the Great Falls Overlook on Olmsted Island. Return by the way you came.

≈   ≈   ≈   ≈

Billy Goat Trail: This trail exists in three sections — A, B, and C — occurring at intervals along the Potomac River downstream from Great Falls, as shown by the bold lines on **Map 18** on page 163. Access to each section is from the towpath of the C&O Canal, shown as a dotted line. The directions below assume that you will follow one or more sections of the trail along the river, getting from one section to the next via the towpath. A circuit from Great Falls along Section A of the Billy Goat Trail and then back to the falls via the canal towpath is about 4 miles. If you continue on Section B of the Billy Goat Trail and then return to Great Falls via the towpath, the distance totals 7 miles. And if you follow Sections A, B, and C of the Billy Goat Trail one after another and then return to Great Falls on the towpath, the distance totals 10.5 miles. Although strenuous, this is a spectacular outing and is a great way to spend a day. **Note**, however, that parts of the Billy Goat Trail, particularly at Sections B and C, are sometimes flooded during spring thaw and after heavy rains. Stay off the trail during high water.

Section A of the Billy Goat Trail: Starting at the Great Falls Tavern, cross the canal on the footbridge at lock 20. With the canal on the left, head downstream along the towpath. Pass locks 19, 18, and 17. About 30 yards before a high footbridge over the canal (the bridge is located at a stop lock and levee to divert floods), turn right onto the Billy Goat Trail, which is marked with blue blazes.

Follow the rocky blue-blazed trail through the woods, then half-left across rugged terrain at the rim of the gorge. The trail is not so much a path as simply a succession of blazes. For the most part, the trail lies somewhat back from the edge of Mather Gorge.

Continue as the blue blazes cross an area of large, jumbled rocks pitted with potholes, indicating that this terrain was once part of the riverbed. Continue behind an escarpment of jagged rocks at the edge of the gorge. Eventually, descend toward the river, then climb diagonally along a sloping face of rock. (If you are uncomfortable at the prospect of scrambling up this rocky slope, retrace your steps 50 or 60 yards, then follow a faint trail that detours toward the end of the rocks and up through a cleft; once above the rocks, bushwhack to the right until you rejoin the blue-blazed trail at the rim of the gorge.)

Continue up and down over rocky terrain on the blue-blazed trail, sometimes near the edge of the gorge and sometimes at a distance from the rim. Eventually, after passing several ponds and rocky hills, the trail reaches a point of rocks above a large channel of the Potomac that is dry during low water. The hill beyond is Sherwin Island; beyond that on the heights of the opposite shore is the Madeira School, with its conspicuous brick auditorium.

At the bend in the river opposite the Madeira School, follow the blue-blazed trail toward the left. Keeping the large channel on the right, continue up and down across rocky hills and ravines. Eventually, follow the blue blazes to the left away from the channel and up to the C&O Canal towpath at the lower end of Widewater.

With the canal on the right, follow the towpath back to the starting point at Great Falls — or, for a longer outing, follow the towpath downriver to Section B of the Billy Goat Trail, as described below.

Section B of the Billy Goat Trail: With the canal at Widewater on your left, follow the towpath downriver. After passing a causeway that leads to the Cropley parking lot, continue on the towpath for 160 yards to the west end of Section B of the Billy Goat Trail, which is marked with blue blazes.

Follow the narrow trail for 80 yards into the woods, then bear left to stay on the blue-blazed path, which soon follows the crest of the bluff before eventually descending to the river. Follow the blue-blazes downstream. At one point the trail veers sharply inland in order to pass around a gully, then returns to the river's edge. Eventually, opposite a large island, the blue-blazed trail bends left away from the river and climbs to the canal towpath at the east end of Section B of the Billy Goat Trail.

MAP 19 — Great Falls Park, Maryland: Berma Road and Gold Mine Loop

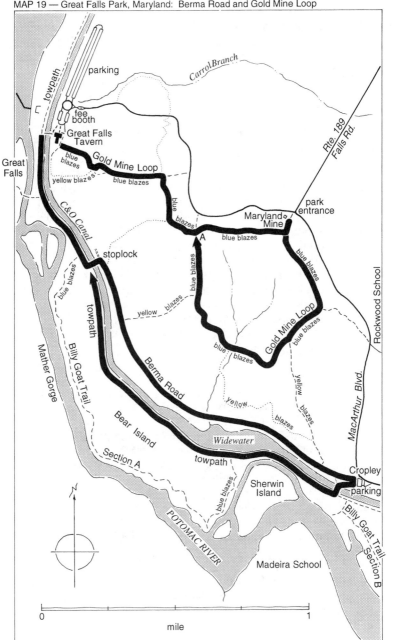

With the canal on the right, follow the towpath back to the starting point at Great Falls — or, for a still longer outing, follow the towpath downstream to Section C of the Billy Goat Trail, as described below.

Section C of the Billy Goat Trail: With the canal on your left, follow the towpath downriver. Soon after the river veers right away from the canal, you will reach milepost 11. Continue 75 yards to the west end of Section C of the Billy Goat Trail, which is marked with blue blazes.

Follow the blue-blazed trail into the woods and past a trail intersecting from the left. Part way down a hill, bear left uphill. Pass another trail intersecting from the left. Follow the blue-blazes behind rocks near the Potomac, then along the top of the cliff above the river. Continue as the trail veers inland and down through a ravine, then returns to the river's edge.

For nearly half a mile the trail borders the river. At another ravine, bear inland, then to the right across a footbridge and back to the river. Eventually, opposite a large house on the Virginia shore, turn sharply inland and follow the blue blazes to the towpath at the east end of Section C of the Billy Goat Trail.

With the canal on the right, follow the towpath back to the starting point at Great Falls.

≈ ≈ ≈ ≈

Berma Road and towpath: This easy 4-mile circuit is shown on **Map 19** on page 167.

Starting at the Great Falls Tavern, cross the canal on the footbridge at lock 20. With the canal on the left, head downstream along the towpath. Pass locks 19, 18, and 17 and continue to a high footbridge over the canal. (The bridge is located at a stop lock and levee to divert floods.) Cross the bridge, then turn right onto the Berma Road, which is a wide path located atop the Washington Aqueduct.

With the canal toward the right, follow the Berma Road about 1.5 miles to a parking lot at MacArthur Boulevard opposite Old Anglers Inn. (This location is called Cropley.) At the parking lot, make a hairpin turn down to the right, then cross the canal on an earth causeway. With the canal on the right, follow the towpath back to the starting point at Great Falls.

≈ ≈ ≈ ≈

Gold Mine Loop: This 4-mile route is shown on **Map 19** on page 167. The trail leads from Great Falls to a circuit through the woods, where prospecting trenches and mine ruins are still visible. After completing the circuit, return to Great Falls by the same trail that you followed at the outset.

Start at the Great Falls Tavern, where the visitor center is located. Facing the front door, turn left and follow a brick path away from the canal, then turn right on a wide concrete path behind the tavern. Go 70 yards to the trailhead on the left for Gold Mine Loop, which is marked with blue blazes.

Follow the blue-blazed trail uphill through the woods. After several hundred yards, turn left atop the raised roadbed of the old Washington and Great Falls Railroad, which formerly ran trolleys to Great Falls. The roadbed is now overgrown with trees.

Follow the old roadbed through the woods. After the trolley roadbed passes through a cut and starts descending slightly, turn right off the roadbed in order to continue on the blue-blazed trail, which eventually climbs to a T-intersection where the blue swatches lead both left and right. This intersection is marked A on Map 19. Turn left here; you will later arrive back at this intersection via the right-hand trail.

As you continue through the woods on the blue-blazed trail, notice an old prospecting trench on the left. Eventually, the path veers right away from the trench and descends to a T-intersection where the main blue-blazed trail leads right. First, however, head uphill to the left a few dozen yards to the remains of the Maryland Mine. Do not enter the chainlink enclosure.

Return to the trail intersection below the mine ruins and continue on the blue-blazed path. Eventually, at a trail junction where a yellow-blazed path from Rockwood School intersects from the left, turn right downhill to follow the blue blazes along an old woods road.

At a fork in the trail, bear right to continue on the blue-blazed path. (The other fork, marked with yellow swatches, leads to Old Anglers Inn at Cropley.) Follow the blue-blazed woods road gradually downhill, across a stream, and uphill — in the process passing two more yellow-blazed trails on the left. Continue to the intersection at point A on Map 19, where the blue trail completes a loop. Turn left and follow the blue-blazes back to the tavern at Great Falls by the way you came at the beginning of your walk.

11

SCOTTS RUN NATURE PRESERVE

Walking — 3 miles (4.8 kilometers). The route shown on **Map 20** on page 178 follows Scotts Run downstream to a waterfall next to the Potomac River, then continues along the heights and rocky bluffs bordering the Potomac River. The circuit is completed by returning though wooded ravines and upland. For people who want a longer outing, the map shows many other trails to explore. During wet, snowy, or icy weather, the stepping stones at Scotts Run and the rocky path along the bluff overlooking the Potomac River can be slippery, so you may want to stay on the upland trails. Do not under any circumstances swim or wade in the Potomac, where there are strong currents.

Scotts Run Nature Preserve is open daily from dawn until dusk. Dogs must be leashed. The preserve is managed by the Fairfax County Park Authority; telephone (703) 941-5000.

A 1969 PLAT for the 336-acre tract of woods, ravines, and Potomac Palisades that now forms Scotts Run Nature Preserve shows a subdivision plan, complete with curving drives, cul-de-sacs, and lots for 309 houses clustered along the ridges. The plan was sweetened (for consumption by Fairfax County officials and local residents) by a pathway and strip of land comprising twenty-six acres along Scots Run and the Potomac River, to be dedicated to public use. Because the lots were approximately half an acre each, much of the land along the ravines and river bluff would have been excess, titled in a homeowners' association and left undisturbed, but in other respects the subdivision would have resembled the conventional developments of cheek-by-jowl tract mansions that can be seen today on adjacent subdivisions. Just how the entire 336-acre property at Scotts Run became instead a public nature preserve is an instructive story.

Before the subdivision was proposed and the counter-crusade for a public park or nature preserve began, the property was the wooded weekend estate of Edward B. Burling, one of the founders of the Washington law firm of Covington and Burling. Burling had a small cabin at the crest of the bluff, where he regularly invited his friends and acquaintances for Sunday lunch. His guests included many of the top government figures and political thinkers of the 1930s, '40s, and '50s, and his cabin was a sort of rustic *salon*. Burling did not mind if others hiked on his land in his absence, and so the tract served as an unofficial park and nature preserve for the neighborhood, reinforcing the area's tone of low-keyed, woodsy exclusiveness.

Burling died in 1966, and three years later one of the region's largest developers, Miller & Smith, Inc., contracted to buy the land from the Burling family trust, but the sale was contingent on county approval for Miller & Smith's subdivision plan. Submitted in the spring of 1969, the proposal was approved, in most respects, by Fairfax County's professional planning staff, but local residents appealed the matter to the county planning commission. Miller & Smith also appealed, seeking approval of an aspect of their plan that entailed relocating the route for the extension of the George Washington Memorial Parkway. Everyone knew that it was highly unlikely that the parkway would ever be extended outside the Capital Beltway, but plats of future roads showed the parkway running across the middle of the Burling tract, and Miller & Smith wanted the route moved to the southern edge of the property and even, in part, shifted onto neighboring land. And so began what newspaper accounts came to call, as the issues developed, a "heated controversy," a "battle," a "donnybrook," and a "revolution."

According to an account in the Washington *Star* for November 3, 1969, "The revolutionaries, ironically, are the establishment this time. They're the doctors, lawyers, merchants, and chiefs of the 'Gold Coast' area in and around McLean, Va. — the people who care about open space and who have the wherewithal to live in it." Organized into a group called the Georgetown Pike and Potomac River Association, the neighborhood residents conceded that the Miller & Smith plan was far above average (as such plans go) in adapting to the difficult terrain and in preserving wooded slopes, but they asserted that the development nonetheless would create massive erosion and sedimentation, and that the number of lots should be reduced to about a hundred. The planning commission responded by referring the matter to the regional soil and water conservation agency for review. Pressing simultaneously for public acquisition of the land, opponents of the subdivision also managed to attract the interest of the Northern Virginia Regional Park Authority and the Fairfax County Park Authority, which were given the opportunity to consider whether the Burling tract should be placed on the Fairfax County Public Facilities Plan as a park site.

The developers, however, had not yet begun to fight. They pledged to use "the most modern soil erosion techniques that responsible people can devise," and their consultants prepared an erosion and sedimentation control plan that a county official called "the best plan that has been submitted to the county as of this date." The Northern Virginia Park Authority also endorsed the plan after Miller & Smith agreed to give the park authority not only twenty-six acres along Scotts Run and the Potomac River, but also a first option to buy twenty-seven choice lots atop the bluff overlooking the Potomac. The Fairfax County Park Authority acquiesced in this arrangement.

As local agencies moved closer to approving the subdivision plan, the park partisans received a boost from the federal government. After being contacted and even visited by several prominent residents of the Burling area, Secretary of the Interior Walter J. Hickel wrote to the Fairfax County Planning Commission that his department was "interested in this remarkable piece of land." He followed up with an extraordinary offer to pay half the cost of buying the property, up to $1.5 million, using money from his department's contingency fund, but the governor of Virginia and county officials said that the state and local governments could not afford to match the federal offer. Efforts to raise matching funds from The Nature Conservancy and private foundations were stymied by lack of interest among local public officials.

Matters dragged on, but by early March 1970, the struggle appeared to be going irreversibly against the park proponents. One headline declared, "Conservationists Beat on Burling." The Fairfax County Planning Commission finally granted a qualified approval of the subdivision plan, and, on appeal, so did the Fairfax County Board of Supervisors. Although the matter of the route for the George Washington Memorial Parkway was still unresolved, no legal barrier remained to prevent Miller & Smith from beginning construction of the first phase of the project. But the developers hesitated and returned to the supervisors a month later for a ruling on the parkway relocation.

The second hearing before the Board of Supervisors was a turning point. After being inundated by a torrent of testimony in support of the park and presented with a park petition containing 2,300 signatures collected door-to-door by high school students, the supervisors requested the county park authority to advise them whether the Burling tract would be suitable for a Dranesville Magisterial District Park (each district elects a supervisor) for which $600,000 of county funds already had been authorized by a 1966 bond referendum.

As the tide of battle shifted toward those fighting for a park or nature preserve, the controversy began to get ugly. In letters to newspapers and even in some editorials, proponents of the preserve were called snobs who were trying to raid the county treasury in order to keep more residents out of their neighborhood. Student activists, whose interest in a nature-oriented park had been sparked by their parents and by classroom discussions and presentations in the schools, were termed an indoctrinated and unruly mob. The supervisor representing the Dranesville District accused the park advocates, whom she called "a few nearby property owners zealously guarding against new neighbors," of "concealment or distortion of some of the basic facts" about costs, taxes, and the loss of opportunity to buy parkland at other sites that she favored. The Georgetown Pike and Potomac River Association in turn alleged that the deliberations and negative decision of the Northern Virginia Park Authority had been tainted by glaring conflicts of interest by some members of its board who had business ties with the developers, and that Miller & Smith had greatly inflated the number of allowable clustered houselots by counting land allocated to the George Washington Memorial Parkway or that was often flooded or otherwise undevelopable.

At a meeting of the Fairfax County Park Authority on April 29, 1970, the movement for a nature preserve gathered momentum. By a margin of four to one, speakers favored buying the Burling tract, and the owner of a large property nearby offered to loan the park authority $1.5 million for three years at 5 percent interest to make the purchase. A few days later the park authority recommended acquisition of the land to the Board of Supervisors, who eventually decided to hold a referendum among Dranesville District voters on whether they were willing to be taxed additionally to raise $1.5 million toward buying the Burling property.

As the date for the referendum approached, attention was focused on the cost to each taxpayer — about $80 for the average homeowner, according to one county official. The local Chamber of Commerce campaigned against the park, objecting to the extra taxes that would be levied on business property. A few large landowners also objected, saying that they would be taxed far more than most and that they were already, in effect, providing open space for the community free of charge (but failing to point out that the public had no right of access to their large estates and horse farms, and that low taxes were a hidden subsidy of their holding costs until the day they sold their land for huge profits, as many have). Other opponents pointed out that the cost of the Burling tract was likely to be higher than anticipated, and that the development of part of it for even a few public tennis courts, ball fields, a swimming pool, and a nature center (as was talked of) would cost still more money. It was said that the community's need for ball fields

would probably entail the purchase of more land elsewhere, since only a small part of the Burling tract is level. Proponents of the park countered that the availability of federal funds was an extraordinary opportunity that should not be lost, and that the development of the land for houses would itself lead to higher taxes because each additional suburban family typically requires more in government services than its newly-constructed home yields in tax revenue.

After a campaign in which numerous students distributed leaflets door-to-door urging purchase of the land for a park, voters of the Dranesville District approved the special tax. Two weeks later, in a confrontation designed to force speedy negotiations about the terms of sale, the developers sent their bulldozers to the site and began clearing a road through the woods — a move the park proponents termed "bulldozer blackmail." Carrying signs and singing "This Land is Our Land," dozens of youngsters and mothers picketed the entrance to the property. The fracas ended abruptly when Miller & Smith agreed to sell the land to the county for $3.6 million (they had bought it a few months earlier for $2.4 million), provided the price was paid by September 4. For a period there was doubt whether the money could be raised that quickly, but the governor of Virginia agreed to contribute $300,000 of federal funds earmarked for the state, and the rest of the local share was borrowed on a short-term basis.

There was still some unpleasantness after the Burling tract was purchased. A few residents of Dranesville District filed a suit alleging technical irregularities in the referendum and complaining that Dranesville was being specially taxed to create a county facility, but their case eventually failed. Others complained of trash left by fishermen and teenagers. Some called the park a "green-tinged white elephant" that was redundant and useless because of other large parks along the Potomac.

What do you think? After you have been to Scotts Run Nature Preserve, you may want to consider how you would have sided in the controversy over the Burling tract, and what (if anything) you are willing to do for the preservation of similar areas in your own community. Our various local, state, and federal park agencies have by-and-large done a magnificent job in the Washington region, and yet even so, in the face of rapid suburbanization, they sometimes do not defend or implement their plans adequately. And occasionally, as in the instance of the Burling property, they simply fail at first to appreciate what people want and will support. It is in cases such as these that park activists can make all the difference.

≈   ≈   ≈   ≈   ≈

AUTOMOBILE DIRECTIONS: Scotts Run Nature Preserve
is located on the Virginia side of the Potomac River 8 miles
northwest of Washington. (See •11 on **Map 1** on page 6 and
Map 20 on page 178.) There are two parking lots, both
accessible from Route 193 (Georgetown Pike) just outside the
Capital Beltway. The directions below will guide you to the
larger parking lot, but in the process you will pass the smaller
lot to which you may want to go back if there is no room at the
larger lot.

To Scotts Run from Interstate 495 (the Capital Beltway):
Leave the Beltway at Exit 13 for Route 193 (Georgetown Pike).
From the top of the exit ramp, follow Route 193 West. After
only 0.2 mile, pass a small parking lot for Scotts Run Nature
Preserve. Continue another 0.4 mile, then turn right into
another, larger parking lot, next to Scotts Run and opposite an
intersection with Swinks Mill Road.

≈   ≈   ≈   ≈

WALKING: The 3-mile circuit described below is shown by the
bold line on **Map 20** on page 178.
From the gate at the back of the parking lot next to Scotts
Run, follow a wide gravel path gradually downhill. Cross
Scotts Run on the concrete stepping stones — if, that is, the
water is not so high as to flow over the top of the stones. If it
is, or if the posts are covered with snow or ice, simply return to
the parking lot and use Map 20 to explore the upland trails.
After crossing Scotts Run, continue downstream on the
broad path for 300 yards, then turn right back across Scotts
Run on another set of concrete stepping posts. Follow the
wide path straight uphill, then curve left downhill past a flight of
wooden stairs and a trail intersecting from the right. Descend
on the broad trail to the Potomac River and a small waterfall at
the mouth of Scotts Run.
From the waterfall at the mouth of Scotts Run, head back
uphill on the wide path. Near the crest of the slope, fork left in
order to climb the stairs that you passed earlier. Continue
uphill to a chimney that marks the site of Edward Burling's
cabin, and from there turn right and follow a wide path, with the
terrain sloping downhill on both sides. After about 0.3 mile
(where the path takes an abrupt turn half-right) turn sharply
left. Follow the trail gradually downhill to a crag overlooking

MAP 20 — Scotts Run Nature Preserve

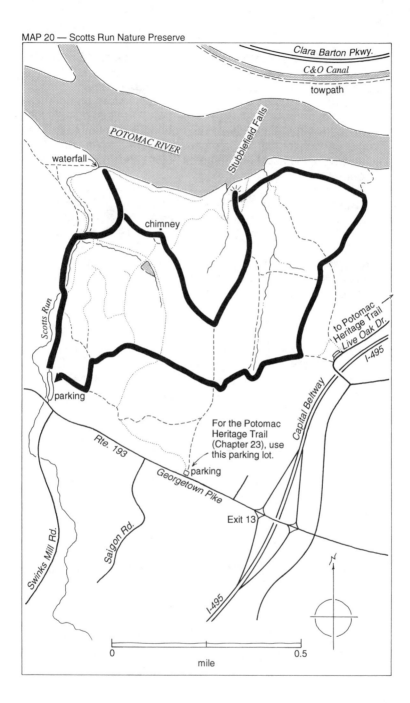

For the Potomac
Heritage Trail
(Chapter 23), use
this parking lot.

Stubblefield Falls, as the rapids are called. Please use caution and don't venture out to the end of the crag if the footing is slippery.

About 40 yards uphill from the rocky overlook above Stubblefield Falls, turn downstream onto a narrow footpath leading along the bluff. With the river downhill to the left, pass other crags. Descend over jumbled rocks and across a small stream. Continue gradually downhill, then up and along the hillside on the narrow footpath. At a T-intersection, turn right uphill.

At the top of the slope, continue straight through a four-way intersection and downhill. Pass a trail intersecting from the right. Continue more or less straight through the woods, then turn sharply right at a slightly skewed T-intersection. Continue as the path passes around the head of a gully. Bear left uphill where a trail intersects from the right. Pass straight through a four-way junction with a wide path. (The path toward the left leads to the small parking lot.)

Continue straight through the woods past obscure trails intersecting from right and left. Eventually, turn left at a T-intersection. Cross a rivulet at the bottom of a broad ravine, then turn right immediately at another T-intersection. With the rivulet on the right, follow the path to the head of a long flight of wooden stairs that descend to the parking lot by Scotts Run.

12

WASHINGTON AND OLD DOMINION TRAIL

Walking, bicycling, and in-line roller-skating. As shown on **Maps 21 and 22** on pages 188 and 189, a paved hike-bike trail follows the former roadbed of the Washington and Old Dominion Railroad for 45 miles through Northern Virginia. The trail's southeastern end is at Arlington in the Shirlington business district, and the northwestern end is at the town of Purcellville, 9 miles short of the Blue Ridge. Between the two end points, the W&OD Trail passes through Arlington, Falls Church, Vienna, Reston, Herndon, Sterling, Ashburn, and Leesburg. Obviously, the farther you get from Washington, the more rural the scenery becomes, but the view from the path is surprisingly attractive even through the close-in suburbs. Although much of the route serves as a right-of-way for the transmission lines of the Virginia Electric and Power Company, the pylons and wires simply reinforce the marching linearity of the trail, which provides a cross-sectional look at Northern Virginia and an interesting transition between city and country.

The W&OD connects with several other hike-bike trails, as shown in schematic outline on **Map 2** on page 7 and also on Map 21. Just east of Herndon at milepost 19 there is a junction with the Fairfax County Parkway Trail, which follows the parkway south to Route 50. In western Arlington there is a junction with the Custis Trail, which follows Interstate 66 and links with the Mount Vernon Trail at Roosevelt Island (see Map 22E). And at Shirlington there is linkage — via local streets and a long hike-bike bridge over Interstate 395 — to the Four Mile Run Trail that in turn connects with the Mount Vernon Trail near Washington National Airport (see Map 22F). For a discussion and map of the Mount Vernon Trail, see Chapter 19.

Because of the considerable length of the W&OD Trail, the automobile directions that start on page 186 provide guidance to five places — Shirlington, Vienna, Route 28, Leesburg, and Purcellville — that are located along the trail at intervals of 10 to 12 miles. Hikers and even cyclists may want to arrange a car shuttle so that they can walk or ride one-way, as discussed briefly in the automobile directions.

The W&OD Trail is open from dawn to dusk. Hikers with dogs must keep their pets on a short leash to avoid accidents with cyclists. Cyclists, in turn, must ride single file, yield to other trail users, and keep their speed to a moderate, safe pace.

The W&OD Trail is managed by the Northern Virginia Regional Park Authority; telephone (703) 352-5900. For the trail office, telephone (703) 729-0596.

NOW CONVERTED TO A HIKE-BIKE TRAIL, the Washington and Old Dominion Railroad stopped running in 1968, after more than 110 years of operation under at least eight names and almost as many corporate owners. During its life the line hauled farm products, Civil War soldiers and supplies, tourists going to and from the Blue Ridge, commuters, and freight for local industries. Toward the end of its existence, the line earned as its nickname, because of its desultory service, the "Virginia Creeper."

Construction of a railroad westward from tidewater on the Potomac was first proposed by a group of Alexandria merchants and bankers concerned about the eclipse of their city by the rival port of Baltimore, through which flowed a lucrative and growing trade with the Ohio Valley. Baltimore was the eastern terminus of the nation's first commercial railroad, the Baltimore and Ohio, which by 1840 already had demonstrated its superiority to the Chesapeake and Ohio Canal, until then the chief hope of the Potomac ports of Georgetown and Alexandria. Accordingly, early in 1847 the Virginia General Assembly chartered the Alexandria and Harpers Ferry Railroad Company. At Harpers Ferry the proposed line would join the Winchester and Potomac Railroad, already serving the Shenandoah Valley. The plan, however, attracted little support, especially after 1848, when the Shenandoah commerce was diverted to Baltimore by a bridge and junction with the B&O at Harpers Ferry.

In 1853 the Virginia legislature amended the charter of the stillborn railroad by specifying a new route running from Alexandria through Leesburg and across the Blue Ridge to the coal fields of Hampshire County (later incorporated into West Virginia). The enterprise was rechristened the Alexandria, Loudoun and Hampshire Railroad Company. Again, however, the promoters had trouble attracting capital, and it was not until the Commonwealth of Virginia undertook to buy three shares of stock for every two purchased by other investors that the company obtained the money to survey the line, compensate owners whose land was condemned for the right-of-way, and begin construction. Between 1855 and 1859, the roadbed was graded from Alexandria to Clarkes Gap west of Leesburg, and a single track laid down as far as Herndon. The ties were white oak, used at the rate of 2,700 per mile. Although the contractors agreed to take 25 percent of the company's stock as part of their payment, progress was slowed nonetheless by lack of cash. In May 1860, service was established once a day each way — later increased to twice and then four times daily — for the two-hour, 38-mile trip between Alexandria and Leesburg.

The line had been in operation barely one year when it was devastated by the Civil War — history's first war in which railroads were a major factor. From the war's outset, railroads were recognized as crucially important for the transportation of troops and supplies, and accordingly they became prime objectives either for seizure or destruction. On May 24, 1861, a few weeks after Virginia had seceded from the Union, Federal forces crossed the Potomac River and took possession of Alexandria and its several railroad terminals. Junctions were soon constructed between the railroad out to Leesburg and two other lines in Alexandria. (Later these railroads were linked to Washington and the North by tracks laid across the Long Bridge at 14th Street.) To prevent the use of the railroads as invasion routes, Confederate troops tore up tracks and burned bridges throughout the southern and western fringes of Fairfax County. On June 17, Confederates ambushed a Union troop train near Vienna station. From there west to Leesburg the Alexandria, Loudoun, and Hampshire Railroad remained a wreck throughout the war. East of Vienna, however, the line was operated by the Federals as part of the U.S. Military Railroads. In particular the railroad played an important role in the buildup of supplies before the first and second battles of Manassas, and it also served various Union forts that were erected to shield Washington. Thousands of Federal troops camped along the tracks in the vicinity of Four Mile Run, which became so polluted with soap from Union wash that the train engineers complained that their locomotive boilers, when filled with water from the stream, frothed with suds.

Lewis McKenzie, president of the Alexandria, Loudoun and Hampshire Railroad, was a Unionist who posted Federal flags on his locomotives the day Alexandria was occupied. In this he was conspicuously unlike the secessionist president of the Alexandria and Washington Railroad, who anticipated the Federal takeover by transferring his engines and rolling stock to the Orange and Alexandria Railroad and fleeing south to the Confederacy. McKenzie urged the War Department in Washington to repair his railroad as far as Leesburg and even to extend it westward for military use, but nothing was done. During the course of the war he repeatedly requested that the line be released from Federal control, but instead it was retained for the use of the Union army longer than any other Virginia railroad.

After the war the railroad company slowly repaired the line. During the course of 1866 and '67, service was reintroduced at Herndon, Sterling, Ashburn, and Leesburg as bridges were rebuilt, including the 278-foot span at Goose Creek. In 1870 West Virginia authorized the railroad to extend its line to the Ohio River, and the company optimistically changed its name to the Washington and Ohio Railroad. The company already had borrowed heavily by issuing corporate bonds paying 7 percent interest; now the capital stock was expanded and then expanded again. By the end of 1874 the track reached Round Hill west of Purcellville, and grading had begun on the roadbed toward Winchester, beyond the Blue Ridge. This objective, however, was never reached. Burdened by its huge construction debt, the railroad sank into bankruptcy, and a receiver was appointed at the beginning of 1878.

In 1882 the railroad's entire property was sold to a new corporation, which promptly collapsed. The next year, the railroad again changed hands and names. Then, in 1886, the line came under the control of a rival railroad company that wanted to put an end — and did — to the plans to extend the line west of the Blue Ridge.

In 1894 the railroad emerged from a period of financial confusion when it was acquired by the newly-chartered Southern Railway Company, which in 1900 extended the tracks to Bluemont at the foot of the Blue Ridge. By being part of the Southern's vast system, the line benefited from a rail link into Washington. Operating as the Bluemont Branch of the Southern Railway, the road for the first time did a good business, carrying vacationing families, hunters, and fishermen to the numerous boarding houses and summer hotels that were popular in Loudoun County. Among others, President Grover Cleveland is said to have taken the train often to Leesburg to fish in Tuscarora Creek.

In 1911 the Southern Railway leased the Bluemont Branch to the Washington and Old Dominion Railway Company. The W&OD already ran a newly-constructed trolley line from Washington through Rosslyn and McLean to the company-owned park on the Virginia side of the Potomac at Great Falls, and it soon electrified the Bluemont Branch as well. The new company continued to promote the tourist traffic, publishing in 1916 an illustrated booklet entitled *Resorts — From the Capital to the Blue Ridge on the Washington and Old Dominion Railway*, extolling the inexpensive accommodations and cooling breezes to be found only a short train ride away from the summertime miasma of Washington. The price of a round-trip ticket between the capital and Bluemont was a dollar. Despite the amenities and low cost, however, passenger revenue fell from 1919 onward as automobiles became commonplace. Although freight revenue rose, on balance the company eventually began losing money. In 1932, when the shareholders refused to meet further deficits, the line again went into receivership.

The receivers drastically reduced services and expenses. The Great Falls Branch was abandoned. In 1936 a new corporation was formed with a slightly different name — the Washington and Old Dominion Railroad — and bought the leasehold rights, rolling stock, and other assets of the old company for a mere $35,000. The reborn railroad negotiated a new lease with the Southern Railway at a greatly reduced rent, and the line west of Purcellville was abandoned. Unable to afford the cost of repairing its system of overhead wires, the company converted to diesel locomotives. Passenger service was terminated, but freight revenues rose as the country pulled out of the Great Depression.

The outbreak of World War II brought sudden prosperity to the line. In 1942 freight revenue reached $335,503, which was 245 percent greater than three years earlier. Gasoline rationing restricted the use of automobiles, and so passenger service — ordered as an emergency measure by the Office of Defense Transportation — was resumed and for a period proved profitable. In 1945 the company managed to buy the line outright from the Southern Railway for only $70,000, the equivalent of less than two years' rent. Passenger service was again terminated in 1951. Four years later the company had only sixty-nine employees, but its revenues were at an all time high of $545,452. In 1956 the shareholders sold the line to the Chesapeake and Ohio Railroad for $445,000 of C&O stock.

The line's future, however, remained doubtful. Throughout the newly-suburbanized region of northern Virginia, a process of de-industrialization was occurring as higher land values and restrictive zoning forced many businesses to leave the area. The railroad nonetheless prospered for few years in the late 1950s during the construction of Dulles International Airport, which required the delivery of immense quantities of sand for the concrete runways. Even so, the lion's share of construction materials for the airport was brought in by truck, and when the new town of Reston was begun in 1961, the railroad received virtually no business from the project, despite the fact that the line passed through the town. At the same time the Virginia Highway Department condemned a spur of the line for part of Interstate 66 and other road projects near Rosslyn, where many of the railroad's industrial customers were located.

The final blow came when the Virginia Electric and Power Company, in a transaction that used the state's Department of Highways as an intermediary (and according to some, as a screen to conceal what really was going on), agreed to buy almost all of the railroad's right-of-way for an undisclosed price — but at least $3.5 million — if the State Corporation Commission of Virginia and the Interstate Commerce Commission approved the railroad's petition to abandon the line. In 1968, over the objection of several local governments and business groups, the petition was approved and the trains stopped running. Nine years later, the Virginia Electric and Power Company sold the roadbed, subject to an easement for its power lines, to the Northern Virginia Regional Park Authority for creation of the present-day hike-bike trail.

≈   ≈   ≈   ≈

METRO: The W&OD Trail passes the East Falls Church Metrorail station (Orange Line) near milepost 5 on the south side of Interstate 66. (See **Map 22D** on page 189.) Turn right out the station and follow Sycamore Street to 19th Street. Turn right uphill on 19th Street and go one short block to Tuckahoe Street, *which is the trail.* To go east toward Washington, turn downhill on Tuckahoe and continue on the paved hike-bike trail. To go west toward Purcellville, turn right uphill on Tuckahoe Street and then, just after bearing left at the top of the hill, turn right on the hike-bike trail, which passes behind a power sub-station.

In addition, a variety of Metrobus routes, including 7A, 7F, 10B, 22A, 22B, 23A, 23B, and 23T, pass through Shirlington. (See **Map 22F**.) And in Vienna, Metrobus 2C follows Maple Avenue (better known as Chain Bridge Road - Route 123) across the trail between Center Street and Park Street.

Telephone (202) 637-7000 for current Metro information, including schedules, routes, and connections.

≈   ≈   ≈   ≈

AUTOMOBILE DIRECTIONS: Located in Northern Virginia, the **W&OD Trail** runs through Arlington, Falls Church, Vienna, Reston, Herndon, Leesburg, and the rural countryside as far as Purcellville. (See **Maps 21 and 22** on pages 188 and 189.) The directions below are to five places located along the trail at intervals of 10 to 12 miles.

So that you do not have to turn around and retrace your route, you may want to arrange a **car shuttle**. Obviously, a shuttle involves either two cars and two hiker-bikers, or a driver who drops you off at the start (after you have left your car at the end) or who simply meets you at the end. To navigate your shuttle, use Map 21 in combination with the following automobile directions. Route 7 parallels the trail, more or less, and is a good shuttle corridor.

≈   ≈   ≈   ≈

SHIRLINGTON, located at milepost 0 on the W&OD Trail, is a commercial district in Arlington. Two approaches via Interstate 395 southbound and northbound are described below. Parking is discussed in the third paragraph.

To Shirlington from Washington via I-395: In Washington, 14th Street leads to I-395 South, which is also accessible from the southbound lanes of the **George Washington Memorial Parkway**. Leave I-395 at Exit 7 for Shirlington, then fork right for Shirlington Road. At a traffic light, turn right onto Shirlington Road itself, and then — at another light — turn left onto Four Mile Run Drive next to the W&OD Trail.

To Shirlington from Interstate 495 (the Capital Beltway): Leave the Beltway at Exit 4B for Interstate 395 North. (This is the same interchange where Interstate 95 from Richmond reaches the Beltway.) Follow I-395 North past **Route 7**, then take Exit 6 for Shirlington. After curving left over the expressway, fork right for Shirlington Road. At a traffic light, pass through an intersection with Arlington Mill Drive, and then — at the next light — turn left onto Four Mile Run Drive beside the W&OD Trail.

Parking on Four Mile Run Drive next to the W&OD Trail: For the first quarter mile, roadside parking places are usually occupied by trucks, but you should be able to find a spot farther up the road. If you cannot find room to park along Four Mile Run Drive, turn right at Walter Reed Drive, then immediately turn left onto the frontage road, where there is ample space. Another option is to follow Four Mile Run Drive for 1 mile to some ball-field parking lots on the left just before the intersection with George Mason Drive.

≈   ≈   ≈   ≈

Map 21 — Washington and Old Dominion Railroad Trail (including cross-references to various details and associated trails shown on Map 22)

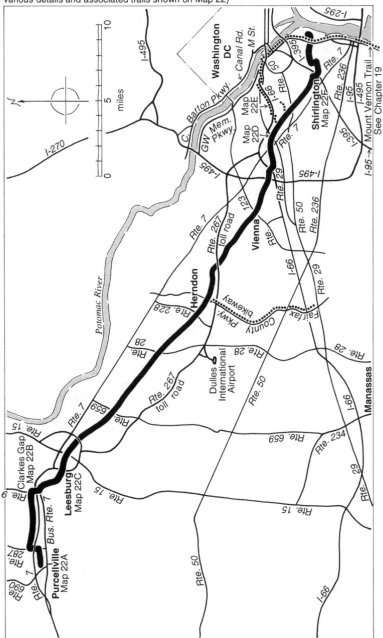

188

Map 22 — Showing various details of the Washington and Old Dominion Railroad Trail. Also shown is the Custis Trail (Map 22E) and the Four Mile Run Trail (Map 22F), each of which links the W&OD to the Mount Vernon Trail (Chapter 19).

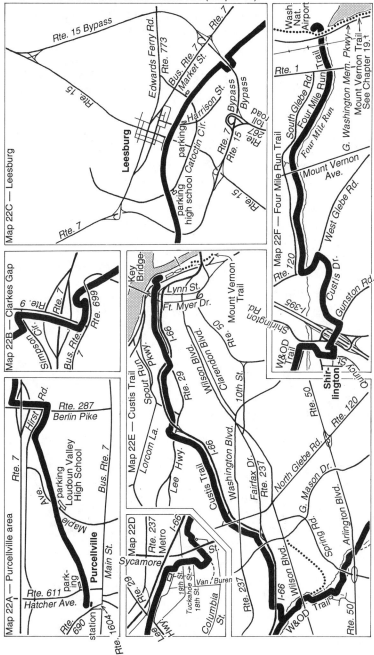

189

VIENNA is located at milepost 12 on the W&OD Trail. Two approaches are described below. While you are in Vienna, you may also want to stop in at Freeman's Store and Museum. This old general store is located on Church Street near the caboose that is on display at the railroad park. Freeman's Store and Museum is open Saturday from 12 noon to 4 P.M. and Sunday from 1 P.M. to 5 P.M.

To Vienna from Interstate 495 (the Capital Beltway): Leave the Beltway at Exit 10 for Route 7 West (Leesburg Pike). From the top of the ramp, follow Route 7 West less than a mile, then take the exit for Route 123 South toward Vienna. Follow Route 123 South 2 miles, then turn right at a traffic light onto Park Street. Go one block, then turn left onto Church Street. Follow Church Street two blocks, then turn right onto Dominion Road. Go one block (passing the old Vienna train station), then turn right onto Ayrhill Avenue. Cross the trail, then immediately turn right into the W&OD parking lot by the station.

To Vienna from Interstate 66: Leave I-66 at Exit 6 for Route 123 North. Follow Route 123 North for more than 3 miles, then turn left onto Center Street, right onto Church, left onto Dominion, right onto Ayrhill, and right again into the W&OD parking lot.

≈   ≈   ≈   ≈

ROUTE 28 is at milepost 24 on the W&OD Trail. There is a very large parking lot here. Several approaches are described below.

To Route 28 (Sully Road) from Interstate 495 (the Capital Beltway): Leave the Beltway at Exit 10 for Route 7 West (Leesburg Pike). From the top of the ramp, follow Route 7 West more than 14 miles, then take the exit for Route 28 South. Follow Route 28 South 2.5 miles to an intersection at a traffic light with Steeplechase Drive, and turn right into the W&OD parking lot within sight of the trail bridge.

Route 28 is also accessible from **Interstate 66** at Centreville, from **Route 50** at Chantilly, and from the **Route 267 toll road** near Dulles International Airport. Follow Route 28 North; you will know that you are approaching the W&OD Trail after passing intersections with Route 846, Cedar Green Road, and Waxpool Road. At an intersection with Steeplechase Drive, turn left into the W&OD parking lot.

≈   ≈   ≈   ≈

LEESBURG is at milepost 34 on the W&OD Trail. (See **Map 22C** on page 189.) Two approaches are described below. Parking is discussed in the third paragraph.

To Leesburg from Interstate 495 (the Capital Beltway) via Route 7: Leave the Beltway at Exit 10 for Route 7 West (Leesburg Pike). From the top of the ramp, follow Route 7 West about 22 miles. As you approach Leesburg, use the left-hand lane to continue straight on Business Route 7. After just 0.6 mile on Business Route 7, turn left at a traffic light onto Catoctin Circle. Go 0.5 mile (crossing the W&OD Trail in the process), then turn right at a traffic light onto Harrison Street. Follow Harrison Street only 0.2 mile, then turn right into a parking lot. The trail itself crosses Harrison Street about 100 yards farther north.

To Leesburg from Interstate 495 (the Capital Beltway) via the Route 267 toll road: Leave the Beltway at Exit 12 for Route 267 West and follow the toll road for 25 miles all the way to its end at Leesburg. Fork left for Exit 1A to Route 7 West. From the bottom of the ramp, go only 0.2 mile to the exit for Business Route 15 North toward Leesburg. Follow Business Route 15 for 0.4 mile, then turn right at a traffic light onto Catoctin Circle. Go 0.3 mile, then turn left at a traffic light onto Harrison Street. Follow Harrison Street 0.2 mile, then turn right into a parking lot. The trail itself crosses Harrison Street about 100 yards farther north.

If there is no room at the parking lot, you should be able to find a parking spot farther up Harrison Street. On weekends, another alternative is to return to Catoctin Circle, then turn right and go 0.9 mile to the parking lot for the Loudoun County High School on the left. The W&OD Trail crosses Catoctin Circle just beyond the high school. Do not park in the high school lot during school hours or school events.

≈   ≈   ≈   ≈

PURCELLVILLE is located at milepost 45 on the W&OD Trail and is its western terminus. (See **Map 22A** on page 189.) Two approaches are described below. Parking is discussed in the third paragraph.

To Purcellville from Interstate 495 (the Capital Beltway) via Route 7: Leave the Beltway at Exit 10 for Route 7 West (Leesburg Pike). From the top of the ramp, follow Route 7 West about 22 miles. At a highway interchange where *Business* Route 7 continues straight into Leesburg, exit to the right in order to continue on Route 7 West. After 10 more miles, leave Route 7 at the exit for Route 287 and Purcellville. At the bottom of the exit ramp, turn left onto Route 287 South. Go 0.7 mile, then turn right at a T-intersection onto Business Route 7 West. Go 1.3 miles into Purcellville, then turn right onto Route 1604 (21st Street). If you miss this turn (as is easy to do), simply continue to Route 690 and turn right. In either case, go 0.1 mile to the old Purcellville station.

To Purcellville from Interstate 495 (the Capital Beltway) via the Route 267 toll road: Leave the Beltway at Exit 12 for Route 267 West. Follow the toll road for 25 miles all the way to its end at Leesburg. Fork left for Exit 1A to Route 7 West. Go 8.4 miles, then leave Route 7 at the exit for Route 287 and Purcellville. At the bottom of the exit ramp, turn left onto Route 287 South. Go 0.7 mile, then turn right at a T-intersection onto Business Route 7 West. Go 1.3 miles into Purcellville, then turn right onto Route 1604 (21st Street). If you miss this turn (as is easy to do), simply continue to Route 690 and turn right. In either case, go 0.1 mile to the old Purcellville station.

There are a few parking spaces adjacent to the station, which may eventually be turned into a visitor center and museum. When the station is open, trail users should not take the parking spaces intended for museum visitors. Map 22A shows other parking areas in Purcellville that are near the trail.

≈   ≈   ≈   ≈

WALKING and BICYCLING: Map 21 on page 188 gives an overview of the 45-mile W&OD Trail. Once you are on the trail, the route is for the most part obvious; the paved path and W&OD signs show the way. Occasionally, however, the trail follows local roads for short distances, or there are obscure twists and turns. These places are shown in detail on **Map 22** on page 189 and are cross-referenced from Map 21.

Mileposts start at Shirlington Road (milepost 0) and ascend to the northwest. For the first few miles northwest of Shirlington, the W&OD Trail is paralleled by the Four Mile Run Trail, which some people prefer. (The Four Mile Run Trail is located mostly on the west side of the stream. There are many places to switch back and forth between the two trails, and near Route 50 they are briefly congruent.)

West of Vienna, the W&OD Trail is bordered by a bridle path that some hikers prefer to the hard-paved trail.

Along the trail there are many road crossings that obviously require caution. If you bring your kids, make sure that they wait for you before crossing. At some busy roads, signs will direct you to cross at the nearest traffic light.

Links to other trails: The **Custis Trail** (Map 22E) and the **Four Mile Run Trail** east of Shirlington (Map 22F) provide two different ways — useful but not scenic — to get back and forth between the W&OD Trail and the Mount Vernon Trail (which is discussed in Chapter 19). In turn, the Mount Vernon Trail provides a connection, via Arlington Memorial Bridge, with the Rock Creek Trail (Chapter 26) and the C&O Canal towpath (Chapter 7). A schematic overview of the entire system of interconnected hike-bike trails is shown on **Map 2** on page 7.

A bench, sign board, and drinking fountain near milepost 4 on the W&OD Trail help to mark the junction with the Custis Trail, which at its other end joins the Mount Vernon Trail via the hike-bike bridge over the George Washington Memorial Parkway just north of the Roosevelt Island parking lot. Near its eastern end, the Custis Trail is simply a sidewalk where caution must be used at street crossings.

The connection through Shirlington between the W&OD Trail and the easternmost segment of the Four Mile Run Trail follows sidewalks and local streets where cyclists must use great caution. In turn, the Four Mile Run Trail meets the Mount Vernon Trail at a junction bordering the George Washington Memorial Parkway near Washington National Airport. The intersection is marked by a sign and occurs just north of the parkway bridge over Four Mile Run.

13

WAKEFIELD - LAKE ACCOTINK TRAIL

Walking — 5 miles (8 kilometers). Starting at Wakefield Park, a broad path follows Accotink Creek downstream through the woods to Lake Accotink Park, then hooks around the reservoir and returns upstream along the bluff above the river. To close the loop, the route shown on **Map 23** on page 200 follows suburban streets for 0.4 mile.

Wakefield Park and Lake Accotink Park are open daily from 7 A.M. until dusk. Dogs must be leashed; swimming is prohibited. The parks are managed by the Fairfax County Park Authority; telephone (703) 569-3464 or 569-0825 for information on boating, fishing, guided walks, and other programs.

THIS WALK FOLLOWS PART of the original roadbed of the Orange and Alexandria Railroad where it weaves along the bluff west of Lake Accotink. The path is smooth and easy. Rails and ties have been removed and the railroad relocated to a less sinuous route a few hundred yards away. But during the Civil War, Confederate troops and guerrillas repeatedly wrecked and sabotaged the railroad in this vicinity, and some recorded actions (described below) occurred at sites passed by this walk.

When the railroad was built, Alexandria was still a port of significance, vying with Georgetown to handle goods shipped to and from the Potomac region. In 1848 a group of Virginia planters successfully petitioned the state's General Assembly to grant them a charter for a new railroad to run southwest from Alexandria to Gordonsville in Orange County. There the line would connect with the Virginia Central Railroad, which later became the Chesapeake and Ohio Railroad. In 1850 a force of Irish immigrants began construction of the O&A line, which was completed to Gordonsville in 1853.

At first the line was used primarily to move farm products and supplies. Although their average speed was only twenty miles per hour, the trains were far faster and cheaper than wagons. Inexpensive transportation reduced the cost of imported guano fertilizer and enabled the owners of small farms and exhausted, moribund plantations in the region south of Washington to convert to intensive truck and dairy farming. Small hamlets sprang up along the line, and new residents moved to parts of Fairfax County that previously were said to have been "as unknown as the wilds of Kansas," according to the editor of the Alexandria *Gazette.* In a fit of enthusiasm for the new railroad, he wrote, "Men worship their idol with a perfect love. . . . In their dreams the ringing of the alarm bell, and the shrill neighing of the iron horse as he prances on his rapid journeys, fall upon the ears as the most delightful music."

At the outbreak of the Civil War, the Orange and Alexandria Railroad ran through Charlottesville to Lynchburg. It provided a rail link with Richmond via the Virginia Central Railroad and with Strausburg in the Shenandoah Valley via the Manassas Gap Railroad. After the Union army crossed the Potomac River and seized the O&A yards in Alexandria on May 24, 1861, control of the railroad and its use as a supply line for the advance on Richmond became a major military objective for the North.

As Confederate troops were concentrated at Manassas to defend the rail junction there, the region served by the railroad north to Alexandria became a no man's land. Southern troops tore up the track and destroyed bridges east of Bull Run. Union efforts to seize Manassas led to the North's eye-opening defeat in the first battle of Manassas on July 21, 1861 (see Chapter 1). For a period Confederate forces occupied Fairfax Station 5.5 miles west of Accotink Creek. Southern pickets were even posted at Springfield Station just east of Accotink.

In 1862 the Union army advanced to the Rappahannock River and rebuilt the O&A line. However, when Union forces retreated from the second battle of Manassas at the end of August, fighting again approached Washington along the track of the Orange and Alexandria Railroad. Hundreds of wounded Union soldiers were taken by train to Fairfax Station, where they were cared for by a small group of nurses headed by Clara Barton, who later founded the American National Red Cross. The last of the wounded were evacuated only a few hours before Confederate troops recaptured Fairfax Station. Following Lee's first invasion of Maryland and the Battle of Antietam, however, the Confederate army withdrew south of the Rappahannock River.

Some skirmishes and other actions occurred in the immediate vicinity of Accotink Creek within what is now the park. On December 24, 1862, J. E. B. Stuart led 1,800 Confederate cavalrymen north across the Rappahannock. Two days later the raiders were in Fairfax County, where they tore up sections of the Orange and Alexandria line and seized Union military supplies, wagons, and mules. On December 28, Stuart paused at Burke Station immediately west of Accotink Creek to eavesdrop on the Union telegraph wire. Some of his troops followed the track east along the section followed by this walk and burned the railroad bridge over the creek near the present-day park dam.

After the Battle of Gettysburg in July 1863, General George Meade pursued General Robert E. Lee to Culpeper, which was served by the Orange and Alexandria Railroad. The O&A was rebuilt again and became Meade's principal supply line, carrying as many as a hundred cars per day.

Confederate guerrillas and sympathizers frequently sabotaged the railroad in the rear of the Union army. On July 26, 1863, guerrillas stopped and attacked a supply train immediately west of what is now Lake Accotink. The incident is described in a report from the commander of the Alexandria depot to Herman Haupt, chief of the Union's military railroads:

> No. 1 train this a.m. found, when a mile and one-half east of Burke's, a rail taken out of the track and horseshoes on trail. Engine was reversed and brakes put hard down. Engine jumped the break, and with two cars passed over. Had it been rail on opposite side [i.e., the outside of the curve], the whole train would have run off the track down a 12-foot bank. Before train was checked, 12 rebels in gray and blue coats and pants, all with guns, pushed out of the bushes, whilst the guard of the Fourth Delaware then took a hand, and, after a few shots, jumped off the train, and had a foot-race through the woods after the rebels. One fat rebel particularly distinguished himself in getting out of sight. The guard saved the train and its convoy, and Providence saved a smash-up, which for some time would have prevented the Army of the Potomac from receiving supplies.

Haupt, in turn, reported to army headquarters that "these attempts to throw off trains are made daily" and that "I am confident that those who appear to be farmers during the day are the parties who injure us at night." Haupt recommended harsh reprisals, and in response General Meade issued the following proclamation:

HEADQUARTERS ARMY OF THE POTOMAC

July 30, 1863

> The numerous depredations committed by citizens, or rebel soldiers in disguise, harbored and concealed by citizens, along the Orange and Alexandria Railroad and within our lines, call for prompt and exemplary punishment. Under the instructions of the Government, therefore, every

citizen against whom there is sufficient evidence of his having engaged in these practices will be arrested and confined for punishment, or put behind the lines. The people within 10 miles of the railroad are notified that they will be held responsible in their persons and property for any injury done to the road, trains, depots, or stations by citizens, guerrillas, or persons in disguise; and, in case of such injury, will be impressed as laborers to repair all damages.

If these measures should not stop such depredations, it will become the unpleasant duty of the undersigned, in the execution of his instructions, to direct the entire inhabitants of the district of country along the railroad be put across the lines, and their property taken for Government uses.

Geo. G. Meade
Major-General, Commanding

Confederate sabotage continued, but without significantly hampering the transport of supplies and without prompting drastic reprisals.

Following the Civil War, the Orange and Alexandria Railroad merged with the Manassas Gap line to form the Orange, Alexandria and Manassas Railroad, later called the Virginia Midland Railroad. In 1894 the Virginia Midland became part of the newly organized Southern Railway. A few years later the old track in the vicinity of Accotink Creek was abandoned in favor of a straighter route laid nearby. The railroad's new route crosses the creek on the high bridge next to the dam and is still used as part of what is now the Norfolk Southern Corporation's main line into Alexandria.

The dam and lake were created by the U.S. Army Corps of Engineers in the 1930s to supply water to Fort Belvoir. In 1965 the federal government gave the lake and surrounding land to Fairfax County for park use.

≈   ≈   ≈   ≈

AUTOMOBILE DIRECTIONS: The Wakefield - Lake Accotink Trail starts at Wakefield Park, located in Virginia about 12 miles southwest of Washington and just outside the Capital Beltway. (See •13 on **Map 1** on page 6, and also **Map 23** on page 200.)

To Wakefield Park from Interstate 495 (the Capital Beltway): Leave the Beltway at Exit 5 for Route 620 West (Braddock Road). At a traffic light located only 0.3 mile west of the Braddock Road bridge over the Beltway, turn right into the entrance for Wakefield Park opposite Queensberry Avenue. (From the Beltway's Outer Loop, the exit ramp joins Braddock

MAP 23 — The Wakefield - Lake Accotink Trail

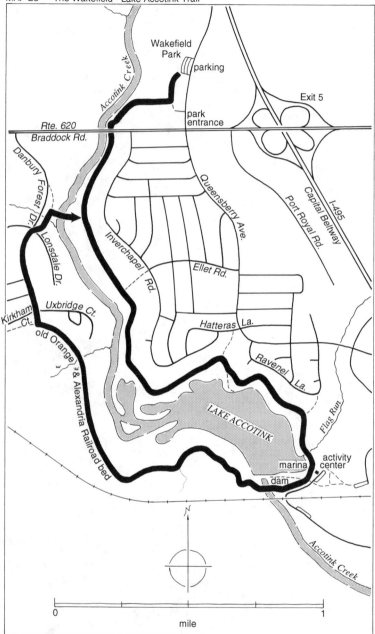

Road only 0.1 mile before the traffic signal and park road.) Follow the entrance road 0.2 mile. Park in the lot on the left.

≈   ≈   ≈   ≈

WALKING: The route described below totals 5 miles and is shown by the bold line on **Map 23** opposite.

From the back-left corner of the Wakefield parking lot, join the Wakefield - Lake Accotink Trail. Follow the trail through the woods. Turn right to avoid a maintenance area, then bear left as the trail approaches Accotink Creek. With the creek on the right, follow the path under Route 620 (Braddock Road) and downstream past houses on the left. Eventually, pass a trail that joins from the right — and by which you will return after circling the lake.

Continue straight through the woods. After awhile, the path borders the creek, then again veers away to the left. Pass houses on the left. Bear sharply right on the main trail where a path intersects from the left. Continue along the slope at a distance from the water. Pass more houses and another path intersecting from the left before arriving at the Lake Accotink activity center and marina.

Follow the shore through the marina. Climb a flight of steps and cross straight through an oblique four-way junction of paths. Follow a paved path next to a road. Fork right to cross Accotink Creek below the dam. If water is flowing across the low bridge, do not attempt to cross; instead, return the way you came.

After crossing Accotink Creek, climb steeply to a wide, well-worn path that snakes along the bluff, then eventually joins the old bed of the Orange and Alexandria Railroad. Follow the former railbed for more than a mile. After passing houses on the right, turn right onto a narrow asphalt path that leads steeply downhill for 50 yards to the intersection of Uxbridge Court and Danbury Forest Drive.

Follow Danbury Forest Drive straight. Pass an intersection with Clydesdale Road on the left and Kings Glen School on the right. Continue downhill on Danbury Forest Drive. Immediately after an intersection with Lonsdale Drive, bear right downhill on a paved path to a flight of concrete steps. Cross a stream on a small bridge. Go 40 yards, then turn right at a trail junction. After crossing Accotink Creek, go 120 yards, then turn left at a T-intersection to return to your starting point at Wakefield Park.

14

BURKE LAKE PARK

Walking, ski touring, and bicycling — 4.5 miles (7.2 kilometers).
Map 24 on page 206 shows the multi-use trail around Burke
Lake, which is located in Virginia southwest of Washington and
Alexandria. Paved mostly with finely crushed rock, the wide and
level path provides easy walking and frequent views out across
the reservoir. The trail is also suitable for fat-tired or hybrid
bicycles.

Burke Lake Park is open daily from 7 A.M. until dark.
Swimming is prohibited and dogs must be leashed. From
approximately May through September, non-residents of Fairfax
County are charged an entrance fee on weekends and holidays.
A campground and boat rental operate during the warmer
months.

Burke Lake Park is managed by the Fairfax County Park
Authority; telephone (703) 323-6601. Burke Lake itself is owned
and managed by the Virginia Department of Game and Inland
Fisheries; telephone (703) 899-4169.

BURKE LAKE PARK is a multi-use area offering a smorgasbord of
recreational activities. Facilities include not only the waterside trail,
which is popular with walkers, joggers, and some cyclists, but also a
campground, a fishing pier, a boat rental, a miniature railroad, a
carousel, playgrounds, picnic areas, a golf course and driving range, a
Frisbee® golf course, sand-lot volleyball courts, and even an ice-cream
parlor. Don't, however, be put off by this fardel of features; nine-tenths
of the waterside trail is far removed from the activity centers where
crowds congregate.

The wide range of activities at Burke Lake Park is typical of munici-
pal and county parks, which traditionally have been called upon to
provide facilities for every age group and interest. And, of course, local
parks are often sports oriented, featuring ball fields and even major

facilities like swimming pools and skating rinks that are used by school and club athletic programs.

At the other end of the spectrum from local parks are national parks. According to standards formulated by the National Park Service when it was established in 1916, national parks were supposed to be vast, spectacular examples of unspoiled natural grandeur, like the Grand Canyon, designated a national park in 1919. (Even before the park service was organized, Congress had already set aside from federal lands a dozen national parks, starting with Yellowstone in 1872.) In order to preserve national parks in pristine condition forever, their use was intended to include only low-keyed forms of nature appreciation, such as sightseeing, camping, horse trekking, and hiking.

During the 1930s, however, the responsibilities of the National Park Service expanded rapidly, sometimes in directions that had little to do with its original mission. The park service was assigned responsibility — by transfer from other federal agencies — for managing many small historic sites (chiefly battlefields and forts). In the decades that followed, the National Park Service acquired numerous houses and other structures and even whole hamlets of historic value, such as Hopewell Furnace National Historic Site in Pennsylvania and Colonial National Historic Park, which includes Yorktown, Virginia. This growth was in addition to the stewardship the National Park Service already exercised over a lengthening list of "national monuments," consisting mainly of outstanding natural landmarks, like Devil's Tower in Wyoming, and areas of scientific interest, such as Dinosaur National Monument in Colorado and Utah. Thus the National Park Service has gradually become what might be described as a sort of Smithsonian Institution of American land, charged with acquiring, preserving, and presenting to the public a diversified roster of scenically, historically, and scientifically important places.

To be sure, there are many exceptions, particularly in the Washington region, where there are now a number of federally administered parks established as an adjunct to other projects, as at Greenbelt Park (Chapter 32). Similarly, in 1936 the first "national recreation area" was designated to take advantage of the opportunity for swimming and boating at Lake Mead (which is the reservoir creating by the construction of Hoover Dam), and now the National Park Service runs a number of such water-oriented recreation areas that were developed incidental to other federal dam projects. Also, at the national seashore parks, the federal government administers immensely popular bathing beaches, as on Maryland's Assateague Island. Still, however, the National Park Service strives (wisely, I think) to maintain emphasis on historic preservation and on the same low-keyed activities — sightseeing, hiking, wildlife observation, and camping — that have long been associated with our great national parks.

As for state parks, throughout the country they are usually based on the federal example. Typically, state park agencies have focused on the preservation of outstanding scenic areas and historic sites, again with emphasis on sightseeing, walking, camping, and nature appreciation — but also recognizing the public's passion for swimming and boating. As suburban sprawl has engulfed many state parks that once were considered remote from big cities, there has been some pressure to "improve" these sites with golf courses, swimming pools, skating rinks, community multi-purpose centers, and the like. The advent of the environmental movement in the 1960s has made clear, however, that such facilities are rarely the sorts of things that the public wants to see when they go to a state park, and in any case worsening budget constraints in the 1980s and '90s have contributed to the trend toward less elaborate development at state parks.

At Fairfax County's Burke Lake Park, there is also a state component, namely the lake itself, which the Virginia Department of Game and Inland Fisheries created in 1961 by damming South Run. The project was paid for by state fishing license fees and by the federal tax on fishing gear and supplies. (There is a similar federal tax on hunting gear and supplies that is granted back to the states to preserve hunting areas.) One idea that has met with a mixed reception is that the items taxed under these federal programs, or under similar state programs, should include binoculars and bird food on the grounds that birdwatchers should also help to preserve and create wildlife habitat.

≈　　　≈　　　≈　　　≈

AUTOMOBILE DIRECTIONS: Burke Lake Park is located in Virginia about 20 miles southwest of Washington and 7 miles south of Fairfax. (See the corner panel on **Map 24** on page 206.) Three avenues of approach are described below.

To Burke Lake from Interstate 495 (the Capital Beltway): Leave the Beltway at Exit 5 for Route 620 West (Braddock Road). Follow Route 620 West about 1.8 miles to an intersection with Route 645 (Burke Lake Road). Turn left and follow Route 645 for 4.8 miles to an intersection with Route 123 (Ox Road). Turn left onto Route 123 and go 0.5 mile to the main entrance to Burke Lake Park on the left. Follow the entrance road as straight as possible 0.3 mile to the marina parking area.

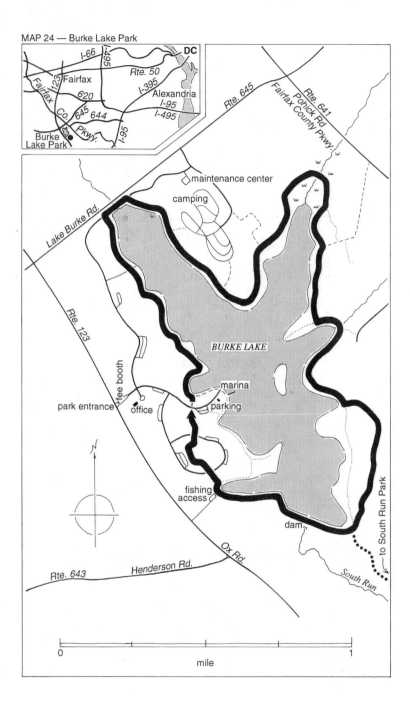

MAP 24 — Burke Lake Park

BURKE LAKE

maintenance center
camping
marina
parking
park entrance
fee booth
office
fishing access
dam
to South Run Park
South Run

Lake Burke Rd.
Rte. 123
Ox Rd.
Rte. 643   Henderson Rd.
Rte. 645
Pohick Rd.
Fairfax County Pkwy.
Rte. 641

N

0   1
mile

Fairfax
Fairfax Co.
Burke Lake Park
I-66
I-495
Rte. 50
I-395
Alexandria
I-95
I-495
I-95
123
620
645
644
Pkwy.
DC

To Burke Lake from Interstate 95 just south of its juncture with the Capital Beltway: Leave I-95 at Exit 169B for Route 644 West (Old Keene Mill Road). This is the Springfield exit, located only 0.4 mile south of the Beltway. Follow Route 644 West for 6.3 miles to a T-intersection with Route 641 (Pohick Road). Turn right and go 0.7 mile, then turn left at a crossroads onto Route 645 (Burke Lake Road). Follow Route 645 for 1 mile to an intersection with Route 123 (Ox Road). Turn left onto Route 123 and go 0.5 mile to the main entrance to Burke Lake Park on the left. Follow the entrance road as straight as possible 0.3 mile to the marina parking area.

To Burke Lake from Interstate 66 near Fairfax: Leave I-66 at Exit 6 for Route 123 South and follow it more than 8 miles, in the process passing through the town of **Fairfax** and crossing Route 620 (Braddock Road). After crossing Route 645 (Burke Lake Road), continue 0.5 mile to the main entrance to Burke Lake Park on the left. Follow the entrance road as straight as possible 0.3 mile to the marina parking area.

≈   ≈   ≈   ≈

WALKING and BICYCLING: A route totaling 4.5 miles around Burke Lake is shown on **Map 24** opposite.

Join the trail where it crosses the park road at the entrance to the marina parking lot. The crossing is marked with white hatch marks on the pavement. I suggest following the trail clockwise around the lake, with the water on your right. Simply stay on the main path.

15

BULL RUN - OCCOQUAN TRAIL

linking Bull Run Regional Park, Hemlock Overlook Regional Park, and Fountainhead Regional Park

Walking — up to 18 miles (29 kilometers) one way. As shown on **Maps 25 and 26** on pages 218 and 219, this long hiking trail, which is located in Virginia about 20 miles southwest of Washington, borders Bull Run and the Occoquan Reservoir. Stretches of easy walking along the river bank alternate with more strenuous sections up and down bluffs and ravines at a distance from the water. For nearly its entire length, the trail is through woods, with little exposure to extraneous development. The best times for a walk here are in fall, at the peak of the color, and in spring, when wildflowers cover the flood plain at the trail's northern end.

Because of the considerable length of the Bull Run - Occoquan Trail, hikers must deal with the problem of how to start at one end, yet have a car at the other end when they are done. Different permutations for car shuttles are discussed briefly on pages 216 and 217 in the automobile directions. There are car directions not only to the trail's end points at Bull Run Regional Park and Fountainhead Regional Park, but also to the approximate midpoint at Hemlock Overlook Regional Park, which makes possible a series of shorter walks back and forth. You can also park and join the trail at Route 28 (Centreville Road) and at Bull Run Marina. Walking directions start on page 220.

The Bull Run - Occoquan Trail is marked with blue blazes. Bicycles are prohibited and dogs must be leashed. During periods of thaw or after rain, parts of the trail can be muddy, and exceptional storms may even flood some sections. If you encounter flooding, do not under any circumstances try to wade though. In wet, snowy, or icy weather, use caution when crossing tributary streams on pedestrian bridges and stepping stones where surfaces may be slick.

The Bull Run - Occoquan Trail is open daily from dawn to dusk. However, the access points at Bull Run Regional Park and Fountainhead Regional Park are closed in winter (call for precise dates), whereas Hemlock Overlook remains open year-round. Non-residents of Northern Virginia may be charged an admission fee at Bull Run Regional Park. The trail and the parks through which it passes are administered by the Northern Virginia Regional Park Authority; telephone (703) 352-5900.

BULL RUN ORIGINATES west of Dulles International Airport and flows southeast across Virginia's gently rolling Piedmont upland, where the stream is sluggish and the banks often low and muddy. But east of Manassas, Bull Run enters a region where the stream — as it descends to join the Occoquan River and eventually the tidal Potomac — has dissected the upland into an intricate system of steep-sided valleys and tributary ravines. Other nearby rivers have similarly eroded the region through which they flow, creating a swath of very uneven terrain along the Piedmont's eastern margin. As you hike the Bull Run - Occoquan Trail, walking up and down the bluffs and along the winding contours, you will have ample time to become familiar with this landscape of ridges and ravines and to contemplate the erosive power of running water, which is the dominate force shaping the earth's surface.

Stream erosion attacks any elevated region and works to reduce it to a lower plain. It is as basic as rain, gravity, and friction, with help too from processes of chemical dissolution. It works slowly but relentlessly, achieving effects over eons. And as the process passes through a sequence of stages, it produces various characteristic landforms that are well illustrated at different parks and along different rivers in the Washington region.

Although the process of erosion is ceaseless, it of course speeds up during periods of peak flow. Most erosion in the eastern United States is attributable to a relatively few heavy rains each year and — even more so — to less frequent but spectacular flood rains. Although these infrequent events may seem freakish, over millions of years they are commonplace and may be said to occur with regularity.

Going hand in hand with erosion — or really as a necessary precursor to it — is the process of weathering, by which a region's rocky foundation is, near the surface, broken down into smaller and smaller pieces that can be carried away by water, which is itself a powerful weathering agent. For example, through *frost action*, water can enter cracks in the rocks and split them apart when the water freezes, eventually reducing rocks near the surface to crumbly fragments. This is the chief form of *physical weathering*, but there are other physical processes, including penetration into rock fissures by roots of trees and other plants, which as they grow pry the rocks apart.

As rocks are reduced to smaller fragments by physical processes, *chemical weathering* becomes increasingly important, and again water is a major agent. Through *hydrolysis*, water reacts with minerals in the rocks, creating clay and freeing some elements which are carried away in solution. Through *carbonation*, carbon dioxide in soil (where it is produced by bacteria) or in the air combines with water to form a weak acid called carbonic acid, which dissolves limestone. Through *oxidation* some minerals, of which iron is the chief, react with oxygen in air and in water, thus contributing to the disintegration of the parent rock of which the oxidized minerals were formerly part. Acting together, physical and chemical weathering convert bedrock to soil or to an intermediate, crumbly substrate called *saprolite,* on which the process of erosion can then work, as discussed below.

Wherever rain falls on land, any downward-pitched trough or swale, even though at first shallow or insignificant, is self-aggrandizing, collecting and channeling the water that flows off a broad area, as may be seen, for example, at Greenbelt Park (Chapter 32), where a branching system of small streams — little more than gullies that are nearly dry between rainfalls — weaves through the woods. Even in the absence of such troughs, rainwater flowing in sheets down a "smooth" hillside tends to organize itself into runnels that in turn erode little rills, some of which may develop into gullies and eventually into ravines that carry away the runoff. Initially, many minor watercourses are dry between rains, but some may be fed seasonally by melting snow or even continuously by springs or the outflow from wetlands where precipitation is stored for a period before continuing its journey to the sea. Gradually, the gullies and ravines deepen with erosion, and once they penetrate the water table, they are fed by a steady seepage of groundwater. Now and again steep slopes may simply slump downhill, or a steep embankment may collapse directly into a stream, where the loosened material is easily carried away.

As a stream extends itself by developing tributaries, its erosive power rapidly increases. The larger drainage area concentrates more water in the main channel downstream, where stream energy is swelled by the greater mass of moving water. The increase in energy is more than directly proportional to stream volume. As the volume increases, an ever-smaller fraction of the river's energy is consumed in overcoming friction with the streambed, and in consequence the speed of the river increases and so does its ability to carry fine clay, silt, and sand in suspension, to abrade and wear down rocks, and to push and role pebbles and cobbles downstream.

Obviously, the ocean constitutes a base level below which a river cannot erode.* Nonetheless, even as a river approaches sea level, the current continues to erode the bank laterally wherever the stream is deflected by each slight turn. This tendency to carve wider and wider curves is present along the entire river but is accentuated in the lower, older reaches where stream volume is greatest. As the river approaches the ocean, downward cutting is no longer possible, but sideward cutting can continue as long as there is flow. Gradually, a meandering course develops as the river snakes back and forth, eroding first one side of the valley and then the other, as can be seen on the Patuxent River at the Jug Bay Natural Area and Merkle Wildlife Sanctuary (Chapter 38). When sinuosity becomes so extreme that the curves loop back on themselves, the current will intercept the channel farther downstream, cutting off the looping meander. Thus, as millennia pass, the river migrates in an ever-changing course over a broad floodplain, leaving behind abandoned channels here and there.

At the mouth of the river where it empties into an ocean or estuary, a distinctive geologic feature forms. As the current dissipates in the standing water, the capacity of the stream to carry material in suspension is reduced and then eliminated, so that the river's load of sand and silt is dropped and forms a delta. The same process occurs where streams enter slackwater at reservoirs, as can be seen at Lake Accotink and Lake Frank (Chapters 13 and 28). Because the current slows gradually, the deposits tend to be sorted, with larger, heavier particles dropped first. After the delta has extended itself a considerable distance in one direction, a flood may cut a new and shorter channel to open water, causing the former course to be abandoned, at least for a period. Large deltas typically have several channels or sets of channels among which the stream shifts as deposits are concentrated first in one and then in another.

Meanwhile, the countless gullies and ravines at the river's headwaters continue to fan outward like the branches of a growing tree. As the tributaries extend themselves, the watershed becomes larger and larger.

---

* Submarine canyons, like those along the edge of the Continental Shelf, are not an exception to this principle. Such canyons — and also the valley now occupied by Chesapeake Bay — were carved by rivers during the depths of the Ice Age, when so much water was amassed on land as continental ice that the level of the sea was as much as three hundred feet lower than it is now.

A growing river may even intercept and divert to itself (or *capture*) streams that previously took a different course to the sea. Material eroded from areas far up a river's many tributaries is redeposited downstream in alluvial floodplains, sandbars, and mudbanks, as at Bull Run Regional Park. Such deposits are re-eroded, transported downstream, and redeposited over and over again as the river's capacity to carry sand and silt in suspension fluctuates with the volume of runoff.

According to one conceptual model of stream erosion developed in the nineteenth century by William M. Davis, an examination of several variables — including stream gradient, valley depth, valley width, and number of meanders — will indicate the stage of development that has been reached by any stretch of river. In the earliest stage, gullies and ravines eat into the elevated land surface. Because the dominant direction of cutting is downward, the gullies and ravines are steep-sided and V-shaped, and even after they join to form larger valleys, the gradient of the streambed is steep compared to navigable waterways. Rapids are common. There are only minor flats in the valley bottom. The ratio of valley depth relative to width is at its maximum. Such a stream was said by Davis to be in *youth*.

As a stream's elevation approaches base level, the gradient diminishes and downward cutting slows. Bends in the course of the stream become accentuated, meanders start to develop, and the width of the valley increases relative to its depth. Sideward cutting produces a continuous floodplain. Such a stream is said to be in *maturity*.

Finally, when downward cutting has become so slow as virtually to cease and the stream is as close to base level as it can get, sideward cutting may eventually produce a nearly flat and featureless valley, much wider than it is deep, across which the river meanders from side to side. The gradient is low, and the broad bottomland is marked only by the scars, swamps, and lakes left by former channels. Perhaps a few rock hummocks and hills — more resistant to erosion than were their surroundings — are left rising above the low valley floor. This stage of river development is *old age*. The ultimate (and largely theoretical) expression of old age is what Davis called a *peneplain*, meaning "almost a plain" and denoting a surface of regional extent and low elevation, with only small variations in relief, produced by long-continued fluvial erosion. Most geologists today, however, think that even if other geologic events (such as fluctuations in sea level and movements in the earth's crust) did not occur, prolonged erosion would create a landscape in which low, rolling hills occupy far more of the region than Davis postulated, especially where vegetation protects the land surface.

Of course, never does all of a river reach old age. The gullies and ravines at the river's headwaters remain youthful as they continue to spread out and consume the upland. The river is also likely to have a mature midsection.

The terms *youth, maturity,* and *old age* can also be applied to an entire region to describe the extent to which it has been acted upon by stream erosion. As an upland region experiences the headward erosion of a stream system, more and more of the landscape is given over to a branching system of gullies, ravines, and valleys. Eventually, the upland lying between different branches or even different watersheds is cut away until the divide changes from a wide plateau to a narrow ridge, and then to a low, rounded rise. Meanwhile, the valleys slowly widen and develop broad, flat floodplains. For as long as an area is mostly upland, it is said to be in youth. During the period that valley walls and slopes occupy most of the landscape (as is the case along the Bull-Run - Occoquan Trail), the region is said to be in maturity. And when most of the landscape is given over to bottomland, the area is said to be in old age. Of course, the terms *youth, maturity,* and *old age* do not describe the actual age of a river or landscape, but only its stage of erosional development — and even so, the terms are rather inexact. Nonetheless, the analogy to a living organism is helpful if one's main goal is to understand the general tendency or sequence of stream erosion in the absence of various other factors and forces mentioned below.

Chief among these complicating factors is the effect produced by varying degrees of resistance to erosion among the different kinds of rocks that underlie a river's watershed. It is a common thing for rivers to show a profile passing from youth to maturity to old age (at this last stage, complete with a wide valley and meandering course), then to re-enter a relatively narrow valley with a steep gradient before once again transitioning to an older landscape. This pattern may occur several times along a single river, and in each case the sections characterized by a wide valley and meandering course are in areas of relatively unresistant rock compared to what is found next downstream. As a local example, the Potomac River above Great Falls has a relatively gentle profile compared to the youthful gorge downstream. This anomaly is traceable to the fact that at Great Falls there occurs a barrier of particularly obdurate rock that acts as a base level for the river upstream. In theory, prolonged erosion should eventually eliminate such anomalies by wearing away even the resistant rocks that cause them.

The varying degrees of resistance to erosion among different kinds of rocks also affects stream patterns. Where differences in resistance are minimal, a river, if viewed from the air, tends to branch out into tributaries like a tree viewed in profile, as at Bull Run and throughout the Washington region. This pattern is called *dendritic.* But where some

rocks are more easily eroded than others, the stream pattern will reflect this fact. For example, a *trellis pattern* — like a grape vine strung on parallel wires or a fruit tree espaliered to a garden wall — is characteristic of areas where alternating hard and soft beds of rock have been tilted or folded by movements in the earth's crust and then partially eroded away. Where the hard layers intersect the land surface, they remain as high ridges. Where the softer layers intersect the surface, they are eroded into valleys by streams that sometimes manage to link from one valley to the next. Such trellis patterns are seen in the Valley and Ridge geologic province of western Maryland and western Virginia. Stream patterns can also reflect the tendency of some rocks to split into rectilinear joints, as does sandstone.

Finally, tectonic movements in the earth's crust can, for protracted periods, cause the land to rise at rates less than, equal to, or greater than the countervailing rate of erosion, thus retarding or even renewing the sequence of erosion outlined in this discussion. Some such movements may be isostatic adjustments by which pieces of the crust, which are "floating" on softer layers below, rise as the surface is worn away, much as an iceberg would rise if only the part above water were subject to melting. Another theory is that crustal plates, spreading from rifts in the ocean basins, sometimes collide with the continental margins, causing the land to bow, buckle, and rise even as it erodes. Careful studies have shown that if present rates of erosion are applied to the past, the Appalachian Mountains should have been worn away long ago, but upward movement has enabled them to endure despite erosion. Whatever the cause for the uplift, one result is that the general contours of the land surface — especially in areas of middling relief like the Piedmont province of Maryland and Virginia — are far more stable than the ongoing process of stream erosion would indicate.

≈　　　≈　　　≈　　　≈

AUTOMOBILE DIRECTIONS: The Bull Run - Occoquan Trail is located near Manassas, Virginia, about 20 miles southwest of Washington. (See •15 on **Map 1** on page 6, and also **Maps 25 and 26** on pages 218 and 219.) The trail's upper end is at Bull Run Regional Park near Interstate 66. The trail's lower end is at Fountainhead Regional Park near Lorton and Interstate 95. In its middle section, the trail passes through Hemlock Overlook Regional Park near the village of Clifton. Directions to the trail's two end points and its approximate midpoint are provided below.

If you plan to walk all (or even half) of the 18-mile trail in one day, you presumably will want to arrange a **car shuttle**. Obviously, a shuttle involves either two cars and two driver-hikers, or a driver who drops you off at the start (after you have left your car at the end) or who simply meets you at the end. To navigate your shuttle, use Maps 25 and 26. You may also want to refer to the following automobile directions.

To Bull Run Regional Park from Interstate 495 (the Capital Beltway): Leave the Beltway at Exit 9 for **Interstate 66 West** (which also, of course, is accessible from downtown Washington via Constitution Avenue and the Roosevelt Bridge). From the Beltway, follow I-66 west nearly 13 miles, then take Exit 52 for Route 29. At the bottom of the exit ramp, turn right onto Route 29 South and go 2.1 miles, then turn left onto Bull Run Post Office Road. Go 1.1 miles, then (immediately after a sharp left bend) bear right onto Bull Run Drive and follow it 0.9 mile to the fee station at the entrance to Bull Run Regional Park. Follow the park road as straight as possible 1.4 miles to the parking lot on the left for the swimming pool. Park as near as possible to the road.

To Hemlock Overlook Regional Park from Interstate 495 (the Capital Beltway): Leave the Beltway at Exit 5 for Route 620 West (Braddock Road). Follow Route 620 West for 10.7 miles to a crossroads at a traffic light with Clifton Road. Turn left onto Clifton Road and follow it 3.7 miles to the center of the nineteenth-century village of Clifton. From the railroad crossing in Clifton, continue straight south 0.9 mile out of town on Main Street (which turns into Kincheloe Road), then turn right onto Yates Ford Road. Follow Yates Ford Road 1.5 miles to the entrance to Hemlock Overlook Regional Park at the end of the road. There are parking areas just outside and inside the gate, plus another parking area 0.1 mile back up Yates Ford Road.

To Fountainhead Regional Park from Interstate 95: Leave I-95 at Exit 163 for Route 642 (Lorton Road). This exit is located about 6 miles south of I-95's junction with **Interstate 495 (the Capital Beltway) and Interstate 395**. At the bottom of the exit ramp, turn right and follow Route 642 for 1.9 miles, then turn sharply right onto Route 123 (Ox Road). Go 1.9 miles, then bear left onto Route 647 (Hampton Road). Follow Hampton Road for 3.2 miles, then turn left into Fountainhead

MAP 25 — Bull Run - Occoquan Trail: upper section

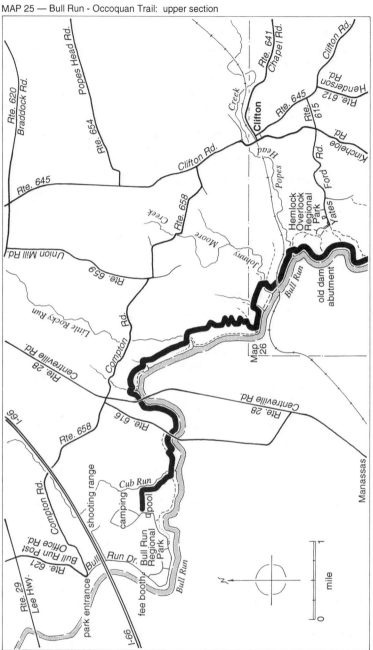

218

MAP 26 — Bull Run - Occoquan Trail: lower section

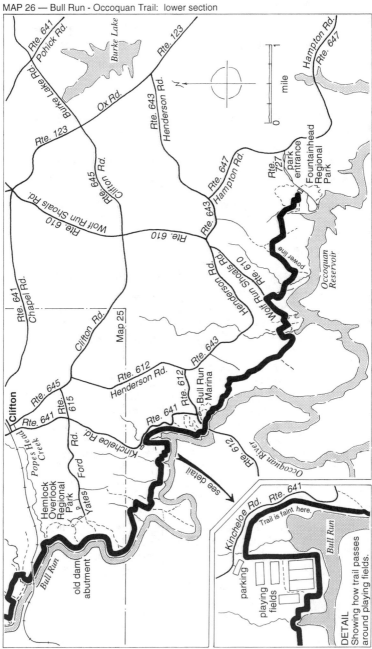

DETAIL
Showing how trail passes around playing fields.

219

Regional Park. Follow the entrance road 0.6 mile to a large parking lot on the right, just beyond the park maintenance area.

≈   ≈   ≈   ≈

WALKING: The 18-mile Bull Run - Occoquan Trail is shown on the two overlapping **Maps 25 and 26** on pages 218 and 219. Directions for getting started from Bull Run Regional Park, Hemlock Overlook Regional Park, and Fountainhead Regional Park are provided below, but once underway your best course is simply to follow the blue blazes closely. At times the trail borders the river, and at other times it climbs and descends along the valley's bluffs and through tributary ravines. South of Bull Run Marina, the trail is rarely within sight of the water.

Hiking downstream from Bull Run Regional Park: See Map 25. From the swimming pool parking lot, turn left onto the park road. With caution, follow the park road 100 yards to the Bull Run - Occoquan trailhead on the right.

Follow the blue-blazed trail through woods and across several boardwalks. At Cub Run bear right. Pass under a power line. At a T-intersection near two sewer manholes, turn left. Cross Cub Run near its confluence with Bull Run. With Bull Run on the right, follow the blue-blazed trail downstream.

To reach the parking lot at Hemlock Overlook Regional Park, go 7 miles to and across Popes Head Creek. Continue along the river to the concrete abutment of an old dam, then turn left uphill off the blue-blazed trail. At camp dormitories at the top of the hill, fork right to the road and parking areas.

For Fountainhead Regional Park (see Map 26), follow the blue-blazed trail 18 miles to its end.

Accessing the Bull Run - Occoquan Trail at Hemlock Overlook Regional Park: Head downhill into the woods on a trail that starts just outside the entrance gate to Hemlock Overlook Regional Park. Pass a junction with a yellow-blazed footpath on the left. Continue straight downhill on the main path.

Join the blue-blazed Bull Run - Occoquan Trail at the bottom of the valley next to Bull Run. The trail's upper end at Bull Run Regional Park is about 7.5 miles upstream. Bull Run Marina is about 4.5 miles downstream, and Fountainhead Regional Park is 10.5 miles downstream .

If you intend just to walk up and down the river and then return to your car at Hemlock Overlook, I recommend going as far downstream as the soccer fields off Kincheloe Road near Bull Run Marina and as far upstream as Popes Head Creek — about 7 miles round-trip.

Hiking upstream from Fountainhead Regional Park: See Map 26. The Bull Run - Occoquan trailhead is near the upper end of the main parking lot.

Enter the woods on the blue-blazed trail. After 160 yards, fork right to stay on the blue-blazed trail, and at all subsequent trail junctions follow the blue blazes.

To reach the parking lot at Hemlock Overlook Regional Park, go to milepost 10, then — after a few dozen yards — turn right uphill on a narrow, yellow-blazed footpath, which eventually leads to the park entrance at Yates Ford Road.

To reach Bull Run Regional Park, follow the blue-blazed trail 18 miles to its end.

16

PRINCE WILLIAM FOREST PARK

Walking and bicycling. Totaling 17,000 acres (more than 26 square miles), Prince William Forest Park is located near Dumfries and Interstate 95 in Virginia, 30 miles southwest of Washington. As shown on **Map 27** on pages 228 and 229, the park has a very extensive trail system. This is a place to which you can return repeatedly and explore new trails each time.

Two of the park's most attractive trails are the North and South Valley trails, and you could easily spend a pleasant day just walking up and down either of them. One possible circuit of 10.5 miles (17 kilometers) that follows both valleys is shown on **Map 28** on pages 230 and 231. If this is too long, the route can easily be shortened by using other trails to cut off part of the loop. A short loop of 3 miles (4.9 kilometers) that passes beaver dams and ponds is the Farms to Forest Trail and Extension in the park's northwest sector near the Oak Ridge Campground.

For bicyclists there are two main options. The Scenic Drive includes a loop of 8.5 miles (13.8 kilometers) that is suitable for cyclists who are experienced at sharing the road with vehicles. There are also a number of dirt and gravel roads that are suitable for fat-tired bikes. Bicycles are prohibited on foot trails.

Prince William Forest Park is open daily from dawn to dark. The visitor center is open daily (except Thanksgiving, Christmas, and New Year's Day) from 8:30 A.M. to 5 P.M. An admission fee, good for one week, is charged. Dogs must be leashed. The park is administered by the National Park Service; telephone (703) 221-7181 for information on activities and programs, including camping and guided hikes.

AS ITS NAME IMPLIES, Prince William Forest Park is nearly all woods, most of which have grown up during the twentieth century. For more than two hundred years before that, the area was cleared and cut repeatedly for farms and timber.

223

Throughout most of the seventeenth century, tobacco was the chief crop of the Chesapeake region. The cultivation of tobacco was at first so profitable that it nearly precluded other crops. As the colonial population increased and each planter's effort remained fixed on tobacco, the Virginia House of Burgesses enacted a law in 1647 requiring that every planter also grow, as a precaution against famine, three acres of corn for each of his tithables, or that is, people (such as indentured laborers) on whom taxes were paid. Because hard currency was scarce, tobacco was used for barter, so that debts, fines, and the prices of goods were commonly expressed in terms of pounds of tobacco. Cultivated by virtually every settler, tobacco quickly exhausted the soil, with the result that throughout the tidewater region, fields were typically left fallow every decade or so and allowed to grow up in brush and young woods for ten, twenty, or thirty years before again being cleared and planted.

Passed over at first because of its broken terrain of ridges and ravines, the Quantico watershed began to be farmed late in the seventeenth century. Early in the next century, Scottish merchants built general stores and tobacco warehouses at the head of navigation on Quantico Creek, and by the mid-1700s, the place — named for Dumfries in Scotland — was a busy port where tobacco was gathered and inspected prior to shipment and where import and export duties were collected. Dumfries' harbor could accommodate deep-draft vessels that sailed directly to and from Great Britain, the Caribbean, and other foreign parts. However, by the time of the American Revolution, which caused an interruption in trade, business at Dumfries started to slacken. Farming and timbering in the Quantico watershed contributed to soil erosion and in turn to siltation of the river where it reaches tidewater. By the end of the eighteenth century, Dumfries had become a shallow backwater. Economic decline continued during the nineteenth century as the region's output of farm and forest products dwindled. Throughout the fall zone between the Potomac River and the Piedmont plateau, farms were abandoned because of depletion and erosion of the soil.

In the vicinity of Dumfries, those farms that remained at the beginning of the twentieth century were economically marginal The typical farm — for example, the 100-acre Taylor farm at the center of the present-day park — had one or two small barns, an orchard for fruit and cider, a vegetable garden, chickens and some cows and pigs, plus a few fields for cultivation of a cash crop. Many farmers were tenants on the land, and many also worked outside the farm to earn income.

The biggest local employer was the Cabin Branch Pyrite Mine, located on the main (or north) branch of Quantico Creek. Pyrite (or iron disulfide) is popularly termed "fools' gold" because of its pale, brass-yellow color and brilliant metallic luster. It can be burned to produce sulfuric acid, used for making phosphate fertilizers, dyes, explosives (especially nitroglycerine), and other products. The Cabin Branch Mining Company opened the mine in 1889. In 1916 during World War I, when sulphur was in great demand, the works were acquired by the American Agricultural Chemical Company. Its Cabin Branch crews totaled about three hundred miners who were exempted from military service. The mine had three main shafts and operated around the clock. Photographs of the works show a series of connected sheds and inclines atop trestlework stilts along the side and rim of the bluff. From the mine a conveyor carried the ore to a mill where it was crushed, sorted by children paid fifty cents per day, and washed before being loaded onto a narrow gauge railroad and shipped out to a siding on the main railroad. The mine operated until 1919, by which time the price of pyrite had fallen because of cessation of the war and the discovery of other, cheaper sources of ore. When the workers went on strike, the mine was simply closed and never reopened. Even today, more than three-quarters of a century after mining stopped, there is still a smell of sulphur at the site.

During the Great Depression of the 1930s, the federal government selected the Quantico watershed as one of forty-six Recreational Demonstration Areas to be located throughout the country. Each such project was near a major city and was intended to show how areas where the soil or other natural resources had become depleted could be reforested and developed into large nature-oriented parks that featured cabins for group camping. To make way for the park in the Quantico watershed, nearly 150 families were relocated with the help of the Agricultural Resettlement Administration.

Providing vocational training and useful work for unemployed single young men, units of the Civilian Conservation Corps dismantled the Cabin Branch Pyrite Mine, planted trees, and built roads, trails, bridges, and cabins on the Quantico land. Run on a semi-military basis by the War Department and assigned to projects selected and supervised by the Departments of Agriculture and Interior, CCC companies usually had about two hundred men. Base pay was $30 per month, and if a man's family at home was on relief, most of his wages were sent there. Many CCC workers were able to take high school and even college level courses in the camps, and for recreation various athletic teams were organized. At its peak in 1935 (two years after its establishment), the CCC had more than half a million men in over 2,600 camps working on forest and wildlife protection, flood control, soil conservation, and the development of federal, state, and local parks.

225

Among the CCC projects at the Quantico watershed was construction of five model camps, each with cabins (some of them built from mine timbers), washhouses, and a central kitchen and dining hall. Once completed, the camps were used by youth groups under the aegis of various service organizations in the Washington metropolitan area. Camp Goodwill was sponsored and used by the 12th Street branch of the Washington YMCA, Camp Mawavi (**M**aryland, **Wa**shington, and **Vi**rginia) by the Girl Scouts of Alexandria, Camp Orenda and Camp Pleasant by Family Services of Washington, and Camp Happyland by the Washington Salvation Army. Now identified as Cabin Camps 1 through 5, these clusters of cabins still stand (in fact, they are on the National Register of Historic Places) and in some cases are used by their original sponsors to bring kids from the city out to the country. For reservations, which are required far in advance, call (703) 221-7181 or inquire at the visitor center.

≈   ≈   ≈   ≈

AUTOMOBILE DIRECTIONS: Prince William Forest Park is easily reached via Interstate 95 in Virginia, 30 miles southwest of Washington. (See •16 on **Map 1** on page 6.)

To Prince William Forest Park from Interstate 95: Leave I-95 at Exit 150 (from Washington, Exit 150B) for Route 619. This exit is located about 19 miles south of I-95's junction with **Interstate 495 (the Capital Beltway)** and **Interstate 395.** At the bottom of the exit ramp, follow Route 619 West a few hundred yards to the entrance to the park, just beyond the intersection with Forestburg Lane. From the fee station, follow the entrance road straight 0.5 mile to the visitor center, where there are exhibits and orientation materials.

≈   ≈   ≈   ≈

WALKING and BICYCLING: The park's roads and trails are shown on **Map 27** on pages 228 and 229. **For cyclists,** the 8.5-mile Scenic Drive is a popular circuit (go counter-clockwise). **For hikers,** one possible excursion that follows some of the best trails is the 10.5-mile circuit shown on **Map 28** on pages 230 and 231, for which directions are provided below. **Please note,** however, that the lowermost sections of both trails are closed until mid-1997 because of reclamation work at the site of the old Cabin Branch Pyrite Mine.

MAP 27 — Prince William Forest Park

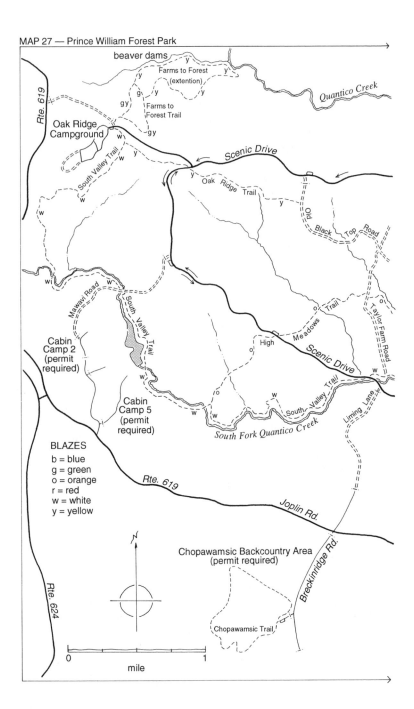

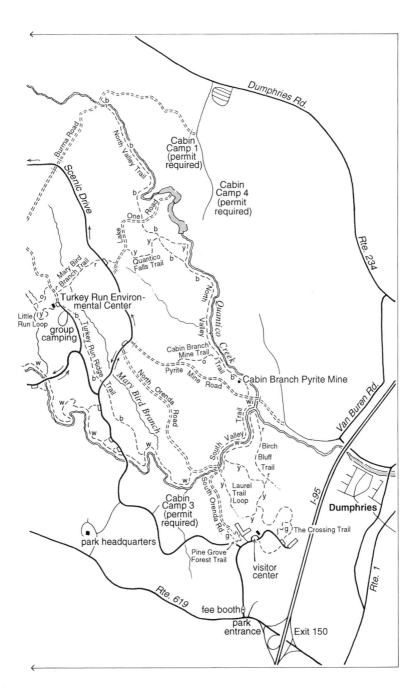

Dumphries Rd.

Burma Road

Scenic Drive

Rte. 234

North Valley Trail

Cabin Camp 1 (permit required)

Cabin Camp 4 (permit required)

Lake One Road

Quantico Falls Trail

Mary Bird Branch Trail

Turkey Run Environmental Center

Little Run Loop

group camping

Turkey Run Ridge Trail

North Valley Trail

Quantico Creek

Cabin Branch Mine Trail

Pyrite Mine Road

Cabin Branch Pyrite Mine

North Orenda Road

Mary Bird Branch

South Valley Trail

Birch Bluff Trail

Laurel Trail Loop

I-95

Van Buren Rd.

Dumphries

Cabin Camp 3 (permit required)

park headquarters

South Orenda Rd.

Pine Grove Forest Trail

The Crossing Trail

visitor center

Rte. 619

fee booth

park entrance

Exit 150

Rte. 1

MAP 28 — Prince William Forest Park: 10.5-mile loop

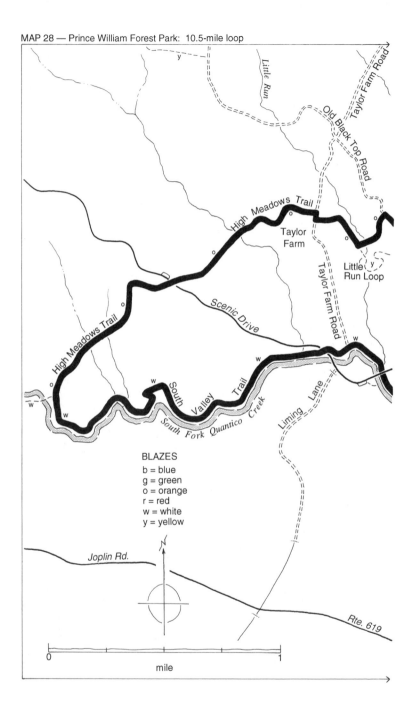

Little Run

Taylor Farm Road

Old Black Top Road

High Meadows Trail

Taylor Farm

Little Run Loop

Taylor Farm Road

Scenic Drive

High Meadows Trail

South Valley Trail

South Fork Quantico Creek

Liming Lane

BLAZES
b = blue
g = green
o = orange
r = red
w = white
y = yellow

Joplin Rd.

N

Rte. 619

0   1
mile

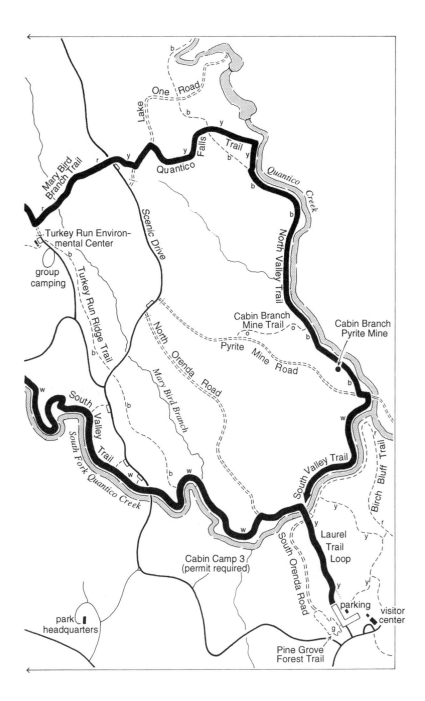

Lake One Road

Quantico Falls Trail

Quantico Creek

Mary Bird Branch Trail

Turkey Run Environmental Center

group camping

Scenic Drive

Turkey Run Ridge Trail

North Valley Trail

Cabin Branch Mine Trail

Cabin Branch Pyrite Mine

Pyrite Mine Road

North Orenda Road

Mary Bird Branch

South Valley Trail

South Fork Quantico Creek

South Valley Trail

Birch Bluff Trail

Cabin Camp 3 (permit required)

South Orenda Road

Laurel Trail Loop

parking

visitor center

park headquarters

Pine Grove Forest Trail

231

Most of the trails are marked with paint blazes and are identified by names. (Years ago, the trails were identified by numbers, and you may occasionally still see outmoded signs referring to numbered trails.) At trailheads and trail junctions, concrete posts provide information on trail names and distances.

The 10.5-mile circuit shown on Map 28 starts at the Pine Grove Picnic Area, the entrance to which is located a few hundred yards south of the visitor center (i.e., back towards the fee station). As you can see on the map, the Pine Grove parking lot is shaped like a capital L; leave your car as far toward the top of the L as you can.

From the top of the L-shaped Pine Grove parking lot, cross a grassy field and — at the far right corner — enter the woods on the yellow-blazed Laurel Trail. Descend more or less straight to a bridge across the South Fork of Quantico Creek.

After crossing the bridge, turn left. With the creek on the left, follow white blazes 270 yards along North Orenda Road, then turn left to continue on the white-blazed South Valley Trail. Follow the white blazes about 4 miles upstream, occasionally passing other trails intersecting from the right and three times crossing (or passing under) the park's Scenic Drive. At times the trail climbs the bluff but then returns downhill to the creek.

Eventually, the white-blazed South Valley Trail reaches an intersection with the orange-blazed High Meadows Trail. Bear right uphill on the High Meadows Trail and follow it 2 miles, in the process crossing the Scenic Drive at parking lot H. Continue to and across Taylor Farm Road (an unpaved track) near the Taylor Farm site. Follow the orange-blazed trail all the way to its end at Old Blacktop Road (not paved now; the surface crumbled long ago).

Turn right on Old Blacktop Road and go only 125 yards, then turn left onto the red-blazed Mary Bird Branch Trail. Follow the red-blazed trail 0.5 mile to the Scenic Drive at parking lot E.

From parking lot E, head through a picnic area for 40 yards, then enter the woods toward the right on the yellow-blazed Quantico Falls Trail. Go 100 yards, then turn left onto Lake One Road. Go 130 yards, then turn right to continue on the yellow-blazed Quantico Falls footpath. Follow the yellow blazes through a junction with the blue-blazed North Valley Trail and then steeply downhill to Quantico Creek. Turn right downstream and continue to another junction with the blue-blazed North Valley Trail.

With Quantico Creek on the left, follow the blue-blazed North Valley Trail downstream past various mine pits and eventually past the site of the Cabin Branch Pyrite Mine. At Pyrite Mine Road, turn left downhill. In front of the bridge, turn right on the white-blazed South Valley Trail.

With the South Fork of Quantico Creek on the left, follow the white-blazed trail upstream 0.7 mile to the bridge that you crossed near the outset of your walk. Turn left across the bridge and follow the yellow-blazed Laurel Trail more or less straight uphill to your starting point at the Pine Grove Picnic Area.

17

GUNSTON HALL
MASON NECK NATIONAL WILDLIFE
REFUGE
MASON NECK STATE PARK

Walking. Mason Neck is located about 20 miles south of Washington on the Virginia shore of the Potomac River. **Maps 29 and 30** on pages 242 and 244 show Mason Neck and three sites there that for most of the eighteenth century were owned by George Mason IV of Gunston Hall.

Gunston Hall Plantation itself is shown on the bottom panel of Map 29; automobile directions start on page 241. In addition to the architecturally distinguished house, there are outbuildings, formal gardens, a museum, and a foot trail leading about 2 miles (3.2 kilometers) round-trip to the Potomac River. As an example of a colonial plantation belonging to a member of Virginia's tidewater aristocracy, Gunston Hall ranks with nearby Mount Vernon. The Gunston plantation is open daily (except Thanksgiving, Christmas, and New Year's Day) from 9:30 A.M. to 5 P.M. An admission fee is charged. Dogs must be leashed and left outside the buildings. The property is owned by the Commonwealth of Virginia and is managed by a Board of Regents of the National Society of the Colonial Dames of America; telephone (703) 550-9220 for information. The schedule of seasonal events and activities includes historic reenactments and lectures, garden seminars, sheep shearing, eighteenth-century games, and a wide variety of other programs for adults and children.

The Woodmarsh Trail at **Mason Neck National Wildlife Refuge** is shown on the top panel of Map 30. Passing through level woods and along the edge of Great Marsh, the trail is 3 miles long (4.8 kilometers) round-trip. This is one of the best places near Washington to see bald eagles, especially in winter. The trail is open daily from sunrise to sunset. Dogs must be leashed; off-road bicycling is prohibited. The refuge is managed by the U.S. Fish and Wildlife Service: telephone (703) 690-1297 or (703) 491-6255.

Mason Neck State Park is shown on the bottom panel of Map 30. The two best trails are the Bay View Trail and the Kanes Creek Trail. The first is about 1 mile long (1.6 kilometers) and the second 2 miles (3.2 kilometers). The observation blind at the end of the Kanes Creek Trail is another good place for spotting bald eagles. The park is open daily from 8 A.M. to dusk. An admission fee is charged. Dogs must be leashed; swimming and off-road bicycling are prohibited. The park is managed by the Virginia Department of Conservation and Recreation; telephone (703) 550-0362 or (703) 550-0960 for information, including the schedule of guided hikes, canoe trips, and other events.

I HAD MANY occasional and strenuous coadjutors in debate, and one most steadfast, able and zealous . . . . This was George Mason, a man of the first order of wisdom among those who acted on the theatre of the Revolution, of expansive mind, profound judgment, cogent in argument, learned in the lore of our former constitution, and earnest for the republican change on democratic principles. His elocution was neither flowing nor smooth, but his language was strong, his manner most impressive, and strengthened by a dash of biting cynicism when provocation made it seasonable.

So wrote Thomas Jefferson in his *Autobiography*, describing George Mason IV, a wealthy Potomac planter. As justice of the Fairfax County Court and vestryman of Truro parish, Mason exercised considerable influence in local affairs. For three years beginning in 1758, he represented Fairfax County in the House of Burgesses, Virginia's colonial legislature. When the British Parliament imposed taxes on the American colonies, Mason joined other prominent Virginians in resistance. Although not a lawyer, he developed a capacity for the exacting labor of drafting resolutions and plans for practical action. In 1765 he contrived a scheme to circumvent, in part, the Stamp Act, which required commercial and legal documents, pamphlets, newspapers, and other publications to bear revenue stamps like those now found on liquor bottles. In 1768 he prepared a series of resolutions, adopted by the Burgesses, urging that British goods be boycotted until Parliament repealed the Townshend import duties. As conflict with England intensified, Mason drafted the Fairfax Resolves in 1774, developing the issue of taxation without representation and again calling for a boycott of British imports; the resolves were approved by a meeting in Fairfax County and later by the House of Burgesses, which had been dissolved by the royal governor but continued to meet nonetheless. As a delegate to Virginia's revolutionary legislature in 1775 and '76, Mason was the dominant figure on the committee that prepared the Virginia declaration of rights — a forerunner of the federal Bill of Rights — and the Virginia Constitution. During the Revolutionary War, he represented Fairfax County in the state's House of Delegates, taking the place of George Washington, who had left to lead the Continental Army. In 1787 Mason was one of the most active speakers at the convention in Philadelphia to draft the federal Constitution, which he opposed in its final version, in part because of the lack of a bill of rights, later added as amendments.

Mason was born in 1725, probably on the plantation at Dogue's Neck (now called Mason Neck) where he later built Gunston Hall. When he was ten, his father drowned during a boat accident while crossing the Potomac River. At age twenty-one, Mason came into the property on Dogue's Neck, as well as other large plantations in Virginia and Maryland, representing the wealth accumulated by his family over the period of a century. His great-grandfather, George Mason I, had emigrated from England in 1651 or '52, and had acquired land on the Potomac a few years later, when most of the area was still unsettled woods. Each succeeding generation of Masons had enlarged the family's holdings, and the fourth George Mason was no exception. To his five sons who survived to maturity, George Mason IV left thousands of acres of farmland, most of which he had purchased himself. Each son received a plantation when he turned twenty-one, so that he could enjoy from youth the same life of independent means that the father had known.

In 1750 Mason married Ann Eilbeck of Mattawoman, Maryland, and about five years later he began construction of Gunston Hall. He obtained the services of William Buckland, a carpenter and joiner who, at age twenty-one, had just completed his apprenticeship in England. Under articles of indenture to last four years, Mason paid Buckland's passage to America, plus wages of £20 per year and room and board. Put in charge of completing the house, Buckland supervised the workmen and designed the interior treatment, including the ornate carving, which is thought to have been executed by William Bernard Sears, another indentured English craftsman.

Mason and his family finally moved into Gunston Hall in 1759. At that time, the Dogue's Neck plantation totaled more than five thousand acres, organized into four adjacent farms, each worked by groups of slaves under an overseer. By the 1780s, the plantation's population numbered about 120 people, mostly slaves. Aside from the usual farm buildings, there were several scattered quarters of hewn log buildings for the hands and their families, as well as workshops for carpenters, coopers, blacksmiths, tanners, shoemakers, spinners, weavers, and other artisans — free and slave — who served the needs of the plantation. In the immediate vicinity of the house were the kitchen yard outbuildings and the resident tutor's schoolhouse, as seen from the present-day reconstructions. A road from the house led downhill past an open park for a domesticated herd of deer and through the woods to Mason's wharf, where tobacco and wheat were loaded onto river craft for shipment along the Potomac or transfer to ocean-going vessels. Mason managed the plantation without the aid of a steward and also attended to the insurance, shipment, and marketing of his crops. Much of the plantation's output was sent to England, so that during the Revolution Mason suffered heavy losses from the curtailment of trade — a small price, he said, to pay for liberty.

As a conspicuous member of Virginia's gentry, Mason was a friend and confidant of other nearby planters, including George Washington, who with his family sometimes dined at Gunston Hall or received the Masons at Mount Vernon. On April 18, 1770, Washington noted in his diary that "Patsy Custis and Milly Posey went to Colo. Mason's to the Dancing School," an itinerant affair conducted in turn at the homes of different patrons. Typically, the children were brought from the surrounding plantations by their parents, who stayed to dinner and had dancing of their own after the lessons were over. At Gunston Hall dancing was most likely done in the central hall, which during the summer also served as a family gathering place, cooled by breezes that swept through the door at each end.

Other rooms also served multiple functions. According to the recollections of John Mason, the seventh of nine Mason children, the left closet in the master bedchamber served as the upper pantry. "It held the smaller or more precious stores for the Table" and was under the control of Mrs. Mason, who managed the household and directed the servants. The room most closely associated with George Mason is his office, used also as a family dining room and an informal parlor when Mason did not require to be by himself. Mason, in fact, called this room the "Little Parlor." It was here, according to John Mason, that his father "absented himself as it were from his family sometimes for weeks together, and often until very late at night during the Revolutionary War." Describing his father's absorption in his work and books — for Mason read widely — John also wrote: "I have frequently known his mind, tho' always kind and affectionate to his children, so diverted from the objects around him that he would not for days together miss one of the family who may have been absent, and would sometimes at table inquire for one of my sisters who had perhaps been gone a week on a visit to some friend, of which he had known but forgotten." Of the garden which the Little Parlor overlooks, John Mason said, "It was here that my Father in good weather would several times a day pass out of his study and walk for a considerable time wrapped in meditation, and return again to his desk, without seeing or speaking to any of the family. And in these walks we all well knew that he was not to be disturbed . . . ."

To the extent that public events and duties permitted, Mason lived a retiring life. From the age of thirty, ill-health became an increasingly obtrusive theme in his life. He suffered from gout, a painful and at times crippling affliction of the joints, especially in the feet, ankles, and knees. Mason also complained of a bad stomach. His chronic pain made him hypochondriacal and at times irritable. His wife's death in 1773 reinforced his crusty disposition, producing in him "a settled melancholy from which I never expect or desire to recover" — although he eventually did remarry.

In poor health, exasperated by the cliquishness and petty self-interest of many public officials, and bearing heavy responsibilities at home, Mason regularly turned down offices that were pressed on him — most notably an appointment as United States senator in 1790, when a vacancy occurred. For the most part, he confined his public service to his immediate community. Yet when he thought that his involvement could make a difference at the state or national level, he exerted himself without stint. Anticipating work on the committee to prepare an enumeration of rights and a state constitution, he wrote to Richard Henry Lee on May 16, 1776:

> We are now going upon the most important of all subjects — government!
> The committee appointed to prepare a plan is, according to custom,
> overcharged with useless members. You know our Convention. I need not
> say that it is not mended by the recent elections. We shall, in all probability,
> have a thousand ridiculous and impracticable proposals, and of course a plan
> formed of heterogeneous, jarring and unintelligible ingredients. This can be
> prevented only by a few men of integrity and abilities, whose country's
> interest lies next to their hearts, undertaking this business and defending it
> ably through every stage of opposition.

Mason was as good as his word, drafting the Virginia Declaration of Rights himself and managing to get it adopted with very few changes of substance, "some of them," he said, "not for the better." The state constitution was also substantially his work, although the absence of a first draft in his handwriting prevents comparison between his proposals and the plan finally adopted.

Following the Revolution, Mason retired from state politics. In October 1782, he wrote to Edmund Randolph:

> I quitted my seat in the House of Delegates, from a conviction that I was no longer able to do any essential service. Some of the public measures have been so contrary to my notions of policy and of justice that I wished to be no further concerned with, or answerable for them; and to spend the remnant of my life in quiet and retirement. Yet with all her faults, my country will ever have my warmest wishes and affections; and I would at any time, most cheerfully sacrifice my own ease and domestic enjoyment to the public good.

One subsequent occasion that he apparently felt demanded his attention was the convention in Philadelphia in 1787 to prepare the federal Constitution. Making 136 major speeches, Mason was one of the most active delegates. Mistrustful of the centralization of power in the federal government and unable to secure a bill of rights, he refused to sign the final draft. After returning home, he urged rejection of the Constitution by Virginia. He even circulated handwritten copies of his objections, probably knowing (given his stature) that they would be printed in newspapers and promulgated in pamphlets. In his opposition to the Constitution, Mason opposed many of his lifelong friends, including George Washington, who strongly supported the federal plan. At the first Congress convened under the Constitution, twelve amendments were submitted to the states for ratification, of which ten — now commonly termed the federal Bill of Rights — were approved by 1791.

When Mason died the following year, his will, written about twenty years earlier, summarized his attitude toward public affairs:

> I recommend it to my sons from my own experience in life, to prefer the happiness of independence and a private station to the troubles and vexation of public business, but if either their own inclinations or the necessity of the times should engage them in public affairs, I charge them on a father's blessing never to let the motives of private interest or ambition induce them to betray, nor the terrors of poverty and disgrace, or the fear of danger or of death, deter them from asserting the liberty of their country and endeavoring to transmit to their posterity those sacred rights to which themselves were born.

Some of Mason's sons did in fact go on to become prominent in local affairs, as discussed in Chapter 18 on Huntley Meadows and Chapter 22 on Roosevelt Island, both of which were once Mason properties.

As for Gunston Hall, it remained in the Mason family until 1866. Most of the Masons who still resided in Virginia sided with the Confederacy, and their fortunes suffered accordingly. Nearly fifty years later, the Gunston property was acquired by Louis and Eleanor Hertle, who began restoration of the house and eventually gave it and 556 acres to the Commonwealth of Virginia, to be administered by The National Society of The Colonial Dames of America.

≈ ≈ ≈ ≈

MASON NECK is one of the best places in the Chesapeake region to see bald eagles. In winter as many as sixty eagles may be present. Most migrate north in spring, but a dozen or more remain and some nest and breed at Mason Neck. It was chiefly to preserve habitat for endangered bald eagles that land was purchased for the state park starting in 1967, and that the national wildlife refuge was established in 1969.

A mature bald eagle is easily identified by its large size (wingspan up to seven feet), dark body, and white head and tail. Bald eagles live for as long as thirty years and mate for life, although if one of a pair dies the survivor will often mate again. From February through May, one to three eggs (usually two) that take seven weeks to hatch are laid in huge nests that are located in the upper branches of trees overlooking the marsh or open water where the eagles hunt and scavenge. It takes both parents about thirty days to build a new nest, which typically measures five feet across. Year after year, nests are reused and enlarged. Some reports assert that nests that have been in use for many years measure as much as nine feet across and fifteen or even twenty feet from top to bottom and weigh about two tons. Much of the weight is from water, since at the core of the nest is a sodden mass of decaying compost. The debris recovered from fallen eagle nests consists mainly of sticks (some up to six feet long), clumps of sod, stalks of corn and cattails, marsh grass (with which the birds line their nests), and undigested food fragments such as muskrat bones, duck feet, and fish heads. Bald eagles pick up most of these animals dead. Fish is their main food, and although most fish are scavenged dead, eagles also catch live fish by swooping close to the surface of the water and snatching them out with their talons. Both eagle parents care for their fledglings, and by the twelfth week after hatching, the young eagles are ready to fly.

≈ ≈ ≈ ≈

AUTOMOBILE DIRECTIONS: Gunston Hall and the federal refuge and state park at **Mason Neck** are located about 20 miles south of Washington on the Virginia shore of the Potomac River. (See •17 on **Map 1** on page 6, and also the top panel on **Map 29** on page 242.) Directions are provided below to Gunston Hall, and from there to the nearby Mason Neck National Wildlife Refuge and Mason Neck State Park.

To Gunston Hall from Interstate 95: Leave I-95 at Exit 163 for Route 642 (Lorton Road). This exit is located about 6 miles

MAP 29 — Mason Neck sites (top) and Gunston Hall Plantation (bottom)

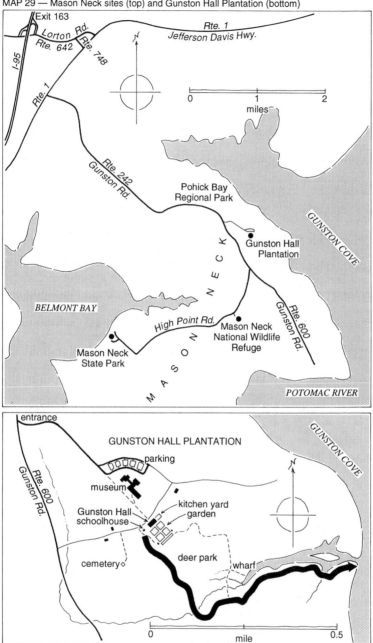

south of I-95's junction with **Interstate 495 (the Capital Beltway) and Interstate 395.** At the bottom of the exit ramp, turn left and follow Route 642 East nearly a mile to an intersection with Route 748. Turn right and follow Route 748 only 0.2 mile to a crossroads with Route 1 (Richmond Highway). Turn right onto Route 1 and go 0.8 mile to an intersection with Route 242 (Gunston Road). Turn left and follow Route 242 for 3.6 miles to the entrance for Gunston Hall on the left.

From Gunston Hall to Mason Neck National Wildlife Refuge and Mason Neck State Park: Refer to the top panel of Map 29. If you went first to Gunston Hall, turn left out the entrance. Otherwise, simply pass the entrance to Gunston Hall on the left. Follow Gunston Road (now designated Route 600) south 0.8 mile, then fork right onto High Point Road. The parking lot for the Woodmarsh Trail at Mason Neck National Wildlife Refuge is located on the left 0.7 mile down High Point Road. From there it is another 2 miles to Mason Neck State Park at the end of High Point Road.

≈   ≈   ≈   ≈

WALKING AT GUNSTON HALL: After visiting the museum and the house, garden, and outbuildings, you may want to walk down to the Potomac River and back. The trail is shown on the bottom panel of **Map 29** opposite. The round-trip distance is nearly 2 miles.

The trail to the river starts behind the schoolhouse, about 50 yards from the gravel lane that runs past the front of the main house. Descend into the woods at the head of a ravine. (Do not confuse the trail with a rutted track that follows the top of the slope and leads to one of the garden gazebos.) Follow the trail as it winds downhill to the river, at one point passing a trail that intersects from the left.

≈   ≈   ≈   ≈

WALKING AT MASON NECK NATIONAL WILDLIFE REFUGE: The 3-mile Woodmarsh Trail is shown on the top panel of **Map 30** on page 244.

There are two parking lots at the Woodmarsh Trail, one behind the other and connected by a road a few dozen yards

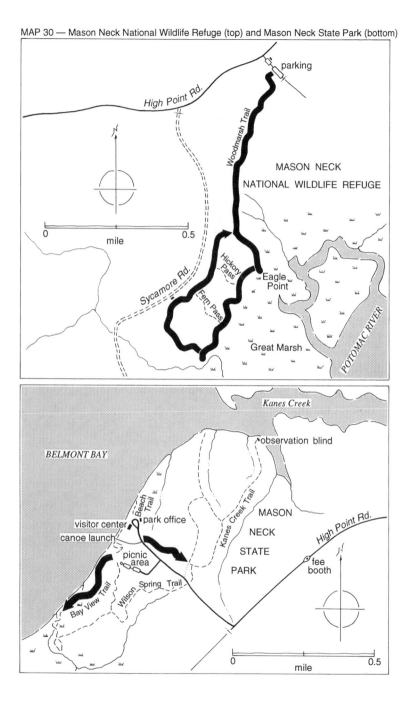

long. The trailhead is on the right-hand side of the second parking lot and is marked by a trail sign.

Follow the Woodmarsh Trail 0.8 mile through the woods. At a T-intersection, turn left toward Eagle Point, and from there continue clockwise around the circuit and then back to the parking lot. Obviously, you can shorten your walk by taking the Hickory Pass or Fern Pass, but if you do, you will miss a short spur that leads to a good vantage point at the bottom of the map, and also a display shelter near Sycamore Road. Please note that Sycamore Road is closed to the public.

≈   ≈   ≈   ≈

WALKING AT MASON NECK STATE PARK: The park is shown on the bottom panel of **Map 30** opposite. The two best trails are the Bay View Trail (1 mile) and the Kanes Creek Trail (2 miles). These two trails are linked by the Wilson Spring Trail and also by a short trail along the water's edge between the visitor center and the picnic area, so that it is possible to make a combined circuit of about 4 miles.

The Bay View Trail starts at the picnic area. The trailhead is next to Belmont Bay, where the Occoquan River flows into the Potomac River. (The truss bridge visible in the distance across the bay is the railroad bridge over the Occoquan next to Route 1.) With the water toward the right, follow the trail along the top of a bluff overlooking Belmont Bay and around the circuit.

The Kanes Creek Trail starts at the main park road near the visitor center, across from the lane leading down to the canoe launching area.

18

HUNTLEY MEADOWS PARK

Walking — 2 miles (3.2 kilometers). There is also limited provision for bicycling, as described below.

Shown on **Map 31** on page 252, the nature preserve at Huntley Meadows is located south of Alexandria, Virginia in an area called the Hybla Valley, where there is a wide swath of flat, low land carved by an ancient meander of the Potomac River. The park includes 1,424 acres of level woods and open wetlands bordering Barnyard Run, a tributary of Dogue Creek. More than two hundred species of birds have been seen here.

A footpath (no bikes) starts at the visitor center and leads through the woods to a large marsh, where a boardwalk continues across the wetlands to an observation tower. Other trails, some of which are accessible only from a different entrance to the park, are shown on the map, but first try the boardwalk trail, which is the best of its kind In the Washington region.

Bicycling is permitted on a paved trail that starts at the park's northwest corner near the intersection of Routes 611 and 633 and leads 1 mile to an observation tower at the edge of the wetlands. This short ride is a good spot for small children.

The park is open daily from dawn until dark. The visitor center, where there are many interesting exhibits, is open daily, except Tuesday, during hours that vary with the seasons; call for precise times. Dogs must be leashed and are not permitted on the boardwalk, so it is best to leave your pet at home.

Huntley Meadows Park is managed by the Fairfax County Park Authority. Telephone the visitor center at (703) 768-2525 for information, including a schedule of events.

IN THE LATE EIGHTEENTH CENTURY, the land at Huntley Meadows Park was part of the vast holdings of George Mason IV. Mason lived at Gunston Hall, which overlooks the Potomac River about five miles downstream from Mount Vernon. (Gunston Hall and Mason Neck are the subject of Chapter 17.) Mason was a leading Virginia statesman and author of the Virginia Declaration of Rights. Thomas Jefferson called him "the wisest man of his generation." Born rich, Mason was a landowner and planter on a large scale. He gave thousands of acres of Potomac farmland, most of which he had purchased himself, to his five sons who survived to maturity. (See Chapter 22 for a discussion of Analostan Island, now Roosevelt Island, which Mason gave to his son John.)

To his son Thomson, who had served briefly in the Virginia militia during the Revolutionary War, George Mason gave land at what is now Huntley Meadows. "He Commanded a Platoon, in a pretty close Action at Williamsbourg, & behaved with proper Coolness & Intrepidity," the father wrote of his son in 1781. According to George Mason's will, the land that was left to Thomson consisted of about 3,300 acres bordering Dogues Run and Little Hunting Creek. Of this slightly more than half had been bought by George Mason from the holder of the original patent. At its southern edge the plantation abutted George Washington's holdings of eight thousand acres. Washington's will refers to "the back line or outer boundary of the tract between Thomson Mason and myself . . . . now double ditching with a post and rail fence thereon." (The remnants of this kind of drainage ditching — two parallel troughs separated by a berm — can still be seen in places running through the woods at Huntley Meadows.) Another nearby plantation was Belvoir, home of the Fairfaxes, who were the leading family of the Northern Neck, as the peninsula between the Potomac and Rappahannock rivers is called.

As was the case with each of the plantations set aside for his sons, George Mason's provision for Thomson was more than a bequest: it was an outright gift when the young man turned twenty-one. The elder Mason had himself come into his property as a youth and thought that his sons should enjoy the same lifelong independence that he had known. By 1787 Thomson and his wife were building a house on the plantation in an area east of the present park. They called their home Hollin Hall after the Yorkshire house of the ancestors of Thomson's grandmother. At the end of 1788 George Mason wrote to his son John that "Your brother Thomson and his family have just moved from Gunston to his own seat at Hollin Hall."

For a period Thomson managed the estate of an older brother and manufactured snuff. In 1789 he became a collector of customs for the port of Alexandria. He also served as a Fairfax County justice, carried the honorary title of "General," and was active in organizing local banks and transportation companies. According to Elijah Fletcher, a

Yankee tutor hired to educate Thomson's children, Mason was "a man of note and respectability, his family very agreeable, social, affable, and easy . . . . Our living is rich and what in Vermont would be called extravagant." In 1825 Thomson died at Hollin Hall. That same year his son, Thomson Francis Mason, completed construction of his own country house at the family plantation, which in 1817 had been divided between himself and his brother, Richard Chichester Mason. By then the plantation was known as Hunting Creek Farm, and the new house — a small, Federal-style summer villa with terraced landscaping in front — was called Huntley. Like all such plantations, the farm was worked by slaves. An advertisement in the Alexandria *Gazette* for August 5, 1828, offered a reward for the return of a slave who had run away from Thomson F. Mason's farm. An overseer managed the property. Mason's principal residence, Colross, was in Alexandria, where he practiced law. In 1827, and again in 1836, Mason was elected Mayor of Alexandria; and shortly before his death in 1838 he was appointed a judge in the District of Columbia. Upon his death, Huntley and a thousand acres of land went to his widow and then, in 1859, to two of his sons, who mortgaged the property. In 1862 the farm was auctioned by creditors and passed from Mason ownership. The Huntley house still stands as a boarded-up shell on the west side of Harrison Lane 0.3 mile north of the entrance to Huntley Meadows Park. Owned by the Fairfax County Park Authority, it occupies a small parcel overlooking a subdivision.

Another Mason house at Huntley Meadows was Okeley, built by Richard Chichester Mason on that part of the property that he had inherited. Okeley stood west of Huntley house within what is now the park. Used by the Union army as a hospital for victims of infectious diseases during the Civil War, Okeley was deliberately burned as a health measure shortly afterward. As for Hollin Hall east of the park, it burned in 1824.

According to a notation on an 1862 military map of the area, the low and level land at Huntley Meadows consisted of a "Wide fertile Valley with but little Timber." By means of an extensive system of ditches, such as that noted earlier in George Washington's will, the flats had been drained for agricultural use in colonial times. During the latter part of the nineteenth century, cultivation of the land here gave way to dairy farming. In the late 1920s, an entrepreneur named Henry Woodhouse purchased 1,500 acres from ten owners in order to establish a Zeppelin terminal, but nothing was built. The Federal government purchased much of this land in 1941, and from 1943 to 1953 the U.S. Bureau of Public Roads operated a facility to test paving materials at

what is now the northwest corner of the park. During the 1950s an anti-aircraft battery for the defense of Washington was located at Huntley Meadows, followed during the 1960s by a secret facility for testing naval radio communications. In 1975 ownership of 1,261 acres was transferred to Fairfax County under the federal government's Legacy of Parks Program, by which surplus federal property is donated to local governments provided that the land is used for recreation. Fairfax County has since acquired a smaller adjacent tract for addition to the park. During the long period of federal ownership, most of the land at Huntley Meadows reverted to woods, except for a large area at the center that now is flooded by water impounded by beaver dams. These wetlands, traversed by boardwalks, are by far the most interesting part of the park.

Freshwater wetlands such as those at Huntley Meadows provide outstanding habitat for waterfowl and other wildlife. Long regarded as wastelands as far as human activity is concerned, they in fact support human settlement and commerce in ways that have come to be appreciated only as they have been drained, filled, and developed. Many marshes and swamps replenish groundwater that ultimately feeds wells for drinking, industry, and irrigation. They are also settling and filtering basins, collecting silt from upland erosion and reducing turbidity and siltation in rivers and estuaries downstream. Wetlands are often called natural sponges because they absorb immense quantities of stormwater runoff, then release it slowly over a period of weeks. In this way they prevent or moderate floods and also keep streams flowing that otherwise would dry up after each rainfall like a southwestern arroyo. In fact, many urban streams that are fed by storm sewers from extensively paved areas have, in effect, become arroyos, immediately discharging a huge volume of turbid water after each rainfall, then lying nearly empty until the next rain.

To prevent this surge of stormwater runoff, some engineers and public officials are urging that subdivision requirements for costly storm sewers and curbs be relaxed and that instead, greater use be made of grassy swales, permeable rip-rap drainage channels, infiltration basins, and even man-made wetlands in order to slow stormwater runoff, filter out dirt and debris, and increase percolation into the ground.

≈ ≈ ≈ ≈

METRO: Metrobus routes 9A, 9B, and 9C to and from Alexandria and the Huntington Metrorail station (Yellow Line) follow Route 1 near Huntley Meadows Park. (The southern

MAP 31 — Huntley Meadows Park

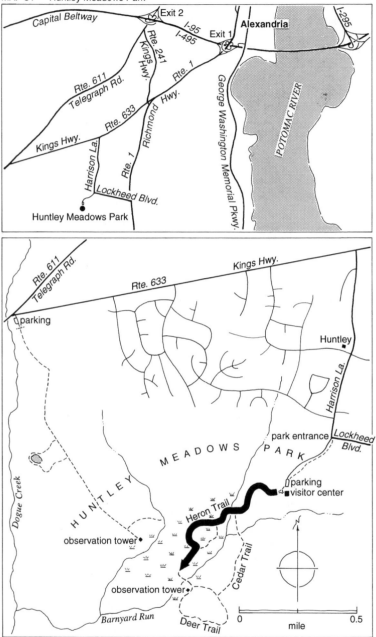

bus terminus is Fort Belvoir.) Get off the bus at the intersection with Lockheed Boulevard and follow Lockheed half a mile west to the park entrance. (See **Map 31** opposite.) Telephone (202) 637-7000 for current Metro information, including schedules, routes, and connections.

≈   ≈   ≈   ≈

AUTOMOBILE DIRECTIONS: Huntley Meadows Park is located in Virginia about 5 miles south of Alexandria. (See the top panel of **Map 31** opposite.)

To Huntley Meadows Park from Interstate 495 (the Capital Beltway): Leave the Beltway at Exit 1 for Route 1 South. Follow Route 1 South for 3.1 miles to an intersection at a traffic light with Lockheed Boulevard. Turn right onto Lockheed Boulevard and go 0.6 mile to the entrance to Huntley Meadows Park on the left at the corner with Harrison Lane. Turn left into the park and follow the entrance drive 0.3 mile to the parking lot and visitor center.

As shown on Map 31, there is another entrance to Huntley Meadows near the intersection of Route 611 and Route 633 at the park's northwest corner. To get there from the visitor center, follow Harrison Lane north 0.9 mile to a T-intersection with Route 633. Turn left and follow Route 633 for 1.5 miles to the park entrance on the left. This entrance serves the mile-long hike-bike trail and several other trails that are not linked to those that start at the visitor center.

≈   ≈   ≈   ≈

WALKING: The trails at Huntley Meadows Park are shown on the bottom panel of **Map 31** opposite. As you can see, the trail system is not extensive, but it includes an excellent boardwalk through the open wetlands at the center of the park.

After stopping by the visitor center, follow a broad, winding path through the woods. At an intersection where the Cedar Trail and the Heron Trail split, fork right to follow the Heron Trail directly to the boardwalk and open wetlands.

Eventually the boardwalk leads to an observation tower. By continuing past the tower, you can, if you want, follow the Deer Trail in a loop through the woods, then bear right to take the Cedar Trail back to the visitor center.

19

MOUNT VERNON TRAIL
DYKE MARSH TRAIL
MOUNT VERNON

Walking and bicycling. As shown on **Map 32** on page 267, the **Mount Vernon Trail** stretches along the Virginia shore of the Potomac River, parallel with the George Washington Memorial Parkway. The northern end of this paved hike-bike trail is at Roosevelt Island, and the southern end is at Mount Vernon. The trail is about 17.5 miles long one-way (28 kilometers), but that distance includes 2 miles through Alexandria, where the route simply follows local streets. For cyclists, the round-trip of 35 miles makes a good half-day's outing, with plenty of time for a visit to Mount Vernon and for watching the airplanes at Gravelly Point.

For a shorter excursion, you may want to focus on just the part of the Mount Vernon Trail that is north or south of Alexandria. For example, the distance from Roosevelt Island to Pendleton Street in Alexandria and then back again is 14 miles. Similarly, from Belle Haven Park south of Alexandria to Mount Vernon and back again to Belle Haven is 15 miles. From Fort Hunt Park to Mount Vernon and then back to Fort Hunt is 6 miles. This is a popular walk that includes sweeping views across the Potomac River. Automobile directions to these various points along the trail start on page 266, and walking and cycling directions start on page 268.

The Mount Vernon Trail is open from dawn to dusk. Dogs must be leashed. If you cycle to Mount Vernon, bring a lock for your bike so that you will not be inhibited from going in when you get there. The trail is administered by the National Park Service; telephone (703) 285-2601. For connections to other hike-bike trails, see page 269.

At Belle Haven Park just south of Alexandria, the Mount Vernon Trail passes the **Dyke Marsh Trail**, shown on the lower-right panel of Map 32. This wide footpath leads south along the Potomac shore and then out across freshwater wetlands. The round-trip distance is 2.5 miles (4 kilometers). A bird list available at the trailhead includes more than two hundred species that have been seen at Dyke Marsh.

At the southern end of the Mount Vernon Trail is **Mount Vernon** itself, home of George Washington. Because of its association with Washington, Mount Vernon survives as an outstanding example of an eighteenth-century tidewater plantation belonging to a member of the top stratum of colonial society. Here are the mansion house, walkways, drives, and gardens on which Washington lavished his care and enthusiasm — and here, too, are the slave quarters and other plantation outbuildings. There is also a reconstructed threshing barn highlighting Washington's role as an innovative and progressive farmer of his day.

Mount Vernon opens daily at 9 A.M. From March through October, the gates close at 5 P.M. From November through February, the gates close at 4 P.M. An admission fee is charged. Dogs must be leashed and are not permitted in the buildings. Mount Vernon is managed by The Mount Vernon Ladies' Association of the Union; telephone (703) 780-2000.

MOUNT VERNON is the real Washington Monument. The plantation reflects the civilian interests and work of George Washington and the life he wanted to lead both before and after his services as Revolutionary general in chief and first President of the United States.

For sixteen pleasant years before he was called upon to head the Continental Army during the Revolution, Washington cultivated, expanded, and improved his property on the Potomac River. After eight years of war, during which he saw his home only twice, Washington resigned his commission and returned to Mount Vernon in 1783. He was determined to devote himself again to managing his estate. "I think with you, " he wrote to an English friend in 1788, "that the life of a husbandman is the most delectable. It is honorable, it is amusing, and, with a little judicious management, it is profitable." When the presidency was pressed on him in 1789, Washington described it as "the greatest sacrifice of my personal feelings and wishes that ever I have been called upon to make." Again, he was mostly absent from Mount Vernon for eight years, although he sometimes lived there during summers when Congress was in recess. In March 1797 Washington returned to Mount Vernon, where he managed his several farms until his death two years later.

Mount Vernon was not only Washington's home but also, for the most part, his creation. He was his own architect and landscape gardener, deriving from books a familiarity with principles of eighteenth-century landscape design in the English manner. "The whole plantation, the garden, and the rest prove that a man born with natural taste may guess a beauty without ever having seen its model," wrote a European visitor in 1798, when the estate was at its peak of development. "The General has never left America [actually, he went once to Barbados]; but when one sees his house and his home and his garden it seems as if he had copied the best samples of the grand old homesteads of England."

The nucleus of the Mount Vernon estate had been granted to George Washington's great-grandfather in 1674 by Thomas, Lord Colepeper, the colonial proprietor of the entire peninsula between the Potomac and Rappahannock rivers. In 1726 George Washington's father, Augustine, purchased the land from his sister, who had inherited it, and later built a house that included the four ground-floor rooms at the center of the present-day mansion. George Washington spent part of his youth here following his father's death in 1743. He lived in the household of his older half-brother, Lawrence, to whom the property had been deeded in 1740. It was Lawrence who named the place Mount Vernon in honor of Admiral Edward Vernon. Vernon had been Lawrence's commanding officer during an unsuccessful English expedition in 1741 against Spain's fortified city of Cartagena, in what is now Colombia.

When Lawrence died childless in 1752, his widow retained a life interest in Mount Vernon. Lawrence's will directed that after her death the estate was to go to George Washington. In 1754 George bought his sister-in-law's life interest for an annual payment of fifteen thousand pounds of tobacco and so came into immediate possession of the property. However, he had already undertaken to follow in Lawrence's footsteps in another way also — by becoming a soldier — and his appointment as commander of Virginia's frontier forces kept him in the Shenandoah Valley and later the Ohio Valley during the French and Indian War. After the French abandoned Fort Duquesne at present-day Pittsburgh, Washington resigned his commission in 1758, by which time he had acquired a reputation as one of the leading officers in the American colonies. The next year he married the wealthy Martha Custis and finally settled at Mount Vernon. A few months after his arrival he wrote to an English acquaintance, "I am now, I believe fixd at this Seat with an agreeable Consort for Life and hope to find more happiness in retirement than I ever experienc'd admidst a wide and bustling World."

When George Washington acquired Mount Vernon, the property included 2,126 acres and eighteen resident slaves. By his marriage he received one-third of his wife's very considerable assets. But the purchase of adjoining land, more slaves, and household goods, wrote Washington, "swallowed before I knew where I was, all the money I got by my marriage. Nay more, brought me into debt." In later years he bought still more land. By 1786 Washington's Mount Vernon estate totaled more than eight thousand acres divided into five adjacent farms. About half the land was in cultivated crops, meadow, and pasture; the rest was woods. Each farm was a complete unit, with its own buildings, equipment, livestock, workers, and overseer.

An inventory in 1786 showed about ninety people living at the Mansion House Farm and about 150 people on the four outlying farms. This population included 216 slaves — men, women, and children — of whom Washington owned about half and his wife the others. By the time of his death, the slaves numbered 317, including 40 hands leased from another owner and 132 who were either too young or too old to work. About a third of the working slaves were skilled in trades or crafts. Washington also hired various artisans who lived on the estate with their families.

To feed this community, pork was produced or purchased by the thousands of pounds. Indian corn was grown and milled, fish were seined from the Potomac and salted down, and liquor was distilled. Washington had his own carpenters and painters to erect and maintain his buildings. He had blacksmiths to shoe his horses and to fashion iron tools; he had spinners, weavers, seamstresses, and shoemakers to clothe his workers. For transport, he had carters and even his own freight sloop on the Potomac. As the production of household manufactures increased at Mount Vernon, he sold goods and services to his neighbors.

Washington was a progressive farmer for his day. Since tobacco depleted the soil and produced little or no profit after being shipped to Great Britain and sold there by agents whom he did not entirely trust, by 1766 Washington turned to wheat and corn as his principal crops. For these there was a domestic market. His flour, ground at his own mill, gained a reputation for high quality. At times he exported flour and salt fish to the Caribbean. He rotated crops, including flax, hemp, oats, hay, and clover. He tried different kinds of plows, including one of his own design. In 1792, at the beginning of his first term as President, he designed and had built a two-story, sixteen-sided threshing barn, of which there is now a carefully authenticated reconstruction at Mount Vernon. He read widely in agricultural magazines and manuals and maintained a botanical garden and other plots where various plants were grown experimentally.

In spite of Washington's close attention to farming, Mount Vernon showed very little profit and sometimes none at all. Throughout his life Washington frequently was strapped for cash. His considerable wealth was derived from, and tied up in, land speculation on the frontier. At Mount Vernon the modest proceeds from the four outlying farms were offset by the expense of improvements and daily life at the Mansion House Farm. This area, about five hundred acres, was largely ornamental. "I do not hesitate to confess that reclaiming, and laying the grounds down handsomely to grass, and in woods thinned, or in clumps, about the Mansion house is among my first objects and wishes," Washington wrote. Many entries in his diary reflect his concern for the improvement of the home estate:

Wednesday, 12th [January, 1785]. Road to my Mill Swamp, where my Dogue Run hands were at Work, and to other places in search of the sort of Trees I shall want for my Walks, groves, and Wildernesses.

At the Sein Landing and between that and the point at the Old Brick Kiln I found about half a dozn. young Elm trees, but not very promising ones. Many thriving Ash trees on high (at least dry) ground of proper size for transplanting, and a great abundance of the Red-bud of all sizes.

Wednesday, 19th. Employed untill dinner laying out my Serpentine road and shrubberies adjoining . . . .

Tuesday, 22 [February]. Removed the pretty large and full green Lilacs to the No. Garden gate, one on each side, taking up as much dirt with the root as cd. be well obtained. Also a mock orange to the walk leading to the No. Necessary.

I also removed from the Woods and the old fields several young Trees of the Sassafras, Dogwood, and Red Bud, to the shrubbery on the No. side of the grass plat . . . .

Washington also greatly enlarged the house. Prior to his marriage he raised the structure from one and a half to two and a half stories. Just before the outbreak of the Revolution, he undertook to add the study and bedroom at the south end of the house, the large dining room at the north end, and the piazza at the back. The piazza was an architectural innovation of his own, although he may have seen similar features in Barbados, where he had accompanied his dying half-brother Lawrence in 1751. During the summer of 1774, while work progressed on his new study and master bedroom, he wrote to a friend, "I am very much engaged in raising one of the additions to my house, which I think (perhaps it is fancy) goes on better whilst I am present, than in my absence from the workmen."

Absent, however, he was required to be. During the Revolution the estate was managed by his distant cousin Lund Washington, to whom

George frequently wrote detailed instructions and inquiries that provided a measure of relief from his military concerns. On September 30, 1776, he wrote:

> The amazement which you seem to be in at the unaccountable measures which have been adopted [by Congress] would be a good deal increased if I had time to unfold the whole system of their management since this time 12 months .... In confidence I tell you that I never was in such an unhappy and divided state since I was born. To lose all comfort and happiness on the one hand ... and to be told on the other that if I leave the service all will be lost, is at the same time I am bereft of every peaceful moment, distressing to a degree. But I will be done with the subject, with the precaution that it is not a fit one to be publicly known or discussed.
>
> With respect to the chimney, I would not have you for the sake of a little work spoil the look of the fireplaces, tho' that in the parlor must, I should think, stand as it does; not so much on account of the wainscotting, which I think must be altered (on account of the door leading into the new building) as on account of the chimney piece and the manner of fronting into the room .... The chimney in the new room should be exactly in the middle of it — the doors and everything else to be exactly answerable and uniform — in short, I would have the whole executed in a masterly manner. You ought surely to have a window in the gable end of the new cellar (either under the Venetian window, or one on each side of it) ....

In another of his letters later in the war, Washington inquired:

> How many Lambs have you had this Spring? How many Colts are you like to have? Is your covered ways done? What are you going about next? Have you any prospect of getting Paint and Oyl? are you going to repair the Pavement of the Piazza? is anything doing , or like to be done, with respect to the Well at the edge of the Hill in front of the House? Have you made good the decayed Trees at the ends of the House and in the Edges &ca., &ca? Have you made any attempts to reclaim more Land for meadow &ca., &ca? An account of these things would be satisfactory to me and infinitely amusing in the recital, as I have these kinds of improvements very much at heart ....

When in residence, Washington was his own manager. "He has about 4,000 acres, well cultivated, and superintends the whole himself," wrote an English visitor in 1785, after England and the United States had resumed normal relations following the Revolution:

> Indeed, his greatest pride now is to be thought the first farmer in America. He is quite a Cincinnatus [the Roman general who according to legend alternated between farming and soldiering], and often works with his men himself; strips off his coat and labors like a common man.

The General has a great turn for mechanics. It's astonishing with what niceness he directs everything in the building way, condescending even to measure the things himself, that all may be perfectly uniform. The style of his house is very elegant, something like the Prince de Conde's at Chantilli near Paris, only not quite so large. But it's a pity he did not build a new one at once, as it has cost him nearly as much repairing his old one. His improvements, I'm told, are very great within this last year. He is making a most delightful bowling green before the house, and cutting a new road through the woods to Alexandria . . . .

It's astonishing what a number of small houses the General has upon his estate for his different workmen and Negroes to live in. He has everything within himself — carpenters, bricklayers, brewers, blacksmiths, bakers, etc., — and even has a well-assorted store for the use of his family and servants.

The store, complete with its own ledger, was intended to reduce pilfering by making the workmen and slaves accountable for the supplies that they were issued, which they were all too often tempted to sell on the side or to use for their own purposes.

In 1786 the servants and other slaves at the house included the mulatto body-servant and butler Billy, waiters Frank and Austin, cooks Hercules and Nathan, seamstresses Betty, Charlotte, and Lame Alice, housemaids Sall and Caroline, and washers Sall Brass and Dolly. The rest of Washington's household, and also his daily routine, were described by Tobias Lear, Washington's private secretary, in a letter dated March 1788.

Major [George Augustine] Washington, a nephew of the General's about my age, with his Lady, reside here; his business is almost solely upon the farms, but we mutually assist each other in our different employments when anything in either requires immediate dispatch. — our affection for each other is reciprocal & we live in the happiest friendship — His Lady is one of those superior beings who are sent down to bless good men. — Mrs. Washington, the Gen'l.'s Lady, is everything that is benevolent & good — I honor her as a second mother & receive from her all those attentions which I should look for from her who bore me — a little Grandson [George Washington Parke Custis] of Mrs. Washington's by a former husband, & his sister [Nelly Parke Custis], the one of 6 & the other of 8 years old, afford me no small pleasure & amusement in instructing them, they are, without partiality, as fine children as were ever seen, I never thought I could be so much attached to children as I am to them . . . . General Washington is, I believe, almost the only man of an exalted character who does not lose some part of his respectability by an intimate acquaintance. — I have lived with him near two years, have received as many marks of his affection & esteem as perhaps any young man ever did — and have occasion to be with him in every situation in which a man is placed in his family — have ate & drank with him constantly, and almost every evening play at cards with him, and I declare I have never found a single thing that could lessen my respect for him. — a compleat knowledge of his honesty, uprightness, & candor in all his private transactions have sometimes led me to think him more than a man — His industry is unparalled — he rises every day before the sun — writes till breakfast (which never exceeds 1/2 after 7) then mounts his horse & rides round his farms til 1/2 past 2, sees that everything is in proper order — and if there is no company he writes till dark & in the Evening — plays a game at whist, or, if pressed with business writes till 9 in the Eveng — this is the general round which he pursues with little variation . . . .

Writing to James McHenry, the Secretary of War under President John Adams, Washington himself described his daily routine in 1797:

I begin my diurnal course with the Sun; if my hirelings are not in their places at that time I send them messages expressive of my sorrow for their indisposition; then having put these wheels in motion, I examine the state of things further; and the more they are probed, the deeper I find the wounds are which my buildings have sustained by an absence and neglect of eight years; by the time I have accomplished these matters breakfast (a little after seven O'clock, about the time I presume you are taking leave of Mrs. McHenry) is ready. This over, I mount my horse and ride round my farms, which employes me until it is time to dress for dinner; at which I rarely miss seeing strange faces; come, as they say, out of respect to me. Pray, would not the word curiosity answer as well? and how different this, from having a few social friends at a cheerful board? The usual time of sitting at Table; a walk, and Tea, brings me within the dawn of candlelight; previous to which, if not prevented by company, I resolve that, as soon as the glimmering taper supplies the place of the great luminary, I will retire to my writing Table and acknowledge the letters I have received; but when the lights are brought, I feel tired, and disinclined to engage in this work, conceiving that the next night will do as well: the next comes, and with it the same causes for postponement, and effect, and so on.

This will account for *your* letter remaining so long unacknowledged, and having given you the history of a day, it will serve for a year . . . .

As Washington's letter indicates, a constant stream of visitors, both friends and strangers, flowed though Mount Vernon. In 1787 Washington compared his home to "a well resorted tavern, as scarcely any strangers who are going from north to south, or from south to north, do not spend a day or two at it." The tavern comparison, however, was not altogether apt, for Washington bore the expense of boarding these visitors, their servants, and horses. In 1797 he noted in a letter, "Unless some one pops in, unexpectedly — Mrs. Washington and myself will do what I believe has not been done within the last twenty years by us — that is to set down to dinner by ourselves."

One visitor in June of 1798 was the Polish Count Julien Ursyn

Niemcewicz, a friend of Count Thaddeus Kosciuszko, who had served as a volunteer soldier of fortune under Washington during the Revolution. In his diary Niemcewicz wrote:

> The General is often censured for his reserve and taciturnity. It is true that he does not talk much; but he does not avoid conversation when one advances a subject worthy of remark . . . . At table, after the ladies' departure, or when sitting under the portico, he often talked with me for hours. His favorite subject is agriculture; but he answered with great kindness all questions put to him on the Revolutionary war, armies, and so on . . . . Mrs. Washington is one of the most delightful persons one can meet. Good, sweet, and exceedingly pleasant, she likes to talk and talks well, of old times . . . .

Washington died in 1799 and Martha Washington in 1802. By the terms of Washington's will, the estate was then divided among various nephews and grandnephews, for Washington had no children of his own. By Washington's directions his slaves were freed as an example to other slaveowners, for in his later years Washington advocated that slavery be abolished "by slow, sure, and imperceptible degrees." The Mansion House Farm and four thousand acres were bequeathed to Bushrod Washington, the son of Washington's favorite brother, John Augustine.

Bushrod Washington was a successful lawyer and later an Associate Justice of the United States Supreme Court. He died in 1829, leaving the house and one thousand acres to his nephew John Augustine Washington. The estate passed to John Augustine's widow and later to his son, John Augustine Washington, Jr., who found owning Mount Vernon a burden. To an even greater extent than in Washington's day, uninvited strangers thronged to see the house. The income from farming dwindled, and the buildings and even the mansion fell into disrepair. A visitor in 1852 described "rooms with the paint cracking off" and noted that the "gardens untrimmed look poverty stricken." The proprietor tried to persuade the federal government to acquire the estate for $200,000, which was $100,000 less than he had been offered by speculators who wanted to commercialize the property as a tourist attraction. When Congress declined, he approached the Virginia legislature, again without success.

In response to official indifference, Miss Ann Pamela Cunningham of South Carolina organized The Mount Vernon Ladies' Association of the Union to collect donations throughout the country to purchase and preserve Mount Vernon. Her campaign was successful, and in 1858 the association acquired the mansion and a tract of two hundred acres. Since then the association has worked to restore the mansion, its contents, the outbuildings, gardens, and grounds to their appearance in

Washington's time, and to operate the whole as a museum open to the public. Adjacent land has been purchased, so that the boundaries today closely correspond to those of the old Mansion House Farm.

≈   ≈   ≈   ≈

As for the Mount Vernon Trail, it was constructed in 1973 along the edge of the right-of-way for the George Washington Memorial Parkway. The parkway, in turn, was started in 1932 to commemorate the bicentennial of George Washington's birth. The parkway — or at least the part built before World War II — was also a Depression-era jobs project and a federal model demonstrating modern highway design.

≈   ≈   ≈   ≈

METRO: The Rosslyn Metrorail station (Blue and Orange lines) provides good access to the northern end of the Mount Vernon Trail at Roosevelt Island. Turn left (downhill) out the station and follow Moore Street one block to 19th Street. Turn right downhill and follow 19th Street one short block to and across Lynn Street. Turn left and follow Lynn Street over Interstate 66 and across Lee Highway, then turn right onto the paved Custis Trail, which soon leads downhill and across the George Washington Memorial Parkway to the Roosevelt Island parking lot. The Mount Vernon Trail starts at the far end of the parking lot.

Also close to the Mount Vernon Trail is the Arlington Cemetery Metrorail station (Blue Line). From the station, follow the broad sidewalk along the south side of Memorial Drive (i.e., with the road on your left) toward Arlington Memorial Bridge and the distant Lincoln Memorial. After passing a traffic circle (and about 60 yards before Arlington Memorial Bridge), bear right onto a paved hike-bike trail and follow it gradually downhill to the riverside Mount Vernon Trail.

Metrobus routes 28A, 28B, 29K, and 29N run to Fairfax and Pendleton streets in Alexandria. Follow Pendleton Street east toward the Potomac River. Just before Union Street, the hike-bike trail appears on the left, leading north. To go south, follow Union Street to the right through Alexandria.

Also in Alexandria, Metrobus routes 10A, 10B, and 10C terminate at Hunting Towers next to the George Washington Memorial Parkway at the intersection with South Street.

Alongside the parkway is the Mount Vernon Trail, which at this point is simply a sidewalk but quickly becomes very attractive as you head south (i.e., with the parkway on your right).

Telephone (202) 637-7000 for current Metro information, including schedules, routes, and connections.

≈   ≈   ≈   ≈

AUTOMOBILE DIRECTIONS: The Mount Vernon Trail more or less follows the Virginia shore of the Potomac River between Roosevelt Island in the north and Mount Vernon in the south. (See **Map 32** opposite.) The directions below are to several places located at intervals along the trail: Roosevelt Island, Belle Haven Park (Dyke Marsh), Fort Hunt Park, and Mount Vernon. All are accessible from the George Washington Memorial Parkway, although it should be noted that the entrance to Roosevelt Island is from the parkway's northbound lanes.

To Roosevelt Island: Please see the directions to Roosevelt Island starting on page 302 in Chapter 22.

To Belle Haven Park and Dyke Marsh
　Fort Hunt Park
　Mount Vernon
from Interstate 495 (the Capital Beltway):
　From the Inner Loop of the Capital Beltway, take Exit 1 for the Mount Vernon Highway. (This is the first exit after crossing the Wilson Bridge from Maryland into Virginia.) Curve sharply right and then turn right onto the George Washington Memorial Parkway.

　From the Outer Loop of the Capital Beltway, take Exit 1B for Route 1 North, Alexandria, and the Mount Vernon Highway. Go about 0.3 mile north, then turn right at a traffic light onto Franklin Street. Go three blocks, then turn right again onto South Washington Street, which soon crosses a bridge over the Capital Beltway and becomes the George Washington Memorial Parkway.

　For Belle Haven Park and Dyke Marsh, follow the parkway south 1.1 miles, then turn left. From the entrance road, turn left again to reach a series of parking lots.

　For Fort Hunt Park, follow the parkway south 5.5 miles, then exit to the right. In rapid succession, fork right and then

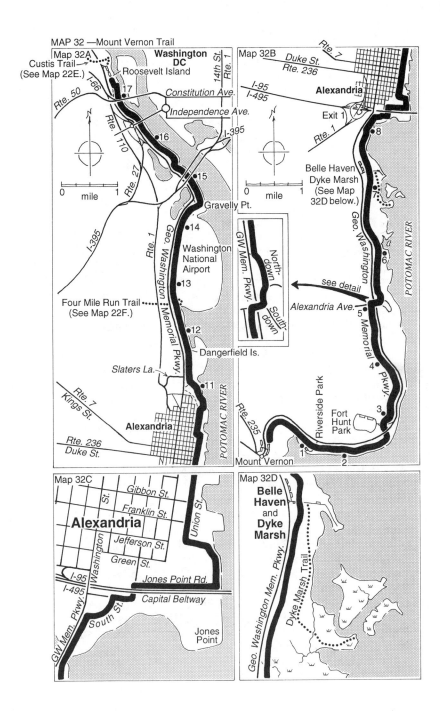

MAP 32 —Mount Vernon Trail

Map 32A
Custis Trail
(See Map 22E.)

Washington DC
Roosevelt Island

17

Rte. 50
I-66
7-I-70

Rte. 110

14th St.
Rte. 1

Constitution Ave.

Independence Ave.

I-395

16

Rte. 27

Rte. 1

Geo. Washington Memorial Pkwy.

15

Gravelly Pt.

14

Washington National Airport

13

Four Mile Run Trail
(See Map 22F.)

12

Slaters La.

Rte. 7
Kings St.

Alexandria

Rte. 236
Duke St.

11

POTOMAC RIVER

Map 32B
Duke St.
Rte. 236

Rte. 7

I-95
I-495

Alexandria

Exit 1

Rte. 1

8

Belle Haven
Dyke Marsh
(See Map 32D below.)

Geo. Washington

see detail

Alexandria Ave.

GW Mem. Pkwy.

North-down

South-down

Dangerfield Is.

6

5

Memorial Pkwy.

4

3

Riverside Park

Fort Hunt Park

Rte. 235

Mount Vernon

1

2

POTOMAC RIVER

Map 32C

Gibbon St.

Franklin St.

St.

Union St.

Alexandria

Jefferson St.

Green St.

I-95
I-495

Washington

Jones Point Rd.

Capital Beltway

GW Mem. Pkwy.

South St.

Jones Point

Map 32D
Belle Haven and **Dyke Marsh**

Geo. Washington Mem. Pkwy.

Dyke Marsh Trail

267

bear left into the park. Follow the park road 0.3 mile to the first parking lot.

For Mount Vernon, follow the parkway south 8.4 miles. At the traffic circle at Mount Vernon, circle left past the entrance and then bear right into a parking lot. If you are interested in the Mount Vernon Trail, the trailhead is at the far end of the parking lot. There is another large lot on the other side of the parkway.

≈   ≈   ≈   ≈

WALKING and BICYCLING ON THE MOUNT VERNON TRAIL: The 17.5-mile Mount Vernon Trail is shown on **Map 32** on page 267. For the most part, the trail is a wide paved path. The route is obvious except at Alexandria, where the trail is interrupted and the route follows local streets. To navigate through Alexandria, refer in part to Map 32C (i.e., the lower-left panel). Note also the detail on Map 32B showing how the route crosses the parkway at Alexandria Avenue near milepost 5.

Cyclists must ride single file, yield to other trail users, and keep their speed to a moderate, safe pace. In particular, cyclists should go slowly on the trail's wooden bridges, where the surface can be very slick when wet.

Getting started: If you start at the **Roosevelt Island** parking lot, the Potomac River, of course, will be on your left. At the end of the parking lot, pass the bridge to Roosevelt Island. After a few dozen yards, bear left onto a boardwalk and continue south along the river.

If you start at **Belle Haven Park**, you can join the Mount Vernon Trail where it crosses the entrance road a few dozen yards from the George Washington Memorial Parkway.

If you start at **Fort Hunt** with the intention of walking or cycling 6 miles round-trip to Mount Vernon, bear right as you pass out the park gate. Join the paved trail on the far side of the road, which almost immediately descends through an underpass below the George Washington Memorial Parkway. There is no path under the parkway, so be cautious as you walk on the side of the road. Once through the underpass, the hike-bike trail is continuous to Mount Vernon.

If you start at **Mount Vernon**, the trailhead is at the north end of the east parking lot, as shown at the bottom of Map

32B. For cyclists, one advantage of starting at Mount Vernon is that you can lock your bike inside your car while you visit Mount Vernon itself before or after your excursion on the Mount Vernon Trail.

Connections to other hike-bike trails: As shown on Map 32A, the Mount Vernon Trail is linked to other Washington-area hike-bike trails. The entire system of interconnected trails is shown in schematic outline on **Map 2** on page 7.

At Roosevelt Island the Mount Vernon Trail connects with the Custis Trail leading to the Washington and Old Dominion Trail (see Chapter 12).

South of Arlington Memorial Bridge, the Mount Vernon Trail passes a spur that leads up to the bridge and across to Washington, where paths go downriver to Potomac Park and upriver to the Rock Creek Trail (Chapter 26) and the C&O Canal towpath (Chapter 7).

At Four Mile Run just southwest of Washington National Airport, the Mount Vernon Trail connects with the Four Mile Run Trail, which links — via local streets — to the southern end of the Washington and Old Dominion Trail at Shirlington. (Again, see Chapter 12.)

Finally, as you pass through Alexandria, you may notice signs referring to the Cameron Run Trail. This trail might more aptly be called a bike route. It follows streets and sidewalks for miles (mostly along Eisenhower Avenue parallel with the Capital Beltway) before eventually reaching a short hike-bike trail along Cameron Run and Holmes Run in western Alexandria.

≈   ≈   ≈   ≈

WALKING ON THE DYKE MARSH TRAIL: The Dyke Marsh Trail at Belle Haven Park is shown on **Map 32D** on page 267. The round-trip distance is 2.5 miles. The trailhead is directly off the entrance road about a hundred yards from the George Washington Memorial Parkway.

20

NATIONAL COLONIAL FARM
R. W. STRAUS ECOSYSTEM FARM
ACCOKEEK CREEK at Piscataway Park

Walking and ski touring. The three sites described here feature a variety of trails, most of them only 1 or 2 miles long (1.6 or 3.2 kilometers). There are, however, obvious opportunities to combine these short trails into a longer excursion lasting two or three hours.

Located about 12 miles south of Washington on the Maryland shore of the Potomac River directly across from Mount Vernon, Piscataway Park comprises 4,700 acres spread along six miles of river front. The park was established by a series of Congressional acts in the 1960s and '70s to preserve the view from George Washington's home as it was in his time.

Part of Piscataway Park is occupied by the **National Colonial Farm,** where there are several miles of lanes and footpaths shown at the west (or left) end of **Map 33** on page 281. With the Potomac River and Mount Vernon as a backdrop, visitors can explore a typical eighteenth-century farm, where costumed docents or interpreters are usually on hand to demonstrate the daily tasks of farm life. The plantation features a house, tobacco barn, outkitchen, herb garden, fields, and pastures, and also historically authentic varieties of crops, livestock, and fowl. Outlying trails lead to a native tree arboretum, groves of chestnut saplings that are maintained in the hope of overcoming the blight that kills mature chestnut trees, and the **Robert Ware Straus Ecosystem Farm**, which demonstrates techniques for high-yield, organic agriculture.

To the east of the two farms is a park trail — shown at the right end of Map 33 — that crosses the marshy mouth of **Accokeek Creek** on a long boardwalk and then follows the Potomac shore past broad fields to Mockley Point and Piscataway Creek. The round-trip distance is 2.5 miles (4.0 kilometers).

The gates at the National Colonial Farm and other sections of Piscataway Park are open daily year-round from early morning until dusk. The farm, to which a small admission fee is charged, operates year-round Tuesday through Friday from 10 A.M. to 4 P.M. and Saturday and Sunday from 12 noon to 5. Both the National Colonial Farm and the Straus Ecosystem Farm are run by the Accokeek Foundation, a non-profit organization dedicated to preserving the historic and natural heritage of the Potomac River, in cooperation with the National Park Service. Telephone (301) 283-2113 for information, including the schedule of events, such as demonstrations on colonial cooking, livestock care, crop maintenance and harvesting, and other farm tasks.

AS AN HISTORIC RE-CREATION of a typical tobacco farm of the 1770s, the National Colonial Farm provides a counterpoise to such estabishments as Gunston Hall down the Potomac and Mount Vernon directly across the river (see Chapters 17 and 19). Obviously, the elegant houses and large plantations of George Mason, George Washington, and others of their high social rank were in no way typical of the vast majority of colonial farmers, who were men of modest means cultivating relatively small farms such as that seen at Piscataway Park.

The eighteenth century was, of course, the second century of English colonization in North America. During the Chesapeake land rush of the prior century, when the tidewater region was one of the frontiers of the New World and its English inhabitants were essentially pioneers in a wilderness, every settler tried to acquire as much land as he could at his first patent or claim. The size of most plantations of the mid-1600s substantially exceeded the 50-acre headright quota, but the land actually cultivated was far less. Three acres of tobacco — and every tidewater planter grew tobacco for export to Great Britain — was about the upper limit for even the hardest worker, who first had to clear the land of woods that covered virtually all of the region's arable land to the water's edge. Settlers who had capital at the time of their immigration brought with them indentured laborers (termed "servants") with whom to claim more land and to cultivate larger fields. Still other freemen who worked alone or with their sons used the profits from their first successful harvests to acquire indentured servants as quickly as possible. Some seventeenth-century writers condemned the system of indenture, but others agreed with one observer who wrote, "The work of their servants and slaves is no other than what every common freeman does." Another observer similarly noted that many masters and their sons worked alongside their bondsmen.

More than three-quarters of the immigrants to the Chesapeake region in the 1600s came as indentured servants, required by their contracts (called articles of indenture) to work for a number of years in exchange for having their passage to the New World paid by merchant recruiters, who then sold the servants to planters who could afford them. Some recruiters dealt in servants on a large scale, but most servants were transported by numerous merchants and mariners primarily engaged in other business and who had perhaps been requested by their agents and customers in the Chesapeake region to supply a few indentured laborers. Even if no such request had been received, merchants and shipmasters knew that transporting a bondservant for resale in Maryland or Virginia was a safe speculation.

In this way, even many of the smaller planters of the tidewater region in the seventeenth century acquired one or two indentured servants. Eventually, the system of indenture became so commonplace that local statutes governed the practice in cases where there were no individualized contracts. Typically, upon completion of his or her term of servitude (often five years for adults, longer for minors), each servant was paid freedom dues consisting of various items, such as new clothes, tools, and even land early on when ample land was still available. For women, the end of their indenture meant marriage to their pick of a multitude of suitors (men outnumbered women by nearly three to one) and in all probability the continuation of a workaday life not unlike what they had known as servants. For men the end of servitude meant the opportunity to set up for themselves as small tobacco planters and to develop, if they, their sons, and grandsons survived and were successful, the kind of middle-class, eighteenth-century plantation represented by the National Colonial Farm.

The flow of indentured immigrants to Maryland and Virginia in the mid-1600s reflected depressed economic conditions in England. A variety of factors — rapid population growth, the consolidation of farms and their conversion from cultivated fields to pastures and orchards, and finally the disruption in commerce caused by the Thirty Years War and the English Civil War — all combined to create widespread unemployment in England. In consequence, many young people, mostly with family backgrounds in farming and textile manufacture, and mostly between the ages of fifteen and twenty-four, chose to go as indentured servants to the Chesapeake region, where there was at least the certainty of gainful employment and the touted prospect of becoming planters after their servitude was over.

From the 1630s through the 1650s, when tobacco prices were high and free land was available, many indentured laborers who had completed their terms of servitude did indeed manage to set up immediately as small growers on good land. By 1660, however, most land suitable for growing tobacco had already been claimed and so became something that had to be purchased from a prior owner. Under these less favorable circumstances, some newly-freed indentured servants took up less desirable land that did not offer much opportunity for economic advancement. Other former servants often got a start by tenant farming for established landowners — perhaps even their former masters — before eventually accumulating the means to become freeholders. Still others became hired workers or sharecroppers, typically living as members of a freeholder's household, but these men rarely improved their status, even after years of laboring. Toward the end of the seventeenth century, economic prospects for former bondsmen dimmed still further as rising land prices and periodic slumps in the tobacco economy condemned most freed servants to the perpetual status of landless, voteless, voiceless tenants, sharecroppers, or hired hands — if, that is, they chose to stay in the tidewater region.

As economic opportunity declined in the Chesapeake country, so too did the flow of indentured servants willing to immigrate from England, where by the closing decades of the 1600s the economy was recovering and employment among the poor was rising. In consequence, the practice of importing African slaves became a way to supply labor to the tidewater plantations. Once started, the conversion to slaves was speeded by the perceived anomaly of working whites and blacks together, and also by the advantages of owning slaves, who, of course, never became free and whose children too belonged to the master. After 1698, when the African slave trade was thrown open to all English firms that wished to engage in the traffic, slaves were transported to the tidewater region in great numbers.

While the flow of English immigrants to Maryland lasted, however, the population grew from somewhat more than 100 in 1634, when the *Ark* and the *Dove* arrived at St. Mary's River at the mouth of the Potomac, to 8,000 settlers in 1660, 15,000 in 1675, and 25,000 in 1688. From freed servants and other immigrants of slender resources came the bulk of pioneer planters, each drudging with his ax and his hoe to grow tobacco, which he traded with shipmasters and merchants for necessary implements and for a very few luxuries — perhaps sugar and occasionally rum. Inventories of probated estates show that the typical planter made every possible article that he could with his own hands; bowls and cups from dried gourds, trenchers and plates from slabs of wood, benches and bedsteads from hewn logs, and mattresses from corn shucks. For his own use he tended also a cornfield, a vegetable garden, and possibly an orchard that he had planted. He supplemented his diet by hunting and fishing. Nearly every seventeenth-century planter family kept a few guinea fowl, cows, and hogs (usually allowed to roam freely in the woods) and perhaps provided board and lodging to an unmarried indentured servant, sharecropper, or hired hand. Most planters were illiterate — they signed their names with an X or some other mark — and very few had even a single book.

Because tobacco rapidly exhausted the soil, the typical planter was always clearing new land. The best land could grow tobacco for about eight years, but poor, sandy soil would support tobacco for only three years, after which the exhausted fields might be planted in corn for a few years more and then left fallow for a decade or two or three. As one seventeenth-century traveler noted, "As fast as the ground is worn out with tobacco and corn, it runs up again in underwoods; and in many places of the country that which has been cleared is thicker in woods than it was before the clearing." Scattered at intervals through the forest and overgrown fields were small houses, many of them ramshackle or even abandoned by planters who had moved to be nearer new fields.

The houses of the seventeenth-century planters were small wooded boxes. Most had only one room, shared by the master, servants, and lodgers alike. More prosperous planters might have houses of two or three rooms and perhaps a separate dwelling for servants, and a very few planters had houses with as many as six rooms. All structures were framed with wooden posts sunk into the ground. Covering the frame were boards, more often split than sawn, chinked with mud. As for the interior walls, "The best people plaster them with clay," explained two visiting Dutchmen in 1680, but some dwellings were so wretchedly constructed "that if you are not so close to the fire as almost to burn yourself, you cannot keep warm, for the wind blows through everywhere." The houses were of one story, often with an earthen floor. Windows had shutters or perhaps panes of oiled paper, but no glass. Chimneys were usually of wood daubed with mud. Roofs were at first of thatch; later shingles were used. In 1686 a visiting Frenchman observed that even the wealthier planters lived in simple structures of this kind, and added, "They build also a separate kitchen, a house for the Christian slaves [or that is, indentured servants], another for Negro slaves, and several tobacco barns, so that in arriving at the plantation of a person of importance, you think you are entering a considerable village."

The National Colonial Farm, of course, represents a plantation of a century later, by which time living conditions had improved, although the essential farm elements remained unchanged. An outkitchen separate from the chief dwelling was still the norm, partly as a precaution against the spread of fire, but also because the kitchen was a major work center serving the whole farm. Tobacco was still grown, then hung to dry in barns before being packed in barrels called hogsheads and sold to merchants with whom the farmers traded for imported goods or (by that time) locally manufactured items. One improvement was that after 1747 in Maryland, the hogsheads of tobacco were subject to inspection by government officials in order to prevent adulteration with trash growth and even earth and stones. Corn, too, was still grown, but cornmeal was eaten mainly by slaves and the poor. The middle and upper classes ate wheat bread. By the mid-1700s, wheat and corn and corn fed livestock had become important cash products, not only to feed the tidewater population but also for shipment from the Chesapeake region to the growing cities, to New England, and to the West Indies, where sugar so dominated the economy that most food for the Caribbean plantations was imported. In the West Indies, grain, salt pork, and salt fish were exchanged for sugar, molasses, rum, salt, and cash, chiefly in the form of Spanish coins. Wheat was shipped also to South America and even southern Europe (but not to Great Britain, which maintained a high tariff). Yet another innovation was the increased use by some farmers of fertilizers, including livestock manure from farm herds, lime, and imported guano. Also, dwellings improved. The National Colonial Farm has a house that, although small, is far superior to the wood-and-mud structures of the 1600s. Called "Laurel Branch," this dwelling was reconstructed in part from a house built nearby in about 1780. It has two stories plus a garret, glass windows (these would have been prohibitively expensive a century earlier, when all glass was imported), interior walls coated with real plaster, and a massive brick chimney. During the eighteenth century, the land at what is now the National Colonial Farm was part of a plantation named "Hansonton," and a 1798 tax assessment of the property lists two dwellings, one of which was 26 by 20 feet with seven windows. These dimensions are almost identical to the Laurel Branch house seen today.

≈   ≈   ≈   ≈

Hard work, command of bound or hired labor, and ownership of fertile land were not the only ingredients for prosperity during the colonial period in the Chesapeake region. Gloria L. Main, in her book *Tobacco Colony*, points out that good health, or more precisely, a long life, was also an important factor. With its abundant marshes and suffocatingly hot summers, the tidewater region was a very unhealthful climate for most English settlers. Malaria often weakened the immigrants and left them in poor condition to survive the dysentery, typhoid fever, pneumonia, and influenza that were also common. In Maryland during the middle of the seventeenth century, white male immigrants who reached age twenty-one (many died earlier) could expect on average to remain alive only into their early forties. A mere third of the marriages in seventeenth-century Maryland lasted as long as a decade before one or the other spouse died. In southern Maryland between 1658 and 1705, 67 percent of married men and widowers who died left children who were all of minor age, while only 6 percent left all adult children. Consequently, the life of the typical planter was often cut short before he had accumulated more than very modest assets to pass on to the wife and children who may have survived him.

By living to old age, however, some planters were able to accumulated expertise and wealth over a protracted period. The first generation of successful planters eschewed spending their profits on consumption goods and instead invested in more and more land and laborers, while continuing to live in a manner that was spare, unostentatious, and frugal. In this way a few planters — perhaps one in twenty — rose to something like affluence by the standards of the time, and a still smaller number laid the foundations for major family fortunes. As a result of marriage gifts and bequests (which fathers commonly distributed well before their deaths), the children of such long-lived planters started adult life with a huge advantage over those without similar patrimony.

Gradually, however, mortality rates among settlers declined during the seventeenth century, and by way of explanation some historians have pointed to the increased consumption of cider, beer, rum, and pure water from deep wells, as opposed to the polluted and sometimes even slightly brackish surface water drunk by the early settlers. The popular notion at the time was simply that the survivors had become "seasoned," or that is, had adjusted to the new environment, but historians with a medical bent point out that the local diseases were such that no lasting immunity was possible, thus again suggesting that sanitation improved.

Some historians have gone so far as to argue that the decline in mortality diminished economic opportunity for newly-freed indentured servants. During the middle third of the seventeenth century, the lottery of longevity had favored a few, who acquired sizable and sometimes even very large landholdings. Had the likelihood of an early death continued to be the norm, such holdings would have been without long-term consequence, because much good land would soon have become available for redistribution as the descendants of big landowners died young like most other people. But instead, improved sanitation and lengthening life expectancies enabled families that already had much land to retain it permanently, shutting out newcomers.

It has also been suggested that increased longevity speeded the conversion to a slave labor force, inasmuch as permanent slaves became preferable to temporary servants once it was observed that the slaves, who were more expensive to acquire than servants, were likely to survive as long-term assets. Furthermore, it became worthwhile to do with some slaves what was not worthwhile with short-term bondsmen, namely to teach them, through a system of in-house apprenticeship, a variety of valuable skills, such as carpentry, coopering, weaving, boat building, and blacksmithing, that would then remunerate the master throughout each slave's lifetime and enable the plantation to become more self-sufficient and profitable.

The stratification of society and the emergence at the top of a small, wealthy elite was reinforced by a pattern of wide fluctuations in the price of tobacco during the seventeenth and eighteenth centuries. At first tobacco prices were high because of limited output, but later, as production soared and the tidewater region was wracked by periodic and precipitous drops in the price of tobacco, many growers who had not yet acquired an adequate cushion of capital failed, and their crops, land, and other useful assets were bought by those with spare money. In particular, two periods of deep depression from 1686 to 1696 and from 1703 to 1716 eroded the holdings of the middle stratum of planters and drove away to Pennsylvania and the Carolinas (where good land was still available at low prices) the poor, the young, and the newly-freed indentured servants.

In other ways also wealth begot more wealth. Tobacco planters with adequate capital were in a position, especially after about 1680 and into the 1700s, to diversify into other fields, such as trade, moneylending, shipping, or the practice of law. Wealthy planters corresponded with English consignment houses for the sale of their tobacco, thus obtaining higher prices than did those smaller growers who simply sold their crops locally. Well-capitalized planters purchased imported goods — cloth, shoes, hats, tools, nails, salt, and other necessities — for resale at a markup of about 50 percent to the numerous smaller planters and tenant farmers. These merchant-planters sold their goods on credit throughout the year, eventually receiving crops in payment, for tobacco served as a substitute for money. Some large planters bought shares in ships, or opened sawmills, gristmills, iron mines, tanneries, and other enterprises often manned by slaves. A few planters even began to experiment with manufacturing items, such as shoes, or with new agricultural pursuits, such as growing wheat or raising large herds of cattle, hogs, and sheep.

Finally, of course, the families of well-to-do planters intermarried, consolidating their wealth among themselves. And they came also to monopolize government power. For a long time the high death rate prevented the emergence of a ruling class, but after 1700, election or appointment to county and provincial offices depended increasingly on the aspiring man's family name, connections, and high — or at least middling — economic status. Wealth enabled the patriarchs of leading families to educate their sons and grandsons in the skills necessary to assume governmental posts, judicial responsibilities, militia officerships, and church positions that were created in increasing numbers as the society expanded and matured. According to the historian Douglas Southall Freeman, by the time of the American Revolution, colonial society in Maryland and Virginia was divided into eight distinct classes. At the top were the gentry and at the bottom were the slaves, both "supposed to be of immutable station," and between them were the small farmers, merchants, seafaring men, frontiersmen, servants, and convicts (who could be purchased, like indentured laborers, for a term of servitude).

Although the National Colonial Farm offers a vision of plantation life as lived in the latter 1700s by the numerous class of ordinary, small farmers, research by James Musgrove suggests that the place belonged in fact to people who were members of southern Maryland's gentry. Prior to his death in 1734, John Fendall, son of Josias Fendall, a former governor of Maryland, deeded Hansonton and another estate called "Surebind" to his daughter Elizabeth, who was married to John Beall Jr. Hansonton, it is thought, included either all or most of the present-day farm, plus more land just to the east. Beall had other properties of his own, including land that he gave to his son Josias Beall while that man was still young. Josias Beall served in the Lower House of the Maryland Assembly. On the 1755 tax roll he was listed as having interests in eight properties in Prince George's County, plus a principal dwelling estate near Hansonton in Charles County. He never, however, inherited Hansonton itself. After his father died in 1757, the elder Beall's estate was valued at £1,360, a considerable sum for the time. The lengthy and detailed estate inventory included silver, furniture, spinning wheels, weapons, "a small diamond," a large stock of wheat and corn, and twenty-nine slaves. There is also evidence that John and Elizabeth Beall housed indentured servants, but there is no record of the size or type of dwelling that the Bealls lived in at Hansonton.

After John Beall's death, his wife Elizabeth never remarried. She and her two daughters resided at and managed Hansonton and Surebind. Totaling 535 acres, the two farms were deeded by Elizabeth to her daughters in 1782, twelve years before Elizabeth's death.

Together John and Elizabeth Beall had family ties to many prominent families and individuals in Maryland and Virginia. They were closely related to the Marshalls and Lees. Elizabeth Beall was the half-sister of Thomas Marshall, a member of the Virginia House of Burgesses and a Revolutionary War leader (and father of Secretary of State and Chief Justice John Marshall). Elizabeth was also the aunt of Phillip Fendall, a Maryland legislator and "Chief Tobacco Agent" on the Potomac River, and she was a step-aunt of Benjamin Stoddert of Charles County, Maryland, a prominent businessman, secretary to the Revolutionary board of war, and first U.S. Secretary of the Navy.

≈   ≈   ≈   ≈

AUTOMOBILE DIRECTIONS: Piscataway Park — which includes the **National Colonial Farm,** the **Robert Ware Straus Ecosystem Farm,** and **Accokeek Creek** — is located about 12 miles south of Washington on the Maryland shore of the Potomac River. (See the corner panel on **Map 33** opposite.)

To Piscataway Park from Interstate 495 (the Capital Beltway): Leave the Beltway at Exit 3A for Route 210 South (the Indian Head Highway). This exit is located not far from the Wilson Bridge — and if you are coming from the direction of the bridge, you can also take Exit 2 then 2A. Follow Route 210 South about 9 miles to an exit for Bryan Point Road and the National Colonial Farm. At the top of the exit ramp, turn left and go 0.5 mile to a T-intersection with Bryan Point Road, and there turn right. (After this turn, you will almost immediately pass a road that intersects from the left. On the way back from the park, you will have to turn at that intersection in order to get onto Route 210.)

Follow Bryan Point Road. After 3 miles you will reach the somewhat obscure entrance on the right for the **Accokeek Creek** trailhead at Piscataway Park. For the **National Colonial Farm** and the **Robert Ware Straus Ecosystem Farm**, continue on Bryan Point Road 0.6 mile to the farm parking lot.

≈   ≈   ≈   ≈

WALKING: Various trails and farm features are shown on **Map 33** opposite.

At the **National Colonial Farm,** I like best the wide lanes bordered by hedgerows and fences. The Bluebird Trail west to

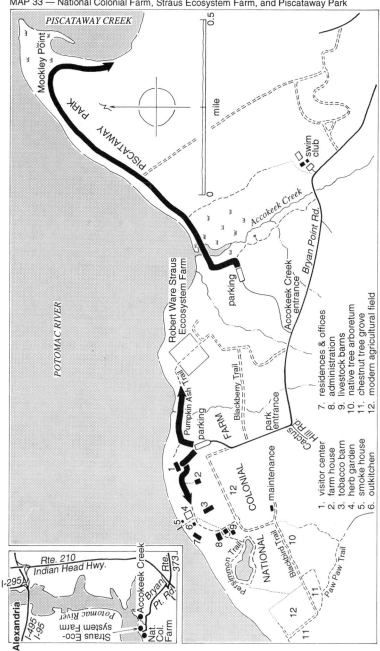

PISCATAWAY CREEK

Mockley Point

PISCATAWAY PARK

POTOMAC RIVER

swim club

Accokeek Creek

Bryan Point Rd.

Robert Ware Straus Eccosystem Farm

parking

Accokeek Creek entrance

Pumpkin Ash Trail

parking

FARM

Blackberry Trail

park entrance

Cactus Hill Rd.

7. residences & offices
8. administration
9. livestock barns
10. native tree arboretum
11. chestnut tree grove
12. modern agricultural field

1
2
3
4
5
6
maintenance

COLONIAL

12

NATIONAL

Blackbird Trail

10

Persimmon Trail

11

Paw Paw Trail

12

11

1. visitor center
2. farm house
3. tobacco barn
4. herb garden
5. smoke house
6. outkitchen

Rte. 210
Indian Head Hwy.

I-295

Alexandria

I-495 / I-95

Potomac River

Straus Eco-system Farm

Accokeek Creek

Bryan Pt. Rd.

Rte. 373

Nat. Col. Farm

mile

0.5

0

281

the Native Tree Arboretum and the Chestnut Tree Groves is attractive. Some of the more narrow footpaths have to be maintained by periodic mowing and so may not be clear when you are there.

For the **Straus Ecosystem Farm**, follow the Pumpkin Ash Trail from the farm parking lot and return by the Blackberry Trail.

At **Accokeek Creek**, a paved path leads from the parking lot east to a boardwalk that crosses a freshwater tidal marsh at the mouth of Accokeek Creek. At the far side of the marsh, a trail continues east along the shore of the Potomac River past Mockley Point to Piscataway Creek. Return by the way you came. The round-trip distance is 2.5 miles.

≈   ≈   ≈   ≈

AT THE TIME OF ENGLISH SETTLEMENT, the level land between Accokeek Creek and Mockley Point was the site of Moyaone, the largest of several Piscataway Indian villages along the Maryland shore of the Potomac River. In 1608 Captain John Smith visited the stock-aded village, where he estimated there to be about a hundred fighting men, which perhaps indicates a population of four or five hundred people. The entire Piscataway population of southern Maryland is thought to have been only about three thousand. The influx of English settlers did not at first adversely affect the Indians — indeed, a mutually beneficial trade developed, and sometimes the Piscataway petitioned the English for protection against the Susquehannocks and Senecas to the north. But as the tide of immigration swelled, friction developed between the settlers and even the friendly Indians, who by the mid-1700s were substantially outnumbered. When the Indians complained that the settlers' livestock foraged in their fields, they were told to erect fences, which were sometimes torn down by pioneer planters eager to see the Indians leave. Quarrels that resulted in the deaths of settlers were invariably followed by bloody reprisals. The colonial government encouraged the Piscataway to concentrate in settlements with other clans and fragments of tribes, and some Indians did so. Although these native Americans lost their tribal structure, their descendants have survived to the present day in southern Maryland and on the Eastern Shore. Most Indians, however, responded to English encroachment by moving inland beyond the frontier.

During the 1620s Moyaone was burned twice — the first time by English settlers in retaliation for the massacre of some white traders, and the second time by northern Indians. After the second fire, the

Piscataway Indians at Moyaone established a new village farther up Piscataway Creek. Excavations at the site of Moyaone have revealed traces of a circular stockade as well as middens and ossuaries.

Toward the end of the seventeenth century, the Piscataway who still lived as a tribe moved to Virginia — but not for long; Governor Andros told them to return to Maryland. Then the Piscataway settled at Canoy Island in the Potomac River near Point of Rocks. In 1700 their head man came to Annapolis and asked Governor Blakiston for permission to bring his people back, either to Accokeek Creek or Mattawoman Creek. The request was granted, but the Piscataway never returned. In 1711 some were at Conejhola on the Susquehanna, and in 1793 a band of fifty Piscataway Indians appeared at a conference in Detroit, where they used the figure of a wild turkey as their signature.

21

FORT WASHINGTON PARK

Walking — 3 miles (4.8 kilometers). The bold line on **Map 34** on page 293 outlines a tour around the perimeter of this remarkable historic site located on the Maryland side of the Potomac River below Washington. The circuit starts at a massive masonry fort built during the first half of the nineteenth century to guard the water approach to the nation's capital. After exploring the parapets, casemates, and living quarters of the old fort, follow a hiking trail along the wooded shore of Piscataway Creek, then continue around the perimeter of the former military reservation. The route also passes concrete batteries (now abandoned) built at the end of the nineteenth century.

Please note that the trail along Piscataway Creek is steep in some places and can be muddy during wet weather or periods of thaw. At intervals, the route occasionally and briefly follows park roads where cars are present. Nonetheless, the circuit provides a pleasant way to see this old military reservation.

While in the vicinity, history buffs may also want to visit nearby **Fort Foote**, where Civil War earthworks are still discernible, and where two huge 15-inch Rodman guns remain. Directions from Fort Washington to Fort Foote are provided on page 294.

Fort Washington Park is open daily from 7:30 A.M. until sunset. The old fort itself, and the visitor center and museum at the former commandant's house, are open daily (except Christmas and New Year's Day) from 9 A.M. to 5 P.M. An admission fee is charged. Tours are provided on Saturdays and Sundays and by arrangement on weekdays. Dogs must be leashed. Off-road bicycling is prohibited. Please do not climb on the fort's parapets or gun emplacements. The park is managed by the National Park Service; telephone (301) 763-4600.

WRITTEN FROM MOUNT VERNON, September 26, 1798, to Benjamin Stoddert, Secretary of the Navy:

With respect to security against the attacks of an Enemy, no place can have advantages superior to the Federal City and Alexandria. Should proper works be erected on Diggs' point, (which you well know) at the junction of the Potomac and Piscataqua creek, it would not be in the power of all the navies in Europe to pass the place, and be afterward in a situation to do mischief above; for every vessel, in passing up the River, must, from the course of the Channel (and the channel is so narrow as to admit but one vessel . . . abreast) present her bows to that point long before she comes within gun shot of it, and continue in that direction under the point, from whence shot may be thrown upon her deck allmost in a perpendicular direction. Should she be so fortunate as to pass the works, she must expose her stern to the fire from them, as far as shot can reach. Thus exposed to be raked fore and aft, for such a distance, without once being able to bring her broadside to bear upon the fort, you can readily see how allmost impossible it will be for a vessel to pass this place; provided it be properly fortified and well supplied. And what makes it the more important, is, that it cannot be attacked by land with any prospect of success; for it has the River on one side, Piscataqua Creek on another side (each nearly a mile wide)and the opposite Banks very low, a deep Ravine (level with the Creek) on the third side from whence the height is almost if not altogether inaccessible. And a very narrow approach on the fourth side. In a word the works might be insulated, and one range of Batteries over another constructed sufficient for an hundred or more pieces of Cannon.

Such were George Washington's comments and recommendations concerning the location of a fort to guard the water approach to the nation's new capital, where the federal government was scheduled to take up residence in 1800. It was not Washington's first communication on the subject; since 1794 he had been urging the federal government to acquire and fortify Digges Point. He was, of course, closely familiar with the site, since it lay within view from his estate at Mount Vernon, which is located downstream across the Potomac River.

Washington was also personally acquainted with the Digges family. As a substantial Potomac planter and man of business, Washington often traded and visited at the Digges estate, called Warburton, where the plantation house stood on the plateau just northwest of the large, present-day parking lot. Like Washington, the Digges were prominent among the local gentry and engaged in commerce on a large scale. A letter to Washington dated April 7, 1775 states:

Dear Sir,

My Father and Mr. Hawkins will take four hundred Bushel of your salt, & I will copy a few Advertisements to be put up in this Neighborhood — your Vessel may come along side of our Warf, which I apprehend wou'd be more Convenient for the people that may want to purchase.

The family Join in Complts to all at Mt. Vernon, with
                                        Dear Sir
                                        Your Most Ob. Sert.
                                        Geo Digges

Washington's diaries record frequent visits at Mount Vernon by George Digges, whose nephew later inherited Warburton and was one of the few people whom Martha Washington invited to her husband's funeral. In his *Life of General Washington*, Washington Irving describes the ostentation of the Potomac planters, some of whom had English barges — or that is, large rowboats — and Irving mentions specifically "Mr. Digges, who always received Washington in his barge rowed by six Negroes, arrayed in a kind of uniform of check shirts and black velvet caps."

During Washington's lifetime, nothing came of his proposal for a fort at Digges Point, but in the first decade of the nineteenth century, the need for a system of coastal defense became more acute. Engaged in a protracted struggle with Napoleonic France, England adopted a policy of seizing American vessels that were trading with her enemy. British men-of-war also stopped American merchantmen and warships in coastal waters to remove sailors whom the British surmised to be deserters from their navy or merchant service. In response Congress in 1808 finally appropriated funds for construction of a number of forts to protect American seaports. For the defense of the Potomac, the federal government followed George Washington's recommendation and purchased part of the Digges estate, where a small earthwork mounting twenty-two guns and called variously Fort Warburton or Fort Washington was erected near the water. According to General James Wilkinson, who was one of the highest-ranking American officers of the day, "This work was seated at the foot of a steep acclivity, from the summit of which the garrison could have been driven out by musketry; but this height was protected by an octagonal blockhouse, built of brick, and of two stories altitude, which, being calculated against musketry only, could be knocked down by twelve-pounder . . . . "

Wilkinson was not alone in his low opinion of the fort. At the outbreak of the War of 1812, President Madison ordered an inspection by Major Pierre Charles L'Enfant, who had laid out the streets of Washington in 1791. L'Enfant reported that the works at Digges Point were dilapidated and the guns poorly maintained. Concluding that "the whole original design was bad, and it is therefore impossible to make a perfect work of it by any alterations," he recommended the construction of a new fort, or at least the addition of heavy guns to the old one.

Fiasco followed. The War Department did nothing to strengthen the

287

fort except to send a few men to the site to make repairs. Secretary of War John Armstrong argued that the rocks, shoals, and devious channel in the Potomac River would bar ascent by hostile ships, and that an invading army was unlikely to leave its ships at the mouth of the river and march inland forty miles. "The British would never be so mad as to make an attempt on Washington," Armstrong concluded, "and it is therefore totally unnecessary to make any preparations for its defense."

Armstrong's assertions were put to the test. In mid-August, 1814, a British squadron appeared in Chesapeake Bay, and on August 24 a British force of about 4,400 infantry entered Washington, having marched overland from Benedict on the Patuxent River. (For an account of the American attempt to stop the British at Bladensburg, see Chapter 31.) Another British force in six ships sailed up the Potomac and captured Alexandria, meeting no resistance at Digges Point, where the commander ordered the garrison to abandon the fort after spiking the guns and setting a fuse to the magazine. The action was described by Captain Gordon, commander of the British squadron:

> The following morning, August 27, 1814, to our great joy the wind became fair, and we made all sail up the river, which now assumed a more pleasing aspect. At five o'clock in the afternoon, Mount Vernon, the retreat of the illustrious Washington, opened to our view, and showed us for the first time, since we entered the Potomac, a gentleman's residence. Higher up the river on the opposite side Fort Washington appeared to our anxious eyes, and to our great satisfaction, it was considered assailable. A little before sunset the squadron anchored just out of the gunshot; the bomb vessels at once took up their positions to cover the frigates in the projected attack at daylight next morning and began throwing shells. The garrison, to our great surprise, retreated from the fort; and a short time afterwards, Fort Washington was blown up, which left the capital of America and the populous town of Alexandria open to the squadron, without a loss of a man. It was too late to ascertain whether this catastrophe was occasioned by one of our shells, or whether it had been blown up by the garrison; but the opinion was in favor of the latter. Still we are at a loss to account for such an extraordinary step. The position was good, and its capture would have cost us at least fifty men and more, had it been properly defended; besides an unfavorable wind and many other chances were in their favor, and we could have only destroyed it had we succeeded in the attempt.

After the British had burned the public buildings at Washington and seized ships, supplies, and even stores of tobacco at Alexandria, they returned to Chesapeake Bay. On September 8, Secretary of State James Monroe (who was also Acting Secretary of War after General Armstrong resigned in disgrace) ordered Major L'Enfant to rebuild the fort at Digges Point. For a few months worked progressed on a large

V-shaped water battery, but by the middle of October, when the British squadron left Chesapeake Bay and sailed for Jamaica, considerations of economy reasserted themselves. L'Enfant's intention to remove the old fort was questioned, and he was told to account for funds spent and to submit detailed plans. The temperamental French engineer took offense, and after refusing to comply with the requests of the War Department, he eventually was dismissed in September 1815. Lieutenant Colonel Walter K. Armistead took over responsibility for the project, and work continued in accordance with plans that he submitted. Constructed at a cost of more than $426,000, the fort finally was finished in 1824, although it remained without cannons.

Fort Washington was designed to defend against attack by wooden sailing ships armed with smoothbore cannons and mortars. The high, nearly vertical stone walls and brick parapets reflect the fact that smoothbore guns of the early nineteenth century were inaccurate and lacked penetrating power, especially at more than pointblank range. In any case, the fort's parapets, seven feet thick and providing a height from which shot could be fired far down the river, were substantially stronger than the hulls of warships, which were likely to be sunk or repelled before they could draw close or significantly damage the fort by prolonged bombardment. And even if the fort came under close attack, there was a lower level of casement chambers from which cannons could fire through gunports — although, actually, the casemates overlooking the river were never equipped with guns. A mantle of masonry and earth over the casemate chambers provided protection against explosive bombs lobbed by mortars. L'Enfant's V-shaped water battery, which lay below and outside the high masonry walls, provided a location from which cannons, firing at a low angle relative to the water, could skip shot across the surface of the river in order to hit ships near the waterline. (Most of the water battery was later destroyed to make room for concrete Battery White.)

Other features of the fort are the officers' quarters and soldiers' barracks facing the parade ground on the side farthest from the river. The small size of the barracks reflects the fort's small peacetime garrison of between 40 and 50 men — when it was garrisoned at all. The guardroom and the commandant's office flank the entrance archway, where there are two sets of massive gates and a drawbridge over the dry moat. The commandant's handsome and commodious house — now the visitor center — is located outside the fort on a hill opposite the entrance in order to allow the commandant's family to live at a remove from the somewhat coarse conditions within the fort.

In the 1840s the fort was strengthened. In order to protect against an attack by land from the rear, the height of the east wall was raised, and at its midpoint a caponierre — a small projecting work — was built from which cannons could rake the dry moat and wall to either side. Thirty large guns, with a range of more than a mile, were mounted behind the parapets on swiveling carriages.

Even so, by the time of the Civil War, Fort Washington's usefulness was greatly reduced by the development of ever-bigger, rifled artillery and steam-powered, armored warships. Compared to the old smooth-bores, the new guns had far greater range, accuracy, and penetrating power. Although rifled guns were not at first mounted on ships (and suffered from diminished accuracy when they were), they still raised the specter that works like Fort Washington could be reduced quickly to rubble from a great distance by siege guns transported by ships and placed temporarily on land, as in fact occurred during the Civil War at several massive masonry forts protecting Southern seaports. At Fort Washington there was the additional possibility that an armored ship could simply steam past the works at top speed, then shell Alexandria, Washington, and Georgetown at leisure.

Accordingly, during the course of the Civil War, Fort Foote was built on the Maryland side of the Potomac below Alexandria. This earthen fort, featuring low, sloping ramparts up to twenty feet thick, eventually mounted a formidable array of large rifles — including two 15-inch Rodman guns that still stand in the woods that have enveloped the fort. Fort Foote, however, was not completed until 1864, and until then Fort Washington was the capital's main defense against naval attack that never came. (For automobile directions from Fort Washington to Fort Foote, see page 294 at the end of the chapter, and for a discussion of the ring of earthen forts built around Washington during the Civil War, see Chapter 36.)

In 1872 Fort Washington was placed on unmanned caretaker status, as it had been during the 1850s. But in the 1890s, construction began on a group of new concrete gun emplacements dispersed around the old fort. The largest of the new batteries were armed with 10-inch rifles on disappearing carriages. When fired, the recoil caused these guns to sink back behind the revetment walls for loading, from which the guns were raised again for firing. Until 1921 the new works, still called Fort Washington, were the headquarters of the Defenses of the Potomac, which included minefields in the river that were controlled electronically from an outpost located atop the ramparts of the old fort. Other batteries of guns were located across the Potomac at Fort Hunt.

Eventually, these works in turn became obsolete. In 1939 the military reservation was turned over to the Department of the Interior, which built a Civilian Conservation Corps camp there. During World War II the site was returned to the Department of War, which moved

the Adjutant General's School for officer training to Fort Washington. In 1946 the fort reverted to the Department of the Interior and has been administered as a park ever since.

≈　　　≈　　　≈　　　≈

AUTOMOBILE DIRECTIONS: Fort Washington Park is located south of Washington on the Maryland side of the Potomac River. (See the corner panel on **Map 34** opposite.)

To Fort Washington from Interstate 495 (the Capital Beltway): Leave the Beltway at Exit 3A for Route 210 South (the Indian Head Highway). This exit is located not far from the Wilson Bridge — and if you are coming from the direction of the bridge, you can also take Exit 2 then 2A. Follow Route 210 South about 4 miles to Fort Washington Road. Turn right onto Fort Washington Road and go 3.3 miles to the entrance to Fort Washington National Park. Continue into the park and past roads intersecting from left and right. Follow the main road to a large central parking lot near the old fort and visitor center.

≈　　　≈　　　≈　　　≈

WALKING: The 3-mile route described below is shown on **Map 34** opposite.

From the main parking lot, follow a paved path past concrete Battery Decatur and an observation tower to the visitor center, which occupies the former commandant's house. From there continue to the old fort.

After touring the old fort, return from the main gain for about 80 yards toward the visitor center, then turn left downhill on a wide paved path leading to the water's edge. Continue left to a wooden lighthouse on a point of land.

The River Trail starts about 80 yards inland from the point of land below the fort. With the water on your right, follow the River Trail along the water's edge. Continue as the path narrows and crosses small streams at the mouths of several ravines. Eventually, the trail reaches a concrete trench where targets were mounted for rifle practice. Firing was done from a point of land about 500 yards back along the water's edge.

Continue past the concrete trench. With the water toward the right, follow the trail as it ascends along the bluff. At the

MAP 34 — Fort Washington Park and Fort Foote

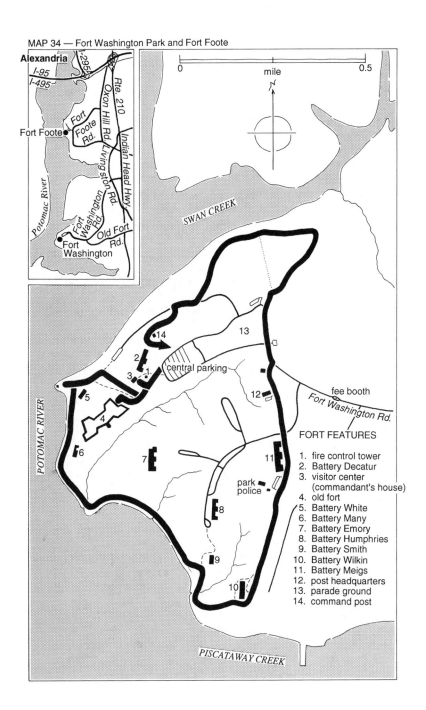

Alexandria

I-95
I-495

Rte. 210

Oxon Hill Rd.

Fort Foote Rd.

Fort Foote●

Indian Head Hwy

Livingston Rd.

Potomac River

Fort Washington Rd.

Old Fort Rd.

●Fort Washington

0   mile   0.5

N

SWAN CREEK

POTOMAC RIVER

●14

2
3   1
central parking

5

13

12

fee booth

Fort Washington Rd.

4

6

7

11

park police

8

9

10

PISCATAWAY CREEK

FORT FEATURES

1. fire control tower
2. Battery Decatur
3. visitor center
   (commandant's house)
4. old fort
5. Battery White
6. Battery Many
7. Battery Emory
8. Battery Humphries
9. Battery Smith
10. Battery Wilkin
11. Battery Meigs
12. post headquarters
13. parade ground
14. command post

293

top of the slope, pass a trail intersecting from the left. Descend steeply, then climb again. (Use the trail farther from the water.) At the top of the bluff, follow the trail away from the water, through a grassy clearing, and to the right around a low, overgrown mound (actually an earth mantle on the front side of Battery Wilkin). Continue along an asphalt road with houses on the right.

Emerge from the woods near the brick park police headquarters. Follow the road past a parking lot on the left. (Here and at other points where the route follows roads, walk on the grass along the left-hand shoulder to minimize the risk of being hit by car approaching from behind.) Pass to the right of Battery Meigs, which mounted 12-inch mortars. At a T-intersection, continue straight across the grass and to the right of the former headquarters. Follow an asphalt drive to the right of another building. At a junction with the main park road, bear half-left, then continue straight past a road intersecting from the left. Follow the main road past the former parade ground on the left.

Where the road curves sharply left, continue straight across the grass to a gravel road leading half-right downhill into the woods. (This gravel road is to the right of a grassy swath that also leads downhill.)

Follow the gravel road downhill, then to the left. Continue past the water at Swan Creek, then gradually uphill. At a T-intersection with a paved road, turn right. With caution, follow the left shoulder of the road 180 yards, then turn left onto a dirt track that climbs through the woods. Follow the path uphill past a brick command post on the left. Continue as the path curves left and emerges from the woods at the central parking lot.

≈　　　≈　　　≈　　　≈

AUTOMOBILE DIRECTIONS FROM FORT WASHINGTON TO FORT FOOTE: Fort Washington and Fort Foote are both shown on the corner panel of **Map 34** on page 293.

After leaving Fort Washington, follow Fort Washington Road 3.0 miles to an intersection at a traffic light with Livingston Road. Turn left onto Livingston Road and go 1.1 miles to a crossroads with Old Fort Road. Turn left and go only 0.5 mile, then turn left at a traffic light onto Fort Foote Road. Go 1.6 miles, then turn left into Fort Foote Park. Follow the gravel road 0.2 mile, then park on the left where signs will guide you to the remains of Fort Foote.

If, when you leave Fort Foote, you want to return to the Capital Beltway, turn left out the fort drive, then left again at an intersection with Oxon Hill Road, which will take you to Route 210 where it crosses the Capital Beltway.

22

THEODORE ROOSEVELT ISLAND

Walking — 1 or 2 miles (1.6 or 3.2 kilometers). Roosevelt Island is located in the Potomac River opposite the Kennedy Center for the Performing Arts. This densely forested, 88-acre retreat provides nearly complete visual isolation from the surrounding city. As shown on **Map 35** on page 303, a footbridge crosses from the Virginia shore to the Roosevelt Memorial. A system of more or less parallel trails provides the opportunity to walk up and down the island without retracing your steps. From the island's northern end, there are dramatic views upstream and across the river to Georgetown.

Roosevelt Island is open daily from 8 A.M. until dusk. Bicycles are prohibited and dogs must be leashed. The island is managed by the National Park Service and is administered from the office of the George Washington Memorial Parkway; telephone (703) 285-2598.

THEODORE ROOSEVELT ISLAND is today a small wilderness dedicated to the President who championed conservation and the rights of the "little man," but in the early nineteenth century it was called Analostan Island and was the landscaped and intensively cultivated estate and summer home of slaveowner John Mason, a wealthy merchant and banker. Mason's wharf and warehouse and many of his other business enterprises were located in Georgetown, and his winter residence was just across Rock Creek where Columbia Hospital is now located. Yet in the fashion of the times, he adopted as a sobriquet the name of his country seat: he was John Mason of Analostan Island. His father was George Mason of Gunston Hall, author of the Virginia Declaration of Rights and the foremost advocate for the federal Bill of Rights. (For more on George Mason, Gunston Hall, and other Mason properties that have become present-day parks and wildlife refuges, see Chapters 17 and 18.)

Wealthy from birth, John Mason was a man of many parts. He engaged in foreign trade, particularly with France, where he had lived for a period. In 1798 he became president of the Bank of Columbia. He was an associate of President Jefferson, who appointed him a brigadier general in the Washington militia — a position that was primarily a social distinction. He was also a Superintendent of Indian Trade. In 1815 he took over Henry Foxall's iron foundry, at that time one of the largest businesses in the District of Columbia, but which gradually declined under Mason's ownership (see Chapter 24). He also served as president of the nearly defunct Patowmack Canal Company until it was superseded by the Chesapeake and Ohio Canal Company in 1828. And, aside from his property and businesses in Georgetown, he owned a plantation of two thousand acres on the Virginia shore opposite his island estate, both of which he had inherited from his father.

John Mason's grandfather, Colonel George Mason III, had purchased the Potomac island in 1717, and for the rest of the century it was known as Mason's Island. The previous owners were heirs of Captain Randolph Brandt, a seafaring man who had called the place "Barbadoes." Before Brandt's tenure it had been My Lord's Island in honor of Charles Calvert, Lord Baltimore, the second colonial proprietor of Maryland. (The island was part of Maryland prior to the creation of the District of Columbia.) A map from 1673 shows the island as Anacostien Isle. Other contemporary variant spellings were Antecostin and Analostan, supposedly corruptions of the name of the Anacostanks or Nacotchtankes, an Indian tribe that had a village nearby.

Not only has the island's name changed over the years, but so have its size and shape. The island has been enlarged by the deposit of sediments carried downstream by the Potomac River and Rock Creek. The sediments settle where the current slackens in the tidewater of the Potomac estuary, particularly in the slight eddy downstream from the core of bedrock at the island's northern end. Successive maps document the gradual deposit of a long, low arm of alluvial soil along the eastern side of the island to enclose a marsh and swamp.

George Mason IV and his son John were alive to the possibility that a bridge from Georgetown to Virginia across the island would greatly increase the value of their land, but nothing came of the proposal. In the absence of a bridge, the Masons profited from a ferry that they owned. Chartered by the Virginia General Assembly in 1748 to replace an earlier ferry, Mason's Ferry ran between Virginia and Georgetown. In 1805 a causeway was built from the Virginia shore to Analostan Island, and the western terminus of the ferry was relocated at the island's upper end.

The main purpose of the causeway, however, was to serve as a dam and thus concentrate the river's current in the channel next to Georgetown. It was hoped that this would flush out the accumulated sediments that threatened to prevent deep-draft vessels from reaching the city, since at that time Georgetown was a thriving port with much to lose if it could not accommodate large ships. Authorized by Congress and by the aldermen of Georgetown, the causeway was built over the opposition of Virginia, which favored its own port of Alexandria. The cost of the causeway — $24,000 — was raised by a tax levied on Mason's Ferry and on vessels using the shipping channel. In 1811 an observer noted, however, that "the Georgetown channel has been but little deepened by the erection of this causeway." The causeway was destroyed by a flood in 1852, rebuilt in 1854, and finally abandoned in 1877 after another flood. As for the ferry, operations ceased shortly after the Washington and Alexandria Aqueduct was converted to a bridge at the time of the Civil War. (The aqueduct carried the C&O Canal across the Potomac so that the canal could continue to Alexandria; two arches of the aqueduct still remain just west of the Key Bridge in Georgetown.)

Following his marriage in 1796, John Mason began to construct an elegant brick mansion on the island. The house, for which he revived the romantic name Analostan, was in the classical style — at that time a novelty in America — and its principal room had large, arched windows. Robert King's 1818 map of Washington locates the house about two-thirds of the way down the island at approximately its highest point. The causeway from the Virginia shore crossed to the island's northwestern corner. A tree-lined driveway ran straight down the island's spine past orchards and cultivated fields on both sides. South of the house were gardens and orchards, through which a walk ran straight to the island's southern tip.

A description of the estate was provided by David B. Warden, a visitor from abroad in the spring of 1811.

Analostan Island, the seat of General Mason, is situated in the river Potomac, opposite Georgetown, and contains nearly seventy acres. A flat boat, of a rude construction, awkwardly impelled by an oar, placed near each extremity, affords a safe conveyance between the island and the main land, a distance of about two hundred yards. . . .

I can never forget how delighted I was with my first visit to this island. The amiable ladies whom I had the pleasure to accompany, left their carriage at Georgetown, and we walked to the mansion-house under a delicious shade. The blossoms of the cherry, apple, and peach trees, of the hawthorn and aromatic shrubs, filled the air with their fragrance, We found Mrs. M. at home, in the midst of her family, composed of nine children. Twin boys, of a healthy mien, and so like each other as scarcely to be distinguished, were tumbling on the carpet of the saloon, full of joy and merriment. Mrs. M. has so youthful an appearance, that a stranger might readily suppose her to be the sister of her daughter rather than her mother.

The house, of a simple and neat form, is situated near that side of the island which commands a view of the Potomac, the President's House, Capitol, and other buildings. The garden, the sides of which are washed by the waters of the river, is ornamented with a variety of trees and shrubs, and, in the midst, there is a lawn with a beautiful verdure.

According to Warden, Mason cultivated yellow Chinese cotton and a species of maize, "the leaves of which, of a deep purple colour, are employed as a dye." The island was irrigated. "By means of an hydraulic machine," Warden noted, "water may be easily raised from the river, and conducted by pipes to every part of the surface."

In the mid-1820s Anne Royall, another traveling journalist, described the island, stating that the "part adjacent to the house is appropriated to flowers, shrubs, grapes, and every rare plant, consisting of the various species of the four quarters of the globe. A great part of the garden, some acres, consists of culinary vegetables. A row of trees leading down to the river divided the garden."

At the semiannual fair of the Columbian Agricultural Society held in Georgetown, Mrs. Mason frequently won prizes for the products of the estate. In May 1810, she won "Premium 6, for the best piece of cotton cloth suitable for pantaloons or small clothes, not less than ten yards." John took honors at the fair held on May 15, 1811: "Premium 1 — to the value of sixty dollars; for the best two tooth ram lamb of the fine wooled breed; adjudged to General John Mason, of Analostan Island, District of Columbia; for his seven-eighths blooded merino ram, Potomac Chief." The following year John Mason won again with Golden Fleece.

The Masons and their children lived on the island during the warmer months. One son was James Murray Mason, later a United States senator and, during the Civil War, the Confederate commissioner to Great Britain, where he strove unsuccessfully to get diplomatic recognition and intervention on behalf of the South. On the way to England, Mason and John Slidell, the commissioner to France, were at the center of the *Trent* Affair when they were removed from a British mail steamer by a Union warship and temporarily detained. James Mason's daughter wrote that her father, aunts, and uncles recalled their childhood summers at Analostan with great pleasure, and that it was "a favorite resort for the young, the gay, and the fashionable."

One social occasion is described by Mr. Warden:

In July, 1811, Mrs. M. gave a rural dance to the friends and acquaintances of her son, at the eve of his departure for France. Though the weather had been excessively warm during the day, in the evening there was a delicious breeze. The young people danced on the lawn. Tea, coffee, cakes, fresh and preserved fruits, were presented to the guests, who sat or walked about conversing, or silently admiring the dance under the shade of trees, illuminated by lamps, which were half obscured by the bright light of the moon. The summer-house is shaded by oak and linden-trees, the coolness and tranquillity of which invite to contemplation. The refreshing breezes of the Potomac, and the gentle murmuring of its waters against the rocks, the warbling of birds, and the mournful aspect of weeping-willows, inspire a thousand various sensations.

The Masons continued at the island until 1833, when financial difficulty forced them to relinquish it. After a disastrous land speculation, Mason had mortgaged the island in 1826 as security for a loan of $28,560, which he did not repay. According to another (and more face-saving) account, the mosquitoes that bred in the growing swamp and in the slackwater behind the causeway were thought to be a menace to the family's health, so they moved their summer residence to Mason's Virginia plantation. In any case, the new owners leased part of the island for public gatherings and used the rest for commercial gardening of vegetables and fruit. A dancing pavilion was erected. During the Civil War, when a Union field hospital and camp were established on the island, the buildings and gardens deteriorated. Among the troops that camped on the island was the 54th Massachusetts Regiment of African-American volunteers. In the 1870s and '80s, the island was leased to the Columbia Athletic Club, which constructed a running track, ball fields, tennis courts, and a grandstand. A photograph from this period shows the Mason house in a very neglected condition. Another photograph taken from the newly completed Washington Monument in 1885 shows the island to be mostly fields with a few clumps of trees. In 1906 the house was gutted by fire, and during the following decades parts of the island became choked with brush.

In 1931 the Theodore Roosevelt Memorial Association purchased the island and gave it to the federal government as a tribute to the former president. A *Washington Post* article from July 3, 1935, carried the headline "CCC Boys Transform Roosevelt Island From Jungle to Park." Since the island was supposed to be a memorial to Roosevelt's love of the American wilderness, the remaining walls of the house were torn down. Vegetation not native to the region was removed, and about thirty thousand trees typical of a climax forest were planted. The Roosevelt Memorial was officially dedicated in 1967.

≈   ≈   ≈   ≈

METRO: The Rosslyn Metrorail station (Blue and Orange lines) is near Roosevelt Island. Turn left (downhill) out the station and follow Moore Street one block to 19th Street. Turn right downhill and follow 19th Street one short block to and across Lynn Street. Turn left and follow Lynn Street over Interstate 66 and across Lee Highway, then turn right onto the paved Custis Trail, which soon leads downhill and across the George Washington Memorial Parkway to the Roosevelt Island parking lot.

Another possibility is to take Metrobus 80 to the Kennedy Center for the Performing Arts. (See **Map 35** opposite.) Once you are at the Kennedy Center, you will have to walk three-quarters of a mile across the Roosevelt Bridge to reach the island — but after all, walking is what this book is all about, and the views from the bridge are excellent. From the main entrance of the Kennedy Center, walk south along the sidewalk opposite the front of the building. (The building should be on your right.) Just beyond the end of the building, bear half-left onto a narrow paved path. With caution, cross an expressway exit ramp and follow the sidewalk across the Theodore Roosevelt Memorial Bridge. Bear right at the far end of the bridge and follow the sidewalk and then a path to the pedestrian bridge leading to Roosevelt Island.

Telephone (202) 637-7000 for current Metro information, including schedules, routes, and connections.

≈   ≈   ≈   ≈

AUTOMOBILE DIRECTIONS: Theodore Roosevelt Island is located in the Potomac River across from the Kennedy Center for the Performing Arts and just upstream from the Roosevelt Bridge. (See **Map 35** opposite.) **The parking lot for Roosevelt Island is accessible only from the northbound lanes of the George Washington Memorial Parkway.** Several avenues of approach that will put you onto the parkway's northbound lanes are described below.

To Roosevelt Island from downtown Washington: Follow Constitution Avenue (Route 50) west along the Mall and across the Roosevelt Bridge. As you cross the bridge, move to the far right lane, then exit to the right onto the George

MAP 35 — Roosevelt Island

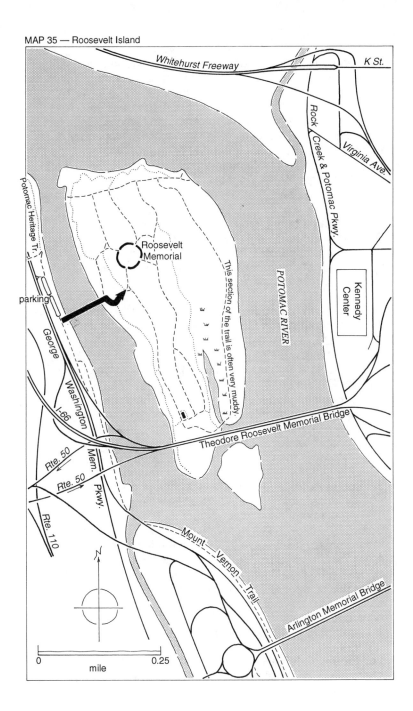

Washington Memorial Parkway — then exit again almost immediately for the Roosevelt Island parking lot on the right.

Another approach from downtown Washington is via 14th Street south to Interstate 395 South. As soon as you cross the Potomac River, take the exit for Arlington National Cemetery. Follow the George Washington Memorial Parkway north 2 miles (stay right in order to remain on the parkway past the exit for Arlington National Cemetery and Memorial Bridge), then exit to the right for the Roosevelt Island parking lot.

To return to downtown Washington, see page 307.

To Roosevelt Island from Interstate 495 (the Capital Beltway): Several major roads and highways that approach Roosevelt Island from different directions are accessible from the Beltway at different exits. These routes are described in turn in the next four sections.

To Roosevelt Island from the south on Route 1 and the George Washington Memorial Parkway: Leave the Capital Beltway at Exit 1 (or Exit 1B from the Outer Loop) for Route 1 North and follow it through Alexandria. After about 1.5 miles — and just before Route 1 crosses a bridge toward the left — fork right for Slaters Lane. Go 0.4 mile, then turn left onto the George Washington Memorial Parkway. Follow the parkway 5.9 miles (taking care to stay right in order to remain on the parkway past the exit for Memorial Bridge), then exit to the right for the Roosevelt Island parking lot.

To return via the GWM Parkway southbound, see page 307.

To Roosevelt Island from the southwest on Interstate 395: I-395 is accessible from the Capital Beltway at Exit 4B. (This is the same interchange where I-95 from Richmond reaches the Beltway.) Follow I-395 North toward Washington. Just before the Potomac River, leave I-395 from the left lane at Exit 11 for Arlington Memorial Bridge. From the bottom of the ramp, follow the George Washington Memorial Parkway north 2.2 miles (taking care to stay right in order to remain on the parkway past the exit for Memorial Bridge), then exit to the right for the Roosevelt Island parking lot.

To return to I-395, see page 307.

To Roosevelt Island from the west on Interstate 66: This approach involves some slight rigmarole toward the end

because of the fact that there is no direct way to get off I-66 onto the George Washington Memorial Parkway. What I recommend doing — as described in detail below — is to cross the Roosevelt Bridge into Washington, and then immediately turn around in order to join the GWM Parkway heading north.

Follow I-66 East toward Washington. (From the Inner Loop of the Capital Beltway, you can get onto I-66 East at Exit 9B; from the Beltway's Outer Loop, you can get onto I-66 East at Exit 12A.) Eventually, I-66 will put you onto the Roosevelt Bridge into Washington. At the far end of the bridge, bear slightly right for Route 50 East (Constitution Avenue). Go only to the second traffic light, then turn left onto 22nd Street. At a T-intersection with C Street, turn left again. At a T-intersection with 23rd Street, turn left yet again, then turn right onto Constitution Avenue and go back across the Roosevelt Bridge. As you cross the bridge, move to the far right lane, then exit to the right onto the George Washington Memorial Parkway — then exit again almost immediately for the Roosevelt Island parking lot on the right.

To return to I-66, see page 307.

To Roosevelt Island from the northwest on the George Washington Memorial Parkway: This approach involves some slight rigmarole toward the end because of the fact that the exit for Roosevelt Island is accessible only from the parkway's northbound lanes. What I recommend doing — as described in detail below — is to exit for the Roosevelt Bridge into Washington, and then immediately turn around in order to rejoin the parkway heading north.

The George Washington Memorial Parkway is accessible from the Capital Beltway at Exit 14 near the Virginia end of the American Legion Bridge across the Potomac River. Follow the parkway toward Washington. After passing the exit for the Key Bridge, take the next exit for the Roosevelt Bridge, which leads across the Potomac River into Washington. At the far end of the bridge, bear slightly right for Route 50 East (Constitution Avenue). Go only to the second traffic light, then turn left onto 22nd Street. At a T-intersection with C Street, turn left again. At a T-intersection with 23rd Street, turn left yet again, then turn right onto Constitution Avenue and go back across the Roosevelt Bridge. As you cross the bridge, move to the far right lane, then exit to the right onto the George Washington Memorial Parkway — then exit again almost immediately for the Roosevelt Island parking lot on the right.

Leaving Roosevelt Island: There is only one way to go when you leave the parking lot, and that is northwest on the George Washington Memorial Parkway. If you want to return to Washington, or to go south to I-395 or Route 1, or west out I-66, follow the parkway only 0.8 mile. Take the first exit (it is from the left lane) for Spout Run Parkway, and then do one of the following:

To return to Washington, follow Spout Run Parkway 0.5 mile uphill, then make a U-turn to the left in a lane provided for that purpose. Once you are back on the George Washington Memorial Parkway, take the exit for the Roosevelt Bridge or Interstate 395 North.

For I-395 South or Route 1 South, follow Spout Run Parkway 0.5 mile uphill, then make a U-turn to the left in a lane provided for that purpose. Once you are back on the George Washington Memorial Parkway, go 2 miles to the exit for I-395 South or continue on the parkway to Slaters Lane and Route 1 in Alexandria.

For I-66 West, follow Spout Run Parkway 0.9 mile, then turn right onto Route 29 South (Lee Highway). Go only 0.2 mile, then turn left up the entrance ramp onto I-66 West.

≈   ≈   ≈   ≈

WALKING: Roosevelt Island is shown on **Map 35** on page 303.

From the parking lot, cross the pedestrian bridge to Roosevelt Island. At the far end of the bridge, bear right and follow the main path uphill and through a four-way intersection. Continue to the Roosevelt Memorial.

From the memorial, explore the rest of the island. Note, however, that the easternmost trail becomes wet, muddy, and slippery — in short, altogether disagreeable — after rain or during periods of high water or thaw.

23

POTOMAC HERITAGE TRAIL

including Turkey Run Park, Fort Marcy, Potomac Overlook Regional Park, and the Key-Chain Circuit

Walking — up to 10 miles (16 kilometers) one way.

As conceived by planners, the **Potomac Heritage Trail** will extend along the Virginia side of the Potomac River from Quantico at least as far upstream as Harpers Ferry. At present, however, the trail has been completed only in the vicinity of Washington. The paved Mount Vernon Trail (see Chapter 19) is part of the Potomac Heritage Trail. And immediately upstream from the Mount Vernon Trail is the 10-mile footpath that is the subject of this chapter.

As shown on **Map 36** on page 316, this part of the Potomac Heritage Trail stretches between Roosevelt Island and Interstate 495 (the Capital Beltway) near Langley. For most of this distance, the riverside footpath follows a narrow shelf of land below the high cliffs and bluffs of the Potomac Palisades. For about 3 miles at the middle, however, the path runs near the George Washington Memorial Parkway in order to avoid privately-owned land and impassable cliffs bordering the river. Although the detour along the parkway is unfortunate, it is only a small segment of what is otherwise a very attractive and at times even spectacular trail. And in any case, the digression from the river has the compensating virtue of leading along Pimmit Run and past **Fort Marcy**, the best-preserved of Washington's earthen Civil War forts. (For a discussion of the Civil War forts, see Chapter 36.)

Although most of the Potomac Heritage Trail is not difficult, parts are rugged and rocky. The main problem is car logistics — or that is, how to start at one end, yet have a car at the other end when you are done. Different permutations for car shuttles are discussed briefly on page 313 in the automobile directions. Walking directions start on page 318.

The Potomac Heritage Trail is open from dawn to dusk. Dogs must be leashed; bicycles are prohibited. Marked with blue blazes, the trail is maintained by the Potomac Appalachian Trail Club and administered by the National Park Service; for the park service telephone (703) 285-2598. The trail is not recommended in wet, snowy, or icy weather, when the rocks can be slippery. During periods of high water, parts of the trail may be flooded. Do not under any circumstances wade or swim in the river, where there are strong currents. Nor, obviously, should you ford tributary streams if they are swollen with stormwater runoff.

As an alternative to hiking the entire trail in one day, another possibility is to take it in sections. **Turkey Run Park**, shown on the top panel of Map 36, includes the trail's upper section. Of the several footpaths at Turkey Run Park, the riverside Potomac Heritage Trail is by far the most attractive and dramatic, so I recommend simply walking up and down along the river, going 1 mile upstream to the cascade at Dead Run and 1.5 miles downstream to the warning signs for the Little Falls Dam. Turkey Run Park is open daily from dawn until dusk. Automobile directions to Turkey Run Park start on page 314. The park is managed by the National Park Service; telephone (703) 285-2601.

Potomac Overlook Regional Park, shown on **Map 37B** on page 317, provides access to the lower section of the Potomac Heritage Trail via a footpath — somewhat rough in places — that follows Donaldson Run to its confluence with the Potomac. From there the Potomac Heritage Trail leads upstream 0.5 mile to Gulf Branch, where the path climbs to the George Washington Memorial Parkway. Downstream from Donaldson Run, the Potomac Heritage Trail passes below high cliffs and — after 3 miles — reaches Roosevelt Island.

Potomac Overlook Regional Park has an attractive, though not very extensive, trail network of its own. There is also an excellent nature center. The park is open daily from dawn until dusk. The nature center is open Tuesday through Saturday 10 A. M. to 5 P.M.; Sunday 1 P.M. to 5 P.M.; and is also usually open Monday holidays. Dogs must be leashed. Automobile directions to Potomac Overlook Regional Park start on page 315. The park is managed by the Northern Virginia Regional Park Authority; telephone (703) 528-5406 for information, including scheduled programs and events.

Finally, **Map 37C** on page 317 shows the 9-mile **Key-Chain Circuit**. This outstanding loop follows the Potomac Heritage

Trail upstream from Roosevelt Island to Chain Bridge, then crosses the river to Maryland and returns downstream via the C&O Canal towpath to the Key Bridge. Directions start on page 320.

UPSTREAM FROM WASHINGTON as far as the Capital Beltway, glimpses of the dramatic scenery along the Potomac River can occasionally be had from the C&O Canal towpath, the George Washington Memorial Parkway, and the Chain Bridge. But for a really close look at this stretch of river, the best vantage is provided by the Potomac Heritage Trail along the Virginia bluffs and bank.

The heights along the Potomac River immediately upstream from Washington represent the eastern edge of the Piedmont Plateau. The cliffs and steep bluffs above the river and the rapid descent of the tributary ravines reflect the hard igneous and metamorphic bedrock through which the river flows immediately before it spills out at Washington onto the soft clay, sand, and gravel of the Coastal Plain.

In 1608 on a voyage of exploration from Jamestown, which had been established the year before, Captain John Smith ascended the Potomac. He described the river as being thick with fish, so much so "that for want of a net we attempted to catch them with a frying-pan, but we found it a bad instrument to catch fish with." Smith and his crew took their small boat as far upstream as they could, presumably to Little Falls above the present-day Chain Bridge.

In the Algonquinian language (the basic Indian tongue of the Atlantic seaboard) Potomac means "something brought," "where something is brought," or more freely, "trading place." Even before permanent English settlements and outposts were established in the Chesapeake region during the early years of the seventeenth century, the Indians used the river corridor to transport goods for trade among themselves. Captain Smith noted that local Indians already had European hatchets and knives and pieces of iron and brass acquired from northern tribes, who, in their turn, had got them from French fur traders in Canada and the Ohio Valley. Smith and his companions secured venison, bear meat, and corn from the Indians, and also traded for beaver, otter, marten, and other furs.

Thereafter the English at Jamestown periodically sent ships to trade for furs with the Piscataway Indians along the upper reaches of the tidal Potomac in Maryland. The Piscataway were friendlier than Indians of

311

the Powhatan Confederacy in Virginia — and friendlier also than the Susquehannocks, Senecas, and other northern tribes that sometimes raided the southern Indians. Often, too, the English bought corn from the Piscataway to supplement the colonists' meager harvests. Even after Jamestown was well established, the English purchased corn for export to other New World settlements and to Europe. Smith relates that in 1619 Iapazous, King of Patawomeck, "came to *James* town, to desire two ships to come trade in his River, for a more plentifull yeere of Corne had not beene in a long time." Eventually, however, as the region was overrun by tens of thousands of English settlers, the tidewater Indians were decimated by famine, disease, and sporadic fighting, both with the settlers and with hostile tribes that vied for control of trade with the English. Some tidewater Indians regrouped in villages that lacked a tribal structure and that were often located on inferior land that the white settlers did not want. Many Indian clans and fragments of tribes, however, moved inland beyond the frontier, where they wandered, dwindled, and vanished.

During the seventeenth century, good cultivable land along the Potomac was patented by English tobacco planters in large and small parcels, but settlement did not at first extend far inland or upriver above tidewater, since water carriage was the chief means of transportation. Early each winter or spring, ships from Great Britain ascended Chesapeake Bay and its tidal rivers, sailing from one plantation landing to the next to trade clothing, tools, and other manufactured goods for tobacco packed in large barrels called hogsheads. Only as waterfront land became unavailable did settlers — former indentured servants and younger sons of established landowners — begin to penetrate the interior. As farming spread to the hinterland during the late seventeenth and early eighteenth centuries, merchants and tobacco factors near the head of navigation on the Potomac built stores and warehouses, some of which provided the nucleus for towns that were established later, such as Alexandria, founded in 1749, and Georgetown, platted in 1751. At the mouth of Pimmit Run near Little Falls (the absolute head of navigation), Thomas Lee built an official tobacco inspection warehouse in 1742, and by 1794 there was a gristmill, brewery, distillery, and cooper and blacksmith shops, and later a woolen factory and paper mill. None of these structures remain. In 1797 the merchants of Georgetown erected a bridge across the Potomac at Little Falls in order to attract trade from Virginia via the Georgetown-Leesburg Road. After this bridge and a subsequent one were destroyed by floods, a chain suspension bridge with a 128-foot span was constructed in 1808. It was mainly to guard the Chain Bridge during the Civil War that the Federal army built nearby Fort Marcy, connected to other forts in Arlington by the Military Road.

Downstream from the Chain Bridge — as the present-day structure is still called, although it is a conventional bridge built in 1936 — the Potomac Heritage Trail occasionally passes below cliffs where stone was quarried, some of it used in Washington buildings. Three large, rusty boilers are remnants of one nineteenth-century quarry operation.

≈ ≈ ≈ ≈

METRO: The Rosslyn Metrorail station (Blue and Orange lines) is near Roosevelt Island at the southern end of the Potomac Heritage Trail. Turn left (downhill) out the station and follow Moore Street one block to 19th Street. Turn right downhill and follow 19th Street one short block to and across Lynn Street. Turn left and follow Lynn Street over Interstate 66 and across Lee Highway, then turn right onto the paved Custis Trail, which soon leads downhill and across the George Washington Memorial Parkway to the Roosevelt Island parking lot. From the parking lot, the blue-blazed Potomac Heritage Trail leads upstream along the river, as discussed starting on page 319.

≈ ≈ ≈ ≈

AUTOMOBILE DIRECTIONS: The Potomac Heritage Trail follows the Virginia side of the Potomac River upstream from Washington. (See **Map 36** on page 316.) The trail's upper end is at **Live Oak Drive** within sight of the Capital Beltway's American Legion Bridge over the Potomac. The Trail's lower end is at **Roosevelt Island** opposite the Kennedy Center for the Performing Arts. At intervals between these two points (which are 10 miles apart) are **Turkey Run Park**, **Fort Marcy**, and **Potomac Overlook Regional Park**. Directions to all these places are provided below.

If you plan to walk the entire trail in one day, you presumably will want to arrange a **car shuttle**. Obviously, a shuttle involves either two cars and two driver-hikers, or a driver who drops you off at the start (after you have left your car at the end) or who simply meets you at the end. To navigate your shuttle, use Map 36. You may also want to refer to the following automobile directions.

To Live Oak Drive from Interstate 495 (the Capital Beltway): Although you can drive to the upper end of the Potomac Heritage Trail at Live Oak Drive, parking is not permitted. For the nearest parking lot, refer to Scotts Run Nature Preserve in the next section below.

For Live Oak Drive, leave the Beltway at Exit 13 for Route 193 (Georgetown Pike). From the top of the exit ramp, follow Route 193 East a very short distance to a crossroads with Balls Hill Road. Turn left onto Balls Hill Road. Go 0.4 mile, then turn left onto Live Oak Drive and follow it across the Beltway. Go 0.8 mile to the cul-de-sac at the end of Live Oak Drive. The trailhead is on the right.

To Scotts Run Nature Preserve from Interstate 495 (the Capital Beltway): This is the nearest parking lot to the upper end of the Potomac Heritage Trail at Live Oak Drive.

Leave the Beltway at Exit 13 for Route 193 (Georgetown Pike). From the top of the exit ramp, follow Route 193 West just 0.2 mile, then turn right into a small parking lot for Scotts Run Nature Preserve.

From this parking lot, you must walk 1.5 miles to the Potomac Heritage trailhead at the end of Live Oak Drive. Although it shows a different excursion, **Map 20** on page 178 may help you to navigate through the woods to Live Oak Drive, which you should then follow to its end. There is no sidewalk along the road, so walk on the left, facing oncoming vehicles, and step off the road as they approach.

To Roosevelt Island: The lower end of the Potomac Heritage Trail is at the parking lot for Roosevelt Island, off the north-bound lanes of the George Washington Memorial Parkway. For directions to Roosevelt Island, please turn to page 302.

≈   ≈   ≈   ≈

TURKEY RUN PARK: Turkey Run Park, through which the northernmost section of the Potomac Heritage Trail passes, is shown on the top panel of **Map 36** on page 316. From Parking Area C-1, a yellow-blazed trail leads steeply downhill to the blue-blazed Potomac Heritage Trail along the river.

To Turkey Run Park from Interstate 495 (the Capital Beltway): Leave the Beltway at Exit 14 for the George Washington Memorial Parkway toward Washington. Follow the parkway about 1.5 miles to the exit for Turkey Run Park. Pass under the parkway, then turn left into Turkey Run Park. After only 0.1 mile, turn left into the first parking lot, Area C-1.

To Turkey Run Park via the northbound lanes of the George Washington Memorial Parkway: The exit for Turkey Run Park is located about 12 miles upriver from Alexandria, 7.1 miles upriver from the Roosevelt Bridge, and 1.8 miles upriver from Chain Bridge Road. After exiting from the parkway for Turkey Run Park, go only 0.2 mile, then turn right into the park itself. After just 0.1 mile, turn left into the first parking lot, Area C-1.

≈   ≈   ≈   ≈

FORT MARCY: As shown on **Map 36** on page 316, the middle section of the Potomac Heritage Trail passes Fort Marcy. By automobile, Fort Marcy is accessible only from the northbound lanes of the George Washington Memorial Parkway 4.3 miles north of the Roosevelt Bridge.

≈   ≈   ≈   ≈

POTOMAC OVERLOOK REGIONAL PARK: The trails of Potomac Overlook Regional Park are shown on **Map 37B** on page 317. From the end of the road north of the nature center, a brown-blazed trail leads to Donaldson Run, where in turn a yellow-blazed trail leads downstream to the blue-blazed Potomac Heritage Trail along the river.

To Potomac Overlook Regional Park from the northbound lanes of the George Washington Memorial Parkway: Leave the parkway at the exit for Spout Run about 1 mile upriver from the Roosevelt Bridge. (The exit is from the left lane.) Follow Spout Run Parkway uphill 0.7 mile, then exit to the right onto Lorcom Lane. Follow Lorcom Lane 0.5 mile, then turn right onto Nelly Custis Drive. After 0.5 mile, bear right onto Military Road and follow it just 0.2 mile to an intersection with Marcey Road. Turn right onto Marcey Road and go 0.3 mile to the entrance to Potomac Overlook Regional Park, just beyond the tennis courts, picnic pavilion, and parking area for Marcey Road Park on the left.

To Potomac Overlook Regional Park from the eastbound lanes of Interstate 66: Leave I-66 at Exit 72 for Route 29 (Lee Highway). At the bottom of the exit ramp, turn right onto Route 29 North, then almost immediately turn left onto Route 124 (Spout Run Parkway). After only 0.2 mile, turn left onto

Map 36 — Potomac Heritage Trail (shown in three overlapping sections)

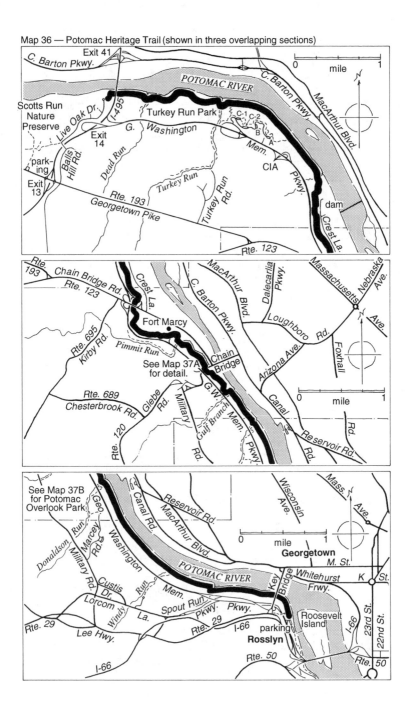

MAP 37 — Top two maps (37A and 37B) show details of Map 36.
Bottom map (37C) shows the Key - Chain Circuit.

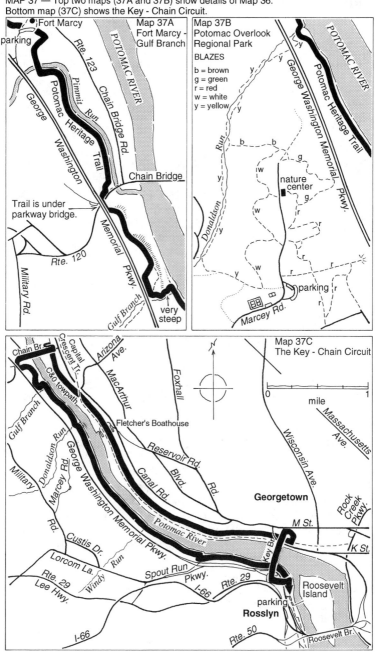

Lorcom Lane. Follow Lorcom Lane 0.5 mile, then turn right onto Nelly Custis Drive. After 0.5 mile, bear right onto Military Road and follow it just 0.2 mile to an intersection with Marcey Road. Turn right onto Marcey Road and go 0.3 mile to the entrance to Potomac Overlook Regional Park, just beyond the tennis courts, picnic pavilion, and parking area for Marcey Road Park on the left.

To Potomac Overlook Regional Park from the Chain Bridge: After crossing the Chain Bridge into Virginia, fork left uphill under the high George Washington Memorial Parkway bridge. After 0.2 mile, exit to the right for Military Road. Pass through an intersection, then turn left and left again to the beginning of Military Road. Follow Military Road 1.4 miles to an intersection with Marcey Road on the left. Turn left onto Marcey Road and go 0.3 mile to the entrance to Potomac Overlook Regional Park, just beyond the tennis courts, picnic pavilion, and parking area for Marcey Road Park on the left.

≈   ≈   ≈   ≈

WALKING the POTOMAC HERITAGE TRAIL: The 10-mile trail is marked with blue blazes and is shown on **Map 36** on page 316. A more detailed view of the section between Fort Marcy and Gulf Branch is shown on **Map 37A** on page 317. Directions are provided below for hiking both downstream and upstream.

Hiking downstream: If you park at Scotts Run Nature Preserve, you must first walk to the Potomac Heritage trailhead at Live Oak Drive, as follows: Take the footpath into the woods, bearing right at each intersection. After 0.7 mile, reach Live Oak Drive where it crosses the Beltway on a bridge. Do not, however, cross the bridge; rather, turn left and follow Live Oak Drive 0.8 mile to its end. Walk on the left side of the road, facing oncoming vehicles, and step off the road as they approach.

At the trailhead at the end of Live Oak Drive, follow the blue-blazed Potomac Heritage Trail steeply downhill and under the American Legion Bridge. With the Potomac River on the left, continue downstream for about 3 miles. A few hundred yards after passing a warning sign for Little Falls Dam, the trail veers right uphill away from the river. At the top of the hill near the

George Washington Memorial Parkway, descend steeply next to a large house. Continue with the parkway on the right and a narrow road (Crest Lane) on the left. At an interchange with Route 123, cross the entrance and exit ramps (be careful) and pass under the bridge next to the parkway. Fifty yards beyond the bridge, veer left up the embankment and into the woods on the blue-blazed trail, which descends along a ravine. When the trail again nears the parkway, turn left and continue with the parkway on the right. Eventually, the trail reaches the parking lot and earthworks at Fort Marcy. The inner fort was triangular. Its parapets, dry moat, and gun platforms are still readily discernible.

At Fort Marcy, the Potomac Heritage Trail continues from the end of the parking lot farthest from the parkway. Follow the blue blazes downhill to Pimmit Run. Cross Pimmit Run and follow it downstream to Glebe Road. Bear right uphill for a few dozen yards. With caution, cross 41st Street and Glebe Road, then follow the blue-blazes steeply uphill under the high parkway bridge. With the Potomac Gorge on the left, continue along the top of the cliffs, but stay back from the edge. Descend under the next parkway bridge to Gulf Branch and follow the blue blazes steeply downhill to the Potomac River.

At the bottom of the slope below the Gulf Branch cascade, follow the blue blazes downstream along the Potomac River. For about half a mile, the path is rough and rocky, but at Donaldson Run it becomes fairly easy and from there continues 3.1 miles to the parking lot at Roosevelt Island.

Hiking upstream: Start at the Roosevelt Island parking lot. With the Potomac River on the right, follow the blue blazes under a pedestrian bridge and across grass and through woods next to the river. Pass under the Key Bridge. Immediately after crossing a short masonry-clad bridge at Spout Run, descend to the river bank and continue upstream, with the Potomac on the right. At 1.7 miles pass a cascade at Windy Run; at 3.1 miles cross Donaldson Run; and at 3.7 miles reach the cascade and big rocks at Gulf Branch. Immediately after crossing Gulf Branch, turn left and climb steeply away from the river on stone steps. Near a high parkway bridge, turn right uphill. With caution, continue along the top of the cliff with the river far below on the right, then descend under the next parkway bridge to Glebe Road.

With caution, cross Glebe Road and 41st Street. Follow the

sidewalk downhill a few dozen yards, then turn left into woods to continue on the blue-blazed Potomac Heritage Trail, which follows Pimmit Run upstream. About a hundred yards short of yet another parkway bridge, cross Pimmit Run on the rocks, then continue straight up a small ravine with the parkway in the distance on the left. After the trail levels off, turn left uphill to the parking lot and earthworks at Fort Marcy. The inner fort was triangular. Its parapets, dry moat, and gun platforms are still readily discernible.

At Fort Marcy, the Potomac Heritage Trail continues from the end of the parking lot nearest the George Washington Memorial Parkway. Follow the blue blazes through the woods, sometimes close to the parkway on the left. At one point very near the parkway, the trail turns abruptly right and follows a ravine, then rejoins the parkway at the bridge and interchange for Route 123. With caution, follow the blue blazes under the bridge and across exit and entrance ramps. Where the entrance ramp joins the parkway, descend slightly to the right across a grassy embankment. Re-enter the woods and continue with the parkway on the left and Crest Lane on the right. Eventually, climb steeply past a large house on the right. At the top of the slope, turn right and follow the trail downhill to the Potomac River.

With the river on the right, continue upstream through Turkey Run Park. Follow the blue-blazed Potomac Heritage Trail all the way to the American Legion Bridge at the Capital Beltway. Immediately after passing under the bridge, cross a drainage swale, then turn left uphill to the cul-de-sac at Live Oak Drive, where the trail ends.

To reach the parking lot at Scotts Run Nature Preserve, follow Live Oak Drive 0.8 mile to a bridge across the Beltway. Walk on the left, facing oncoming vehicles, and step off the road as they approach. Just before the bridge over the Beltway, turn right into the woods on a footpath and follow it 0.7 mile, bearing left at each trail junction.

≈   ≈   ≈   ≈

THE KEY-CHAIN CIRCUIT: This 9-mile loop along both sides of the Potomac River between the Key Bridge and the Chain Bridge is shown on **Map 37C** at the bottom of page 317. The directions below assume that you will start at the Roosevelt Island parking lot, although obviously you can join the circuit at many other places.

Starting at the Roosevelt Island parking lot, head upriver with the Potomac on the right. Follow blue blazes under a pedestrian bridge and across grass and through woods next to the river. Pass under the Key Bridge. Immediately after crossing a short masonry-clad bridge at Spout Run, descend to the river bank and continue upstream with the Potomac on the right. At 1.7 miles pass a cascade at Windy Run; at 3.1 miles cross Donaldson Run; and at 3.7 miles reach the cascade and big rocks at Gulf Branch. Immediately after crossing Gulf Branch, turn left and climb steeply away from the river on stone steps. Near a high parkway bridge, turn right uphill. With caution, continue along the top of the cliff with the river far below on the right, then descend under the next parkway bridge to Glebe Road. Cross Glebe Road, 41st Street, and Route 123. Follow the sidewalk across the Potomac River on the Chain Bridge.

Near the far end of the bridge, descend a ramp to the C&O Canal towpath. With the canal on the left, follow the towpath 3.5 miles to Georgetown. After passing under the Whitehurst Freeway and the Key Bridge, turn left across the canal on a sloping footbridge. Climb some steps, then turn left again and follow an asphalt path up to the Key Bridge. Turn left across the bridge, with views downstream to Roosevelt Island. At the far end of the bridge, continue straight to a four-way intersection at a traffic light, then turn left on an asphalt path toward the Mount Vernon Trail and Roosevelt Island. Follow the path to a pedestrian bridge that leads to the parking lot at Roosevelt Island.

24

CAPITAL CRESCENT TRAIL

including circuits with the Rock Creek Trail and through Battery Kemble Park, Wesley Heights Park, and Glover-Archbold Park

Walking, bicycling, and in-line roller skating. **Map 38** on page 331 shows the **Capital Crescent Trail** as of 1996. It is 7 miles long (11.3 kilometers), one way. From its upper end at Bethesda Avenue, the trail eventually will be extended northeast to Silver Spring, but even the present, shorter version is an outstanding recreational trail.

As shown by the dotted line on Map 38, cyclists can ride from the upper end of the Capital Crescent Trail east on local streets in order to link with the Rock Creek Trail, described in Chapter 26. By following the Rock Creek Trail south, cyclists can then reach the C&O Canal Towpath, which will take them west to the lower end of the Capital Crescent Trail. Altogether the circuit is 20 miles long (32.4 kilometers).

Alternatively, **Map 39** on page 333 shows a 7-mile (11.3-kilometer) circuit for hikers that makes use of part of the Capital Crescent Trail overlooking the Potomac River, plus footpaths through wooded ravines at **Battery Kemble, Wesley Heights, and Glover Archbold parks** in northwest Washington. In one section the route briefly follows residential streets and the old roadbed of the Glen Echo trolley.

The maps show that it is possible to join these excursions at many points. One good place is Fletcher's Boat House, to which there are automobile directions on page 329.

The trails are open daily from dawn until dusk. Dogs must be leashed. In Washington, the Capital Crescent Trail is administered by the National Park Service; telephone the C&O Canal headquarters at (301) 739-4200. In Montgomery County the Capital Crescent Trail is managed by the Department of Parks; telephone (301) 299-0024. Finally, Battery Kemble,

Wesley Heights, and Glover-Archbold parks in Washington are administered by the National Park Service; telephone (202) 426-6909.

THE CAPITAL CRESCENT TRAIL follows the former roadbed of the Georgetown branch of the Baltimore and Ohio Railroad. As originally conceived late in the nineteenth century, the rail line was intended to be much more than just a spur into Georgetown. Rather, the B&O planned to cross the Potomac River and link with other railroads serving the growing markets of the South. Although the Long Bridge at Washington already carried a railway over the Potomac, the tracks there were controlled by the Pennsylvania Railroad, which refused to allow its competitors to use the line. At first the B&O responded by operating a train ferry at Alexandria, but this was slow and costly. Also, the ferry was linked only with railroads serving the southern Piedmont and not the seaboard down to Florida. To remedy this shortcoming, the B&O developed plans for its own bridge and line into northern Virginia, where junctions would be established with *all* the important railroads coming up to Washington from the south.

Downstream from Washington, boat traffic and the great width of the Potomac made a railroad bridge impractical, and so the B&O planned a circuitous route around the city and across the Potomac where it was narrow and there was no river traffic. At Silver Spring the line would leave the B&O's Metropolitan branch linking Washington, Rockville, and Brunswick. After crossing the Potomac River just upstream from the Chain Bridge, the B&O's new branch into Virginia would run forty miles south to Quantico, making junctions with various railroads along the way. As an incidental feature, the line would also have a spur into Georgetown, where there were mills and warehouses along the C&O Canal.

Construction began from Silver Spring in 1892. The railroad was quickly built as far as Chevy Chase, but there the line stopped for seventeen years, during which it delivered building materials to the growing suburbs and coal to an electric street car company's power plant. By the time construction resumed in 1909, the incentive to build a new bridge across the Potomac was greatly reduced by the fact that the Pennsylvania Railroad's former rail link into northern Virginia had come under the joint control of six companies, of which the B&O was one. And so from Chevy Chase the B&O extended its line only as far as Georgetown.

Starting in 1910, one freight train daily transported coal and building supplies to numerous private sidings in Georgetown's waterfront district. The fact that the town had long been a port and terminus of the Chesapeake and Ohio Canal had already made the area between the canal and the river a substantial warehousing, milling, and distribution center. The railroad entered Georgetown by passing under what is now one of the two remaining arches of the Aqueduct Bridge, originally built to carry the Alexandria branch of the C&O Canal across the Potomac. In Georgetown the B&O's railroad tracks ran down the center of Water Street (now K Street) and terminated at Rock Creek. The Capital Traction Company's electric generating plant at K Street and Wisconsin Avenue was the line's largest customer until 1933, when the plant closed. (It was finally torn down in 1968.) Even as recently as the early 1980s, the railroad regularly delivered coal to the federal government's power plant and steam heating station near the mouth of Rock Creek. By then, however, the redevelopment of the Georgetown waterfront for offices, luxury apartments, restaurants, and trendy shops had been underway for two decades, with a corresponding decline in business for the railroad, which ran only two trains weekly. In 1985 the Chessie System (created by merger of the Chesapeake and Ohio and the Baltimore and Ohio in 1963) stopped service on the Georgetown branch after a flood destroyed part of the line near Fletcher's Boat House. Thereafter coal was delivered by truck to the federal government's Rock Creek steam plant. After agreeing to continue these truck deliveries as needed, the railroad company received permission from the Interstate Commerce Commission to abandon the Georgetown branch and to sell the right-of-way to Montgomery County and the National Park Service for development of the Capital Crescent Trail.

≈   ≈   ≈   ≈

HEADING OUT OF GEORGETOWN, the Capital Crescent Trail crosses Foundry Branch near the southern end of Foxhall Road. Together, the stream and road recall the Foxall Foundry, once one of the largest industries in Georgetown. It was situated on a low shelf of land where Foundry Branch flows from the ravine of Glover-Archbold Park into the Potomac River. During the first two decades of the nineteenth century, the Foxall plant was the nation's leading manufactory of all sorts of ordnance for the federal government. When the Chesapeake and Ohio Canal was subsequently built across the company's property, a tunnel was constructed under the waterway to provide access from Canal Road to the foundry works and docks next to the river. Although the casting house, boring mill, and other foundry structures have all been torn down long ago, the tunnel remains and is still used by hikers,

325

joggers, and bicyclists. This is the tunnel through which the circuit shown on Map 39 passes in order to get from Glover-Archbold Park to the Capital Crescent Trail.

The Foxall Foundry was established at the personal request of President Jefferson. When the federal government moved to Washington in 1800, Jefferson asked Henry Foxall, the leading partner in the Eagle Iron Works of Philadelphia, to organize in the new capital a foundry that would be devoted exclusively to casting cannon, shot, and gun carriages for the War and Navy departments.

Foxall himself designed and supervised construction of the plant, which used the latest technology . Instead of being cast around a core to produce a hollow barrel as they were during the Revolution, the cannon were cast as solid pieces, then the barrels were bored out. The solid-cast cannon had much smoother barrels and were far more accurate than hollow-cast pieces. The boring machines were powered by a water wheel turned by Foundry Branch and later by water released from the C&O Canal.

According to an 1803 map, the foundry consisted of a blast furnace, a boring mill, and several other structures; but during the next ten or twelve years the plant was greatly enlarged. Raw materials and finished cannons were shipped in and out on the Potomac River. Construction of the C&O Canal made the site even more advantageous. An inventory from 1836 describes the foundry at its peak of development, although most of the improvements had been made at least twenty years earlier:

> A capacious and lofty casting-house of stone, containing four large air furnaces, with double stacks; an extensive moulding-floor; deep pit for casting cannon vertically; drying-room, with iron doors, for baking gun-moulds; three powered cranes, fitted with the requisite iron pinions, sheaves [i.e., pulleys], and chains; a room for preparing moulding materials; iron railway and carriage for moving guns in and out of the drying-room; railway and carriage for transporting the same from the casting-house to the boring mill. . . .
>
> Two large stone houses for boring cannons, both having four floors, including the basement stories, fitted with large waterwheels, enclosed in tight water chambers to secure their running in time of frost, geared throughout with iron; one mill containing four frames, and the other five, for boring cannon, provided with all the requisite railways, advancing carriages, racks, levers, rods, bits, and other tools for boring and turning cannon of all dimensions. . . . On the exterior, against one of the walls, is fitted a machine, with iron sheaves and chains, for breaking up, by means of heavy drops, old cannon and other massive castings, so as to accommodate the fragments for reception and fusion in the furnace. In both boring-mills are laid, on heavy horizontal timbers extending throughout the houses, on the second story, and

thence into the yard, iron railways and truck-carriages, for moving and hoisting cannon in and out of the boring frame; and in both are, in the second stories, extensive carpenters' shops for preparing patterns, flasks, &c.; and garret stories for storing and preserving patterns and utensils; and basement stories for receiving, as they fall from the guns, and storing, the gun borings.

Foxall's guns were markedly superior to those produced at other foundries. During the fifteen years that he ran the Georgetown plant, it supplied almost all government ordnance. By late 1801 the Foxall works were turning out about a hundred cannon per year. A few years later the foundry's capacity was reported to be three hundred guns per year and thirty thousand shot.

The War of 1812 further stimulated Foxall's business, and he became a very wealthy man. After the British marched into Washington on the evening of August 24, 1814, Foxall feared that they intended to wreck his foundry, just as they had already destroyed other such works in the Chesapeake region, and just as they burned the White House and Capitol during the one day that they spent in Washington. When his foundry was spared — by some accounts, the heavy rain that fell on the 25th flooded Rock Creek and prevented the British from crossing — Foxall was so grateful to Providence that he paid for construction of the Methodist Foundry Church at the corner of 14th and G streets. (The present-day Foundry Church at 16th and P is a later structure.) Foxall himself was a member of the Dumbarton United Methodist Church in Georgetown.

Foxall sold the foundry in 1815 to John Mason of Analostan Island (see Chapter 22). Mason was not a founder, but rather a banker and merchant on a large scale. For him, the Columbia Foundry (as the Foxall works by then were called) was simply an investment. Despite the construction of rival foundries and talk of establishing a government-owned foundry (as was eventually done), the Columbia plant continued to do a thriving business with the War and Navy departments. New forts throughout the vast Louisiana Territory, expeditions against Indians, and a growing navy all created an unceasing demand for ordnance. During the 1820s the Columbia Foundry supplied at least a quarter of the government's needs.

By 1835, however, the prosperity of the Columbia Foundry had begun to wane. John Mason had been in financial difficulty since 1826, after a disastrous land speculation. In 1836 he tried to convince the federal government to buy his foundry. However, in testimony before the House Committee on Military Affairs, a former Columbia Foundry employee said that the machinery was "old and dilapidated" and that the foundry had fallen into disrepair. Although this statement was probably an exaggeration, the plant had not been modernized since Foxall's time. In any case, the government did not purchase the foundry.

Although the Columbia Foundry continued to generate substantial income for Mason during the late 1830s, it lagged far behind its scheduled production. Moreover, the government established quality standards that could not be achieved at older plants. In 1842 a cannon cast at the foundry exploded when it was fired, killing several soldiers. By 1845 the Columbia plant was merely making shells and cannonballs for guns cast at other works. During the Mexican War of 1846-48, other foundries retooled to manufacture modern weapons using the latest technology, but the Columbia Foundry remained unchanged. After John Mason's death in 1849, it produced almost nothing, and operations ceased altogether in 1854.

≈   ≈   ≈   ≈

ANOTHER INDUSTRIAL RELIC passed by the excursions shown on Maps 38 and 39 is the Abner Cloud House, built in 1799 as an adjunct to a flouring mill located in the vicinity of the present-day Fletcher's Boat House. The mill was powered by water supplied by the Little Falls Skirting Canal, which was one of the short waterways with locks built by the Patowmack Canal Company to get around rapids on the river. (For a discussion of the Patowmack Canal, see Chapter 9.)

≈   ≈   ≈   ≈

METRO: The Bethesda Metrorail station (Red Line) is located at the northern end of the Capital Crescent Trail. (See **Map 38** on page 331.) Also, Metrobus J2, which runs between the Silver Spring Metrorail station (Red Line) and Montgomery Mall, passes through Bethesda and stops there at the Metrorail station.

Georgetown is at the southern end of the Capital Crescent Trail. The Metrorail station closest to Georgetown is Foggy Bottom - GWU (Blue and Orange lines). As you exit from the station, turn left and follow 23rd Street north one block to Washington Circle. Circle left across K Street, then bear left onto Pennsylvania Avenue and follow it a few blocks over Rock Creek to M Street in Georgetown. Once you are in Georgetown, turn left downhill a couple of blocks to K Street under the Whitehurst Freeway. Turn right and follow K Street to the Capital Crescent Trail, which starts at the stone arch of the old Alexandria Aqueduct.

Several bus routes, including 32, 34, 35, 36 and 38B, pass through Georgetown on M Street. From M Street, head downhill a couple of blocks to K Street under the Whitehurst Freeway. Turn right and follow K Street to the Capital Crescent Trail, which starts at the stone arch of the old Alexandria Aqueduct.

Finally, Metrobus D4 follows Reservoir Road and MacArthur Boulevard in the vicinity of the excursion shown on **Map 39** on page 333. A good place to get off the bus is at the intersection of Reservoir Road and Foxhall Road.

Telephone (202) 637-7000 for current Metro information, including schedules, routes, and connections.

≈   ≈   ≈   ≈

AUTOMOBILE DIRECTIONS: The directions below are to **Fletcher's Boat House** on Canal Road in northwest Washington. At Fletcher's there is large lot where you can park legitimately for as long as you want — but even so in pleasant weather you should go early to be sure of finding a parking spot.

Fletcher's is a good place to start on the two excursions shown on **Maps 38 and 39** on pages 331 and 333, **provided that you go on a weekend,** when Canal Road is open all day to two-way traffic, and **provided also that you approach from the east**, or that is, from Georgetown, the Key Bridge, or the Whitehurst Freeway. The reason for this second caveat is that the entrance to Fletcher's Boat House forms such an acute angle with Canal Road that you can safely turn into Fletcher's only by approaching from the east — and by afterwards exiting toward the east — as is easily done per the following directions.

On weekdays, Canal Road past Fletcher's Boat House is one-way eastbound from 6 A.M. to 10:15 A.M., and one way westbound from 2:45 P.M. to 7:15 P.M. At other times on weekdays, Canal Road is open to two-way traffic. If you are careful about the clock, you can fit in an excursion from Fletcher's even on weekdays by going between 10 A.M. and 2:45 P.M. or by arriving before a one-way period and leaving afterwards.

To Fletcher's Boat House from Georgetown, the Key Bridge, or the Whitehurst Freeway: From Georgetown, follow M Street west out of town past the Key Bridge and

Whitehurst Freeway, where M Street becomes Canal Road. As a second option, from Virginia via the Key Bridge, turn left onto M Street, which in a hundred yards becomes Canal Road. And as a third option, from the Whitehurst Freeway turn left onto Canal Road.

All three options put you onto Canal Road heading west, with the C&O Canal on your left. Follow Canal Road 0.5 mile, then fork left to remain on Canal Road where Foxhall Road veers right uphill. Continue on Canal Road 1.6 miles to the inconspicuous entrance on the left for Fletcher's Boat House. With caution, follow the narrow ramp down past the white stone Abner Cloud House. If there is no room to park at the bottom of the ramp, continue under the canal to the larger lot by the Potomac River.

≈   ≈   ≈   ≈

WALKING and BICYCLING ON THE CAPITAL CRESCENT TRAIL: The 7-mile trail is shown on **Map 38** opposite. At Fletcher's Boat House, the paved Capital Crescent Trail is located next to the dirt C&O Canal towpath.

To reach Georgetown, which is 2 miles distant, start with the canal towpath on the left.

To reach Bethesda, which is 5 miles distant, start with the canal towpath on the right. Use caution at road crossings.

Together, the bold line and dotted line on Map 38 show a 20-mile bicycle circuit via the Capital Crescent trail, the Rock Creek Trail (see Chapter 26), and the C&O Canal Towpath (Chapter 7). I recommend going clockwise because the steady grade of the Capital Crescent Trail provides an easy way to climb gradually to Bethesda.

≈   ≈   ≈   ≈

WALKING AT BATTERY KEMBLE, WESLEY HEIGHTS, AND GLOVER-ARCHBOLD PARKS: The 7-mile circuit described below is shown on **Map 39** on page 333. The route starts and ends on the Capital Crescent Trail. A short section follows residential streets.

From Fletcher's Boat House, head west on the asphalt-paved Capital Crescent Trail, with the dirt C&O canal towpath on the right. After half a mile, the trail crosses the canal and Canal Road on the old railroad truss bridge. From the far end

MAP 38 — Capital Crescent Trail (with links to the Rock Creek Trail)

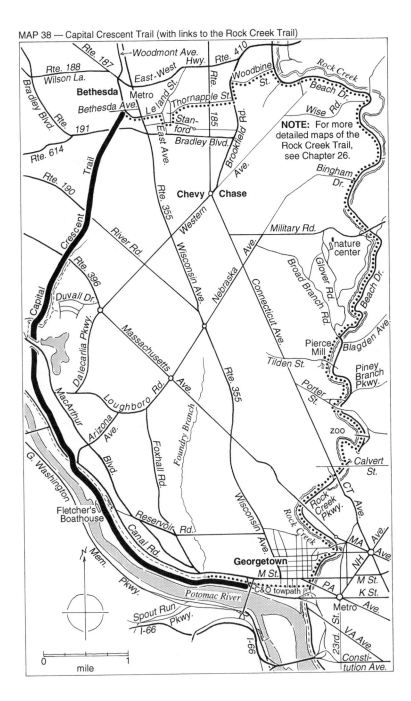

NOTE: For more detailed maps of the Rock Creek Trail, see Chapter 26.

331

of the bridge, continue about three-quarters of a mile, and then — just beyond a wooden railing on the left — turn right onto a narrow dirt track that climbs 50 yards to Potomac Avenue.

Turn right onto Potomac Avenue and follow it along the top of the Potomac Palisades. After passing intersections with Manning Place, Macomb Street, and Cathedral Avenue, turn left onto Galena Place. Cross Carolina Place, then turn right onto Sherrier Place. At the next intersection, turn right up a pedestrian ramp and then left across a pedestrian bridge over Arizona Avenue. (The bridge is a remnant of the former Glen Echo trolley.) Follow the old trolley right-of-way behind some houses and across a cul-de-sac. Continue along the trolley bed, which crosses Chain Bridge Road obliquely and eventually leads to a rough footpath that curves left up a ravine to MacArthur Boulevard and the red 1864 Conduit Road Schoolhouse.

MacArthur Boulevard lies atop the Washington Aqueduct and was originally called Conduit Road. From Great Falls, the aqueduct and road follow the contours of the Potomac Valley to the Georgetown Reservoir, crossing the valleys of Cabin John Creek and Little Falls on high, man-made ridges.

With caution, cross MacArthur Boulevard and re-enter the woods where one path leads straight along the side of the ravine and another path leads half-left slightly uphill. Go straight on the lower path, which eventually reaches a trail junction at a wooden pedestrian bridge. Here the route shown on Map 39 turns right, but first you may want to continue straight for 400 yards to the grassy slopes of Battery Kemble Park, where the indecipherable remains of Civil War earthworks are still visible at the top of the hill next to Chain Bridge Road. (For a discussion of Washington's Civil War earthworks, see Chapter 36.)

Turn right across the pedestrian bridge onto the buff-blazed Wesley Heights Trail toward Foxhall Road and the Glover-Archbold Trail. Cross 49th Street and continue uphill through woods, with Fulton Street toward the left. At the head of the ravine, climb steeply to Foxhall Road.

With caution, cross Foxhall Road to Edmunds Street. Continue on the footpath, which passes through woods below Edmunds Street and then eventually descends steeply to 44th Street.

MAP 39 — 7-mile loop via Capital Crescent Trail, Potomac Palisades, and Battery Kemble, Wesley Heights, and Glover Archbold parks

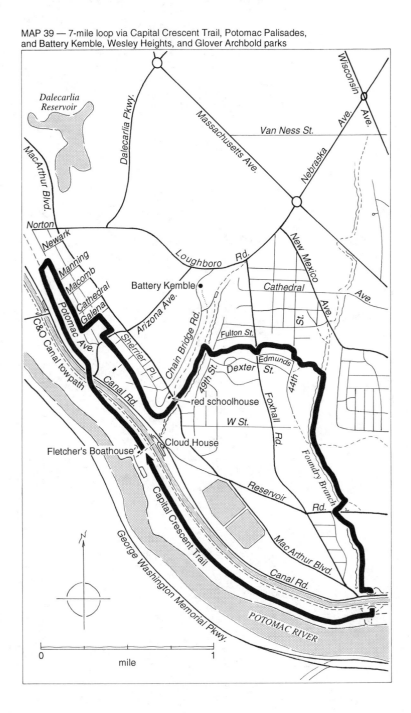

Cross 44th Street and follow it right for 50 yards, then turn left into the woods and follow a footpath downhill. At a trail junction, cross a stream and continue downhill, eventually reaching Foundry Branch. With caution, cross Foundry Branch and then — in 25 yards — turn right onto the blue-blazed Glover-Archbold Trail.

Follow the Glover-Archbold Trail straight downstream along the bottom of the valley past trails intersecting from either side. Eventually, fork right and descend a short flight of log steps in order to cross Foundry Branch. Continue on the blue-blazed trail as it climbs obliquely to Reservoir Road.

Cross Reservoir Road, then bear half-left across a grassy field and downhill into the valley. Continue into the woods and along the bottom of the ravine on the blue-blazed trail, which eventually reaches Canal Road near the intersection with Foxhall Road. Turn left and descend to a tunnel under Canal Road and the C&O Canal itself. At the far end of the tunnel, turn right on the paved Capital Crescent Trail. (This was the site of the Foxhall Foundry.)

With the Potomac River toward the left, follow the Capital Crescent Trail to Fletcher's Boat House.

25

ROCK CREEK PARK in Washington

Walking — 8 miles (13 kilometers). Well-graded paths form a large loop through Washington's famous intown wilderness. The circuit is shown by the bold line on **Map 40** on page 345, but there are also many other trails shown there that can be used to make a shorter loop.

From the Rock Creek Nature Center at the western rim of the valley, descend gradually to Rock Creek, then follow it upstream to the boundary with Montgomery County. Return through deep woods along the side of the valley and eventually past Fort DeRussey, one of the few Civil War defenses of Washington that saw combat.

The trails at Rock Creek Park are open daily from dawn until dusk. Dogs must be leashed; bicycles are prohibited on unpaved paths. Except for federal holidays, the nature center is open from 9 A.M. to 5 P.M., Wednesday through Sunday; it is also open Monday and Tuesday during the summer.

Rock Creek Park and the nature center are managed by the National Park Service. For information, including a schedule of guided walks and other events, telephone the nature center at (202) 426-6829. For the park headquarters, telephone (202) 282-1063.

HIDDEN IN THE WOODS overlooking the valley of Rock Creek about two miles north of the National Zoo is Fort DeRussey, which is passed by the walk described at the end of this chapter. The remains of the fort are hardly more than an irregular, five-sided ridge of earth fronted with a ditch, yet in places the earthworks are twenty feet high. A gun emplacement for a 100-pounder Parrott rifle at the fort's northeast corner is still discernible. The fort was also armed with ten lesser guns and mortars, mostly 32-pounder rifles. Now trees as large as two or three feet in diameter grow within the fort and from the parapets.

Because of the forest, it is impossible to catch more than a glimpse of the valley that the Union fort commanded during the Civil War. Yet when Fort DeRussey was built in 1861, all timber to its front was felled and left to lie on the ground to hinder advancing Confederate troops that might circle around Washington and attack from the north. In a ravine behind the fort was — and still is — the Military Road, built to connect Fort DeRussey with similar earthworks that ringed the national capital. Unlike most of the other works, Fort DeRussey and some of its neighbors, particularly Fort Stevens to the east on the opposite side of Rock Creek, came under attack during Jubal Early's raid on Washington in the summer of 1864. The remains of Fort Stevens are now a small park at the intersection of 13th Street and Piney Branch Road. For a discussion of Washington's Civil War defenses, which included sixty-eight enclosed forts, ninety-three field batteries, and twenty miles of rifle trenches, see Chapter 36.

By the summer of 1864, Washington's defensive works were highly developed, but the garrisons manning the forts were weak. Following Lee's defeat at Gettysburg in July 1863, the likelihood of another Confederate incursion north of the Potomac seemed remote. It was the Confederate capital at Richmond that was threatened as Lieutenant General Ulysses S. Grant, during May and early June of 1864, alternately battled and sidled his way southward. Grant eventually crossed the James River to the east of Richmond and laid siege to nearby Petersburg. If Petersburg were taken, Richmond would fall with it. Although Grant's losses were horrifying, they could be replaced by drawing on the North's vast manpower. Some replacements came from the Washington forts, leaving militiamen and poorly trained recruits to man the works and handle the unfamiliar, heavy guns. This was the situation late in June 1864, when Lee directed Lieutenant General Jubal Early to circle north and attack Washington from the rear in order to draw Union troops away from Petersburg. In addition, if Confederate troops were to occupy Washington, even for only a few days or weeks, Southern leaders hoped — rather forlornly at this late stage of the war — that the English and French governments might use the occasion as a pretext to recognize the Confederacy and lend it aid.

With startling speed Early's 14,000 men gained control of the Shenandoah Valley, crossed the Potomac at Shepherdstown on July 6, exacted a ransom of $200,000 from the city of Frederick, and pushed aside Union forces attempting to block the way at the Monocacy River. General Lew Wallace, the Union commander at Monocacy, wired to the capital: "I have been defeated; the enemy are not pursuing me, from which I infer they are marching on Washington." By July 11 the Confederates were on the outskirts of the capital in a front stretching from Tenleytown to the Seventh Street turnpike (now Georgia Avenue). Only 9,000 untried troops — more than half of whom were stationed south of the Potomac — manned the Washington forts. Miscellaneous units that happened to be in the city constituted another 11,000 men, but they lacked cohesive leadership. From Petersburg Grant wired to Henry Halleck, the army chief of staff, to "get into Early's rear and destroy him." Halleck replied in part:

> What you say about getting into Early's rear is probably correct, but unfortunately we have no forces here for the field. All such forces were sent to you, long ago. What we have here are raw militia, invalids, convalescents from the hospitals, a few dismounted batteries, and the dismounted and unorganized cavalrymen you sent up from the James River. With these we hope to defend our immense depots of stores and the line of intrenchments (extending 37 miles) around the city . . . .

All available manpower was rushed to the forts, but even so some works were left empty. At other forts, no one knew how to operate the artillery. The rumored size and whereabouts of Early's army added to the confusion. In the desperation of the moment, workmen from the Navy Yard were ordered into the trenches at Fort Lincoln. Some of these men did not know even how to load a gun. Among their officers was Asaph Hall, an astronomer (and this writer's great-grandfather). Hall, who worked at the Naval Observatory, had been commissioned the year before in the Corps of Professors of Mathematics, a position that required no military training. He did, however, know how to load and fire a musket, and he spent two days instructing the stopgap troops.

The Battle of the Suburbs occurred on July 11 and 12, 1864. Fort Stevens was the main point of action, with support from the guns at Fort DeRussey to the west and Fort Slocum to the east. For General Early, the key question was whether his army had outpaced the veteran 6th Army Corps that Grant had sent north by boat to defend Washington. All day on July 11 the mile-long Confederate column moved forward from Gaithersburg. There were many stragglers. "No air stirring," Early noted. The day was "an exceeding hot one." By 1 P.M. firing from the direction of Washington indicated that the Confederate vanguard had reached the Union lines outside the city.

Early himself first saw the Federal lines at Fort Stevens near the Seventh Street pike. The fort appeared to be feebly manned by a few home units. Some of its defenders wore linen dusters. Early ordered his troops to deploy in a line of battle and seize the fort; but as his men were moving into position, a cloud of dust approaching from Washington became a column of Union soldiers, who wore the faded blue uniforms of veterans. Early nonetheless ordered his skirmishers to probe the Union line. At first his men pushed back the enemy pickets, but late in the afternoon more bluecoats from the Union 6th Corps filled the trenches and restored the original line of battle.

In his memoirs General Early described the defensive works. They were

> exceedingly strong, and consisted of what appeared to be enclosed forts for heavy artillery, with a tier of lower works in front of each pierced for an immense number of guns, the whole being connected by curtains and ditches in front, and strengthened by palisades and abatis. The timber had been felled within cannon range all around and left on the ground, making a formidable obstacle, and every possible approach was raked by artillery. On the right was Rock Creek, running through a deep ravine which had been rendered impassable by the felling of timber on each side, and beyond were the works on the Georgetown Pike which had been reported to be the strongest of all. On the left, as far as the eye could reach, the works appeared to be of the same impregnable character. The position was naturally strong for defense, and the examination showed, what might have been expected, that every appliance of science and unlimited means had been used to render the fortifications around Washington as strong as possible.

The arrival of the Union 6th Corps nullified any possibility that the Confederates could take Washington. Transport boats carrying the troops had reached the Sixth Street docks at midday. Crowds gathered and cheered as the troops were at first misdirected toward Georgetown and then redirected up the Seventh Street road toward Fort Stevens and Fort DeRussey. Many of the soldiers had been trained on the artillery at the Washington forts.

According to the historian of the 6th Army Corps,

> The column was formed and we marched up 7th Street, past the Smithsonian Institution, the Patent Office, and the Post Office, meeting on our way many old friends, and hearing people who crowded on the sidewalks, exclaiming, "It is the old 6th Corps" — "These are the men who took Mayre's Heights" — "The danger is over now."
>
> Thus we made our way to the north of the city, the sound of cannonading in our front stimulating and hastening the steps of the men.
>
> Families with a few of their choicest articles of household furniture loaded into wagons, were hastening to the city, reporting that their houses were burned, or that they had made their escape, leaving the greater part of their goods to the mercy of the Rebels.
>
> We reached a pine grove in the rear of Fort DeRussey and made our bivouac for the night.

Part of the 6th Corps march to Fort Stevens, where late in the afternoon five hundred men were ordered to push back the Confederate skirmishers near the fort. While General Early watched from his side, President Lincoln, in one of several such visits during the action, arrived at Fort Stevens for a look of his own. He and the other civilians who had managed to reach the fort saw the opposing hills flashing with hundreds of muskets as the Union troops scrambled forward. A few houses that had provided cover for Confederate sharpshooters burned in the twilight after being shelled from Fort Stevens.

On the morning of July 12, General Early decided to retreat. His survey of the front at dawn revealed that Fort Stevens, the trenches stretching west to Fort DeRussey and east to Fort Slocum, and the various field batteries were all fully manned by veteran troops. If one thing had been made clear by three years of war, it was the folly of a frontal attack on well-prepared defenses. Also, Early had received intelligence not only of the arrival of the Union 6th Corps but also of the approach of 6,000 Federals from the 19th Corps. There was danger that his force might be trapped north of the Potomac. To avoid having to fight his way back to Virginia, Early decided to start his withdrawal during the coming night. In the meantime his army was deployed in a line of battle along a two-mile front stretching from Fort Slocum (now a park at 3rd and Nicholson streets) to Fort DeRussey. Once in position, the Confederates lay down out of sight of the Union defenses.

Except for occasional picket and artillery fire, the day progressed uneventfully while the Union generals worked to get still more men to the front. Gideon Welles, U.S. Secretary of the Navy, obtained a pass to Fort Stevens and later described his carriage ride out from the city through what was then farmland:

> Here upon one side in a field of standing corn was the baggage train of a Regiment, the mules enjoying the luxury of green forage — on the other side, perhaps the shelter tents of the men were pitched in an oat field just ready for the sickle — The comfort of man and horse was evidently first consulted — the interest of the farmer was made a matter of secondary consideration. I am obliged to confess moreover that the remarks of the soldiers upon my equipage were in this wise, always answered by us in good temper however and we usually disarmed our assailants. "You are non combatants, You are!" "Coming out here to get up another Bull run ar'nt ye?" "Skedaddle white livers!" &c &c .... On we went past Regiment and division, through the first and second toll gates, passing picket after picket until at length we came to Fort Stevens.

By early afternoon the Union commanders decided to drive back the Confederates in front of Fort Stevens. Rebel sharpshooters and skirmishers were thought to be uncomfortably close. Late in the afternoon a brigade of 1,000 men was sent forward under cover of artillery fire from forts Stevens, DeRussey, and Slocum. The advancing bluecoats were surprised to encounter a solid line of Confederates. Union reinforcements were called in as the sortie turned into a battle. At a cost of about 250 killed (some of whom are buried in the small U.S. National Military Cemetery on Georgia Avenue near Van Buren Street), the Union forces pushed back the Confederates from the area in front of Fort Stevens.

As night fell, the fighting died down. Relieved to be able to disengage from the Union forces, Early started his retreat. Pursuit was weak and on the morning of July 14, the Confederates forded the Potomac and reached safety in Virginia. Of the exploit the pro-Southern London *Times* said on July 25, 1864, "The Confederacy is more formidable as an enemy than ever." But, of course, Washington was not taken nor was Grant distracted from his slow envelopment of Petersburg and Richmond, both of which eventually fell on April 3, 1865. A week later Lee surrendered at Appomatox.

≈   ≈   ≈   ≈

METRO: Metrobus routes E2 and E3 follow Military Road across the Rock Creek Valley. To the west the buses originate at the Friendship Heights Metrorail station (Red Line), and to the east they stop at the Fort Totten Metrorail station (Green and Red lines). Get off the bus at the intersection of Military Road and Oregon Avenue, shown near the left edge of **Map 40** on page 345.

To the east of Rock Creek Park, Metrobus routes S2 and S4 follow 16th Street between the Silver Spring Metrorail station (Red Line) in the north and Federal Triangle (Blue and Orange lines) in the south at 10th Street and Constitution Avenue. A good place to get off the bus is the intersection of 16th and Whittier streets, from which the Whittier Trail descends into the park.

Telephone (202) 637-7000 for current Metro information, including schedules, routes, and connections.

≈   ≈   ≈   ≈

AUTOMOBILE DIRECTIONS: The walk described in this chapter starts at the **Rock Creek Nature Center** in northwest Washington. The nature center is located on Glover Road just south of its intersection with Military Road at the western rim of the valley. (See **Map 40** on page 345.) Several approaches to the nature center are described below.

To the nature center from the south via Connecticut Avenue: After passing the National Zoo, continue north on Connecticut Avenue almost 2 miles, then turn right onto Nebraska Avenue. (You will know that you are approaching Nebraska Avenue after passing Davenport, Ellicott. and Fessenden streets.) Follow Nebraska Avenue northeast 0.4 mile, then turn right onto Military Road and go 0.7 mile to the crossroads where Oregon Avenue intersects from the left and Glover Road intersects from the right. Turn right onto Glover Road. In quick succession, fork left and then turn left again for the nature center. Finally, turn left once more into the nature center parking lot.

To the nature center from the north via Connecticut Avenue: After passing Chevy Chase Circle, continue south on Connecticut Avenue 0.5 mile, then turn left onto Military Road. (You will know that you are approaching Military Road after passing Morrison, Livingston, and Legation streets.) Follow Military Road 1.1 miles to the crossroads where Oregon Avenue intersects from the left and Glover Road intersects from the right. Turn right onto Glover Road. In quick succession, fork left and then turn left for the nature center. Finally, turn left once more into the nature center parking lot.

To the nature center from Interstate 495 (the Capital Beltway): Although Connecticut Avenue provides access from the Beltway, you will probably encounter less congestion if you leave the Beltway at Exit 31B for Route 97 South (Georgia Avenue). Follow Route 97 South 0.4 mile, then turn right for Route 390 South (16th Street). Follow 16th Street south 3.1 miles, then turn right down the ramp onto Military Road. Follow Military Road 0.9 mile to the crossroads where Oregon Avenue intersects from the right and Glover Road intersects from the left. Turn left onto Glover Road. In quick succession, fork left and then turn left again for the nature center. Finally, turn left once more into the nature center parking lot.

To the nature center from Georgia Avenue: About half way between downtown Washington and Silver Spring, Georgia Avenue intersects with Military Road. Follow Military Road west 1.5 miles across Rock Creek Valley to the crossroads where Oregon Avenue intersects from the right and Glover Road intersects from the left. Turn left onto Glover Road. In quick succession, fork left and then turn left again for the nature center. Finally, turn left once more into the nature center parking lot.

To the nature center from Virginia via the Roosevelt Bridge: The bridge is accessible from Route 66 East, Route 50 East, and the southbound lanes of the George Washington Memorial Parkway. At the District of Columbia end of the bridge, fork left toward Route 66 East. Stay left toward the Whitehurst Freeway and Rock Creek Parkway, but after just a few tenths of a mile, exit to the left for the Kennedy Center, then immediately turn right onto Virginia Avenue and right again onto the Rock Creek Parkway.

Follow the Rock Creek Parkway 2 miles, then bear right onto Beach Drive and follow it 2.2 miles. After passing an intersection with Blagden Avenue, turn left across Rock Creek. In quick succession, bear left for Broad Branch Road, then turn right onto Glover Road toward the nature center. Follow the nature center signs 1.4 miles uphill (along the way forking left and then right). Turn right into the nature center entrance, and then left for the parking lot.

≈   ≈   ≈   ≈

WALKING: The 8-mile route described below is shown on **Map 40** opposite. The walk starts at the Rock Creek Nature Center.

With your back to the nature center, follow the parking lot left. Continue straight to the horse center and stables (which have a first story of concrete block and a second story of wood siding painted red). Stay on a paved road and pass immediately to the left of the stables. Join a broad bridle path as it circles two-thirds of the way around a corral, passing a trail that intersects from the left. Stay on the broad horse path as it enters the woods.

Follow the path across an entrance drive serving the park headquarters and continue through the woods. After crossing Glover Road, continue on the path 90 yards, then fork right downhill on a green-blazed bridle path. Follow the path as it gradually curves left. Within sight of Glover Road, turn right on the green-blazed trail to continue parallel with the road. Follow the trail just below the edge of the lawn and then along the rim of the valley. Continue straight where the green-blazed bridle path forks right opposite a riding ring.

MAP 40 — Rock Creek Park: 8-mile loop

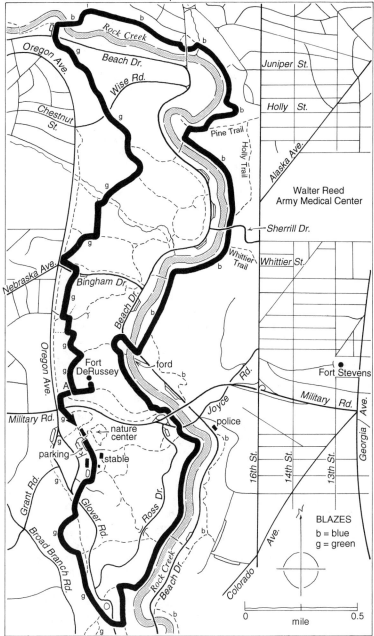

With Glover Road toward the left, re-enter the woods and then cross Glover Road. Continue through the woods to a trail intersection. Bear left and follow the path along the side of the valley, with Rock Creek downhill to the right. At another trail junction, turn right downhill. At the bottom of the valley, bear left.

With Rock Creek on the right, continue upstream. Pass a trail intersecting from the left and a footbridge on the right. With the stream on the right, continue to Joyce Road. Cross Joyce Road and follow an asphalt path along the edge of the creek. About 100 yards after passing under the Military Road bridge, turn right onto the horse path. In another 40 yards, fork right at a three-way intersection of horse paths. With Rock Creek in the distance downhill to the right, continue upstream.

At Milkhouse Ford follow the paved road left, then turn right across the bridge. At the far end of the bridge, turn sharply left onto a horse path, which soon joins the blue-blazed Valley Trail. With Rock Creek on the left, follow the trail upstream along the bottom of the valley. At times the trail is at a distance from the creek. Continue past a bridge on the left and the Whittier Trail intersecting from the right. Continue under the Sherrill Drive bridge and along the edge of the creek. Pass the Holly Trail intersecting from the right.

At a T-intersection, turn right away from a bridge over Rock Creek. Following the blue blazes, turn right again at a bluff above the creek. Continue with the stream downhill on the left. Fork left along the side of the valley where the Pine Trail leads straight. Pass below some houses and then along the edge of a steep bluff above the creek. Pass more houses on the right as the trail continues through a wooded floodplain. After crossing a small bridge, fork left to pass under a road bridge. (If the water is high, detour to the right across the road.) With the river a few dozen yards off to the left, continue along the foot of a bluff. Eventually, after crossing Rock Creek on a bridge at the boundary with Montgomery County, turn left toward a parking area next to Beach Drive.

Cross Beach Drive and bear left uphill on a horse path (the Western Ridge Trail) marked occasionally with green blazes. Follow the trail up and down as it winds along the side of the valley and through tributary ravines. Cross Wise Road and continue through the woods past two trails intersecting from the left. Descend into a ravine and then, after crossing a stream, pass through a four-way trail junction. About 50 yards after the junction, turn left uphill at a T-intersection. At the top of the slope, bear right at a trail junction. After only 40 yards, pass a trail intersecting from the right. Continue more or less straight through the woods to an intersection with a paved bicycle path near the corner of Oregon Avenue and Nebraska Avenue. Turn left onto the asphalt bike path, but after just 20 yards, fork right toward Bingham Drive where another bike path veers left toward the valley.

Cross Bingham Drive above a parking bay, then curve right uphill through the woods on the paved bike path . When the bike path reaches a paved road, turn left. Go 70 yards, then turn right across a wide grassy swath below a fenced enclosure of garden plots on the right. Go 80 yards alongside an old fence overgrown with vines on the left, then turn left in front of the woods in order to continue on the green-blazed Western Ridge Trail, which soon curves right downhill into the woods. At a trail junction, turn right uphill. Just beyond the crest of the hill, turn left at a T-intersection. Go 150 yards to Fort DeRussey in the woods on the left.

From Fort DeRussey, retrace your steps 150 yards, then continue straight downhill. Pass a bicycle path intersecting from the left-rear. Go straight on a paved path to a T-intersection opposite a large school on the far side of Oregon Avenue. Turn left and follow the paved path to the intersection of Military Road and Oregon Avenue. Continue straight across Military Road . Follow the paved path uphill through the woods to the parking lot at the nature center.

26

ROCK CREEK TRAIL in Washington and Montgomery County, Maryland

Walking, bicycling, and in-line roller skating. As shown on **Map 41** on page 357 — and in greater detail on **Maps 42-45** on pages 358-361 — the Rock Creek Trail stretches nearly 24 miles (39 kilometers) through Washington and Montgomery County. The southern end is at the Potomac River, where the trail links with other hike-bike paths, as discussed on page 365. The northern end is at Lake Needwood above Rockville.

A brief overview of the Rock Creek Trail is as follows: For 5.5 miles between the Arlington Memorial Bridge and the middle of Washington's Rock Creek Park at Blagden Avenue (located just north of Pierce Mill), the trail consists of a paved path. Although sometimes immediately adjacent to Rock Creek Parkway, the trail is nonetheless an attractive and interesting way to walk or ride between the Potomac River and the trail's more idyllic sections in northern Washington and Montgomery County. Although Pierce Mill no longer operates, it serves as a ranger station and museum open (during the warmer months) from 9 A.M. to 5 P.M. Wednesday through Sunday.

For 5 miles between Blagden Avenue and the East-West Highway in Montgomery County, the Rock Creek Trail consists of Beach Drive and Meadowside Lane. Sections of Beach Drive are closed to cars from 6 A.M. Saturday to 6 P.M. Sunday. This portion of the trail is very popular with cyclists and in-line skaters. It is not well suited to walking except on the relatively short sections that are closed to cars.

For 13 miles between the East-West Highway and Lake Needwood, the Rock Creek Trail consists of a paved path through Rock Creek Regional Park. Near Washington, the path is located fairly close to Beach Drive or other local roads. Some bicyclists who want to ride fast prefer to use the roads instead of the path, which is narrow and popular with walkers. North of Garrett Park Road, the path is no longer bordered by roads, and north of Aspen Hill Park near Viers Mill Road, the path crosses only three roads in 4 miles as it follows Rock Creek through deep woods to Lake Needwood.

There are many parking lots along the trail. Automobile directions to some of these parking areas, located at intervals of 5 to 8 miles, are set forth on pages 362-364.

The Rock Creek Trail is open from dawn to dusk — but as noted above, only for part of each weekend are sections of Beach Drive in Washington closed to cars. Hikers with dogs must keep their pets on a short leash to avoid accidents with cyclists. Cyclists, in turn, must ride single file, yield to other trail users, and keep their speed to a moderate, safe pace.

The section of the trail in Washington is administered by the National Park Service; telephone the Rock Creek Park headquarters at (202) 282-1063; the nature center at (202) 426-6829, and Pierce Mill at (202) 426-6908. The section of the trail in Montgomery County is administered by the county's Department of Parks, Maryland-National Capital Park and Planning Commission; telephone (301) 948-5053 (weekdays only).

BEFORE AMERICAN INDUSTRY converted from water power to steam during the second half of the nineteenth century, Rock Creek, like Northwest Branch, Cabin John Creek, Four Mile Run, and other streams in the Washington area, was the site of a chain of water-driven mills and factories, recalled now by the names of various roads, such as Adams Mill Road, Pierce Mill Road, and Shoemaker Street (after a Pierce descendant). Eight mills of various types — gristmills, sawmills, a woolen and cotton mill, plaster mills, bone mills, and a paper mill — stood at intervals along Rock Creek within what is now the District of Columbia. Another eighteen mills operated at one time or another farther upstream in Montgomery County. The Rock Creek Trail, featured in this chapter, passes the sites of some of these works.

Of the mills that once stood along Rock Creek within the District of Columbia, the southernmost was a paper mill on the east bank near the P Street bridge. According to an old advertisement, "P Street intersects Boundary Street [now Florida Avenue] opposite the front door." The mill was built in about 1800, next to a ford reached by a steep road down the sides of the ravine. Later a wooden covered bridge, the Paper Mill Bridge, crossed the creek at the former ford. In 1805 the paper mill was purchased by Edgar Patterson, and so it was known for a few years as the Patterson Paper Mill before being sold again in 1811. An

350

advertisement from 1820 calls it the Columbian Paper Mill. It was offered for sale yet again in the *National Republican*, December 29, 1821, where it was described as having two vats housed in a three-story structure 120 feet long. The first story was of stone. A sluice and waterwheel were located where the milldam abutted the building. Employing six men, twelve women, and two boys, the mill consumed 30,000 pounds of rags per year to make writing paper. The building still stood in 1868, but now the site reveals no traces of the dam or mill.

Not far upstream from the paper mill was the Georgetown Wool and Cotton Manufactory, a carding and spinning mill that was operating in 1813, according to an advertisement. Its owner was Richard Parrott, whose estate, Ellerslie, is now Montrose Park.

Lyons Mill stood on the Washington side of Rock Creek, across the stream from Oak Hill Cemetery. From Georgetown the mill was reached by Mill Road (of which only a truncated spur remains off Q Street) and a bridge (now a concrete span for the Rock Creek Trail built on the old stone abutments). The mill was constructed in 1780 by Pigman and Crow, partners who built and operated a number of mills in the vicinity of Washington. Under new ownership in 1795, it was called Federal Mill. After 1811 it was operated by John Kurtz and John Lyons, and after 1826 by Lyons alone, who lived on the property. Apparently, Lyons was prosperous; in 1820 his household totaled nineteen persons, including eight slaves. Fifty years later the mill was still managed by the Lyons family. Evans Lyons employed five hands at the mill, where, in 1880, three pairs of millstones reduced 90,000 bushels of wheat to 20,000 barrels of flour. Annual output also included 45,000 bushels of livestock feed and 449 tons of plaster.

In 1873 Evans Lyons died. A foreclosure advertisement stated that the plant was a large merchant mill with modern equipment and a capacity of 140 barrels of flour per day. The phrase *merchant mill* indicates that the plant produced flour for sale in the commercial market, including the thriving export market. In *custom mills* or *country mills*, on the other hand, the miller ground flour and feed on demand for local farmers, who paid him a fee or a share of what he ground. The Federal Mill property of sixty-five acres included a large house, a miller's cottage, and a small farm with a barn, smokehouse, and stable. Evans Hughes, who last operated the mill, died in 1875. A photograph of the abandoned mill in 1908 shows a plain, almost severe, rectangular brick structure, two and a half stories high, with a peaked roof. The mill sat on a stone foundation set into the bluff. Its millrace extended nearly half a mile upstream, making it the longest in the federal district. In 1913 the mill collapsed, and nothing now remains of the structure.

About one and a half miles upstream from Lyons Mill was Adams Mill, another merchant operation. It stood near the lower ford, also called Adams Mill Ford, a few hundred yards upstream from the present-day Calvert Street bridge near the Beach Drive tunnel. Originally called the Columbian Mill, it was built in the early 1790s by Benjamin Stoddert, who during the Revolution had served as secretary to the board of war. Later Stoddert was a confidential agent for the national government when it needed to buy land within the new federal district. After the U.S. Navy Department was created in 1798, he became the first Secretary of the Navy under President John Adams, whose son eventually invested in the Columbian Mill. An advertisement in 1821, before Adams' involvement, provides a description of the property. The tract of thirty-two acres included a miller's house, a small plaster mill, and a brick flour mill, four stories high, fifty by fifty-four feet, and equipped with three pairs of six-foot stones powered by a waterwheel sixteen feet in diameter. Two other pairs of stones ground corn and plaster. At that time the mill was owned by George Johnson, who claimed to have invested $60,000 in the property. Johnson said the mill's annual output was 60,000 bushels of wheat, 20,000 bushels of corn, and 40,000 pounds of plaster of Paris.

Johnson's business, however, did not prosper. In 1823 he persuaded his cousin's husband, Secretary of State John Quincy Adams, to purchase a half-share in the mill for $20,000 in order to pay off a mortgage that the Bank of Columbia was threatening to foreclose. Johnson remained manager of the mill. And so Adams entered an investment that he later said preyed on his spirits "like gangrene." To buy into the mill, he sold $9,000 in government bonds and mortgaged his Washington house. But during the first year of his co-ownership, the mill was damaged by a flood and required extensive repairs. Production should have been 80 to 100 barrels of flour per day but was only 100 barrels per week. During the years of Adams' presidency, which started in 1825, the mill continued to be unprofitable. In 1830 Johnson was eased out of active participation in the business, and one of Adams' sons took over management, running the mill on a break-even basis until the son's early death in 1834.

Part of the difficulty at Adams Mill was traceable to the fact that in the 1830s the flour industry in Washington began to shift to the banks of the new Chesapeake and Ohio Canal in Georgetown. There grain could be unloaded from barges directly into mills built into the hillside below the canal, from which water flowed through sluices to power the machinery. John Quincy Adams wanted to dispose of the Rock Creek property — in 1825 his son unsuccessfully advertised it for rent, directing responses to "the President's, Washington" — but a number of failed mills were on the market and he received no acceptable offers. After his son's death the mill was managed by his wife's brother-in-law, who eked out a small profit that helped support the former President until he died in 1848. The mill continued to operate during the settlement of Adams' estate and the subsequent settlement of George Johnson's estate, but by 1867 the buildings must have been in ruins inasmuch as they were struck from the tax records that year.

The only surviving mill in Rock Creek Park is Pierce Mill, located on the west bank about three-quarters of a mile upstream from the National Zoo (photograph: page 348). A sawmill was adjacent to the gristmill. When Isaac Pierce, a Pennsylvania Quaker, bought the property in 1794, it already included a mill. Earlier Pierce had worked as millwright at Abner Cloud's mill on the Little Falls skirting canal, where he not only built the machinery but also courted Cloud's daughter, whom he married. After moving to Rock Creek, Pierce rapidly acquired land, and by 1800 he owned nearly two thousand acres, which he farmed with a dozen or more slaves. In 1820 Pierce and his son Abner, a master mason, replaced the old mill on their property with the granite structure seen today, which houses three sets of millstones: one for wheat and rye, one for buckwheat, and one for corn. As with most mills, the owners did not operate Pierce Mill themselves, but leased it to a miller for an annual rent, which during the mill's most prosperous years was $1,200 to $1,500. As payment for grinding grain, the miller kept one-eighth of every bushel. According to Louis Shoemaker, a Pierce descendant, it was a daily occurrence at Pierce Mill during the 1860s and '70s to see ten or twelve wagons loaded with wheat from the surrounding farm country, as well as a number of boys carrying sacks of grain on horseback. By 1880 the mill was producing mainly livestock feed. It went out of business in 1897 when the main shaft broke. The works, however, are still intact, having been renovated by the National Park Service in the 1930s. Since then the machinery has again deteriorated and now no longer runs, but the waterwheel, wooden gears, millstones, rolling screen, belt-and-bucket elevators, augers, bolters, and other devices — and also drawings and models — show how a fairly sophisticated gristmill worked. If the mill is open, as it usually is Wednesday through Sunday during the warmer part of the year, be sure to stop in.

Less than half a mile upstream from Pierce Mill was Blagden Mill on the west side of Rock Creek. This gristmill was also called Argyle Mills, after the original land grant. Built in the 1820s by Thomas Blagden, a prosperous merchant — he at one time owned an entire block on New Jersey Avenue, SE, and his wharf was at the foot of Third Street — the stone mill was two and a half stories high. A bone mill, where livestock bones were ground into fertilizer, adjoined the gristmill. The milldam was located near present-day Boulder Bridge about a third of a mile upstream from the mills. The millrace produced an eleven-foot fall of water that drove an overshot wheel at thirty revolutions per minute. In 1850 the mill was grinding primarily wheat and some rye for flour, but by 1880 the mill's output was over-whelmingly livestock feed. Although the walls of Blagden Mill still stood when the land was condemned for park use in 1890, the remains were torn down to make way for Beach Drive.

Perhaps the oldest mill within the present-day park was located in the narrow valley between Blagden Avenue and the Military Road, where Rock Creek drops more than seventy feet in less than two miles. This area was called White's Mill Seat when it was patented in 1756. In 1800 it was resurveyed as Peter's Mill Seat, but by then the mill may have ceased operating. In 1872 Thomas Peter advertised to sell his undivided share in 450 acres on Rock Creek, with an excellent mill seat. Construction of Beach Drive obliterated remains of the millrace and mill foundation.

Continuing upstream along Rock Creek from Washington into Montgomery County, Jones Mill (of which nothing now remains) was built before the Revolution by Charles Jones, owner of Clean Drinking Manor. The site was on Jones Mill Road near what is now the bound-ary with the District of Columbia. Because of the gentle gradient in this section of valley, the mill required a long headrace. In 1777 the place was called Jones Saw Mill, but by 1813 (if not earlier) it was operating as a gristmill, for in that year the owner was successfully sued by Oliver Evans for using, without payment, patented devices and procedures for milling flour. In 1795 Evans had revolutionized milling by publishing *The Young Mill-Wright's and Miller's Guide*, which described machinery — as seen today at Pierce Mill — that made milling a more-or-less automated process.

About eight miles upstream from Jones Mill was Veirs Mill, which stood where Veirs Mill Road crosses Rock Creek. Samuel C. Veirs built the gristmill in 1838. It was called Rock Creek Mills on Simon J. Martinet's 1865 map, and Rockville Flouring Mills in an advertisement placed in the *Sentinel*, August 11, 1880, by the Viers Brothers (as the name was spelled before *Veirs* became the accepted spelling). In 1879 the G. M. Hopkins atlas of Montgomery County showed Edwards Viers Grist Mill just south of Rockville Road (later Veirs Mill Road) and the Viers residence to the north. "Viers Family" and "Bouquet" were the names of two brands of flour produced at the mill. According to the 1880 census, the gristmill employed fourteen hands and had an annual payroll of $3,500. Three pairs of millstones were powered by a water wheel nine feet wide, which in turn was driven at eight revolutions per minute by a fall of water twelve feet high. Maximum daily output was 100 bushels. Annual output was 6,000 barrels of flour, 32.4 tons of cornmeal, and 226.2 tons of feed, altogether worth $54,200. Veirs Mill, of which nothing now remains but its name, operated until about 1915. An old photograph shows merely a large clapboard structure standing on the wooded bank of the stream.

Two miles above Viers Mill on Rock Creek was Horner's Mill, located just below the bridge at Avery Road. Upstream from the bridge, the berm and ditch of the millrace are still plainly visible from the Rock Creek Trail, following the side of the valley for about 300 yards to the site of the former dam and mill pond. Downstream from Avery Road, the millrace follows the side of the valley for about 150 yards to the mill site, where all that is left is a jumble of rocks at the former foundation and wheel pit. Charles Beckwith operated a mill here prior to his death in 1799. Apparently the miller and mill deteriorated together, for the mill was said to be out of repair at the time of Beckwith's death. Subsequent owners repaired or rebuilt the mill, but by 1830 it was again described as dilapidated. For a period the mill was owned by the Prather family, whose small cemetery — called Walnut Grove and now overgrown with brush and cedars — is located above the valley upstream. The mill was conveyed by the Prathers to the brothers J. W. and F. B. Horner, whose residence and a "G. & S. Mill" — or grist and sawmill — is shown on the 1879 G. M. Hopkins atlas. The mill had an overshot wheel, which later was replaced by a small turbine, but despite this modern innovation, the mill ceased operating about 1890.

By the end of the nineteenth century, most of the mills along Rock Creek had been abandoned. Development of the roller-milling process used today made millstones obsolete, and new and larger mills were built to accommodate the new technology. Efficient steam engines and steam-generated electricity freed manufacturers from the need to locate their factories in narrow stream valleys, where the works were subject to periodic flooding. Also, the shift in wheat cultivation from the eastern states to the northern Great Plains and beyond doomed the many small gristmills of the mid-Atlantic region.

As early as 1866, twelve years after New York's Central Park was established north of what was then the city, a report prepared for Congress recommended that Washington similarly anticipate future recreational needs by creating a park along Rock Creek in what was then the rural northwest quadrant of the District of Columbia. In 1890, after years of pleading by civic leaders, Congress finally authorized purchase of the valley as "a pleasuring ground for the benefit and enjoyment of the people of the United States." The mill sites and industrial relics along the creek within the District of Columbia were condemned by the federal government. Since then Rock Creek Park has been enlarged from time to time by the acquisition of land along both the main valley and its tributaries. Also, in accordance with recommendations of the Maryland-National Capital Park and Planning Commission — created in 1927 to coordinate planning among Washington and Montgomery and Prince George's counties — Montgomery County (with the help of grants from the federal government) started buying land along Rock Creek in 1931 in order to continue the greenway that now extends from the Potomac River north past Rockville and even Gaithersburg.

≈   ≈   ≈   ≈

METRO: Near the southern end of the Rock Creek Trail is the Arlington Cemetery Metrorail station (Blue Line). From the station, follow the broad sidewalk along the south side of Memorial Drive (i.e., with the road on your left) toward Arlington Memorial Bridge and the distant Lincoln Memorial. Cross the Potomac River. At the far end of the bridge, follow the path down and around to the right, in the "loop-the-loop" manner suggested by the corner panel on **Map 2** on page 7, then follow the riverside path upstream along the Potomac River to Rock Creek, as shown on **Map 42** on page 358.

It is also easy to join the Rock Creek Trail via the C&O Canal towpath at Georgetown. Metro service to Georgetown is discussed on page 117. Follow the canal downstream to the junction with the Rock Creek Trail.

Metrobus routes H2 and H4 cross the Rock Creek Trail at Porter Street, about half a mile below Pierce Mill.

In Montgomery County near the boundary with Washington, Metrobus route J2 follows the East-West Highway across the Rock Creek Trail at the intersection with Meadowside Lane. (See the corner detail on **Map 43** on page 359.) And a couple of miles upstream, Metrobus route L8 on Connecticut Avenue crosses the trail at the intersection with Beach Drive.

Metrobus route Q2 on Veirs Mill Road crosses the northernmost section of the Rock Creek Trail at the intersection with Aspen Hill Road. (See the corner detail on **Map 45** on page 361.) Metrobus C8 also passes this intersection.

Telephone (202) 637-7000 for current Metro information, including schedules, routes, and connections.

MAP 41 — Overview of the Rock Creek Trail

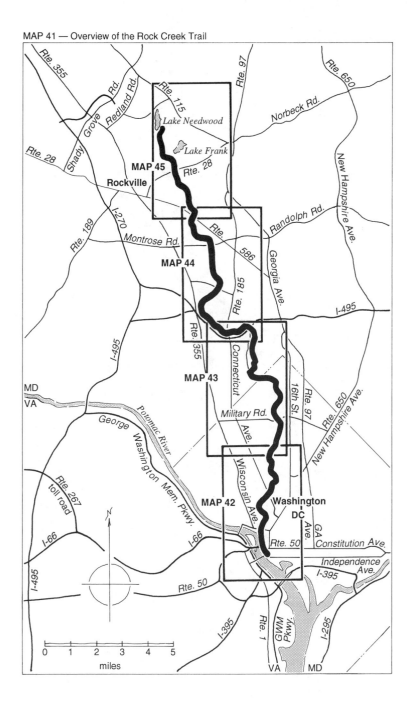

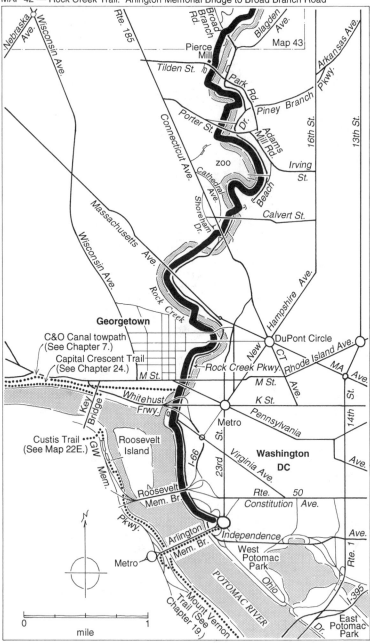

358

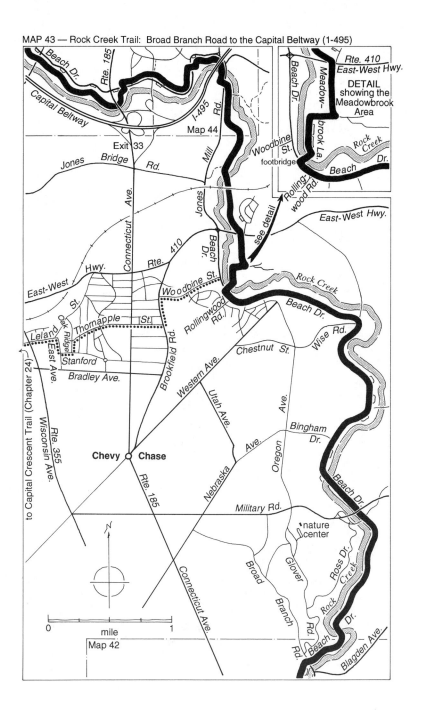

DETAIL
showing the
Meadowbrook
Area

Map 44

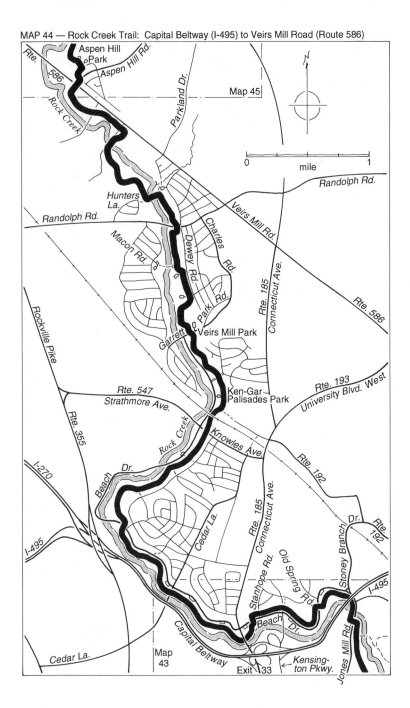

MAP 45 — Rock Creek Trail: Veirs Mill Road (Route 586) to Lake Needwood

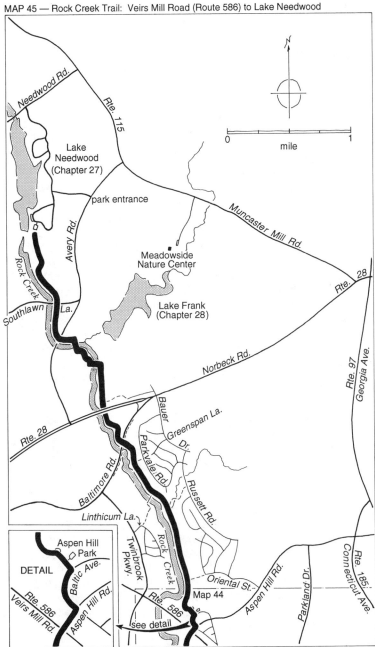

361

≈   ≈   ≈   ≈

AUTOMOBILE DIRECTIONS: The Rock Creek Trail, which runs through Washington and south-central Montgomery County in Maryland, is shown on **Maps 41-45** on pages 357-361. Obviously, there are many places to join the trail. The following directions lead to parking areas at the trail's two end points and to some other parking areas in-between.

Parking lots at the southern end of the Rock Creek Trail near the Potomac River in Washington: You may be tempted to use the parking lot for the Thompson Boat House, located where Virginia Avenue meets Rock Creek Parkway at the southern end of the Rock Creek Trail. However, not only do signs declare that this lot is for boat house patrons only, but also finding a parking spot here is impossible on any day when there is a boating event.

Ample parking, however, is available at **West Potomac Park** and **East Potomac Park,** shown in the lower-right corner of Map 42, and from which a riverside path leads a mile north past the Arlington Memorial Bridge to the trail upstream along Rock Creek.

Another possibility for parking is Roosevelt Island, from which the Mount Vernon Trail leads downriver to the Arlington Memorial Bridge, which in turn provides access to the Rock Creek Trail.

Parking lots in the midsection of Washington's Rock Creek Park: The parking lots described here are in the vicinity of Tilden Street, **Pierce Mill**, and Blagden Avenue, which are shown near the top of Map 42. Two approaches to these parking lots are described below:

From the vicinity of the Potomac River: Take Rock Creek Parkway north. The western end of Independence Avenue (south of the Lincoln Memorial), the northwestern end of Virginia Avenue, and the western end of K Street all provide access to the parkway. (The ramps off K Street are somewhat obscure. From K Street westbound, there is a ramp on the right just before the Whitehurst Freeway. From K Street eastbound, there is a ramp on the right immediately after the end of the Whitehurst Freeway.)

Follow Rock Creek Parkway north, then fork right for Beach

Drive. Follow Beach Drive 1.8 miles to a crossroads at a traffic light near Pierce Mill, where Park Road intersects from the right and Tilden Street from the left. Turn left across Rock Creek and then — just beyond Pierce Mill — turn left onto Shoemaker Street and left again into the parking lot. The Rock Creek Trail borders the creek.

If there is no room in the parking lot at Pierce Mill, go back to Beach Drive and turn left. Almost immediately there is another parking lot on the left. If it too is full, follow Beach Drive 0.3 mile north. After passing the intersection with Blagden Avenue, bear left across Rock Creek and then immediately turn left into a parking lot. The Rock Creek Trail actually passes through this parking lot, so be alert for hikers and bicyclists.

From Connecticut Avenue: Go to the intersection with Tilden Street. Connecticut Avenue crosses Tilden 1.5 miles north of the long, high Taft Bridge and 4.5 miles south of Exit 33 off Interstate 495 (the Capital Beltway). On Connecticut Avenue, you will of course know that you are approaching Tilden Street by watching the two-syllable alphabetized cross streets: Rodman and Sedgewick are just to the south and Upton and Van Ness are just to the north. (One syllable cross streets are farther south; three syllable cross streets farther north.) If you are approaching from the south on Connecticut Avenue, turn right onto Tilden; if you are approaching from the north on Connecticut, turn left onto Tilden.

Follow Tilden Street 0.5 mile downhill into Rock Creek Park. Within sight of the stone Pierce Mill, turn right onto Shoemaker Street and then left into the parking lot. The Rock Creek Trail borders the creek.

If there is no room in the parking lot across the road from Pierce Mill, continue on Tilden Street across Rock Creek, then turn left onto Beach Drive. Almost immediately there is another parking lot on the left. If it too is full, follow Beach Drive 0.3 mile north. After passing the intersection with Blagden Avenue, bear left across Rock Creek and then immediately turn left into a parking lot. The Rock Creek Trail actually passes through this parking lot, so be alert for hikers and bicyclists.

Parking lots along Beach Drive in Montgomery County: As shown at the bottom of Map 44, Interstate 495 (the Capital

Beltway) provides quick access to the Rock Creek Trail in Montgomery County. For walkers, the trail in Montgomery County is far preferable to the trail in Washington.

Leave the Beltway at Exit 33 (Exit 33A off the Inner Loop) for Route 185 North (Connecticut Avenue). At the bottom of the exit ramp, turn north onto Route 185, but almost immediately turn left onto Beach Drive. The paved hike-bike trail is on the left, but eventually crosses Beach Drive. Most road bikers prefer Beach Drive itself, so drive slowly.

Park in one of the lots along Beach Drive. If you cannot find a satisfactory parking spot within the first mile, don't worry. Keep following Beach Drive north and eventually you will find a parking lot with room. If you reach a T-intersection with Garrett Park Road, turn right and then left into the parking lot for Veirs Mill Park.

Parking at the northern end of the Rock Creek Trail: The northern terminus is at **Lake Needwood**, as shown on Map 45. For walkers, this is an excellent place to start, providing immediate access to the trail's most rural and attractive section. The trail here is also suitable for cyclists who are prepared to ride slowly and share the path with hikers. Road bikers are better off starting at the parking lots described in the previous paragraph.

To reach Lake Needwood, leave the Beltway at Exit 31A for Route 97 North (Georgia Avenue). Follow Route 97 North for 7.4 miles to an intersection at a traffic light with Route 28 (Norbeck Road). Turn left (west) onto Route 28, but go only 0.2 mile, then turn right at another traffic light onto Route 115 (Muncaster Mill Road). Follow Route 115 West 2.1 miles, then turn left at a traffic light onto Avery Road toward Rock Creek Regional Park. Go only 0.4 mile, then turn right into the entrance for Lake Needwood. Follow the entrance road 0.3 mile, then turn left at a T-intersection and continue 0.4 mile to the parking lot for the hike-bike trail on the right.

≈   ≈   ≈   ≈

WALKING and BICYCLING: The 24-mile Rock Creek Trail is shown on **Maps 41-45** on pages 357-361. For the most part, the trail is a paved path. However, in northern Washington the trail follows Beach Drive for 5 miles, and in Montgomery

County the trail occasionally follows local streets for short distances. Detailed insets are provided on the maps to help navigate two places where the route is less than obvious.

Connections to other hike-bike trails: As shown on Map 42 and — in schematic outline — on **Map 2** on page 7, the Rock Creek Trail is linked to other Washington-area hike-bike trails.

Just south of Pennsylvania Avenue near the Potomac River, the trail connects with the C&O Canal towpath (see Chapter 7). The towpath, in turn, links with the Capital Crescent Trail (Chapter 24).

By crossing the Potomac River via the Arlington Memorial Bridge (see the corner panel on Map 2), hikers and cyclists can pass back and forth between the Rock Creek Trail and the Mount Vernon Trail (Chapter 19). And from the northern end of the Mount Vernon Trail at Roosevelt Island, the Custis Trail runs west to join the W&OD Trail (Chapter 12).

27

LAKE NEEDWOOD

including access to the Rock Creek Trail

Walking and ski touring. **Map 46** on page 370 shows a short route (2 miles; 3.2 kilometers) that follows easy trails along the side of the valley overlooking Lake Needwood.

For a longer walk, Lake Needwood also provides access to the most rural and attractive section of the Rock Creek Trail, which is shown extending southward at the bottom of Map 46. The distance to Veirs Mill Road is 3 miles (4.8 kilometers) one way, but you can go much farther if you want. For a discussion and maps of the entire Rock Creek Trail, including not only the 13-mile hike-bike path in Montgomery County, but also another 10 miles through Rock Creek Park in Washington, see Chapter 26.

Lake Needwood is open daily from dawn until dusk. Dogs must be leashed. Swimming is prohibited. The park is managed by the Montgomery County Department of Parks, Maryland-National Capital Park and Planning Commission; telephone (301) 948-5053 (weekdays only). For information about boat rentals during summer and on spring and fall weekends, call (301) 762-1888.

THE LARGE EARTH DAMS creating Lake Needwood and nearby Lake Frank (see Chapter 28) were constructed by the Soil Conservation Service during the mid-1960s in order to reduce flooding and sedimentation in the Rock Creek Valley downstream to Washington. Lake Needwood impounds water on Rock Creek's main branch, and Lake Frank on the river's North Branch, which joins the main river about a mile south of Lake Needwood. Of the seventy-seven square miles within the Rock Creek drainage area, about one third is upstream from the dams. The high elevation of the spillways and dam crests reflects the enormous volume of stormwater runoff that occurs during exceptionally heavy rains. For example, during Tropical Storm Agnes in 1972, the water reached within a foot or two of the Lake Needwood spillway, which is twenty-eight feet above the normal level of the reservoir.

When the plan for the two reservoirs was developed in 1962, most of the land in the upper Rock Creek watershed was still devoted to farming. Since then rapid land development throughout the area has increased erosion from construction sites — although there has been a corresponding (and permanent) reduction in erosion from cultivated fields. In any case, much of the sediment ends up in the reservoirs, which act as giant settling basins for mud that otherwise would flow into the Potomac River. The extent of sedimentation is especially evident at the eastern end of Lake Frank during periods of low water; there the North Branch of Rock Creek has carved a gully across the bed of accumulated sand and silt, showing sediments as much as ten feet thick. After studying the rate of sediment delivery into Lake Needwood from the time of its creation until 1968, the Soil Conservation Service projected a mere fifty-year life for the reservoir before its capacity would be so far reduced that it would no longer store enough water to prevent flooding downstream. The long-term outlook for the two lakes is that sediments will eventually fill them to the level of the concrete "risers" or large drain pipes that maintain normal water level. As this happens, the lakes will slowly change into marsh and swampy woods.

Partly to reduce sedimentation and turbidity in lakes Needwood and Frank, Montgomery County was among the first local governments in Maryland to enact an ordinance requiring land developers to take measures to reduce erosion from construction sites. Subsequently, in 1970 Maryland adopted a Sediment Control Law requiring that all construction projects be carried out in accordance with a grading and sediment control plan approved by the local Soil Conservation District. City and county development permit agencies are supposed to inspect construction sites and enforce the required sediment control measures, such as dikes to divert stormwater runoff around the sites, straw mulch and cellulose fiber to cushion the impact of rain and to slow runoff, holding ponds to allow sediments to settle, and gravel sediment traps and low, fence-like barriers of permeable fabric to filter rain water before it flows from the site. If installed and maintained properly, the various control measures are estimated to reduce the outflow of sediments from construction sites by about 70 percent. At first, enforcement of such measures was lax, but government agencies and development contractors have been more observant of the law in recent years, so that now, in the law's third decade, the required procedures have become a normal and accepted part of the development process.

≈   ≈   ≈   ≈

The route shown on Map 46 on page 370 passes near the Needwood Mansion, located at the rim of the valley west of the lake. The main body of the handsome brick house was built in 1857 by William George Robertson on land inherited by his wife, Harriet. Her grandfather, John Cooke, had received a patent for one thousand acres in 1758. George Robertson had also inherited extensive land holdings in the area, and he and his wife established a prosperous farm that they called Sunnyside. In 1861 Robertson was killed by lightning as he turned his horse into the main gate at Needwood. His widow and children — including a son who fought for the South during the Civil War as one of Colonel John S. Mosby's Rangers — continued to live in the house until 1881, when it was acquired by George Washington Columbus Beall. His family owned the property until 1948.

In 1962 Needwood became part of Rock Creek Regional Park and now serves as the administrative headquarters for Lake Needwood and Lake Frank. Although not open on weekends, the house is worth looking at from the outside as you pass nearby.

≈   ≈   ≈   ≈

AUTOMOBILE DIRECTIONS: Lake Needwood is located in Maryland 15 miles north of downtown Washington and only 3 miles north of Rockville. (See the corner panel on **Map 46** on page 370.) Three avenues of approach are described below.

To Lake Needwood from Interstate 495 (the Capital Beltway: Leave the Beltway at Exit 31A for Route 97 North (Georgia Avenue). Follow Route 97 North 7.4 miles to an intersection at a traffic light with Route 28 (Norbeck Road). Turn left (west) onto Route 28, but go only 0.2 mile, then turn right at another traffic light onto Route 115 (Muncaster Mill Road). Follow Route 115 West 2.1 miles, then turn left at a traffic light onto Avery Road toward Rock Creek Regional Park. Go only 0.4 mile, then turn right into the entrance to Lake Needwood. Follow the entrance road 0.3 mile, then turn left at a T-intersection and continue 0.4 mile to the parking lot for the hike-bike trail on the right.

To Lake Needwood from Interstate 270 near Rockville and Gaithersburg: Leave I-270 at Exit 9A for Interstate 370 East toward the Gaithersburg Metro Station. Pass the exit for Shady Grove Road to Route 355; continue on the expressway

MAP 46 — Lake Needwood
The northern end of the Rock Creek Trail (which is described
in Chapter 46) is shown at the bottom of the map.

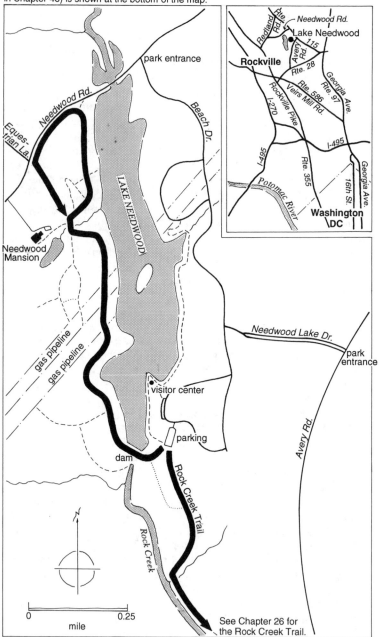

for another 1.3 miles to the exit for Shady Grove Road East.

Follow Shady Grove Road East 1.5 miles to an intersection at a traffic light with Route 115 (Muncaster Mill Road), and there turn right. Follow Route 115 East 2.6 miles to an intersection at a traffic light with Avery Road, and there turn right toward Rock Creek Regional Park. Go only 0.4 mile, then turn right into the entrance to Lake Needwood. Follow the entrance road 0.3 mile, then turn left at a T-intersection and continue 0.4 mile to the parking lot for the hike-bike trail on the right.

To Lake Needwood from Rockville: From Route 355 (Rockville Pike) or Route 586 (Veirs Mill Road) in Rockville, take Route 28 East (Norbeck Road) for about 1 mile, then turn left onto Avery Road. Go nearly 2 miles, then turn left into the entrance to Lake Needwood. Follow the entrance road 0.3 mile, then turn left at a T-intersection and continue 0.4 mile to the parking lot for the hike-bike trail on the right.

≈   ≈   ≈   ≈

WALKING: A route totaling only 2 miles along the western side of Lake Needwood is shown on **Map 46** opposite and is described below. The line extending south at the bottom of the map shows how to get started on the **Rock Creek Trail**, discussed in Chapter 26.

For the 2-mile walk along the lake's western side, start at the hike-bike parking lot. Follow a gravel track across the large grassy spillway, with the reservoir to the right. Continue uphill and across the crest of the Lake Needwood dam. With the reservoir downhill to the right, follow the main track along the slope. After crossing several pipeline rights-of-way, the path veers left. At a trail intersection, turn right and go 50 yards, then turn right again and continue as Lake Needwood once more comes into view on the right.

At Needwood Road, follow the path as it curves left uphill. Turn left away from Needwood Road opposite an intersection with Equestrian Lane. With Lake Needwood downhill on the left and the Needwood Mansion visible on the right, follow the path to a four-way intersection of trails. To return to the parking lot by the way you came, continue straight 50 yards, then turn left.

28

LAKE FRANK

including the Meadowside Nature Center

Walking and ski touring — 1.5 or 4 miles (2.4 or 6.4 kilometers), depending on whether you take a short circuit through woods and fields at the Meadowside Nature Center or a longer loop around Lake Frank. Both excursions are shown on **Map 47** on page 377, and both start by following the North Branch of Rock Creek from the nature center downstream to Lake Frank. After circling the lake, the longer route eventually follows the North Branch upstream to Muncaster Mill Road, then back down the opposite bank to the nature center.

About 1.5 miles of the trail along the south side of Lake Frank is paved and provides a pleasant country setting for pushing your child in a stroller. Direct access to the paved path is from the parking lot off Avery Road.

The park entrance at the Meadowside Nature Center is open daily from sunrise to sunset. The nature center building is open Tuesday through Saturday from 9 A.M. to 5 P.M. Dogs must be leashed. Swimming and bicycling are prohibited.

The park is managed by the Montgomery County Department of Parks, Maryland-National Capital Park and Planning Commission; telephone (301) 948-5053 on weekdays. For the Meadowside Nature Center, which offers a variety of programs and guided walks, call (301) 924-4141 Tuesday through Saturday.

THE OVERGROWN FIELDS at the Meadowside Nature Center provide a hint of the farm landscape that characterized Montgomery County before it was overspread by suburbia. Other vestiges of the farm economy that lasted well into the twentieth century are the region's many gristmills, several of which stood along Rock Creek and its North Branch in the vicinity of what is now Lake Frank.

A few stone pillars and foundation walls overgrown with brush are all that is left of Muncaster Mill. Powered by the North Branch of Rock Creek, this small country gristmill stood on the west bank just south of where Muncaster Mill Road now crosses the stream on a concrete and steel bridge of recent vintage. A photograph taken in the 1930s, however, shows a dirt road leading across a small kingpost truss bridge a dozen yards downstream from the present bridge. The road then passed between the frame and clapboard gristmill and an open-sided shed that housed a sawmill. The gristmill fronted directly on the road. Its facade was two stories high, topped by a steep gambrel roof. In the back the roof sloped down two and a half stories like that of a New England saltbox. From a dam about half a mile upstream, the millrace ran along the side of the valley and into a wooden flume that fed an overshot water wheel at the side of the gristmill.

Muncaster Mill was built about 1820 by the millwright Joseph Elger, Jr. His father, Joseph Elger, Sr., had built an earlier mill about a mile downstream on land that he obtained by means of a writ *ad quod damnum* filed on February 19, 1763. Such writs were a way for individuals to condemn private property for their own use, provided that they built a mill, as Elger eventually did in the 1770s. Intended to assist local agriculture, the writs were authorized by the Acts of 1660, "An Act for Encouragement of Such Persons as Will Undertake to Build Water Mills." Entrepreneurs who obtained the writs were required to post a bond of fifty thousand pounds of tobacco to ensure that they intended to erect a mill. If the writ was approved, the applicant received ten acres along each bank of the stream, and the landowner was awarded appropriate compensation. Sometimes owners even condemned their own land in order to establish well-defined, court-approved mill sites, which they could use themselves or sell to a millwright. Without court approval — and sometimes even with it — there was danger of running afoul of conflicting mill and water rights farther upstream or down.

The Elgers built a third mill on the North Branch of Rock Creek in about 1800. It stood about five hundred yards downstream from the site subsequently selected for Muncaster Mill and was disassembled when the later mill was erected by Joseph Elger, Jr. for a landowner named Robertson, who had bought Elger's "Milton Farm." Other substantial landowners in the vicinity were the Muncasters, and by 1879 the mill was shown as William E. Muncaster's gristmill and sawmill on the G. M. Hopkins atlas of Montgomery County. For a period, wool carding was also done at the mill.

Leased to various millers, Muncaster Mill was the last mill on Rock Creek to cease operating. When it finally closed in 1925, it had been run for the five previous years by a Mr. Dove, who also farmed nearby. He and his young son William operated the mill two or three times a week year round. According to the recollections of William Dove, Jr., the mill served thirty or forty families in Olney, Rockville, Gaithersburg, Redland, and Norbeck. Farmers would leave their grain one week and pick it up the next. Most customers paid, or promised to pay, in cash; but sometimes the Doves accepted one bushel out of five as payment. The flour and cornmeal were packaged in five-pound bags and sold in nearby towns. The younger Dove's duties included collecting delinquent accounts that exceeded fifteen or twenty dollars. The Doves charged sixty cents per bushel to grind grain. To lease, operate, and maintain the mill cost them about $300 annually. During their tenure the mill had three pairs of millstones driven by a water wheel fifteen feet in diameter and six feet wide. One pair of stones ground corn; another, wheat, barley, and oats to a coarse texture; and the third ground wheat and buckwheat for fine flour.

The Doves also operated the sawmill, which sat on stone piers and was powered by a small turbine. The mill originally had an oscillating saw that later was replaced by a circular saw. The family filled orders for wagon tongues, furniture pieces, truck beds, and other custom work.

After Muncaster Mill closed, it was partially dismantled so that its heavy timbers could be used to build a stable. What was left burned in 1935, but not until after the mill had been photographed for inclusion in the federal government's survey of historic buildings and the machinery examined by workers engaged in the restoration of Pierce Mill in Washington.

≈   ≈   ≈   ≈

AUTOMOBILE DIRECTIONS: Lake Frank and the **Meadowside Nature Center** are located in Maryland 14 miles north of downtown Washington and only 2 miles northeast of Rockville. (See the corner panel on **Map 47** on page 377.) Three avenues of approach are described below.

To Lake Frank from Interstate 495 (the Capital Beltway):
Leave the Beltway at Exit 31A for Route 97 North (Georgia Avenue). Follow Route 97 North 7.4 miles to an intersection at a traffic light with Route 28 (Norbeck Road). Turn left (west) onto Route 28, but go only 0.2 mile, then turn right at another traffic light onto Route 115 (Muncaster Mill Road). Follow

Route 115 West 1.5 miles to the entrance to the Meadowside Nature Center on the left at Meadowside Lane. Follow Meadowside Lane 0.4 mile to the parking lot and nature center building at the end of the road.

To Lake Frank from Interstate 270 near Rockville and Gaithersburg: Leave I-270 at Exit 9A for Interstate 370 East toward the Gaithersburg Metro Station. Pass the exit for Shady Grove Road to Route 355; continue on the expressway for another 1.3 miles to the exit for Shady Grove Road East.

Follow Shady Grove Road East 1.5 miles to an intersection at a traffic light with Route 115 (Muncaster Mill Road), and there turn right. Follow Route 115 East 3.3 miles to the entrance to the Meadowside Nature Center on the right at Meadowside Lane. Follow Meadowside Lane 0.4 mile to the parking lot and nature center building at the end of the road.

To Lake Frank from Rockville: From Route 355 (Rockville Pike) or Route 586 (Veirs Mill Road) in Rockville, take Route 28 East (Norbeck Road) about 3 miles to an intersection at a traffic light with Route 115 (Muncaster Mill Road). Turn left and follow Route 115 West for 1.5 miles to the entrance to the Meadowside Nature Center on the left at Meadowside Lane. Follow Meadowside Lane 0.4 mile to the parking lot and nature center building at the end of the road.

≈   ≈   ≈   ≈

WALKING: Map 47 opposite shows a short loop and a long loop. At a point marked A on the map, the short route returns to the nature center, for a total distance of only 1.5 miles. The longer route continues around Lake Frank for a total distance of 4 miles.

Both loops start at the trailhead located at the end of the nature center parking lot near a bulletin board. Follow the Rocky Ridge Trail into the woods for 25 yards, then turn left onto the Sleepy Hollow Trail. Zigzag downhill to the edge of Rock Creek's North Branch.

With the creek on the left, follow the Sleepy Hollow Trail downstream. Pass the Backbone Trail leading right uphill. Continue along the bottom of the bluff near the creek. After crossing a footbridge, bear right away from the creek. Follow a tributary stream uphill 100 yards, then turn left uphill onto the

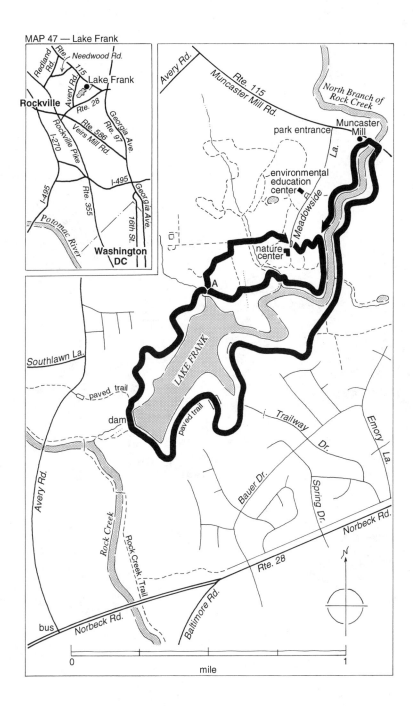

MAP 47 — Lake Frank

Redland Rd.
Rte. 115
Needwood Rd.
Avery Rd.
Lake Frank
Rockville
Rte. 28
Georgia Ave.
Rte. 586
Rte. 97
Veirs Mill Rd.
Rockville Pike
I-270
I-495
Rte. 355
I-495
Georgia Ave.
16th St.
Potomac River
Washington DC

Avery Rd.
Rte. 115
Muncaster Mill Rd.
North Branch of Rock Creek
park entrance
Muncaster Mill
Meadowside La.
environmental education center
nature center
A
LAKE FRANK
Southlawn La.
paved trail
dam
paved trail
Trailway Dr.
Emory La.
Bauer Dr.
Spring Dr.
Norbeck Rd.
Avery Rd.
Rock Creek
Rock Creek Trail
Rte. 28
Baltimore Rd.
bus
Norbeck Rd.
N

0   mile   1

Big Pines Trail. At a slightly skewed T-intersection, bear left. Soon Lake Frank comes into view on the left. Continue along the edge of the water to an intersection (marked A on the map) with the Old Nasty Trail.

To return directly to the nature center, turn right uphill. Near the top of the slope, turn right at a T-intersection, then descend gradually. Turn left at a slightly skewed T-intersection, then right at the next trail junction. Descend straight through a four-way trail junction, then cross a steam and climb to a picnic area by the nature center.

For the circuit around Lake Frank, continue straight past the junction with the Old Nasty Trail. Turn left across a stream. Continue through woods, then return to the vicinity of the water, with the lake toward the left. Eventually, the trail makes a long detour to the right around a ravine, then again returns to the bluff above the lake. Continue to an intersection with an asphalt path. Follow the paved path downhill to the left and along the crest of an earth dam.

At the far end of the dam, continue on the paved path around the lake. Pass through a parking lot and out the far end, then follow the road as it curves left downhill. Pass an entrance road on the right. With the lake toward the left, continue on the park road to another parking lot.

From the far end of the parking lot, enter the woods on a dirt path. With Lake Frank on the left, continue along the slope. After passing around a ravine, follow the path across a hill covered with scrubby, young woods. Pass trails intersecting from the right. Eventually, the North Branch of Rock Creek comes into view on the left. With caution, cross a tributary stream and continue on the main path all the way to Muncaster Mill Road.

Turn left across the Muncaster Mill Road bridge, then immediately descend the embankment on the log steps to a path that leads downstream past the site of Muncaster Mill. With the creek on the left, follow the path to the intersection with the Sleepy Hollow Trail, where you first descended into the valley from the nature center. Turn right and follow the Sleepy Hollow Trail as it zigzags uphill to the parking lot by the nature center.

29

WHEATON REGIONAL PARK
including Brookside Nature Center
and Brookside Gardens
SLIGO CREEK TRAIL

Walking — 3 miles (4.8 kilometers) at Wheaton Regional Park; walking and bicycling — up to 18 miles (29 kilometers) round-trip on the Sligo Creek Trail. The trail along Sligo Creek is a paved hike-bike path that will link (when it is finished) with other bikeways, as discussed below.

Wheaton Regional Park provides access to several very different walking and bicycling opportunities. The park itself has a network of footpaths and horse trails through wooded, rolling terrain in the vicinity of **Brookside Nature Center**. The park also includes **Brookside Gardens**, featuring ponds, lawns, a Japanese teahouse, conservatory, specialty gardens, and many paths for strolling. Wheaton Regional Park is shown on **Map 48** on page 386. The route shown by the bold line on the upper part of the map makes a short pass through the woods (avoiding areas of residential and recreational development at the park's periphery) and then enters Brookside Gardens. To avoid the crowds on spring weekends, go early in the day.

Wheaton Regional Park is also a good place to start on the paved **Sligo Creek Trail**, which is shown on **Map 49** on page 388. The bold line trailing off the bottom of Map 48 shows the start of this hike-bike trail. When it is finished, the Sligo Creek Trail will run 9 miles southeast to a juncture with the paved trails along Northwest Branch, the Anacostia River, Northeast Branch, Paint Branch, and Indian Creek, which are discussed in Chapter 31 — but as of 1996 the section of the Sligo Creek Trail between Maple Avenue and Riggs Road was unfinished. Near Wheaton Regional Park, the trail makes use of residential streets for 0.5 mile, and it occasionally crosses major roads.

Wheaton Regional Park is also at the northern end of the Northwest Branch Trail, as noted on the right edge of Map 48. The Northwest Branch Trail is discussed in Chapter 30.

Wheaton Regional Park is open daily from dawn until sunset. The Brookside Nature Center is open Tuesday through Saturday from 9 A.M. to 5 P.M. and Sunday from 1 to 5; it is closed Monday and holidays. Brookside Gardens is open daily (except Christmas) from 9 A.M. to 5 P.M. Dogs must be leashed at Wheaton Regional Park and are altogether prohibited within Brookside Gardens.

If your interest is to walk at Wheaton Regional Park, use the automobile directions that lead to the Glenallan Road entrances for Brookside Gardens or Brookside Nature Center. For the Sligo Creek Trail, use the automobile directions that lead to the Shorefield Road entrance.

Wheaton Regional Park is managed by the Montgomery County Department of Parks, Maryland-National Capital Park and Planning Commission; telephone (301) 946-7033. For information on programs at Brookside Nature Center, telephone (301) 946-9071. For Brookside Gardens call (301) 949-8230 or 8231.

WHEATON REGIONAL PARK lies near the eastern edge of Mary-and's Piedmont, which is one of several physiographic provinces that run parallel with the Atlantic shore in belts of varying width from New York southward almost to the Gulf of Mexico. Starting at the water's edge, the land rises gradually across the Coastal Plain, then more rapidly over the Piedmont, which in Maryland includes the depression of the Frederick Valley. West of Frederick is the abrupt line of the Blue Ridge, followed by the Valley and Ridge province of Washington and Allegany counties and the high Appalachian Plateau of Garrett County and West Virginia.

Disregarding soil, most of the Piedmont province is composed of hard crystalline rock, including shist, granite, gneiss, quartzite, serpentine, and gabbro, although occasionally there are areas — both large and small — of relatively soft limestone, as in the Frederick Valley. In the vicinity of Wheaton Regional Park, the bedrock is part of a massive complex of coarse-grained schist rich in mica, quartz, feldspar, and garnet. White quartzite rocks occasionally are visible at the surface, and flat pebbles of shist speckled with mica are present in the stream beds. Between 1882 and 1916 the Kensington Mica Mine operated across Kemp Mill Road from Wheaton Regional Park.

To the east of Wheaton Regional Park, the Piedmont bedrock dips seaward below the unconsolidated sediments of the Coastal Plain, which — together with the underwater Continental Shelf — is an apron of clay, silt, sand, and gravel eroded from the Piedmont and Appalachian highlands. Also contributing to the thick mantle of deposits along the mid-Atlantic coast are immense quantities of rock flour and sand scoured by continental glaciers from regions farther north and carried to the sea by huge rivers of meltwater that today survive in the relatively trivial trickle of the Hudson, Delaware, and Susquehanna rivers. Across the coastal sediments the ocean shore has advanced and receded repeatedly as the sea has risen and fallen, depending on how much of the planet's water has been amassed in the polar ice caps and in continental ice sheets.

The Coastal Plain sediments were laid down in relatively recent geologic time — that is, within the last 135 million years — during periods when the coastal region was submerged beneath the sea or under shallow inland lakes, swamps, and slowly meandering rivers. Seashells and the bones and teeth of marine animals are common in some layers of sediment. In the vicinity of Beltsville, Muirkirk, and Bladensburg, the deposits contain many dinosaur bones and teeth.

The layers of sediment all dip toward the southeast. Although the angle of dip is very slight — generally less than one degree — the sediments have accumulated to a depth of more than a mile beneath the present Atlantic coastline. Even near the boundary with the Piedmont, the coastal deposits are hundreds of feet thick, giving rise to large sand and gravel strip mines in the vicinity of Interstate 95 north of the Capital Beltway.

Marking the transition between the Piedmont and the Coastal Plain is the so-called Fall Line, which is not really a sharp boundary but rather a zone of considerable width. Within the fall zone, streams descend from the Piedmont plateau in a series of rocky rapids and falls to the low elevation of rivers flowing across the easily eroded sediments of the Coastal Plain. The descent through the fall zone involves such a concentrated release of energy that often gorges are carved extending far upstream into the Piedmont, as exemplified by the Potomac River above Washington.

Downstream from their last rapids, most rivers of the mid-Atlantic region are at or near sea level, so that the Fall Line also marks, more or less, the heads of navigation. Washington (like its older neighbor, Georgetown) was sited at the head of navigation on the Potomac River, four miles downstream from Little Falls, the first rapids. Other East Coast cities, including Albany, Trenton, Baltimore, and Richmond, were located similarly at the heads of navigation on their respective rivers at sites where the nearby Fall Line also provided abundant water power for industrial development. A walk along Northwest Branch (see Chapters 30 and 31) provides a good opportunity to follow a stream as it descends from the Piedmont near Wheaton Regional Park, passes through the fall zone in a gorge of its own making, reaches the Coastal Plain just below Adelphi Mill near College Park, and from there flows gently within low banks through Hyattsville to the head of navigation at Bladensburg. Sligo Creek shows a similar profile.

Except in major river valleys, where the transition from Piedmont to Coastal Plain is fairly clear, the boundary between the two physiographic provinces is sinuous and ill-defined. It is marked by a feathering out of the deposits of coastal sand, silt, and clay as they lap up onto the soil and underlying bedrock of the Piedmont. North of Washington the transition very roughly corresponds to the boundary between Montgomery and Prince Georges counties. Farther north between the Patuxent River and Baltimore, the boundary moves east to the vicinity of Route 1. Somewhat surprisingly, however, topography is often not a clue. Despite its name, the Coastal Plain west of Chesapeake Bay is not at all flat. To some extent, the coastal deposits reflect the uneven surface on which they were laid down. More significantly, the sedimentary deposits now stand far above sea level and therefore have been shaped by stream erosion. In consequence, the Coastal Plain near Washington forms a rolling upland resembling the Piedmont landscape much more closely than the low plain of the Eastern Shore. For example, the topography of Wheaton Regional Park, which is located about three miles west of the boundary between the Piedmont and Coastal Plain, is much like that of Greenbelt Park (Chapter 32) and the National Arboretum (Chapter 34), each located several miles east of the boundary. Nonetheless, the transition into the Coastal Plain is reflected in the almost rockless stream banks and in the more frequent occurrence of Virginia Pine and other trees that thrive in areas where the coastal soils are particularly sandy.

≈　　　≈　　　≈　　　≈

METRO: Metrobus routes Y4, Y5, and Y8 originate at the Wheaton Metrorail station (Red Line) and follow Georgia Avenue north. Get off the bus at the corner with Shorefield Road, which leads east 0.3 mile to Wheaton Regional Park.

The Sligo Creek Trail (which is shown on **Map 49** on page 388) crosses several Metrobus routes, including C2 and C4 on University Boulevard, Z2 and Z8 on Route 29 (Colesville Road), and K6 on New Hampshire Avenue.

Telephone (202) 637-7000 for current Metro information, including schedules, routes, and connections.

≈   ≈   ≈   ≈

AUTOMOBILE: Wheaton Regional Park is located in Maryland directly north of Washington, about 5 miles beyond Silver Spring. (See •29 on **Map 1** on page 6, and also **Map 49** on page 388.) If you plan to walk at the park — or if you want to drive to the upper end of the Northwest Branch Trail (described in Chapter 30) — follow the directions to the Glenallan Avenue entrances for Brookside Gardens or Brookside Nature Center.

The Sligo Creek Trail stretches south from Wheaton Regional Park to the Capital Beltway, then southeast to Takoma Park and Hyattsville. If you plan to walk or bicycle on the Sligo Creek Trail, go to the Shorefield Road entrance at Wheaton Regional Park, as described in the second paragraph below.

To Wheaton Regional Park's Brookside Gardens or Brookside Nature Center from Interstate 495 (the Capital Beltway): Leave the Beltway at Exit 31A for Route 97 North (Georgia Avenue). Follow Route 97 North about 3 miles to Randolph Road; in the process you will pass Shorefield Road, where there is a different park entrance. Turn right (east) onto Randolph Road and go 0.3 mile to an intersection with Glenallan Avenue. Turn right and follow Glenallan Avenue downhill 0.7 mile. Turn right into the parking lot for Brookside Gardens at 1500 Glenallan Avenue or continue 0.1 mile and turn right into the parking lot for Brookside Nature Center at 1400 Glenallan Avenue.

To Wheaton Regional Park's Shorefield Road entrance from Interstate 495 (the Capital Beltway): Leave the Beltway at Exit 31A for Route 97 North (Georgia Avenue). Follow Route 97 North less than 3 miles to an intersection at a traffic light with Shorefield Road. Turn right onto Shorefield Road and go 0.4 mile to the end of the road, then turn right into Wheaton Regional Park and descend to the far end of the parking lot.

≈   ≈   ≈   ≈

MAP 48 — Wheaton Regional Park
The northern end of the Sligo Creek Trail is shown at the bottom of the map.
The entire Sligo Creek Trail is shown on Map 49.

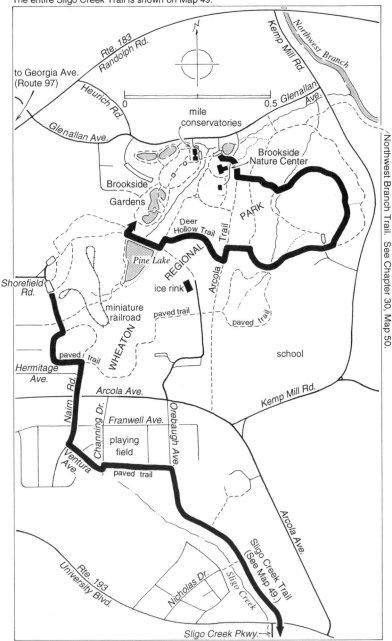

WALKING AT WHEATON REGIONAL PARK: The bold line at the top center of **Map 48** opposite shows the route described below. It starts at the Brookside Nature Center parking lot. If you parked at Brookside Gardens, you can reach the nature center as follows: From the conservatory parking lot, descend steps opposite a brick building between the two greenhouses. Follow the footpath to the parking lot for Brookside Nature Center.

From the parking lot for Brookside Nature Center, follow the paved path 10 yards toward the nature center building (which is well worth visiting), then fork left onto a path leading by a fence enclosing a small pond. Cross a road and fork right uphill on a footpath. After 120 yards, turn left at the first trail junction. Follow the footpath straight through an intersection with a horse trail. At a T-intersection, turn left across a small bridge. Follow the wide trail as it gradually circles right.

Eventually, at a T-intersection with the horse trail, turn right uphill. After 80 yards, cross a paved road at the entrance to a parking lot. Continue on the horse trail down through a valley and steeply up the other side. At the top of the slope, turn left toward the Arcola Trail. At a T-intersection with the Arcola Trail, turn left. Go 65 yards, then turn right onto the Deer Hollow Trail toward Pine Lake. Follow the footpath gradually downhill. At a trail junction, turn left for a few dozen yards to a gravel road at the corner of Pine Lake.

Turn right to follow the road along the crest of an earth dam. (Alternatively, for a slightly longer walk, circle clockwise around the lake to the other end of the dam.) A few dozen yards beyond the end of the dam, turn right onto an asphalt path leading into Brookside Gardens.

≈   ≈   ≈

WALKING and BICYCLING ON THE SLIGO CREEK TRAIL:
The bold line at the bottom of **Map 48** opposite shows how to get started on this hike-bike trail, and **Map 49** on page 388 shows the rest of the trail downstream to Northwest Branch.

From the lower end of the parking lot at the Shorefield Road entrance of Wheaton Regional Park, you can reach the Sligo Creek Trail by following a paved path straight past the end of the miniature railroad. After entering the woods, turn right uphill.

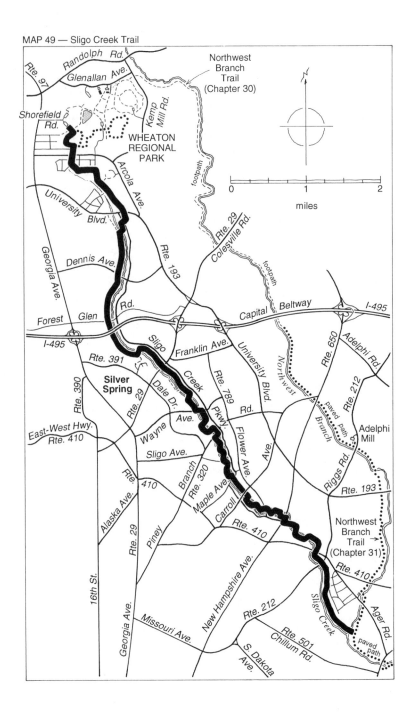

MAP 49 — Sligo Creek Trail

Randolph Rd.

Glenallan Ave.

Rte. 97

Shorefield Rd.

Kemp Mill Rd.

Northwest Branch Trail (Chapter 30)

WHEATON REGIONAL PARK

Arcola Ave.

University Blvd.

Georgia Ave.

Dennis Ave.

Rte. 193

footpath

Rte. 29

Colesville Rd.

footpath

Glen Rd.

Forest Glen

Capital Beltway

I-495

I-495

Sligo

Rte. 391

Franklin Ave.

University Blvd.

Northwest

Rte. 650

Adelphi Rd.

Rte. 390

Silver Spring

Rte. 29

Dale Dr.

Creek

Rte. 789

Rd.

paved path

Rte. 212

Branch

Adelphi Mill

East-West Hwy.
Rte. 410

Wayne Ave.

Pkwy.

Flower Ave.

Ave.

Riggs Rd.

Sligo Ave.

Alaska Ave.

Rte. 410

Branch

Rte. 320

Maple Ave.

Carroll

Rte. 410

Rte. 193

Northwest Branch Trail (Chapter 31)

Rte. 29

Piney

16th St.

Georgia Ave.

Missouri Ave.

New Hampshire Ave.

Rte. 212

Rte. 501
Chillum Rd.

S. Dakota Ave.

Rte. 410

Sligo Creek

Ager Rd.

paved path

0   1   2
miles

At a four-way intersection, turn right. Follow the path, then Nairn Road, uphill. With caution, cross Arcola Avenue and follow Nairn Road downhill. Cross Franwell Avenue, then turn left onto Ventura Avenue. Follow Ventura Avenue to an intersection with Channing Drive, where the paved hike-bike trail starts, with woods on the right and a ball field on the left.

Follow the paved path and bikeway signs downstream. Sometimes at roads — at Wayne Avenue and Piney Branch Road, for example — the trail crosses Sligo Creek on the road bridge before continuing downstream on the opposite bank.

30

NORTHWEST BRANCH TRAIL

Walking — up to 14 miles (22.5 kilometers) round trip. The route shown on **Map 50** on page 396 follows a linear park through the urban fringe of Prince Georges and Montgomery counties in Maryland. Here you can literally drop out of sight of the suburbs into a quiet, wooded valley where, for mile after mile, the trail follows Northwest Branch.

The automobile directions on page 397 are to Adelphi Mill at Riggs Road. From Adelphi Mill the trail leads upstream 3 miles to the gorge and cascade at Burnt Mills on Route 29, then continues along the river 4 miles to Wheaton Regional Park (where you may prefer to start — see Chapter 29). Hike as far as you want and return the way you came. The first 2 miles above Adelphi Mill are a paved path, but the rest is a dirt path that in some places is rough or muddy.

Downstream from Adelphi Mill the paved path eventually connects with other hike-bike trails of the Anacostia watershed. This system of paved paths is the subject of Chapter 31. The present chapter, however, focuses on the section of the Northwest Branch Trail that lies upstream from Adelphi Mill and that is mostly unpaved.

The trail is open daily from dawn until dusk. Dogs must be leashed. North of New Hampshire Avenue, the park is managed by the Department of Parks, Montgomery County, Maryland-National Capital Park and Planning Commission; telephone (301) 946-7033. South of New Hampshire Avenue, the park is managed by the Department of Parks and Recreation, Prince Georges County, Maryland-National Capital Park and Planning Commission; telephone (301) 699-2407.

NORTHWEST BRANCH OF WHAT? Until the end of the nineteenth century, the echo-like answer was Northwest Branch of the Eastern Branch of the Potomac River. Now the Eastern Branch is called the

Anacostia River. Upstream from Bladensburg, the Anacostia splits into Northwest Branch and Northeast Branch.

During the nineteenth century, Northwest Branch — which flows from Ashton through Colesville, Wheaton, and Hyattsville to tidewater at Bladensburg — powered a series of gristmills. This walk passes the sites of three of these works.

The lowermost mill on Northwest Branch was Adelphi Mill, which still stands where Riggs Road crosses the river (photograph: page 395). On the opposite side of the road is the miller's stone cottage. These structures were built by the Quaker brothers Issacher and Mahlon Schofield, who acquired the Adelphi tract in 1796. There may have been an older mill, but the Schofields are thought to have torn it down and erected a new one.

Mill builders, called millwrights, were among the chief industrial entrepreneurs of their day, and for some reason, a disproportionately high number were Quakers. Constructing a gristmill was the equivalent of setting up an automated factory today. Starting at a dam, a millrace carried water at a constant elevation along the side of a ravine or valley — perhaps for hundreds of yards — in order to create a heavy fall of water that turned the waterwheel. (The Adelphi millrace was three hundred yards long.) The wheel, of course, turned the main shaft. Within the mill at the other end of the shaft were wooden gears that transferred the slow rotation of the waterwheel to vertical spindles that rotated perhaps as fast as twice each second. Extending through the floor to the next level up, these spindles turned the millstones.

Millstones were massive, thick disks, typically four to five feet in diameter, and each might weigh more than a ton. Often there were three or more pairs of stones for grinding different types of grain. For each pair of stones, the lower one was called the bedstone, and it was stationary. The upper stone was called the runner, and it rotated. The spindle that turned the runner passed through the center of the bedstone, and atop this spindle the runner was balanced above the bedstone, from which it was separated by only a tiny distance. Grain was fed by gravity through a hole in the center of the runner. In the face of each stone, sharp-edged furrows were chiseled, radiating from the middle (photograph: page 96). The scissors-like effect of these furrows rotating past each other acted to cut the grain, and in this way — rather than by sheer grinding or crushing — the stones reduced the grain to flour, which dribbled out at the circumference. Every three weeks or so the stones were re-dressed by a skilled worker who sharpened the furrows with a narrow-pointed chisel called a millbill

By the end of the eighteenth century, the more technically advanced mills used machinery developed by Oliver Evans', who described his automated system and patented devices in *The Young Mill-Wright's &*

Miller's Guide, first published in 1795. Evans-type mills had mechanical sifters, fans, dryers, and Archimedes screws and belt-and-bucket elevators for processing and moving the grain and flour, all powered by the waterwheel via a system of gears and leather belts. About 60 percent of the energy from the waterwheel was used to turn the millstones and the rest powered the other machinery. By the second quarter of the nineteenth century, virtually all mills used Evans' techniques.

According to John McGrain — an appropriate name for one of Maryland's leading authorities on gristmills — people often stood in awe of the millwright. McGrain cites an old saying: "One drop of a millwright's blood would kill a toad." This tangy aphorism seems to reflect a sort of spiteful respect for the industry and self-interested cunning of the millwright. Once established, a well-managed mill could generate substantial income both for its owner and for the miller who operated the enterprise. But suspicion and resentment were sometimes directed towards those who profited from mills. In 1704 the colonial legislature of Maryland enacted a law "for the prevention of the abuse frequently committed by persons keeping water mills, by taking excessive toll." Limits were set on the share of grain which a miller could keep as a charge for his services; eventually the standard fee for grinding all varieties of grain was fixed at one-eighth of every bushel. Nonetheless, suspicion lingered that when millwrights constructed their mills, hidden funnels and chutes were built to divert part of the grain into secret bins.

Adelphi Mill operated for about 120 years. In the early nineteenth century Adelphi was said to be the largest mill in the vicinity of Washington. The 1798 tax list indicates that the property included a stone mill, fifty-five by forty-six feet, a stone house, and a blacksmith shop. An advertisement dated June 19, 1811, mentions wool carding at Adelphi Mill, although it was primarily a gristmill. The 1820 census shows that the miller employed three hands and that the mill had complete Evans machinery and an annual output worth between $20,000 and $22,000 in flour and meal. In 1839 ownership passed to a family named Logan, and for a period the site was known as Logan's Mill. In 1863 George W. Riggs bought the mill, and the property came to be called Riggs Mill on the Riggs Road. In 1905 its flour won first prize at the Hyattsville Fair. The last miller was H. D. Freeman, who ran the mill until about 1916, largely as a convenience to neighboring farmers. His daughter told the Washington *Daily News* in 1954, "Years ago they held country dances there. They'd put a platform over the corn hopper for the musicians to sit on."

In 1951 Mrs. Leander McCormick-Goodheart, who had acquired the mill in 1928 and who subsequently tore down the milldam, deeded the site and thirty-nine acres to the Maryland-National Capital Park and

Planning Commission. After some restoration the building was dedicated as a community recreation center in 1954.

About three and a half miles upstream from Adelphi Mill is the site of Burnt Mills on the east side of Route 29 (Colesville Road). A large frame structure stood there until 1928, when it was acquired and torn down by the county sanitation commission, now the Washington Suburban Sanitary Commission. The mill name came from a tradition regarding an older mill, which was said to have burned in the early eighteenth century. In any case, a deed of sale reflects that when ownership changed in 1803, the property included a mill. The 1850 census lists a flour and bone mill with two sets of millstones. Four hands were employed. Annual output was 2,385 barrels of flour, 3,300 bushels of bone dust for fertilizer, and 2,200 bushels of meal, altogether worth $17,280. By the time of the 1880 census, the annual output had increased to 3,500 barrels of flour, plus more than 150 tons of meal and feed. The mill then had three pairs of stones powered by a sixteen-inch, thirty horsepower turbine, which in turn was driven by a twenty-five-foot fall of water. The mill was said to represent an investment of $10,000 dollars. In about 1895 the building was expanded to accommodate modern steel rollers to crush the grain rather than to grind it in the traditional manner. Photographs of the modernized mill show a large clapboard structure three and a half stories high. Measurements of the foundation in 1931 indicated that the mill had two sections, forty-one by thirty-seven feet and thirty by thirty-six. A rusted turbine, three feet in diameter, was still to be seen at that time.

Theodore Roosevelt, an enthusiastic hiker and rider, described an excursion to Burnt Mills in a letter to his oldest son:

> White House
> June 21, 1904

Dear Ted,

Mother and I had a most lovely ride the other day, way up beyond Sligo Creek to what is called North-west Branch, at Burnt Mills, where is a beautiful gorge, deep and narrow, with great boulders and even cliffs. Excepting Great Falls it is the most beautiful place around here. Mother scrambled among the cliffs in her riding habit, very pretty and most interesting. The roads were good and some of the scenery really beautiful. We were gone four hours, half an hour being occupied with the scrambling in the gorge.

Ten years after Roosevelt's visit to Burnt Mills, the Washington *Sunday Star* reported that the "mill which stands there now has been grinding and grinding so long that no man's memory runneth to the

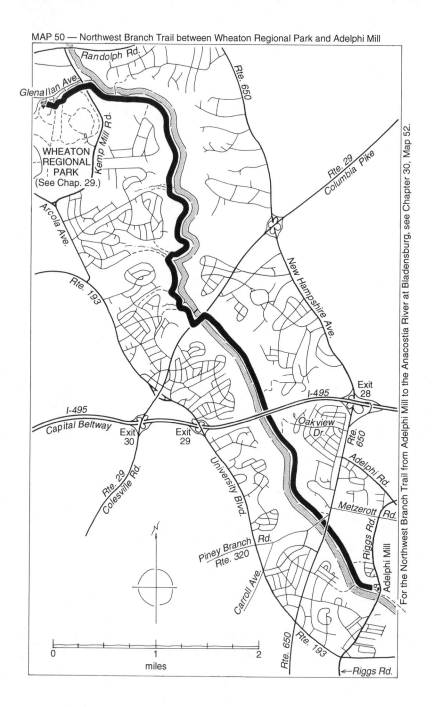

396

contrary." Operations ceased, however, in about 1920. In its last days Burnt Mills was used as a dance hall. The present-day dam at this location was built by the Washington Sanitary and Sewer Commission in 1930.

Finally, yet another gristmill along Northwest Branch was Kemp Mill, memorialized by Kemp Mill Road. In the Rockville *Sentinel*, March 20, 1857, George Kemp offered his mill for sale. He declared that he was "unable to carry on because of delicate health." Whatever the source or precise nature of Kemp's condition, the fact is that milling entailed the inhalation of dust and flour that ultimately caused many millers to suffer respiratory problems. In any case, Simon Martinet's 1865 map of Montgomery County shows the grist and sawmill of Mrs. S. Kemp on Northwest Branch near what is now Wheaton Regional Park, but the mill is not shown in the 1879 G. M. Hopkins atlas. The mill stood on the east side of Kemp Mill Road near the crossing with the Northwest Branch Trail.

≈   ≈   ≈   ≈

METRO: Metrobus route R2, which originates at the Fort Totten Metrorail station (Green and Red lines), follows Adelphi Road past Adelphi Mill at the southern end of the trail shown on **Map 50** opposite.

Metrobus routes Z2 and Z8 from the Silver Spring Metrorail station (Red Line) follow Colesville Road across the trail at its approximate midpoint.

For Metrobus service to the trail's northern end at Wheaton Regional Park, see page 384.

Telephone (202) 637-7000 for current Metro information, including schedules, routes, and connections.

≈   ≈   ≈   ≈

AUTOMOBILE DIRECTIONS: Northwest Branch Park is located in Maryland and runs from northwest to southeast past Wheaton and Hyattsville. The directions below are to **Adelphi Mill**, located 3 miles north of Washington near Silver Spring and Takoma Park. (See •30 on **Map 1** on page 6, and also **Map 50** opposite.)

The northern end of the Northwest Branch Trail is at Wheaton Regional Park. If you want to start there at the Brookside Nature Center, automobile directions are given on page 385 in Chapter 29.

If the 14-mile round trip between Adelphi Mill and Wheaton

Regional Park sounds like too much, you may want to arrange a **car shuttle** that will enable you to walk only 7 miles one way. Obviously, a shuttle involves either two cars and two driver-hikers, or a driver who drops you off at the start (after you have left your car at the end) or who simply meets you at the end. Use Map 50 to navigate your shuttle.

To Northwest Branch at Adelphi Mill from Interstate 495 (the Capital Beltway): Leave the Beltway at Exit 28B for Route 650 South (New Hampshire Avenue). Follow Route 650 South for only 0.5 mile to a crossroads at a traffic light where Dilston Street intersects from the right and Adelphi Road intersects from the left. Turn left onto Adelphi Road and follow it 0.7 mile, then turn right onto Route 212 (Riggs Road) and go almost 1 mile to the entrance and parking lot for Adelphi Mill Recreation Center on the right.

To Northwest Branch at Adelphi Mill from Washington or Takoma Park via Route 650 (New Hampshire Avenue): Follow Route 650 North to the intersection with **Route 193 (University Boulevard).** Turn right and follow Route 193 East about 0.5 mile to an intersection with Route 212 (Riggs Road). Turn left onto Route 212 and go 0.8 mile to the entrance and parking lot for Adelphi Mill Recreation Center on the left.

≈   ≈   ≈   ≈

WALKING: Map 50 on page 396 shows the route described below. It totals 14 miles round-trip between Adelphi Mill and the Brookside Nature Center at Wheaton Regional Park.

From the parking lot at Adelphi Mill, follow the paved path upstream with the river on the left. (On the right are the low embankment and shallow ditch that are the remains of the millrace.) Continue along the paved riverside path and under bridges at New Hampshire Avenue and Piney Branch Road. Eventually, the high Capital Beltway bridge will come into sight, or at any rate, you will hear the Beltway traffic.

Where the pavement ends and the main trail veers uphill to the right to Oakview Drive off New Hampshire Avenue, fork left so as to continue along the river on a narrow, rocky footpath. For about 500 yards the path is rugged as it crosses cobbles next to Northwest Branch, but once you get past the Beltway bridge, the going again becomes easy. Follow the dirt footpath along the high, level bank with the river on the left.

Eventually, the trail climbs past a cascade and through an area strewn with large boulders. The easiest path is along the side of the valley above the rocks. After passing the rocks, the trail reaches Route 29, where Burnt Mills was located.

To continue upstream along Northwest Branch, cross Route 29 using great caution, then turn left over the river. About 40 yards beyond the bridge, turn right and descend across a gully. Follow the path uphill and past the end of the dam. Continue upstream with the river downhill to the right. Where an exposed sewer pipe crosses a tributary ravine, bear left for 60 yards, then turn right across the tributary. With the river on the right, continue along the main valley. Turn right across another tributary where the sewer pipe veers right. Follow the path past yet another tributary where the sewer pipe is elevated. Soon afterward the trail follows a high bank above the stream. Cross an open trough of masonry and rubble, then — in 10 yards — turn right off the main path and descend steeply across a small tributary and past a sewer manhole. In a few dozen yards, veer right where another trail intersects from the left at the bottom of a bluff. Continue with the bluff on the left and the river 50 yards away on the right.

Follow the path with the bluff on the left and the river on the right. Eventually, cross a tributary, where you may have to detour upstream 30 or 40 yards, then continue along the main river. At times, the path is not well-defined, and at times there are two or more tracks, one next to the river and one farther away. Simply continue upstream with the river on your right. Ultimately, the trail becomes a gravel road leading to Kemp Mill Road.

Cross Kemp Mill Road about 100 yards to the left of the intersection with Glenallan Avenue. You are now entering Wheaton Regional Park, where signs mounted on large wooden posts will help to guide you to the Brookside Nature Center. Follow the horse path, forking half-right where a trail intersects from the left. After passing a bridge on the right, go 100 yards, then bear right onto a narrow path that follows a stream to the nature center.

If you have not arranged a car shuttle, return the way you came. Another possibility for long-distance hikers is to take the Sligo Creek Trail (Chapter 29) downstream from Wheaton Regional Park to the Northwest Branch Trail, then follow Northwest Branch upstream to Adelphi Mill. The total circuit is about 20 miles long and can be traced on **Map 49** on page 388.

31

LAKE ARTEMESIA and hike-bike trails to Colmar Manor and Adelphi Mill

Walking, bicycling, and in-line skating. The system of interconnected hike-bike trails discussed in this chapter includes a circuit of 1.5 miles (2.4 kilometers) around Lake Artemesia and also 22 miles (36 kilometers) of paved paths along the branching tributaries of the Anacostia River northeast of Washington in suburban Prince George's County.

Lake Artemesia Park is shown on **Map 51** on page 406, and also in the photograph at left. Its trails are a popular place for walking, jogging, in-line skating, and bicycling with small children. If you have children too heavy to carry but too young to walk far, the paved paths are also an excellent promenade for strollers and buggies.

Connected with Lake Artemesia is the system of paved trails shown on **Map 52** on page 407. From Lake Artemesia, the **Indian Creek Trail, Paint Branch Trail, Northeast Branch Trail, and Anacostia River Trail** lead south 5 miles to Colmar Manor. From a trail junction at Baltimore Avenue (Route 1), the **Northwest Branch Trail** goes 7 miles to and beyond Adelphi Mill, then turns into the hiking trail discussed in Chapter 30. Finally, completion of the **Sligo Creek Trail** between Riggs Road and Maple Avenue will eventually provide a link with the rest of the Sligo Creek Trail discussed in Chapter 29.

Lake Artemesia and the other trails are open from early morning until dusk. Dogs must be leashed. The lake and the hike-bike trails are managed by the Prince George's County Department of Parks and Recreation, Maryland-National Capital Park and Planning Commission; telephone (301) 445-4500.

THIRTY-EIGHT ACRE LAKE ARTEMESIA was excavated at the site of an earlier, smaller lake in order to provide sand and gravel for the railbed and parking lots of Metro's Green Line to College Park and

Greenbelt. By taking alluvial deposits from park property near the confluence of Paint Branch and Indian Creek, Metro avoided the need to buy sand and gravel and to truck it in from a remote location at a cost of up to $10 million. In return, Metro agreed to spend $8 million developing the excavation site according to specifications set by the county recreation department and Maryland Department of Natural Resources. The result is the outstanding park seen today. As for *Artemesia*, it is the first name of three generations of women in the family that gave the property to Prince George's County for park purposes in 1972.

A few miles to the south, at the end of the hike-bike trail leading downstream from Lake Artemesia, Metro also played a role in creation of the large, mounded park at Colmar Manor. Formerly this site was a landfill run by the Washington Suburban Sanitary Commission on bottomland and tidal flats owned by the Maryland-National Capital Park and Planning Commission. By all accounts the dump was mismanaged, and when it was abruptly closed by order of the state department of health in 1970, the site was described as having raw, unstable slopes, poor drainage, and a surface strewn with debris. In 1977 the park and planning commission entered into a four-year contract by which more than two million cubic yards of earth — most of it from the Metro tunnels — was brought in to bury the dump under a thick mantle. Aside from paying $120,000 for permission to dispose of the dirt, the contractor graded the final surface to the planners' specifications. The site now includes softball, baseball, and football fields perched atop a mound that rises eighty-five feet above the Anacostia River to the east and Dueling Branch to the west.

Dueling Brach is named for the dueling grounds located farther upstream near the intersection of 38th Street and Bladensburg Road (see Map 52 on page 407). More than fifty duels were fought there during the nineteenth century before the custom faded in the 1860s. Many of the duels involved U.S. legislators, foreign ministers, prominent military officers, and other notables. Probably the most famous affair was a duel fought on March 22, 1820, between Commodore James Barron and Commodore Stephen Decatur, the hero of the Tripolitan War. Decatur had been one of the judges at Barron's court-martial in 1808. As a navy commissioner, Decatur later opposed Barron's reinstatement in the navy. After an angry correspondence that went on for several years, Barron and Decatur eventually agreed to duel. Firing simultaneously from a distance of eight yards, the two men wounded each other. Decatur died later in the day; Barron soon recovered.

Aside from dueling, the Bladensburg vicinity is notorious for the Battle of Bladensburg, fought August 24, 1814, during the War of

1812. The battle was also called the Bladensburg Races, for the speed with which most of the Americans retreated. Visible from the lower end of the Anacostia River Trail at Colmar Manor is a high hill to the west (now occupied by a cemetery and a large Italianate building with a red-orange tile roof) where Commodore Joshua Barney posted his artillery and force of 620 seamen and marines. They were the only contingent of the 6,000 American defenders — mostly poorly trained militia — who offered more than token resistance to a force of 4,500 British regulars.

After sailing up the Patuxent River and disembarking at Benedict, the British began their march on Washington four days before the battle. By the time the British arrived at Bladensburg at the head of navigation on the east side of the Anacostia River, the Americans were assembled on the opposite bank in three lines of defense, one behind the other. With little delay the British waded across the river in a flanking attack above the Bladensburg bridge. They struck panic into the American front line by firing a volley of Congreve rockets, which were little more than oversized fireworks. Describing the American militia, a British observer wrote:

> But the fact is, that, with the exception of a party of sailors from the gunboats [which the Americans had been forced to abandon on the Patuxent], under the command of Commodore Barney, no troops could behave worse than they did. The skirmishers were driven in as soon as attacked. The first line gave way without offering the slightest resistance, and the left of the main body was broken within half an hour after it was seriously engaged. Of the sailors, however, it would be injustice not to speak in the terms which their conduct merits.
>
> They were employed as gunners, and not only did they serve their guns with a quickness and precision which astonished their assailants, but they stood till some of them were actually bayoneted, with the fuses in their hands; nor was it till their leader was wounded and taken, and they saw themselves deserted on all sides by the soldiers, that they quitted the field.

Wounded and captured, Commodore Barney was visited on the field by General Robert Ross and Admiral George Cockburn, the commanders of the British force. "These officers," Barney wrote a few days later, "behaved to me with the most marked attention, respect and politeness, had a surgeon brought and my wound dressed immediately." Barney was then released. The British, of course, proceeded to Washingon, where they burned the capitol and the president's house before returning to their ships. When news of the victory reached England, General Ross was permitted to add to his family's titles that of Ross of Bladensburg, but by that time Ross was dead, killed in an unsuccessful land attack on Baltimore, during the same engagement that saw the

naval bombardment of Fort McHenry and Francis Scott Key's penning of the Star Spangled Banner.

During the eighteenth century, before the District of Columbia existed or was even contemplated, Bladensburg vied with nearby Georgetown for preeminence as a tobacco port serving Maryland farms of the region. Ocean-going vessels ascended the Anacostia River to the Bladensburg docks. William Wirt, a resident of the town during the Revolution and later U.S. attorney general for twelve years under presidents Monroe and John Quincy Adams, left this description:

> It was then a thrifty, business-driving, little sea-port, profitably devoted to the tobacco trade of which it constituted, at that time, quite an important mart. It was inhabited by some wealthy factors who had planted themselves there in connection with trans-Atlantic houses, and whose mode of living, both in the character of their dwellings and in the matter of personal display, communicated a certain show of opulence to the town.

There were ten or twelve large stores with associated tobacco warehouses, run mostly by Scotsmen. These establishments exported 1,200 to 1,500 hogsheads of tobacco annually and imported all manner of necessities and luxury items for the colonists. In the latter part of the century, flour was also a major export commodity. It was ground at Carlton Mill, Avalon Mill, and other nearby establishments, including Adelphi Mill on Northwest Branch (see Chapter 30).

Bladensburg was on the main post road from Baltimore to Alexandria and Georgetown. The road was very bad; one English traveler in 1796 wrote that passengers in stages often had to lean out of the carriage, first on one side and then on the other, to prevent it from overturning in the deep, sandy ruts. Following the Revolution, when Bladensburg began to decline as a port because of deposits of silt in the river, the town served as a relay point on the stage line. William Wirt wrote:

> During the great portion of this period, Bladensburg was enlivened by the daily transit of some half dozen or more mail coaches plying through to and from the capital of the United States. Twice a day the silence which brooded over its streets was broken by the blowing of horns, the clamor of stable boys hurrying with fresh relays of horses to the doors of rival stage houses, and by the rattle of rapidly arriving and departing stage coaches.

Completion of the railroad between Baltimore and Washington in 1835 closed the stagecoach era in Bladensburg. According to Wirt: "The railroad which touches only on the border of the town, has now displaced the old stage coach, and the village slumbers are no longer broken."

MAP 51 — Lake Artemesia
The route shown here continues on Map 52.

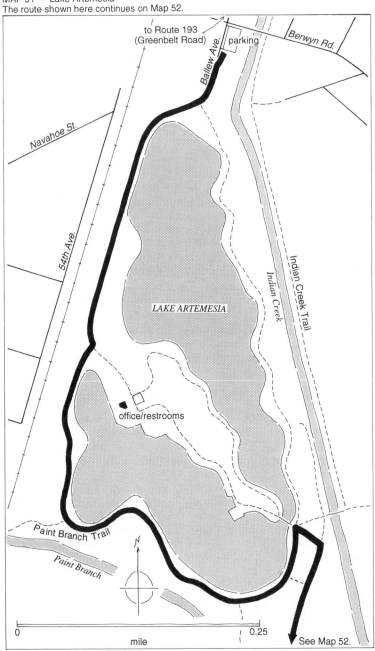

to Route 193
(Greenbelt Road)

Berwyn Rd.

parking

Ballew Ave.

Navahoe St.

54th Ave.

LAKE ARTEMESIA

Indian Creek

Indian Creek Trail

office/restrooms

Paint Branch Trail

Paint Branch

N

0   0.25
            mile

See Map 52.

MAP 52 — Anacostia watershed hike-bike trails

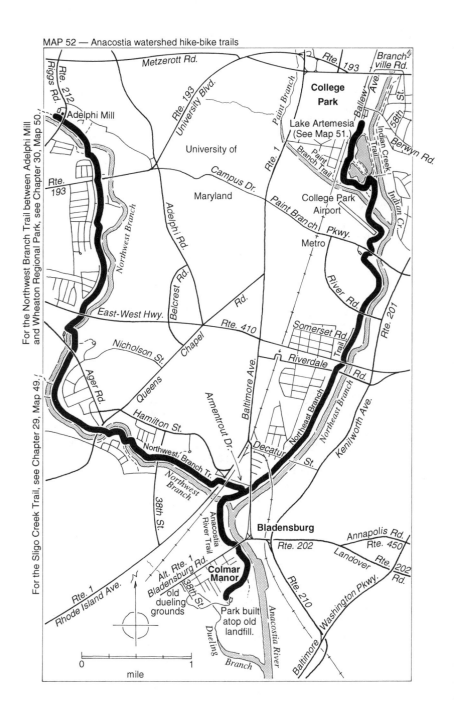

≈ ≈ ≈ ≈

METRO: The College Park - University of Maryland Metrorail station (Green Line) is located at the corner of Paint Branch Parkway and River Road near the northeast end of the trail system shown on **Map 52** on page 407. Exit through the turnstile and bear left out of the station. Pass straight across a parking lot and across River Road. Follow Paint Branch Parkway (it should be on your left) to Northeast Branch, where you can join the hike-bike trail.

For Metrobus service to the northwest end of the paved trail at Adelphi Mill, see page 397.

Metrobus routes T18 and 84 cross the southern segment of the hike-bike trail at Bladensburg Road. To the west these buses stop at the Rhode Island Avenue Metrorail station (Red Line) and to the east they stop at the New Carrollton station (Orange Line).

Telephone (202) 637-7000 for current Metro information, including schedules, routes, and connections.

≈ ≈ ≈ ≈

AUTOMOBILE DIRECTIONS: Lake Artemesia Park is located in Maryland 5 miles northeast of Washington near College Park and Greenbelt. (See •31 on **Map 1** on page 6, and also **Map 52** on page 407.) Even if your interest is not in the lakeside trails but rather in the longer system of watershed hike-bike paths, Lake Artemesia is a good place to start.

Two approaches to Lake Artemesia are described below. Both eventually make use of the entrance at Branchville Road off Route 193 between Route 1 (Baltimore Avenue) and Route 201 (Kenilworth Avenue).

To Lake Artemesia from the Baltimore-Washington Parkway: Leave the parkway at the exit for Route 193 West (Greenbelt Road), which is located just north of the interchange between the parkway and Interstate 495 (the Capital Beltway). Follow Route 193 West across Route 201 (Kenilworth Avenue) and from there continue on Route 193 only 0.8 mile, then turn right at a traffic light onto Branchville Road toward Lake Artemesia. Go 0.6 mile through an industrial area and around to the left (where the road changes name to Ballew Avenue). Pass through an intersection with

Berwyn Road, then immediately turn left into the Lake Artemesia parking lot.

To Lake Artemesia from Interstate 495 (the Capital Beltway): Leave the Beltway at Exit 23 for Route 201 South (Kenilworth Avenue). Almost immediately, exit via the far right lanes for Route 193 West (Greenbelt Road). Follow Route 193 West only 0.7 mile, then turn right at a traffic light onto Branchville Road toward Lake Artemesia. Go 0.6 mile through an industrial area and around to the left (where the road changes name to Ballew Avenue). Pass through an intersection with Berwyn Road, then immediately turn left into the Lake Artemesia parking lot.

≈   ≈   ≈   ≈

WALKING and BICYCLING: Turn left out the Lake Artemesia parking lot and follow the paved path alongside Ballew Avenue to Lake Artemesia.

The trails at Lake Artemesia are shown on **Map 51** on page 406. As outlined there, several trails intersect the waterside circuit at the lake's southern end and provide a link to the system of trails shown on **Map 52** on page 407. To navigate this extensive system of trails, watch for trail names and arrows painted on the pavement. Be careful where the trails cross roads or pass through parking lots.

Five miles from Lake Artemesia, the southern end of the trail system is at Colmar Manor Park on the west side of the Anacostia River opposite Bladensburg. You will know that you have reached the end of the trail — at that point called the Anacostia River Trail — when it rises to the top of the immense mound behind the community of Colmar Manor.

The Northwest Branch Trail intersects with the Anacostia River Trail just downstream from the bridge at Route 1 (Baltimore Avenue). At some places the Northwest Branch Trail is simply a sidewalk, but at others (particularly at its upper end) it is very pleasant. The paved Northwest Branch Trail extends 7 miles upstream to a point just short of the Capital Beltway, where it turns into a hiking trail leading to Wheaton Regional Park (see Chapter 30).

The Sligo Creek Trail intersects with the Northwest Branch Trail between Queens Chapel Road and Ager Road. For a discussion and map of this trail, see Chapter 29.

32

GREENBELT PARK

Walking and ski touring — 4 miles (6.4 kilometers). Located only 5 miles outside of Washington adjacent to the Baltimore-Washington Parkway, this 1,100-acre park is a very pleasant oasis of low, wooded ridges and shallow valleys carved by the tributaries of Northeast Branch.

The trail system at Greenbelt Park includes several circuits, ranging from the 1.4-mile Dogwood Trail at the center of the park to the 6-mile Bridle Trail around the periphery. Combining the best sections of these two trails is the 4-mile circuit shown by the bold line on **Map 53** on page 415, and that is the route described in the walking directions on page 416.

Greenbelt Park is open daily from dawn until dusk. Dogs must be leashed. Bicycles are not permitted on the trails. The park is managed by the National Park Service; telephone (301) 344-3948. Call for information on camping and on various programs, including orienteering.

THE LAND AT GREENBELT PARK was acquired by the national government at the same time that the Federal Resettlement Administration was planning and building the town of Greenbelt. The new suburb was intended to be a model community, complete with its own government, schools, shopping center, services, and open space. The federal experiment in town planning included development of similar "garden towns" at Greenhills, Ohio, outside Cincinnati, and at Greendale, Wisconsin, outside Milwaukee. The projects provided employment during the Great Depression. When construction was finished, the new towns offered low-rent housing for families of modest means. Over the long term, these satellite towns were supposed to prevent congestion in nearby urban areas, to preserve open countryside between the cities and their suburbs, and to demonstrate the soundness of community planning.

The greenbelt towns developed by the federal government in the 1930s are part of a "garden city" movement going back a century earlier, formulated in response to the rampant growth of cities and urban slums spawned by the industrial revolution. In the early nineteenth century in Great Britain, Robert Owen, a wealthy textile manufacturer who had started work at the bottom of his industry at age ten, proposed the formation of cooperative agricultural-industrial communities. He established the model industrial town of New Lanark, Scotland (which was a success) and the communistic town of New Harmony, Indiana (which eventually failed). Other industrialists in England and America built new mill towns in formerly rural areas, combining capitalistic enterprise with reformist (often markedly paternalistic) visions of urban life. Ebenezer Howard's 1902 book *Garden Cities of To-morrow* fully developed the idea of residential and industrial communities surrounded by a rural belt, each town with a predetermined area and population and with ownership vested in a community corporation. To some extent, the new towns of Reston, Virginia and Columbia, Maryland reflect these ideas. However, most satellite towns that were actually conceived and built as part of the garden city movement lacked local industries or other employment opportunities and instead became commuter or "bedroom" communities, as has been the case at Greenbelt, Maryland.

Although the national government has long since ceased development activities at Greenbelt (and at the other garden towns) and has sold the federally built housing at Greenbelt to a local cooperative, the nearby tract of woods remains a federal facility, administered since 1950 by the National Park Service. Now an island of green within the Capital Beltway, the park was conceived as part of the "green belt" that would buffer the town from nearby Washington.

When the federal government purchased the land at Greenbelt, the area consisted of marginally productive or abandoned farms. For centuries tobacco had been the dominant crop, and poor farming practices had contributed to erosion and exhaustion of the soil. In the mid-1930s the government bought more than twelve thousand acres at an average price of $97 per acre. Most of the land was later transferred to the U.S. Department of Agriculture for addition to the National Agricultural Research Center, intended to demonstrate techniques for soil restoration and good farming.

At Greenbelt Park, however, the former fields have grown up in woods. In Maryland, this reversion of farmland to forest typically starts with the incursion of weeds and brush — including crabapples, cherries, plums, hawthorns, persimmons, red cedars, gray birch, sumac, aspens, and Virginia pine, pitch pine, and white pine — most of which eventually give way to large, long-lived, deciduous trees that shade and kill their competitors. Plants themselves can contribute to changes in soil, moisture, sunlight, wildlife, and other conditions, and these changes may favor the rise to dominance of yet entirely different plant species than were formerly present. This displacement of one biotic community by another is called *ecological succession*, and it can continue through several stages until change eventually becomes so slow — depending, perhaps, on shifts in the climate itself — that a virtual equilibrium is achieved between the physical environment and the climax community of plants and animals. At any time, however, hurricanes, ice storms, fires, infestations, floods, and other such events can abruptly undo decades of gradual change and rejuvenate the mix of trees, shrubs, and other plants. At Greenbelt Park, for example, gypsy moths have killed large areas of mature hardwoods, turning back by half a century or more the process of ecological succession. Meanwhile, Virginia pines remain abundant.

The climax plant community of central Maryland and Virginia used to be called the "oak-chestnut" forest, but in the early twentieth century chestnut blight killed all mature American chestnut trees. The disease continues to kill chestnut saplings as they sprout from old root systems. North of the Potomac River, tulip trees (also called yellow poplar and tulip poplar) have filled the gap left by the chestnuts and now occupy a position of co-dominance with the oaks. Beech, black cherry, sassafras, and varieties of ash, hickory, and maple are also common. Dogwood is widespread in the understory. According to a vegetation map prepared by the Department of Geography and Environmental Engineering at Johns Hopkins University, Greenbelt Park falls in an area forested by the tulip poplar association, including red maple, flowering dogwood, sour-gum, white oak, sassafras, black cherry, mockernut hickory, pignut hickory, black oak, American beech, and northern red oak.

Although many trees are tolerant of a broad range of soil and moisture conditions, some are usually found in a particular type of terrain where they flourish and even supplant other species. For example, as its name suggests, swamp white oak generally grows in moist or even soggy soils inimical to other species. Willow oak and pin oak often are found in heavy bottomland soils. Most oaks, however, including white, scarlet, black, and chinquapin oak, prefer drier soils. Southern red oak usually grows in upland regions. Blackjack oak, post oak, and to a lesser extent chestnut oak have a high tolerance for dry, gravelly hilltops or poor, sandy soils. So do the evergreen Eastern red cedar, pitch pine, and Virginia pine.

Each type of terrain is associated with certain groups of trees. Stream banks and bottomland support river birch, boxelder, hornbeam, red and silver maple, sycamore, black locust, American elm, sourgum, witch-hazel, varieties of willow, and black, green, and pumpkin ash.

413

The slopes of hills and valleys sustain white ash, beech, Hercules'-club, mountain maple, striped maple, sweetgum, tulip tree, flowering dogwood, and mountain laurel. Cool, shady ravines and moist, north-facing slopes provide a suitable environment for Eastern hemlock. On upper slopes and ridgetops the balance shifts toward the dry oaks and shagbark and pignut hickory. As you follow the trails up and down the hills and stream valleys described in this book — particularly in areas with more topographic relief than at Greenbelt Park — and as soil changes and the slopes face sometimes north and sometimes south, notice how the vegetation changes.

≈   ≈   ≈

METRO: Metrobus route C2 passes the entrance to Greenbelt Park on Greenbelt Road at the intersection with Walker Drive. The nearest Metrorail station where you can catch bus C2 is Greenbelt (Green Line); board bus C2 for Greenbelt Center.

Telephone (202) 637-7000 for current Metro information, including schedules, routes, and connections.

≈   ≈   ≈   ≈

AUTOMOBILE DIRECTIONS: Greenbelt Park is located only 10 miles northeast of downtown Washington. (See •32 on **Map 1** on page 6, and also **Map 53** opposite.) The entrance is on Route 193 (Greenbelt Road). Two avenues of approach are described below.

To Greenbelt Park from Interstate 495 (the Capital Beltway): Leave the Beltway at Exit 23 for Route 201 South (Kenilworth Avenue), then exit again almost immediately for Route 193 East (Greenbelt Road). After turning left onto Route 193, follow it east 0.3 mile, then turn right at a traffic light into Greenbelt Park. Follow the curving entrance road to a T-intersection, then turn right and go 0.6 mile to the parking area for the Dogwood Nature Trail, located on the right shortly after a road intersects from the left.

To Greenbelt Park from the Baltimore-Washington Parkway: Leave the parkway at the exit for Route 193 West (Greenbelt Road), which is located just north of the interchange between the parkway and the Capital Beltway. Follow Route 193 West 0.8 mile, then turn left at a traffic light

MAP 53 — Greenbelt Park

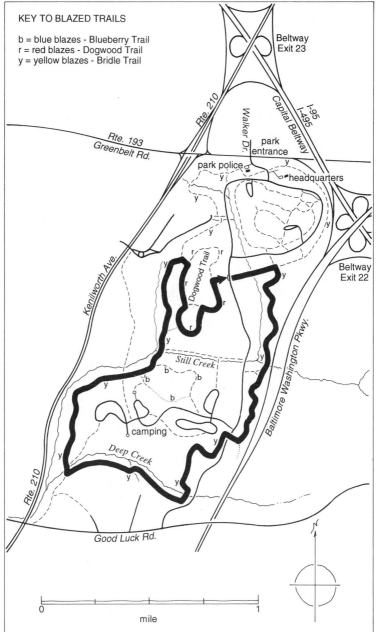

KEY TO BLAZED TRAILS

b = blue blazes - Blueberry Trail
r = red blazes - Dogwood Trail
y = yellow blazes - Bridle Trail

Beltway
Exit 23

Rte. 210

Walker Dr.

Capital Beltway

I-95
I-495

Rte. 193
Greenbelt Rd.

park
entrance

park police

headquarters

y

Kenilworth Ave.

Dogwood Trail

r

Beltway
Exit 22

Still Creek

b b

b

Baltimore Washington Pkwy.

camping

Deep Creek

y

Rte. 210

Good Luck Rd.

N

0   1
                        mile

415

into Greenbelt Park. Follow the curving entrance road to a T-intersection, then turn right and go 0.6 mile to the parking area for the Dogwood Nature Trail, located on the right shortly after a road intersects from the left.

≈　　≈　　≈　　≈

WALKING: The 4-mile route described below is shown by the bold line on **Map 53** on page 415. From the parking area for the Dogwood Nature Trail, cross the road and enter the woods on a wide trail. After crossing a small stream, continue uphill 220 yards to a trail junction where yellow blazes lead both straight ahead and to the right. Turn right to follow the yellow-blazed trail as it winds gradually downhill through the woods. Eventually, the trail approaches the Baltimore-Washington Parkway, with which it runs parallel for some distance. About 100 yards after crossing Still Creek just below the parkway, fork left to continue on the yellow-blazed trail — again more or less parallel with the parkway. Climb across a knoll near the parkway and continue as the yellow-blazed trail winds along a low ridge. At a T-intersection, bear right to follow the yellow-blazed trail past a chainlink fence and across a park road.

About 20 yards after re-entering the woods, turn left to continue on the yellow-blazed trail. After 200 yards the trail turns right. Follow the trail downhill, then to the left. Eventually, pass around the head of a gully on a boardwalk. At a T-intersection, turn right to continue on the yellow blazed trail, which before long passes a new housing development on the left.

Follow the yellow-blazed trail through the woods, with a gully grandly called Deep Creek on the right. Eventually, at a T-intersection turn right across Deep Creek, then fork left in 20 yards to continue on the yellow-blazed trail. Follow the trail as it winds through the woods, at one point passing near Kenilworth Avenue. Eventually, cross a grass and gravel fire road and continue through the woods. After passing an obscure trail intersecting from the right (the Blueberry Trail), continue 115 yards, then fork left on the yellow-blazed trail. Go 160 yards to a bridge over Still Creek.

After crossing the bridge, continue straight past a path intersecting from the right. Follow the yellow-blazed trail though the woods. Eventually, after reaching fairly level terrain, the yellow-blazed path arrives at a trail junction where it bends abruptly left toward two tall apartment buildings visible through the trees. **At this junction, turn right** and go 30 yards to reach the main loop of the red-blazed Dogwood Nature Trail. (If you find yourself getting closer and closer to the apartment buildings and then passing them, you have missed the trail junction. Retrace you steps until you find the junction at a bend in the yellow-blazed trail.)

Once you reach the main loop of the red-blazed Dogwood Nature Trail, you can either bear left to follow it clockwise to your starting point, or — for a slightly longer walk — bear right to follow it counter-clockwise. Map 53 shows the latter route, which is more scenic. At an intersection where the red blazes lead both ways, bear right. Eventually, bear right twice more to follow the red-blazed trail back to the parking area where you started.

33

NATIONAL WILDLIFE VISITOR CENTER
at the Patuxent Research Refuge

Walking — up to 4 miles (6.4 kilometers) for the total trail system. Located about half way between Washington and Baltimore, the National Wildlife Visitor Center features outstanding exhibits that focus on different habitats, research methods and results, endangered species, and various environmental issues. A large window overlooking Lake Redington is equipped with spotting scopes, binoculars, and even sound equipment for viewing and hearing waterfowl and other birds and animals. For walkers there are several short trails, of which the 1.5-mile circuit around Cash Lake is the most varied and attractive. This loop is shown by the bold line on **Map 54** on page 425. From late fall through spring, however, the Cash Lake loop is usually closed, at least in part, to avoid disturbing wintering waterfowl and nesting ducks, so during that period you may want to try some of the other trails shown on the map. There is also a tram that runs on a regular weekend schedule, spring through fall, around Lake Redington.

The building and grounds at the National Wildlife Visitor Center are open daily from 10 A.M. to 5:30 P.M.. Dogs must be leashed. Bicycling is not permitted on the trails, and the tram road around Lake Redington is off limits to walkers.

The Patuxent Research Refuge and the National Wildlife Visitor Center are managed by the U.S. Fish and Wildlife Service within the Department of the Interior. Telephone (301) 497-5760 for information, including the schedule of films, educational programs, and events.

WITH ITS VARIED HABITATS — piney and deciduous woods, meadows, streams, freshwater marsh, small ponds, and larger lakes — the National Wildlife Visitor Center is among the better places in the Washington region to see a wide assortment of birds. More than 260 species of waterfowl, land birds, and migrating shorebirds have been recorded here — or about 85 percent of all species that occur regularly in the Washington region.

Even for fledgling birders, identifying the many species that nest in the Washington region or pass through during migration is easier than might at first be thought. Shape, size, plumage, and other physical characteristics are distinguishing field marks. Range, season, habitat, song, and behavior are other useful keys to identifying birds.

Range is of primary importance for the simple reason that many birds are not found throughout North America or even the eastern United States, but only in certain regions such as the Atlantic and Gulf coasts. For example, Baltimore orioles and Bullock's orioles are two species that closely resemble each other (for a period they were even thought to be two races of the same species), so it helps to know that the latter is not seen near Washington. Good field guides provide range maps based on years of reported sightings and bird counts. Of course, bird ranges are not static; some pioneering species, such as the glossy ibis and house finch, have extended their ranges during recent decades. Other birds, such as the ivory-billed woodpecker, have lost ground and died out.

Season is related to range, since migratory birds appear in different parts of their ranges during different times of year. The five species of spot-breasted thrushes, for instance, are sometimes difficult to distinguish from each other, but usually only the hermit thrush is present in the Washington region during the winter. In summer the hermit thrush is rare near Washington, but the wood thrush is common and indeed nests at the National Wildlife Visitor Center. Swainson's thrush and the gray-cheeked thrush are seen during migration in spring and fall. Again, the maps in most field guides reflect this sort of information, and a detailed account of seasonal occurrence often is contained in local bird lists maintained and disseminated at some of the parks and wildlife sanctuaries discussed in this book.

Habitat, too, is important in identifying birds. Even before you spot a bird, its surroundings can tell you what species you are likely to see. Within its range a species usually appears only in certain preferred habitats, although during migration some species are less particular. (In many cases, birds show a degree of physical adaptation to their preferred environment.) As its name implies, the marsh wren is seldom found far from cattails, rushes, sedges, or tall marsh grasses; if a wren-like bird is spotted in such a setting, it is unlikely to be a house wren or Carolina wren or one of the other species commonly found in thick underbrush or shrubbery. Ducks can be difficult to identify unless you tote a telescope; but even if all you can see is a silhouette, you can start with the knowledge that shallow marshes, ponds, and streams normally attract few diving ducks (such as oldsquaw, canvasbacks, redheads, ring-necked ducks, greater and lesser scaup, common goldeneye, and buffleheads) and that large, deep bodies of water are not the usual setting for surface-feeding puddle ducks (American black ducks, gadwalls, mallards, common pintails, American widgeons, wood ducks, northern shovelers, and blue-winged and green-winged teals).

Some of the distinctive habitats that different bird species prefer are open oceans; beaches; salt marsh; mud flats; meadows; thickets; various types of woods; and creeks, ponds, and lakes. The area where two habitats join, called an *ecotone*, is a particularly good place to look for birds because species peculiar to either environment might be present. For example, both meadowlarks and wood warblers might be found where a hay field abuts a forest. All good field guides provide information on habitat preference that can help to locate a species or to assess the likelihood of a tentative identification.

Song announces the identity (or at least the location) of birds even before they are seen. Although some species, such as the red-winged blackbird, have only a few songs, others, such as the mockingbird, have an infinite variety. Some birds, most notably thrushes, sing different songs in the morning and evening. In many species the basic songs vary among individuals and also from one part of the country to another, giving rise to regional "dialects." Nonetheless, the vocal repertory of most songbirds is sufficiently constant in timbre and pattern to identify each species simply by its songs.

Bird songs, as distinguished from calls, can be very complex. They are sung only by the male of most species, usually in spring and summer. The male arrives first at the breeding and nesting area after migration. He stakes out a territory for courting, mating, and nesting by singing at prominent points around the area's perimeter. This wards off other males of his species and simultaneously attracts females. On the basis of the male's display and the desirability of his territory, the female selects her mate. Experiments suggest that female birds build nests faster and lay more eggs when exposed to the songs of males with a larger vocal repertory than others of their species, and the relative volume of their songs appears to be a way for males to establish status among themselves.

In a few species, including eastern bluebirds, Baltimore orioles, cardinals, and white-throated sparrows, both sexes sing, although the males are more active in defending their breeding territory. Among mockingbirds, both sexes sing in fall and winter, but only males do in spring and summer. Some birds, such as canaries, have different songs for different seasons.

Birds tend to heed the songs of their own kind and to ignore the songs of other species, which, after all, do not compete for females nor, in many cases, for the same type of nesting materials or food. In consequence, a single area might include the overlapping breeding territories of several species. From year to year such territories are bigger or smaller, depending on the food supply. Typically, most small songbirds require about half an acre from which others of their species are excluded.

Bird calls (as distinguished from songs) are short, simple, sometimes harsh, and used by both males and females at all times of year to communicate alarm, aggression, location, and existence of food. Nearly all birds have some form of call. Warning calls are often heeded by species other than the caller's. Some warning calls are thin, high-pitched whistles that are difficult to locate and so do not reveal the bird's location to predators. Birds also use mobbing calls to summon other birds, as chickadees and crows do when scolding and harassing owls and other unwanted visitors. Birds flying in flocks, like cedar waxwings, often call continuously. Such calls help birds migrating by night to stay together.

The study of bird dialects and experiments with birds that have been deafened or raised in isolation indicate that songs are genetically inherited only to a very crude extent. Although a few species, such as doves, sing well even when raised in isolation, most birds raised alone produce inferior, simplified songs. Generally, young songbirds learn their songs by listening to adult birds and by practice singing, called *subsong.* Yet birds raised in isolation and exposed to many tape-recorded songs show an innate preference for the songs of their own species. Probably the easiest way to learn bird songs is to listen repeatedly to recordings and to refer at the same time to a standard field guide. Most guides describe bird vocalizations with such terms as *harsh, nasal, flutelike, piercing, plaintive, wavering, twittering, buzzing, sneezy,* and *sputtering.* Played slowly, bird recordings demonstrate that the songs contain many more notes than the human ear ordinarily hears.

Shape is one of the first and most important aspects to notice once you actually see a bird. Most birds can at least be placed in the proper family and many species can be identified by shape or silhouette, without reference to other field marks. Some birds, such as meadowlarks, are chunky and short-tailed, while others, such as catbirds and cuckoos, are elegantly long and slender. Kingfishers, blue jays, tufted titmice, Bohemian and cedar waxwings, and cardinals are among the few birds with crests.

Bird bills frequently have distinctive shapes and, more than any other body part, show adaptation to food supply. The beak can be chunky, like that of a grosbeak, to crack seeds; thin and curved, like that of a creeper, to probe bark for insects; hooked, like that of a shrike, to tear at flesh; long and slender, like that of a hummingbird, to sip nectar from tubular flowers; or some other characteristic shape depending on the bird's food. Goatsuckers, swifts, flycatchers, and swallows, all of which catch flying insects, have widely hinged bills and gaping mouths. The long, thin bills of starlings and meadowlarks are suited to probing the ground. In the Galapagos Islands west of Ecuador, Charles Darwin noted fourteen species of finches, each of which had evolved a different type of beak or style of feeding that gave it a competitive advantage for a particular type of food. Many birds are nonetheless flexible about their diet, especially from season to season when food sources change or become scarce. For example, Tennessee warblers, which ordinarily glean insects from foliage, also take large amounts of nectar from tropical flowers when wintering in South and Central America.

In addition to beaks, nearly every other part of a bird's body is adapted to help exploit its environment. Feet of passerines, or songbirds, are adapted to perching, with three toes in front and one long toe behind; waterfowl have webbed or lobed feet for swimming; and raptors have talons for grasping prey.

Other key elements of body shape are the length and form of wings, tails, and legs. The wings may be long, pointed, and developed for swift, sustained flight, like those of falcons. Or the wings may be short and rounded for abrupt bursts of speed, like those of accipiters. The tail may have a deep fork like that of a barn swallow, a shallow notch like that of a tree swallow, a square tip like that of a cliff swallow, or a rounded tip like that of a blue jay.

Size is difficult to estimate and therefore not very useful in identifying birds. The best approach is to bear in mind the relative sizes of different species and to use certain well-known birds like the chickadee, sparrow, robin, kingfisher, and crow as standards for mental comparison. For example, if a bird resembles a song sparrow but looks unusually large, it might be a fox sparrow.

Plumage, whether plain or princely, muted or magnificent, is one of the most obvious keys to identification. Color can occur in remarkable combinations of spots, stripes, streaks, patches, and other patterns that make even supposedly drab birds a pleasure to see. In some instances, like the brown streaks of American bitterns and many other species, the plumage provides camouflage. Most vireos and warblers are various shades and combinations of yellow, green, brown, gray, and black, as one would expect from their forest environment. The black and white backs of woodpeckers help them to blend in with bark dappled with sunlight. The bold patterns of killdeers and some other plovers break up their outlines in much the same manner that warships used to be camouflaged before the invention of radar. Many shorebirds display countershading: they are dark above and light below, a pattern that reduces the effect of shadows and makes them appear an inconspicuous monotone. Even some brightly colored birds have camouflaging plumages when they are young and least able to avoid predators.

For some species, it is important *not* to be camouflaged. Many seabirds are mostly white, which in all light conditions enables them to be seen at great distances against the water. Because flocks of seabirds spread out from their colonies to search for food, it is vital that a bird that has located food be visible to others after it has landed on the water to feed.

To organize the immense variation in plumage, focus on different basic elements and ask the following types of questions. Starting with the head, is it uniformly colored like that of the red-headed woodpecker? Is there a small patch on the crown, like that of Wilson's warbler and the ruby-crowned kinglet, or a larger cap on the front and top of the head, like that of the common redpoll and American goldfinch? Is the crown striped like the ovenbird's? Does a ring surround the eye, as with a Connecticut warbler, or are the eye rings perhaps even joined across the top of the bill to form spectacles, like those of a yellow-breasted chat? Is there a stripe over or through the eyes, like the red-breasted nuthatch's, or a conspicuous black mask across the eyes, like that of a common yellowthroat or loggerhead shrike? From the head go on to the rest of the body, where distinctive colors and patterns can also mark a bird's bill, throat, breast, belly, back, sides, wings, rump, tail, and legs.

Finally, what a bird *does* is an important clue to its identity. Certain habits, postures, ways of searching for food, and other behavior characterize different species. Some passerines, such as larks, juncos, and towhees, are strictly ground feeders; other birds, including flycatchers and swallows, nab insects on the wing; and others, such as nuthatches and creepers, glean insects from the crevices in bark. Woodpeckers peck into the bark. Vireos and most warblers pick insects from the foliage of trees and brush.

All of these birds may be further distinguished by other habits of eating. For example, towhees scratch for insects and seeds by kicking backward with both feet together, whereas juncos rarely do, although both hop to move along the ground. Other ground feeders, such as meadowlarks, walk rather than hop. Despite the children's song, robins often run, not hop. Swallows catch insects while swooping and skimming in continuous flight, but flycatchers dart out from a limb, grab an insect (sometimes with an audible smack), and then return to their perch. Brown creepers have the curious habit of systematically

MAP 54 — National Wildlife Visitor Center

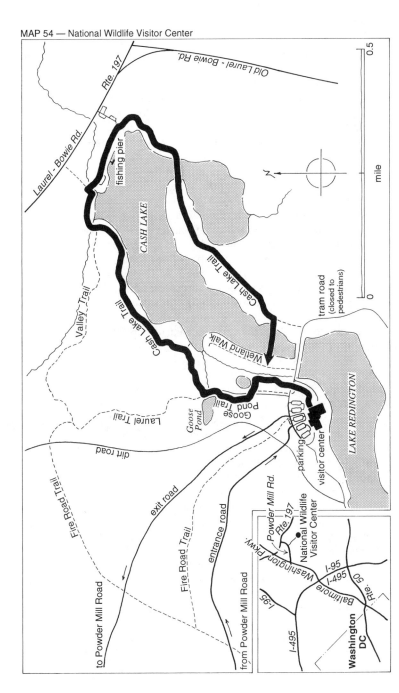

425

searching for food by climbing trees in spirals, then flying back to the ground to climb again. Woodpeckers tend to hop upward, bracing themselves against the tree with their stiff tails. Nuthatches walk up and down trees and branches head first, seemingly without regard for gravity. Vireos are sluggish compared to the hyperactive, flitting warblers.

Many birds divide a food source into zones, an arrangement that apparently evolved to ensure each species its own food supply. The short-legged green heron sits at the edge of the water or on a low over-hanging branch, waiting for its prey to come close to shore. Medium-sized black-crowned and yellow-crowned night herons hunt in shallow water. The long-legged great blue heron stalks fish in water up to two feet deep. Swans, geese, and many ducks graze underwater on the stems and tubers of grassy plants, but the longer necks of swans and geese enable them to reach deeper plants. Similarly, different species of shorebirds take food from the same mud flat by probing with their varied bills to different depths. Various species of warblers that feed in the same tree are reported to concentrate in separate areas, such as the trunk, twig tips, and tree top. Starlings and cowbirds feeding in flocks on the ground show another arrangement that provides an even dis-tribution of food: those in the rear fly ahead to the front, so that the entire flock rolls slowly across the field.

Different species also have different styles of flight. Soaring is typi-cal of some big birds. Gulls float nearly motionless in the wind. Buteos and vultures soar on updrafts in wide circles, although turkey vultures may be further distinguished by wings held in a shallow V. Some other large birds, such as accipiters, rarely soar but instead inter-rupt their wing beats with glides. Kestrels, terns, kingfishers, and burrowing owls can hover in one spot. Hummingbirds, like oversized dragonflies, can also hover and even fly backward. Slightly more erratic than the swooping, effortless flight of swallows is that of swifts, flitting with wing beats that appear to alternate (but do not). Still other birds, such as the American goldfinch and flickers, dip up and down in wavelike flight. Some species, including jays and grackles, fly dead straight. Among ducks, the surface-feeding species launch themselves directly upward into flight, seeming to jump from the water, but the heavy diving ducks typically patter along the surface before becoming airborne.

Various idiosyncrasies distinguish yet other species. The spotted sandpiper and northern waterthrush walk with a teetering, bobbing motion. Coots pump their heads back and forth as they swim. The eastern phoebe regularly jerks its tail downward while perching, but wrens often cock their tails vertically. Herons and egrets fly with their necks folded back; storks, ibises, and cranes fly with their necks outstretched. Still other birds have characteristic postures while sitting or flying or other unique habits that provide a reliable basis for identification.

≈   ≈   ≈   ≈

AUTOMOBILE DIRECTIONS: The National Wildlife Visitor Center is located near Laurel, Maryland 15 miles northeast of downtown Washington. (See the corner panel on **Map 54** on page 425.)

To the visitor center from Interstate 495 (the Capital Beltway): Leave the Beltway at Exit 22A for the Baltimore-Washington Parkway northbound, then follow the directions in the next paragraph.

To the visitor center from the Baltimore-Washington Parkway: Follow the parkway north toward Baltimore. About 3.5 miles north of the Capital Beltway, take the exit for Powder Mill Road. At the bottom of the exit ramp, turn right and go 1.9 miles to the entrance for the National Wildlife Visitor Center. Follow the entrance road (Scarlet Tanager Loop) 1.3 miles to the large parking lots at the Visitor Center building.

≈   ≈   ≈   ≈

WALKING: Trails are shown on **Map 54** on page 425. The most attractive route is the 1.5-mile loop past Goose Pond and around Cash Lake, shown by the bold line.

To reach the trailhead from the main hall of the Visitor Center building, exit through the Gallery.

≈   ≈   ≈   ≈

You may also want to inquire about the National Wildlife Visitor Center's **North Tract**, which is separate from the Visitor Center itself. Mostly woods, the 8,100-acre North Tract was formerly part of Fort Meade and includes about 10 miles of roads that carry little traffic and that pass several ponds, wetlands, and streams.

34

THE U.S. NATIONAL ARBORETUM

Walking — 1 or more miles (1.6 or more kilometers). The United States National Arboretum, located near the eastern corner of Washington, has a wide variety of gardens and plant collections, through which you can walk pleasurably for an hour or all day.

Map 55 on page 435 shows the Arboretum and an introductory 1.5-mile walk that links some of the most popular gardens — including the Azalea Hillside (blooms late April and early May), the National Capitol Columns, the National Herb Garden (including antique and shrub roses), and the Bonsai and Penjing Museum. These features are all in the Arboretum's western half, and from there you can walk or drive to other collections shown on the map. Fern Valley (which includes the Native Plant Collection) has a small trail system of its own, and so do the various Asian collections on the high bluff overlooking the Anacostia River.

The Arboretum is open daily (except Christmas) from 8 A.M. to 5 P.M. There is no admission fee. Dogs must be leashed. Bicycling is permitted on paved roadways, but walking is the only satisfactory way to see the gardens and plant collections.

The Administration Building and the Information Center are open weekdays from 8 A.M. to 4:30 P.M. and — during spring and fall — on weekends and holidays from 9 to 5. The National Bonsai and Penjing Museum is open daily from 10 to 3:30.

The Arboretum is managed by the Agricultural Research Service, an agency of the U.S. Department of Agriculture; telephone (202) 245-2726 for information, including the schedule for horticultural demonstrations, short courses, and lectures.

THE UNITED STATES NATIONAL ARBORETUM in northeast Washington comprises 444 acres of rolling meadows, woods, groves, and gardens. Established by Congress in 1927, the Arboretum conducts research and educational programs on trees, shrubs, and herbaceous plants suited to the different climatic zones of the United States. These activities include plant identification and classification and the development of improved varieties of shrubs and trees for commercial and ornamental use. With its thousands of labeled specimens — most are within the various gardens and collections rather than in the uncultivated natural areas — the arboretum is a perfect place to learn native and foreign trees, or just to stroll in a beautiful setting.

Learning to identify trees in not difficult. Every walk, bicycle ride, or automobile trip is an opportunity for practice. Notice the overall forms and branching habits of the trees, and also the distinctive qualities of their twigs, buds, bark, leaves, flowers, and fruits or seeds. These factors are the key identification features that distinguish one species from another. Finally, when using a field guide, check the maps or descriptions that delineate the geographic range within which a tentatively identified tree or shrub is likely to be found.

Some trees, of course, have very distinctive and reliable forms. Familiar evergreens like balsam fir and eastern red cedar have a conical shape, like a dunce cap, although in dense stands the red cedar tapers very little and assumes the columnar form of the Italian cypress, which it somewhat resembles. The deciduous little-leaf linden, imported from Europe and used as a street tree, is also more or less conical in shape, but with wider-spreading lower branches than the evergreens mentioned above. The American elm displays a spreading form like a head of broccoli. A full-bodied egg-shape is characteristic of sugar maple and beech, although both will develop long, branchless trunks in crowded woods, as do most forest trees competing for light. The vertically exaggerated cigar shape of Lombardy poplar — a form called fastigiate — and the pendulous, trailing quality of weeping willow are unmistakable. (Both Lombardy poplar and weeping willow have been introduced to North America from abroad.)

Branching habit is an important clue to some trees. White pine, for example, has markedly horizontal branches with a slight upward tilt at the tips, like a hand turned with its palm up. Norway spruce (another imported species) is often seen as an ornamental tree dwarfing and darkening a house near which it was planted fifty or a hundred years ago; it is a very tall evergreen — sometimes reminding me of a pagoda — with long, evenly-spaced, festoon-like branches. The slender lower branches of pin oak slant downward, while those of white oak and red oak are often massive and horizontal, especially on mature trees growing in the open. The lower branches of the horse chestnut (yet another European import) also droop but then curl up at the tips in chunky twigs. Elm branches spread up and out like the mouth of a trumpet. The trunk of the mature honeylocust diverges into large branches somewhat in the manner of an elm. Even the reviled *ailanthus* or tree of heaven, which in many East Coast cities springs up in dense groves of spindly, spiky saplings wherever earth has been disturbed, eventually develops a spreading form somewhat like an elm or honeylocust.

A good botanist or forester can identify trees by their twigs alone — that is, by the end portion of the branch that constitutes the newest growth. During winter the shape, color, size, position, and sheathing of buds are important. For instance, beech buds are long and pointed, tan, and sheathed with overlapping scales like shingles. Sycamore and magnolia buds are wrapped in a single scale. The twigs of horse chestnut are tipped with a big, sticky, brown bud, while those of silver maple, and to a lesser extent red maple, end with large clusters of red buds. Some oaks, such as white oak, have hairless terminal buds, while other species, such as black oak, have hairy end buds.

Aside from buds, other characteristics of twigs are color, thorns, odor, hair, pith, and the size, shape, and position of leaf scars marking where the leaf stems were attached. For example, most maple twigs are reddish brown, but the twigs of striped maple and mountain maple are greenish. Thorns and spines are significant because relatively few trees have them, notably honeylocust, black locust, Hercules club, prickly ash, buckthorn bumelia, devil's walking stick, Osage-orange, American plum, some crabapples, and the many varieties of hawthorn. *Ailanthus* twigs, which show huge leaf scars, have a rank odor when broken open. Most oaks have hairless twigs, although some species such as blackjack oak are distinctly hairy. As for pith, it can be chambered, solid, spongy, or of different colors, depending on the species. Oak, hickory, and tulip trees are common forest species in the Washington region, but only the pith of white oak in cross section forms a star. Finally, the location of leaf scars in opposite pairs along the twigs (as with maples) distinguishes a wide variety of trees and shrubs from those with leaf scars arranged alternately, first on one side and then on the other (as with oaks). All these distinguishing features can best be appreciated simply by examining the twigs of different species.

Bark is not always a reliable clue for identifying trees, as the color and texture of bark change with age or from trunk to branches to twigs. Often the distinctive character of bark is seen only in the trunks of large, mature trees. Bark can be smooth, furrowed, scaly, plated, shaggy, fibrous, crisscrossed, or papery. Some trees, of course, may be clearly identified by their bark. The names *shagbark hickory* and *paper birch* speak for themselves. Striped maple has longitudinal, whitish stripes in the smooth green bark of the younger trees. The crisscrossed ridges of white ash, the light blotches on sycamores, and the smooth gray skin of beech are equally distinctive. Birches and some cherries are characterized by horizontal lenticels like random dashes.

Most people notice leaves, particularly their shape. The leaves of the gray birch are triangular; ginkgo, fan-shaped; catalpa, heart-shaped; sweetgum, star-shaped; beech, elliptical (or actually pointed at each end); and black willow narrower still and thus *lanceolate*. Notice also the leaf margin or edge. Is it smooth like rhododendron, wavy like water oak, serrated like basswood, or deeply lobed like most maples? And how many lobes are there? Tulip trees, for example, have easily recognized four-lobed leaves (see the photograph at right); maples have three- or five-lobed leaves. Also, are the lobe tips rounded like white oak or pointed like red oak? Or, maybe, as with sassafras and red mulberry, the same tree has leaves that are shaped differently, the most distinctive being those with a single asymmetrical lobe creating a leaf outline like a mitten. In some trees, such as the large-leaf magnolia with its tobacco-like foliage, the sheer size of the leaves is significant. Similarly, sycamores have leaves resembling sugar maples or red maples, but usually bigger and coarser in texture.

Some leaves such as those of the Japanese maple, horse chestnut, and Ohio buckeye are palmately compound, meaning that they are actually composed of leaflets radiating from the end of the stem. In the fall the whole compound leaf may drop off the tree as a unit, or the leaflets may fall off individually, and then finally the stem. Other leaves, such as ash, hickory, and sumac, are pinnately compound, being composed of leaflets arranged in opposite pairs along a central stalk. With pinnately compound leaves growing from the top of a branchless trunk, the saplings of *ailanthus* resemble little palm trees. Still other leaves are *bi*pinnately compound, somewhat like a fern. The leaflets grow from stalks that, in turn, spread from a central stalk. Honeylocust, Kentucky coffeetree, and the ornamental imported silktree are examples.

Although the needles of evergreens are not as varied as the leaves of deciduous plants, there are still several major points to look for, such as the number of needles grouped together. White pine has fascicles of five; pitch pine, loblolly pine, and sometimes shortleaf pine have fascicles of three; and jack pine, red pine, Virginia pine, Austrian pine, and sometimes shortleaf pine have fascicles of two. Needles of spruce, hemlock, and fir grow singly, but are joined to the twig in distinctive ways. Spruce needles grow from little woody pegs, hemlock needles from smaller bumps, and fir needles directly from the twig, leaving a rounded pit when pulled off. Spruce needles tend to be four-sided, hemlock flat, and fir somewhere in between. The needles of larch (also called tamarack) grow in dense clusters and all drop off in winter. The needles of bald cypress also drop off — hence its name.

Flowers are a spectacular, though short-lived, feature of some trees and shrubs. Three variables are color, form, and (less reliably) time of bloom. Eastern redbud, with red-purple clusters, and shadbush (also called Allegheny serviceberry), with small, white, five-petaled flowers, are among the first of our native trees to bloom, sometimes as early as mid-March in the Washington region. As members of the rose family, apples, cherries, plums, peaches, and hawthorns all have flowers with five petals (usually pink or white) in loose, white clusters, typically blooming in April. The blossoms of flowering dogwood, which also appear in April or early May, consist of four white, petal-like bracts, each with a brown notch at the tip, while the flowers of alternate-leaf dogwood consist of loose, white clusters. These are a few of our native species commonly thought of as flowering trees and shrubs, but the blossoms of other native species are equally distinctive, such as the small but numerous flowers of maples or the tuliplike flowers and durable husks of tulip trees. Unlike most trees, witch hazel — which produces small, yellow, scraggly flowers — blooms in fall or winter.

Finally, the seeds or fruit of a tree are a conspicuous element in summer and fall, sometimes lasting into winter and even spring. Even if a tree is bare, the fruits and seeds (or for that matter, the leaves) can often be found littered on the ground around the trunk. Nobody who sees a tree with acorns could fail to know that it is an oak, although some varieties, such as willow oak and shingle oak (also known as northern laurel oak) are deceptive. Distinctive nuts are also produced by beech trees, horse chestnuts, hickories, and walnuts. Some seeds, like ash and maple, have wings; such winged seeds are termed *samaras*. Others, such as honeylocust, Kentucky coffeetree, and redbud, come in pods like beans and in fact are members of the same general legume family. The seeds of birches, poplars, and willows hang in tassels, while those of sweetgum and sycamore form prickle-balls (as do the shells of horse chestnut and buckeye). Eastern cotton-wood produces seeds that are wind-borne by cottonlike tufts. And, of course, brightly colored berries and fruits are produced by many species, such as crabapples, holly, hawthorn, and hackberry. The female ginkgo has pale pink, globular, and remarkably foul-smelling fruit. Among needle evergreens, spruce and pine cones hang from the twigs, while fir cones stand upright like stubby candles, and the small hemlock cones grow from the twig tips.

In conclusion, the trick to tree identification is to consider, either simultaneously or in rapid succession, a wide variety of features of which the ones discussed here — form and branching habit, twigs, buds, bark, leaves, flowers, and fruits or seeds — are the most obvious and the most readily observed. Don't get hung up pondering any single ambiguous or inconclusive feature; move on to consider other clues.

MAP 55 — National Arboretum

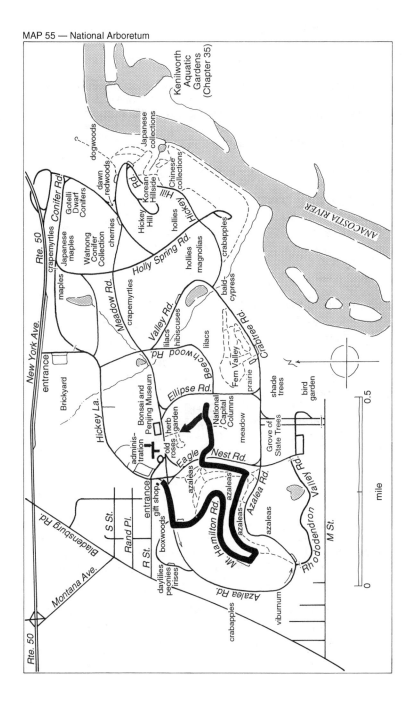

Kenilworth Aquatic Gardens (Chapter 35)

ANACOSTIA RIVER

Rte. 50

Conifer Rd.

New York Ave.

crapemyrtles

Gotelli Dwarf Conifers

Japanese maples

Watnong Conifer Collection

dogwoods

dawn redwoods

cherries

maples

Japanese collections

Korean Hillside

Chinese collections

Hickey Hill

Hickey Rd.

hollies

hollies

magnolias

crabapples

Meadow Rd.

Holly Spring Rd.

crapemyrtles

Valley Rd.

lilacs

hibiscuses

lilacs

bald-cypress

Crabtree Rd.

Beechwood Rd.

Fern Valley

prairie

shade trees

bird garden

entrance

Brickyard

Hickey La.

Ellipse Rd.

Bonsai and Penjing Museum

herb garden

National Capital Columns

meadow

Grove of State Trees

adminis-tration

old roses

Eagle Nest Rd.

Bladensburg Rd.

S St.

Rand Pl.

R St.

entrance

gift shop

boxwoods

azaleas

azaleas

azaleas

Mt. Hamilton Rd.

azaleas

Azalea Rd.

azaleas

Rhododendron Valley Rd.

M St.

Montana Ave.

daylilies
peonies
irises

Azalea Rd.

crabapples

viburnum

Rte. 50

N

0.5

mile

0

435

≈   ≈   ≈   ≈

METRO: Metrobus route B2 follows Bladensburg Road past the west end of the Arboretum. Get off the bus at the intersection with R Street, which leads to the Arboretum. Telephone (202) 637-7000 for current Metro information, including schedules, routes, and connections.

≈   ≈   ≈   ≈

AUTOMOBILE DIRECTIONS: The National Arboretum borders Route 50 (New York Avenue) near the eastern corner of the District of Columbia. (See •34 on **Map 1** on page 6, and also **Map 55** on page 435.) Although there is an Arboretum entrance from the eastbound lanes of Route 50, the directions below will guide you to the R Street entrance near the Administration Building and Information Center. If there is no room in the parking lot at the R Street entrance, there is another large lot at the New York Avenue entrance, which you can reach by following Hickey Lane.

To the Arboretum's R Street entrance from downtown Washington: Follow Route 50 (New York Avenue) east to the intersection with Bladensburg Road. This intersection occurs immediately after a large overhead highway sign gives advance warning for Rte. 50 East to Annapolis. Turn right onto Bladensburg Road. Go 0.4 mile, then turn left onto R Street. Follow R Street 0.3 mile to the Arboretum entrance at the end of the road, then turn left to park.

To the Arboretum's R Street entrance from Interstate 495 (the Capital Beltway): Leave the Beltway at Exit 19B for Route 50 West and follow it for nearly 7 miles. After passing the Arboretum, turn left onto Bladensburg Road. Go 0.4 mile, then turn left onto R Street. Follow R Street 0.3 mile to the Arboretum entrance at the end of the road, then turn left to park.

To the Arboretum's R Street entrance from the north on the Baltimore-Washington Parkway: Follow the parkway south toward Washington. (From the Capital Beltway you can get onto the parkway at Exit 22B.) At the split where I-295 forks left toward Richmond, fork right for New York Avenue and follow it for 2 miles into Washington. After passing the Arboretum, turn left onto Bladensburg Road. Go 0.4 mile, then turn left onto R Street. Follow R Street 0.3 mile to the Arboretum entrance, then turn left to park.

≈   ≈   ≈   ≈

WALKING: The roads, foot trails, and main gardens and collections at the National Arboretum are shown on **Map 55** on page 435. The bold line on the map — and the directions in the next paragraph — delineate a 1.5 mile introductory walk that leads first to Mt. Hamilton and then back past the Azalea Hillside, the National Capitol Columns, the Herb and Rose gardens, and the Bonsai and Penjing Museum.

Start at the Arbor House Gift Shop within sight of the Arboretum's R Street entrance. Facing the gift shop, proceed half-left along the shoulder of Azalea Road. Turn left at the first opportunity onto Mt. Hamilton Road and follow it uphill through the woods. At the end of the road, continue straight through a gap in a barricade. Bear half-left downhill for a few dozen yards, then turn left at a T-intersection. Follow the path gradually down along the Azalea Hillside and past trails that intersect from either side, then turn left up brick steps to the Morrison Azalea Garden. From the far end of the garden, continue along a path for about 130 yards, then turn right downhill to a large Corinthian capital on the far side of Eagle Nest Road. Follow a mown path across the meadow to the distant National Capitol Columns, which were removed when an addition was appended in 1955. From the pool in front of the columns, another mown path leads to the herb garden and — on the other side of Meadow Road — the Bonsai and Penjing Museum. From there, you can return to the parking lot by following the road slightly uphill past the Administration Building.

Fern Valley and the **Japanese and Chinese collections** also provide good strolling. In winter the **hollies, Watnong Conifers**, and **Gotelli Collection of Dwarf and Slow-growing Conifers** remain interesting even when the other gardens are bare. But on that score, even a winter garden can be attractive — for example, the Morrison Azalea Garden, located at the intersection of Eagle Nest and Azalea roads (and one of my favorite places at the arboretum).

35

KENILWORTH AQUATIC GARDENS

Walking — 1 or 2 miles (1.6 or 3.2 kilometers). Located near the eastern corner of Washington, this unique garden specializes in the cultivation of water lilies, lotuses, and other freshwater aquatic plants. A network of dikes topped by paths provides very pleasant strolling through a complex of forty-four lily ponds where the plants are grown. Also, the River Trail (1.5 miles round-trip) leads past a freshwater tidal marsh that borders the Anacostia River. The entire site is shown on **Map 56** on page 443.

The gardens open daily at 7 A.M. and close at 4 P.M. Dogs must be leashed.

Water lilies fall into two broad categories: hardy species (meaning that they are native to temperate climates) and tropical species. Also within these two categories are countless hybridized cultivars. At the Kenilworth Aquatic Gardens, the blooming season for hardy water lilies starts in May and reaches a peak in June, then tapers off as the plants flower intermittently until fall. Stored in greenhouses during winter, the tubers of tropical plants are set out in May. The tropical water lilies bloom from July until frost. Also at Kenilworth are different species and cultivars of lotus, blooming from mid-June into July. From late spring through the end of summer, the best time of day for a visit is morning until 10 or possibly 11 A.M. in order to see night-blooming flowers before they close for the day, and also to see day-bloomers as they open.

Kenilworth Aquatic Gardens is managed by the National Park Service; telephone (202) 426-6905 for information, including the calendar of guided walks and other events.

THE KENILWORTH AQUATIC GARDENS border the east bank of the Anacostia River seven miles upstream from its confluence with the Potomac. Across the Anacostia is the U.S. National Arboretum (see Chapter 34). At Kenilworth, twelve acres of ponds contain a large selection of hardy and tropical water lilies of the genus called *Nymphaea*, after the beautiful water nymphs of classical mythology. Hardy water lilies are distinguishable by the smooth edges on the pads and tropical water lilies by the serrated or rippled edges on the pads. The flowers of hardy water lilies typically ride at the water level (an example is the common North American white water lily, *Nymphaea odorata*), while tropical flowers are borne on stiff stalks six to nine inches — or even a foot — above the water.

Also at Kenilworth are other flowering water plants, including lotuses of the genus *Nelumbo* (which have leaves and flowers that stick four or five feet out of the water) and giant water platters of the genus *Victoria*. The genus *Nelumbo* contains two species: *N. lutea* and *N. nucifera*. The first is the yellow American lotus, also called water chinquapin because of its nutty seeds, and the second is the pink East Indian lotus, or sacred bean, from which Hindus believe Brahma was born and on which, in Buddhist art, the Buddha is often shown seated.

Distinct from the tall *Nelumbo* lotuses are some water lilies of the genus *Nymphaea* that are also commonly called lotuses. (There is, too, a whole genus of entirely different plants of the legume family termed *lotus*.) Among the *Nymphaea* lotuses are the hardy blue African or Egyptian lotus (*N. caerulea*) and the tropical white lotus of Egypt (*N. lotus*). In ancient Egyptian paintings, stylized depictions of these two plants are common, and the forms of their flowers appear in old Egyptian jewelry, chalices, and the sculpted capitals of temple columns. In particular, the day-blooming *N. caerulea* was regarded as sacred and was identified with the sun-god and with the theme of resurrection. Actual desiccated *N. caerulea* and *N. lotus* flowers, woven into funerary garlands that were festooned across mummies, are often found in ancient Egyptian tombs. Another *Nymphaea* lotus is the tropical blue lotus of India (*N. stellata*). To avoid confusing it with the East Indian lotus, keep in mind that there are no blue *Nelumbo* species or cultivars.

The roster of commonplace water plants also includes the so-called pond lilies of the genus *Nuphar*. Most species are native in ponds and sluggish streams in North America. One species seen often in the mid-Atlantic region is *Nuphar advenum*, popularly called cow lily or spatterdock, with yellow globular flowers held above the water. Prolific in some marsh settings and in man-made waterfowl pools at wildlife refuges, it is not usually cultivated as a decorative plant.

Most water lilies grow from tubers or rhizomes rooted in mud at the bottom of shallow, still water. The leaves develop underwater and spread out into floating pads when they reach the surface. The large, showy, and often fragrant blossoms open and shut daily and typically last from three to seven days (or sometimes up to two weeks). When flowering is over and seeds begin to develop, the pods dip below the water to ripen — as opposed to the *Nelumbo* lotuses, which have conspicuous seedpods that, after the petals drop away, resemble shower heads that ripen above water.

The flowers of hardy water lilies are all daytime bloomers, opening in mid-morning and closing in late afternoon. Many tropical water lilies also bloom during daylight, but some bloom at night. Also blooming at night and during early daylight during August and September are the giant water platters of the South American species *Victoria amazonica*; each flower lasts two nights. At the Kenilworth Aquatic Gardens, the platter-like leaves of this species grow up to four or even five feet in diameter before dying during winter, but in the plant's native Amazon region, the leaves grow up to six feet across. The underside of the leaf consists of a network of veins resembling honeycomb that traps air and gives the leaf considerable buoyancy.

The Kenilworth Aquatic Gardens started as the hobby of Walter B. Shaw, a clerk of the U.S. Treasury Department. In 1880, when this part of Washington was still farmland, Shaw bought thirty-seven acres from his father-in-law. In an old ice pond Shaw planted hardy white water lilies from Maine, where he had grown up. Shaw steadily expanded his water garden by dredging and diking new ponds in the tidal freshwater marsh. He also imported foreign plants and developed new hybridized cultivars. Eventually he turned to water gardening on a commercial basis, supplying cut flowers to florists along the East Coast and tubers to gardeners.

In 1912 Shaw's daughter, L. Helen Fowler, became manager of the business, which she expanded further. She imported plants from around the world, including lilies of the Nile from Egypt, lotuses from Africa and the Orient, and *Victoria amazonica* from South America. She built a sales office (the present-day visitor center) and greenhouses for cultivating and wintering tropical water lilies and other plants. She wrote a how-to book called *Water Gardening* that also served as a sales catalogue. During the 1920s and '30s, the W. B. Shaw Aquatic Gardens (Shaw himself had died in 1921) attracted as many as five thousand sightseers and picnickers on summer Sundays.

In the 1930s a dispute arose between Mrs. Fowler and the U.S. Army Corps of Engineers, which was engaged in dredging the Anacostia River and filling the bordering marshes. The Corps of Engineers claimed that the lily ponds were on federally owned tidal land and would have to make way for the reclamation project. The matter was resolved in 1938 when the U.S. Department of the Interior bought the property in order to preserve the water gardens as a federal park named for the nearby community of Kenilworth.

≈   ≈   ≈   ≈

METRO: The Deanwood Metrorail station (Orange Line) is about half a mile from the aquatic gardens. Exit from the station through the turnstile, then turn left out a short tunnel leading to Polk Street. Follow Polk Street away from the station. Cross a pedestrian bridge over the Kenilworth Avenue expressway. Referring to **Map 56** opposite, follow Douglas Street and then Anacostia Avenue to the aquatic gardens.

Also, Metrobus route V6 follows the Kenilworth Avenue frontage road near the aquatic gardens. Get off the bus at the intersection with Douglas Street and follow it to Anacostia Avenue and the garden entrance.

Telephone (202) 637-7000 for current Metro information, including schedules, routes, and connections.

≈   ≈   ≈   ≈

AUTOMOBILE DIRECTIONS: The Kenilworth Aquatic Gardens are located near the juncture of Route 50 and the Baltimore-Washington Parkway at the eastern corner of Washington. (See •35 on **Map 1** on page 6, and also the corner panel on **Map 56** opposite.) Several avenues of approach are described below.

To the aquatic gardens from downtown Washington on Route 50 (New York Avenue): Follow Route 50 east out of the city. After passing the National Arboretum, the *Washington Times* building, and South Dakota Avenue, take the exit for Kenilworth Avenue south toward Interstate 295 and SE Washington — then exit again almost immediately for Eastern Avenue and the aquatic gardens. Pass Eastern Avenue intersecting from the left. Go straight 0.4 mile, then turn right onto Douglas Street. Follow Douglas Street 0.3 mile, then turn right at a T-intersection with Anacostia Avenue. Follow Anacostia Avenue a few hundred yards, then turn left into the parking lot for the aquatic gardens. Note the closing time posted on the gate.

To return to downtown Washington via Route 50, see page 445.

To the aquatic gardens from Interstate 495 (the Capital Beltway): Three different highways — the Baltimore-

MAP 56 — Kenilworth Aquatic Gardens

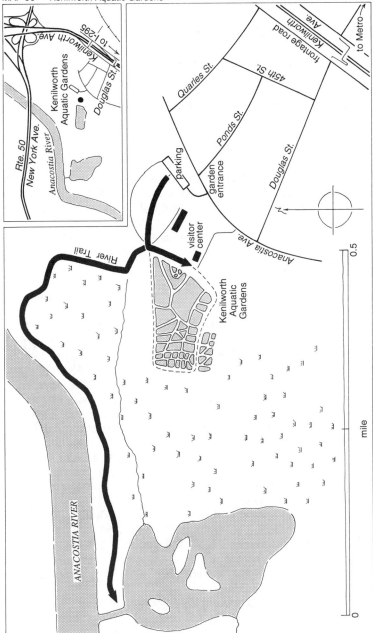

443

Washington Parkway from the north, Route 50 from the east, and Interstate 295 from the south — cross the Beltway at different exits and approach the aquatic gardens from different angles. Each of these routes is described in turn in the next three sections.

To the aquatic gardens from the north on the Baltimore-Washington Parkway: Follow the parkway south toward Washington. (From the Beltway you can get onto the parkway at Exit 22B.) At the split where New York Avenue heads right into Washington, fork left for Interstate 295 toward Richmond. Go only 0.7 mile, then take the exit for Eastern Avenue and the aquatic gardens. Pass Eastern Avenue intersecting from the left. Go straight 0.4 mile, then turn right onto Douglas Street. Follow Douglas Street 0.3 mile, then turn right at a T-intersection with Anacostia Avenue. Follow Anacostia Avenue a few hundred yards, then turn left into the parking lot for the aquatic gardens. Note the closing time posted on the gate.

To return northward on the Baltimore-Washington Parkway, see page 445.

To the aquatic gardens from the east on Route 50: Follow Route 50 West toward Washington. (From the Beltway you can get onto Route 50 West at Exit 19B.) As you near Washington, take the exit for Kenilworth Avenue south toward Interstate 295 and SE Washington. (The signs also say, "To I-95."). From the top of the ramp, go just 0.3 mile, then take the exit for Eastern Avenue and the aquatic gardens. Pass Eastern Avenue intersecting from the left. Go straight 0.4 mile, then turn right onto Douglas Street. Follow Douglas Street 0.3 mile, then turn right at a T-intersection with Anacostia Avenue. Follow Anacostia Avenue a few hundred yards, then turn left into the parking lot for the aquatic gardens. Note the closing time posted on the gate.

To return eastward via Route 50, see page 445.

To the aquatic gardens from the south on Interstate 295 (the Anacostia Freeway): I-295 is accessible from the Capital Beltway at Exit 2B near the Maryland end of the Wilson Bridge across the Potomac River.

Follow I-295 North toward Washington. Stay on the expressway for about 9.5 miles, even after a sign declares that I-295 has officially ended. (You are now on Route 295 in the

District of Columbia.) Take the exit for Eastern Avenue, then make a U-turn to the left across the Eastern Avenue bridge in the lane provided for that purpose. Follow the frontage road 0.4 mile, then turn right onto Douglas Street. Follow Douglas Street 0.3 mile, then turn right at a T-intersection with Anacostia Avenue. Follow Anacostia Avenue a few hundred yards, then turn left into the parking lot for the aquatic gardens. Note the closing time posted on the gate.

Leaving Kenilworth Aquatic Gardens: Return via Anacostia Avenue and Douglas Street to the T-intersection with the Kenilworth Avenue frontage road, where the only way to turn is right. After turning right onto the frontage road, do one of the following:

For I-295 South, simply merge left onto the expressway at the first opportunity.

For Route 50 or the Baltimore-Washington Parkway, follow the frontage road 0.6 mile to Lee Street. Turn left under the expressway, then immediately turn left again onto Kenilworth Avenue north toward Interstate 95 and Route 50. Follow the signs that will guide you north on the Baltimore-Washington Parkway or to Route 50 East toward Annapolis or to Route 50 West toward Washington.

≈   ≈   ≈   ≈

WALKING: The Kenilworth Aquatic Gardens are shown on **Map 56** on page 443. The bold line shows the outlying River Trail, which leads past a freshwater tidal marsh bordering the Anacostia River. Restored from areas that previously were dredged, the 78-acre marsh is an ongoing research project of the National Park Service and other organizations. With its mix of woods, marsh, and open water, the River Trail provides good birding.

36

FORT CIRCLE TRAIL

Walking and bicycling — up to 10 miles (16 kilometers) round-trip. The Fort Circle Trail follows a chain of forested parks southeast of the Anacostia River, where the heights were fortified during the Civil War. Overgrown and obscured by woods and brush, traces of the earthworks remain. Although termed a hike-bike path by the park service, most of the trail is unpaved. A particularly good time for an outing here is mid-May, when the abundant mountain laurel is in bloom.

As shown by the bold line on **Map 57** on page 453, the route described in this chapter climbs the ridge at Fort Dupont Park, then heads southward along deeply wooded hillsides and ravines to Fort Davis and Fort Stanton parks. At times the route necessarily follows park roads for short distances. After 5 miles, the trail ends at the Smithsonian Institution's Anacostia Museum of Afro-American History and Culture. Hike as far as you want and return the way you came. If you do not feel up to the full 10 miles round-trip, the distance to Fort Dupont and back is just 3 miles.

The Fort Circle Trail and the various parks through which it passes are open daily from dawn until dusk. The Anacostia Museum of Afro-American History and Culture is open daily, except Christmas, from 10 A.M. to 5 P.M. For information about the museum's exhibits and programs, telephone (202) 287-3369 weekdays or (202) 357-2700 weekends.

The Fort Circle Trail is managed by the National Park Service; telephone (202) 426-7745.

DURING THE CIVIL WAR the federal government constructed a vast system of earthen forts, trenches, field batteries, and military roads entirely surrounding Washington. About half the forts were in Virginia; a few were in Maryland near the Potomac River above and below the city; the rest were within the federal district in an arc stretching clockwise from the Chain Bridge, across Rock Creek at the Military Road, through northeast Washington, and along the high ridge southeast of the Anacostia River. In this last sector, the chain of forts was intended primarily to prevent the enemy from seizing the Anacostia highlands, from which the Washington Navy Yard, the Arsenal, and two bridges could be bombarded. In other respects the Anacostia forts were not essential to the defense of Washington, since the Anacostia River itself formed an effective barrier against attack south of Bladensburg.

Today the chief legacy of the ring of Civil War forts is about a dozen parks, big and small, and a few military roads that have become modern thoroughfares. In southeast Washington, where forts Mahan, Chaplin, DuPont, Davis, Stanton, and other smaller works stood, the parks form an interconnected chain traversed by the Fort Circle Hiker-Biker Trail, which the walk outlined in this chapter follows in part.

None of the earthworks existed at the outset of the Civil War. In fact, the national capital's only fort when fighting began was Fort Washington, located on the Maryland shore of the Potomac River near Mount Vernon. Obsolete and weakly garrisoned, Fort Washington guarded against a naval attack such as that which the British had mounted a half-century earlier during the war of 1812. (For a discussion of Fort Washington, see Chapter 21.)

As the southern states began to secede from the Union one after another late in 1859 and early in 1860, Washington was gripped by apprehension and intrigue. The city was a southern town surrounded by the slave states of Virginia and Maryland. On Christmas day the Richmond *Examiner* asked, "Can there not be found men bold and brave enough in Maryland to unite with Virginians in seizing the capital in Washington?" Such a stroke appeared altogether possible, especially after Virginia itself seceded on April 17, 1861. Maryland's allegiance continued to be doubtful. For a period food ceased to flow into the capital from the surrounding countryside. Railroad and telegraph lines north of Baltimore were severed, cutting communication between Washington and the northern states that had elected Abraham Lincoln. Only a few hundred federal troops were stationed in the capital. The Washington militia — such as it was and minus various secessionist units — was mustered, and about six hundred men turned out. So matters stood for more than a week until the arrival of three volunteer regiments from New York, Massachusetts, and Rhode Island on April 25 and 26 secured Washington from the immediate threat of betrayal or a *coup de main*. Lines of communication with the North were re-opened. By the end of April there were nearly 10,000 federal troops in Washington. During the following weeks and months, other units poured into the city, transforming the national capital into an armed camp and eventually into an important supply center and staging area. Economically, the war transformed Washington into a boom town.

As federal troops massed in Washington, President Lincoln and his administration took measures against possible attack from Virginia. At 2:00 A.M. on May 24, eight federal regiments crossed the Potomac River and occupied the heights in Arlington and west of Alexandria. During the next few weeks the Union soldiers built six isolated earthworks guarding the southern approaches to Washington. Three forts covered the Georgetown Aqueduct, which carried the Chesapeake and Ohio Canal across the Potomac; two forts guarded the Long Bridge; and one fort was built outside Alexandria.

At first, no forts were built north of the Potomac River. The Union army was supposed to defend Washington in the field if the city were threatened by an attack through Maryland. However, the army's shattering defeat at the first battle of Manassas in July 1861 (see Chapter 1) made it clear that defensive works ringing the capital were necessary. Colonel (later Major General) John Gross Bernard of the army engineers was appointed to supervise construction of a system of forts, redoubts, and batteries. Without regard for private property, lines of rifle trenches and military roads were cut through fields, orchards, and woods. Houses and stands of timber were leveled to provide clear lines of fire. One veteran later wrote, "I remember to have watched from our encampment the disappearance of these forests, and as giant after giant was seen to fall along the edge of the woods, the forest seemed to melt away and disappear as the snow gradually dissolves from the hillsides in springtime." The trees were simply left on the ground, felled so that their branches lay toward the enemy to hinder advancing troops. A soldier noted that "the appearance of thousands of dead trees all lying in the same direction added greatly to the desolate looks of this war afflicted vicinity."

Massive earthworks were erected overlooking stream valleys, roads, and rail arteries entering the city. By the end of 1861 the physical defenses of Washington included forty-eight works armed with 24- and 32-pounder seacoast cannon, 24-pounder siege guns, and smaller field-pieces — over three hundred guns in all. The forward parapets of the forts were twelve to eighteen feet thick. Surrounding each work was an abatis of interwoven branches — a sort of primitive barbed wire. Describing the forts in his vicinity, a solider stationed south of the Potomac wrote: "Every hill is covered with an earthwork or crested with a camp. The plains in all directions are snowed on with tents." However, the forts were simply detached strong points with large gaps between them, especially north of the Potomac, where the works were without permanent garrisons and consequently were poorly maintained.

Union defeat at the second battle of Manassas in August 1862 and Lee's invasion of Maryland caused new alarm for the security of Washington. A commission of army officers recommended constructing still more forts and creating a purely defensive force of 25,000 infantry, 9,000 artillerymen, and 3,000 cavalry. By the end of 1863, the city was guarded by a ring of sixty forts, ninety-three batteries, and 837 guns. Enclosed forts were spaced at intervals of eight hundred to one thousand yards. Approaches and depressions uncovered by the forts were swept by batteries of field guns. The entire periphery was connected by rifle trenches for two ranks of infantry. Circumferential military roads allowed rapid troop movements from one fort to the next. Two especially massive works were Battery Rodgers at Alexandria and Fort Foote on the opposite shore of the Potomac River. These forts had parapets twenty to twenty-five feet thick to absorb fire from naval guns. Armed with 200-pounder Parrott rifles and fifteen-inch Rodman guns, they guarded the water approach to Washington.

Soldiers at the forts followed a routine of drill, artillery practice (firing at old tents for practice), guard duty, work detail, inspections, and meals. Occasionally, they were issued passes into Washington, but most of their time was spent in the immediate vicinity of the forts. Compared to service in the field, life at the forts was safe and relatively comfortable, although the winter months were hard on troops garrisoned in tents or small, overcrowded barracks. In February 1862, a gale flattened most of the tents at the Anacostia forts. During the war hundreds of men died of measles, typhoid, dysentery, and other contagious diseases while garrisoned at the forts. One soldier who at first spoke with enthusiasm of the "immense fortifications" and their big guns (or "big barkers," as he called them), concluded that "a couple of nights' guard duty in the rain and mud, without any kind of shelter, chilled to the bone and as miserable and wretched as it was possible to be, took the romance out of the business of taking care of these forts."

The forts required constant maintenance and improvement. Brush had to be cut from the fields that had been cleared in front of the forts. Because rain and frost caused the earthworks to slump, efforts were made to sod all slopes. As rifled cannons and more powerful shells were developed during the course of the war, the parapets of the forts were thickened. Magazines for ammunition storage also had to be strengthened. Abatis that had rotted or had been used as firewood were replaced. Along the inside of the parapets, board retaining walls were used to hold the earth at a nearly vertical angle, but it became evident that they would have to be replaced with continuous rows of posts. Constructing gun platforms required still more timber. Civilian laborers were often hired to speed completion of the improvements, but the soldiers themselves performed ongoing maintenance.

Even as the war entered its final year and it became obvious that the South was beaten, work on the defenses of Washington continued, justified in part by the important role the forts had played in repelling the Confederate attack led by Jubal Early in July 1864 (see Chapter 25). By the war's end sixty-eight forts had been built and over 900 pieces of artillery and mortars were mounted in the works. Stores of ammunition amounted to 200 rounds per gun. General Bernard thought that his fortifications surpassed anything comparable in Europe at the time.

Once fighting stopped, however, most of the works were quickly stripped of timber and allowed to crumble. For a period, twenty-two of the forts, including Fort Stanton near the southern end of the Fort Circle Trail, were designated for continued use, but soon these were also abandoned. According to Benjamin Franklin Cooling, author of a book and several articles on the Civil War defenses of Washington, the remains of thirty-two forts were still discernible in 1971.

≈   ≈   ≈   ≈

METRO: Metrobus route V6 follows Minnesota Avenue past Randle Circle, located near the northern end of the trail shown on **Map 57** on page 453. The nearest Metrorail station where you can catch bus V6 is Minnesota Avenue (Orange Line).

At the southern end of the trail, Metrobus Route W2 follows Morris Road and Erie Street to the Anacostia Museum near Fort Stanton and Battery Ricketts. The nearest Metrorail station where you can catch bus W2 is Anacostia (Green Line).

Telephone (202) 637-7000 for current Metro information, including schedules, routes, and connections.

≈   ≈   ≈   ≈

AUTOMOBILE DIRECTIONS: The Fort Circle Trail is within Washington southeast of the Anacostia River. (See •36 on **Map 1** on page 6, and also **Map 57** on page 453.) The walk starts at Fort Dupont Park near Randle Circle on Minnesota Avenue. Several approaches are described below.

To the Fort Circle Trail from downtown Washington:
Follow Pennsylvania Avenue southeast across the Anacostia River. At the second traffic light (0.3 mile east of the river), turn left onto Minnesota Avenue and follow it 0.5 mile to Randle Circle. Circle almost 180 degrees, then turn right into Fort Dupont Park. Follow Fort Dupont Drive 0.2 mile to the parking lot for the Fort DuPont Activity Center on the left.

To the Fort Circle Trail from Interstate 495 (the Capital Beltway): Leave the Beltway at Exit 11B for Route 4 North/West (Pennsylvania Avenue). Follow Route 4 North 5.6 miles to an intersection at a traffic light with Branch Avenue. Turn right onto Branch Avenue and go 0.6 mile to Randle Circle. Bear right and go about a quarter of the way around the circle, then turn right into Fort Dupont Park. Follow Fort Dupont Drive 0.2 mile to the parking lot for the Fort DuPont Activity Center on the left.

To the Fort Circle Trail from Interstate 395: Follow I-395 North nearly to its end, then take the exit for Pennsylvania Avenue East. Follow Pennsylvania Avenue southeast across the Anacostia River and under the Anacostia Freeway. At the second traffic light (0.3 mile east of the river), turn left onto Minnesota Avenue and follow it 0.5 mile to Randle Circle. Circle almost 180 degrees, then turn right into Fort Dupont Park. Follow Fort Dupont Drive 0.2 mile to the parking lot for the Fort DuPont Activity Center on the left.

To the Fort Circle Trail from the Anacostia Freeway: The freeway, of course, links the Baltimore-Washington Parkway in the north with Exit 2B of the Capital Beltway in the south. For most of this distance, the freeway is Interstate 295. At its northern end, the freeway is also accessible from Route 50.

Leave the Anacostia Freeway at the exit for Pennsylvania Avenue East. At the second traffic light, turn left onto Minnesota Avenue and follow it 0.5 mile to Randle Circle. Circle almost 180 degrees, then turn right into Fort Dupont Park. Follow Fort Dupont Drive 0.2 mile to the parking lot for the Fort DuPont Activity Center on the left.

≈　　≈　　≈　　≈

WALKING: The route described below is shown by the bold line on **Map 57** opposite. The walk starts at the Fort Dupont Activity Center.

From the corner of the parking lot nearest the Fort Dupont Activity Center, follow an asphalt path downhill 50 yards into a grassy valley. Turn right onto another paved path leading past the side of a summer theater. Follow the path (which after awhile becomes an unpaved track) gradually uphill past minor trails that intersect from either side. Eventually, turn right at a

MAP 57 — Fort Circle Trail

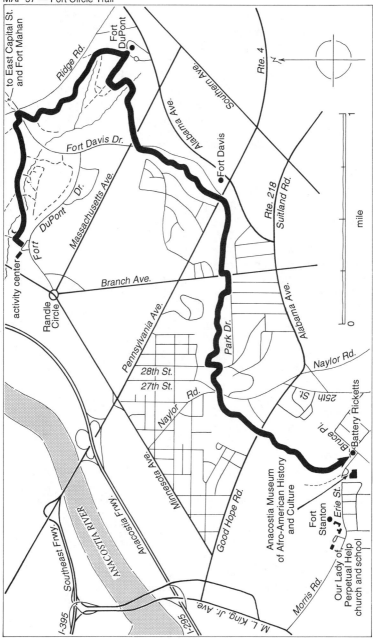

453

T-intersection near the top of the hill. Go 30 yards to Fort Davis Drive, then turn left along the road. Go 40 yards to an intersection with Ridge Road, then turn right across Fort Davis Drive.

Enter the woods on the Fort Circle Park Hiker-Biker Trail. After about 150 yards, fork left uphill to continue on the main track as the trail winds through the woods, at times close to Ridge Road. Pass trails intersecting from either side. Eventually, climb steeply to a loop road, in the center of which are the remains of Fort Dupont.

Fort Dupont was hexagonal in shape, one hundred feet on each side, and fronted with a dry moat eight feet deep. Although the earthworks are severely eroded and covered with brush, the general outline of the fort is evident.

From Fort Dupont, follow a grass and gravel track that re-enters the woods a few dozen yards uphill from where you previously emerged from the woods. At the first intersection, turn left to continue on the wide gravel path (just before another trail intersects from the right). Turn left again in 50 yards. Follow the path along the slope, at one point crossing a small bridge. Continue to Massachusetts Avenue.

With caution, cross Massachusetts Avenue. Follow the path 70 yards through the woods, then cross Fort Davis Drive. Continue to the left on the hiker-biker path, which soon enters the woods. Follow the trail as it winds along the side of the hill. Emerge from the woods at the intersection of Fort Davis Drive and Pennsylvania Avenue.

As shown on the map, Fort Davis is located just uphill from this intersection. A park service sign, located next to a ball field bordering Alabama Avenue, includes a military engineer's drawing of the fort. The fort itself is overgrown by a dense, nearly impenetrable thicket.

With caution, cross Pennsylvania Avenue and re-enter the woods on a wide gravel path. Follow the path to Branch Avenue.

Cross Branch Avenue half-left to an intersection with Park Drive. Follow Park Drive 100 yards, then turn right into the woods. Follow the trail as it winds through ravines to 28th Street.

Turn left at 28th Street. Go 90 yards, then cross the road

and enter the woods. Follow the trail to the intersection of 27th Street and Naylor Road. With caution, cross both roads and continue on the hiker-biker trail to Good Hope Road.

Cross Good Hope Road and continue through the woods on the hiker-biker trail. Cross a ravine on a footbridge and continue uphill to a T-intersection within sight of the brick Anacostia Museum of Afro-American History and Culture on the right, on the other side of Fort Place. Straight ahead in the brush is Battery Ricketts, a small Civil War earthworks.

Battery Ricketts was built during 1861 to sweep the ravine from which you have just climbed. If you want to walk around the thicket to Bruce Place, there is a sign showing a drawing of the fort. The battery protected the eastern approach to Fort Stanton, a major defensive position located about 0.3 mile to the west. Throughout most of the Civil War, Battery Ricketts was armed with three 12-pounder field-pieces and one 8-inch siege mortar. Three more 12-pounder guns were added toward the end of the war. This small position had a perimeter of only 123 yards, yet its authorized garrison was 42 artillerymen and 164 infantry. These numbers were based on standards that specified two men per yard of front perimeter, one man per yard of rear perimeter, and three reliefs of artillerymen per gun.

Fort Stanton was considerably larger than Battery Ricketts. With a perimeter of 322 yards, it mounted eighteen guns and called for a garrison of 270 artillerymen and 213 infantry. In fact, however, both Battery Ricketts and Fort Stanton were manned at less than one-fourth their authorized strength.

The location of Fort Stanton is shown on Map 57. For enthusiasts who don't mind the dense brush, some of its earthworks are still discernible behind Our Lady of Perpetual Help School. On clear days there is a panoramic view of Washington from the brow of the hill west of the school.

If you have not arranged a car shuttle, return to your starting point by the way you came.

≈   ≈   ≈   ≈

From Fort Dupont Park the Fort Circle Hiker-Biker Trail also extends north to East Capitol Street, then still farther north to Fort Mahan Park. However, the southern part of the trail outlined in this chapter is both longer and more attractive than the section north of Ridge Road.

37

CALVERT CLIFFS STATE PARK

Walking — 4 or more miles (6.4 or more kilometers). As shown on the bottom panel of **Map 58** on page 460, various trails lead to and from the Chesapeake shore at Calvert Cliffs State Park. The bold line traces the most direct route (2 miles each way), but hikers who want a longer excursion can explore wooded ravines and ridges on a network of blazed trails.

Please **stay off the cliffs** and even the cliff tops; after all, the cliffs are only clay and are prone to slumping. **Hunting** is allowed in season in the area north of the service road, so if you want to explore that part of the park, you may prefer to walk on Sunday, when hunting is prohibited — or you can call for specific information on the hunting schedule.

The days when Calvert Cliffs State Park is open change with the seasons. From Memorial Day weekend through Labor Day, the park is open daily. From early April through late May, and from early September through October, the park is open Friday, Saturday, and Sunday. And from November through March, the park is closed. On days when the park is open, the hours are 10 A.M. to 6 P.M., but everyone must leave the beach by 5. An admission fee is charged. Dogs and swimming are prohibited. During summer a naturalist is usually at the beach to teach people how to look for fossils and to help identify what they find.

Calvert Cliffs State Park is managed by the Maryland State Forest and Park Service. The park is administered from Point Lookout State Park; telephone (301) 872-5688.

While you are at Calvert Cliffs State Park, you may also want to visit the adjacent Middleham Chapel, built in 1748 on the site of an older chapel established in 1684 (see page 461).

SHARK TEETH. *Ancient* shark teeth. More precisely, shark teeth from the early and middle Miocene Epoch — or that is, from about twenty-four to twelve million years ago. The tangible remains of prehistoric sharks are among the chief attractions of Calvert Cliffs State Park. Just as tourists scour Florida beaches for seashells, so fossil hunters comb the sand along the shore of Chesapeake Bay in Calvert County, looking for pointed, enameled, triangular or Y-shaped objects that range in length from half an inch to five inches and in color from black through gray to white.

The clay cliffs along the Calvert County shore show a marked stratification. The lower, fossil-bearing layers are made of fine sand, silt, and clay deposited as sediment at the bottom of a shallow sea that covered southern Maryland during the Miocene Epoch. Algae and aquatic plants flourished in the sunlit shallows, which formed a rich nursery for marine life. The climate is thought to have been like that of North and South Carolina today, and fossils show that the coastal waters teemed with varieties of coral, snails, clams, oysters, scallops, bony fishes, and other vertebrates, including turtles, crocodiles, sea-cows, porpoises, whales, rays, and sharks.

The fossil remnants of these animals are simply their hard parts — mollusk shells, vertebrate skeletons, and teeth — that did not deteriorate after the creatures died and their bodies settled to the bottom. These remains were covered and preserved by sediments that were carried to the sea by rivers or eroded from the shore by wave action. In the case of the Miocene sharks, only the teeth and larger vertebrae remain today, as shark skeletons are cartilaginous rather than bony and ordinarily disintegrate with the rest of the body. The thick strata of sand, silt, and clay in which the various fossils are buried stand now, in part, above sea level because of shifts in the earth's crust and also because far more water presently is amassed in the polar ice caps than was the case during the relatively warm Miocene Epoch.

The abundance of shark teeth found along the shore of Calvert County reflects the presence of great numbers of sharks, apparently attracted by young whales that made easy prey. A pamphlet prepared by Jeanne D. McClennan of the Maryland Geological Survey mentions that numerous bones of immature whales have been recovered in the area, suggesting that it was a calving ground. Many of these bones show the scratches and scars of shark teeth.

Another reason for the abundance of shark teeth is that sharks have a nearly unlimited supply. Arrayed in row after row, the teeth are anchored not in the jaw but merely in the gums. If a tooth is lost, as often happens, it is soon replaced by another that moves forward from the row behind. Also, young sharks replace their teeth frequently — every seven or eight days in one common present-day species.

It is likely that ancient sharks shared these characteristics, for sharks are among the most successful of nature's creatures, having remained essentially unmodified by evolution during periods that have seen the development and extinction of countless varieties of other animals. As old as the Miocene shark teeth are, they are of relatively recent origin compared to Paleocene and Eocene shark teeth found in places along the Potomac River; these two epochs lasted from sixty-six to thirty-seven million years ago. Even older remains occur in beds of shale near Cleveland, Ohio. Consisting of calcified cartilage and actual impressions of skin and body shape, the Ohio fossils are from a species of shark not very different from those alive today, but dating from more than 350 million years ago, well before the age of the dinosaurs. The fossilized remains of one of these primitive sharks can be seen at the Natural History Museum in Washington.

A final note. If you are bent on finding fossil shark teeth at Calvert Cliffs, the best time of year to look is early spring, after winter storms have exposed a fresh crop to view and before the area is picked over by summer visitors. The fossils are found at the surf line along the beach. If the park naturalist is at the beach during your visit, he can show you how to look for them.

≈　　　≈　　　≈　　　≈

AUTOMOBILE DIRECTIONS: Calvert Cliffs State Park is located on the shore of Chesapeake Bay about 50 miles southeast of Washington. (See the top panel of **Map 58** on page 460; Calvert Cliffs is at the lower-right corner.) Access is provided by Route 4, which is the extension of **Pennsylvania Avenue** out of the city.

To Calvert Cliffs from Interstate 495 (the Capital Beltway): Leave the Beltway at Exit 11A for Route 4 South (Pennsylvania Avenue). This exit occurs about half-way between the interchange with Route 50 and the Wilson Bridge across the Potomac River.

From the Beltway, follow Route 4 South past Upper Marlboro and Prince Frederick for about 45 miles to the exit on the left for Calvert Cliffs State Park. After leaving Route 4, go a few hundred yards to an intersection with Route 765 (Trueman Road); the park entrance is straight ahead.

≈　　　≈　　　≈　　　≈

WALKING: The most direct route to the beach (2 miles each way) is shown by the bold line on **Map 58** on page 460. Called

MAP 58 — Calvert Cliffs State Park

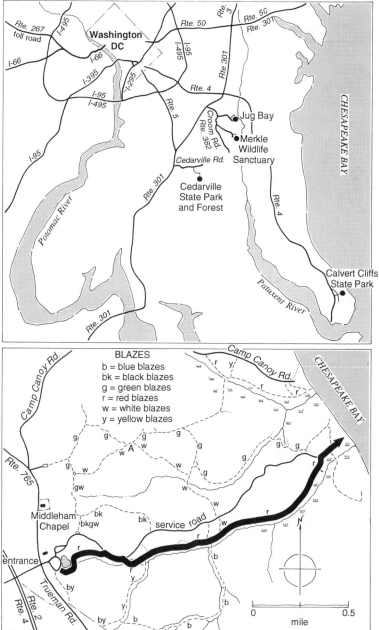

the Cliff Trail, this route is marked with red blazes and is described below.

From the loop road at the park entrance, follow the red-blazed Cliff Trail to the right of a pond on a boardwalk, then to the left across an earth dam and into the woods. Merge with the service road and follow it right 110 yards, then veer right to continue along a brook on the red-blazed foot trail. Continue more or less straight past trails intersecting from right and left. Eventually, after following the edge of swampy woods on the right for more than half a mile, again merge with the service road and follow it right 400 yards straight to the beach.

As Map 58 indicates, there are a number of ways to return to the parking area. The service road is easy and direct. The green-blazed trail is more circuitous and scenic, but in places is not well maintained. One approach is to take the green trail to a point — marked A on Map 58 — where it briefly merges with the white trail, and from there follow the white trail back to the parking lot.

There is another small beach at Calvert Cliffs State Park near the end of Camp Canoy Road. It is accessible via a spur trail off the green trail.

≈   ≈   ≈   ≈

MIDDLEHAM CHAPEL: As mentioned in the introduction to this chapter, while you are at Calvert Cliffs State Park, you may want to stop by briefly at Middleham Chapel, a very small and attractive brick Episcopal church built in 1748 on the site of a wooden chapel of ease first established here in 1684. To see Middleham Chapel, turn right out the park entrance and go north on Trueman Road just 0.3 mile.

461

38

JUG BAY NATURAL AREA
at Patuxent River Park
MERKLE WILDLIFE SANCTUARY

Walking and bicycling. Amounting together to nearly 4,000 acres, the Jug Bay Natural Area and the adjacent Merkle Wildlife Sanctuary are located in rural Prince George's County, Maryland, 20 miles southeast of Washington. **Map 59** on page 469 shows the various trails, ranging from short loops in the immediate vicinity of the Jug Bay and Merkle visitor centers to a more far-flung system where you can easily walk for hours.

Another feature is the **Chesapeake Bay Critical Area Driving Tour**, shown by the bold line on Map 59. The tour road is four miles long (6.4 kilometers) and links the Jug Bay and Merkle areas. The road is open to cars each Sunday year-round (weather permitting) from 10 A.M. to 3 P.M. and is open to hikers and bicyclists each Saturday, May through mid-September, from 10 to 4. Within the Merkle refuge, the tour road is not hard-paved and is unsuitable for thin-tired bicycles. For cars, the tour road is one-way southbound, starting at Selby's Landing in the Jug Bay area. Hikers and cyclists, however, may start at either end and go back and forth as necessary.

For hikers willing to walk 8 miles (12.9 kilometers) round-trip between Jug Bay and the observation platform at the Mattaponi Creek bridge, the dotted line on Map 59 shows a route that passes though a variety of habitats, including freshwater marsh, wooded uplands and ravines, and cultivated fields. If you go on a Saturday when the tour road is open to walkers, you can continue into the Merkle area, where there is an observation tower that overlooks the big bend in the river.

The Jug Bay Natural Area is open daily from 8 A.M. until dusk; the precise closing time is posted at the gate and of course changes with the seasons. At Jug Bay, dogs must be leashed and off-road bicycling is permitted only on trails that are identified by signs as horse paths. In addition to the trails there are the Patuxent Village and the Duvall Tool Museum, both focusing on life on the region's farms and along the river during the nineteenth century. Call ahead of time for information on museum hours, guided walks, and boat tours. The Jug Bay area is managed by the Department of Parks and Recreation, Prince George's County, Maryland-National Capital Park and Planning Commission; telephone (301) 627-6074. The Merkle Wildlife Sanctuary is open daily from 8 A.M. to 5 P.M. Dogs and off-road bicycling are prohibited. The excellent Merkle Visitor Center is open daily from 10 A.M. to 4 P.M. and features a variety of exhibits. The Merkle area is managed by the Maryland Department of Natural Resources; telephone (301) 888-1410 for the schedule of upcoming group programs (reservations are required).

ABOUT EIGHT THOUSAND CANADA GEESE (identified by their large size, black heads and necks, and white cheeks) winter along the Patuxent River, mostly at the Jug Bay Natural Area and neighboring Merkle Wildlife Sanctuary. In January 1995, about 17,500 Canada geese were counted on Maryland's Western Shore and 242,000 on the Eastern Shore — many times more than during the first three or four decades of the twentieth century, but less than half the 600,000 that wintered in Maryland during the early 1980s.

The increase in wintering Canada geese in Maryland prior to the mid-'80s was in part fostered by the establishment of large wildlife refuges, including the federal government's Blackwater refuge in 1932 and Eastern Neck Island in 1962. Private efforts were also effective, as at Edgar Merkle's 400-acre farm, where in the 1930s Merkle inaugurated a program of habitat improvement and crop management that eventually resulted in thousands of wintering geese. With the understanding that the area would continue to be managed for Canada geese, the Maryland Department of Natural Resources acquired the Merkle property in 1970 (partly by purchase and partly by gift) and has since bought adjoining tracts to create a state wildlife sanctuary of more than 1,600 acres.

The increase in wintering Canada geese in the Chesapeake region before the mid-1980s was also the result of changes in agriculture, principally the planting of more corn and soybeans starting in the 1930s and '40s. The mechanical reapers that harvest these crops leave as much as 10 percent of the kernels and beans on the ground, where they are eaten by geese that graze on the stubble fields. The result was so-called "short-stopping," meaning the tendency for goose populations that formerly wintered farther south in the Carolinas to stop and stay for the winter in the Chesapeake region, as most Canada geese migrating southward along the Atlantic flyway now do. Maryland alone accounted for two-thirds of the Atlantic population in the early 1980s. Since then the population of migratory Canada geese that winter on the East Coast from New England to the Carolinas has declined from 900,000 to 650,000, of which about 40 percent are counted in Maryland.

The recent precipitous decline of migratory Canada geese is thought to be the result of over-hunting, particularly on the Eastern Shore, where marshaling hunting rights on private farm fields and accommodating and feeding visiting hunters has become big business. Hunting is estimated to cause about 85 percent of deaths among Canada geese. In particular, hunting early in the season kills off a disproportionately large number of unwary juvenile birds and chases the rest away. Studies show that from 1962 to 1974, when the winter population of Canada geese was increasing in Maryland, the adult survival rate from one year to a subsequent year was about 82 percent; but during the mid-1980s, the survival rate dropped below 70 percent as Maryland attracted large numbers of hunters from other states. To counter the decline in wintering Canada geese, Maryland shortened the hunting season, set lower bag limits, and started a program (funded by revenues from non-resident hunting licenses) to pay farmers whose fields are not leased for hunting to leave crops standing in order to attract and feed geese in relatively safe places. As a result, the decline in the number of wintering Canada geese appeared to have been arrested, at least in Maryland. However, responding in 1995 to a very poor breeding season, the federal Fish and Wildlife Service declared a moratorium, subject to annual review, that bars the hunting of Canada geese wintering along the entire East Coast.

Although a distinct subspecies of Canada goose is now fairly common in the Chesapeake region even during summer, migrating Canadas do not begin to arrive in great numbers until late September, reaching a peak in November. Some continue farther south for the winter, and even within the Chesapeake area there is a good deal of movement throughout the winter, as flocks exhaust one food source and move to another.

Northward migration begins as early as the second week of February, and the vast majority of migratory Canada geese are gone by the end of March. The trip from the Chesapeake region is about 1,900 miles and lasts four to six weeks. The birds fly several hundred miles at a jump, then rest and feed for two or three days in preparation for the next flight. The path of migration is more or less straight north to the Ungava Peninsula east of Hudson and James bays, where the birds nest and breed. The number of young that hatch and survive depends greatly on how early the snow and ice melt on the breeding grounds, but unseasonably late storms, predation by foxes, hunting by Innuit, and even the activities of caribou (which are known to eat goose eggs) are also factors. The geese stay at the breeding grounds until August, when they begin to mass along the shores of the bays for the flight south.

The recovery of banded birds has shown that the Canada geese that summer in Ungava and winter in the Chesapeake region form a sub-group (or subspecies or geographic race) among all those Canada geese that breed across the whole width of the continent. According to ornithologists, there are at least thirteen distinct populations of Canada geese. For the most part, they do not mix, and each population has its own breeding and wintering grounds and migration route between the two. The interaction of genetics and persistent behavior over thousands of years has led to substantial differences in the size of birds belonging to the different groups. Mid-continental Canada geese weigh up to eighteen pounds, while those seen in the Chesapeake region weigh up to nine pounds, and those found along the Pacific coast weigh just three pounds. The genetic differences that have developed among subspecies are both a cause and effect of the fact that young Canada geese adhere closely to family groups and learn from parent birds where to breed, where to winter, and where to migrate. Of geese that are banded in Maryland and later recovered, about 90 percent are found in the locality — often even the same pond — where they were banded one or more years earlier. Even so, geese are adaptable enough to react to changed circumstances, as demonstrated by the previously-mentioned fact that most of the geese of the Atlantic flyway have shifted their wintering grounds northward to the Chesapeake during the mid-1900s, and yet other populations that winter in Pennsylvania, New Jersey, New York, and Connecticut are developing.

Another recent phenomenon has been the increase among Canada geese that spend the entire year in Maryland and other East Coast states, residing not only at refuges like the Merkle Wildlife Sanctuary (where Edgar Merkle introduced breeding pairs in the 1930s) but also at parks, golf courses, public watershed areas, and other places where they are relatively safe from hunters — and where their droppings are problematic. These year-round residents are another genetically distinct sub-group, somewhat larger than the Canada geese that migrate to the Chesapeake region for the winter. In Maryland the population of resident Canada geese, which are sometimes called "street geese" because of the frequency with which they show up even in suburban residential areas, was estimated at ten thousand in 1991 and at twenty-five thousand in 1995. On the East Coast as a whole, the stay-at-home geese are now thought to outnumber the migratory geese. Because they are present during the growing season, the resident Canada geese can do considerable damage to crops. To reduce their numbers, Maryland has instituted a short hunting season during the first half of September, before the migratory geese arrive.

Another large bird seen virtually without fail at the Jug Bay and Merkle areas from spring through early fall is the osprey, or fish hawk. Its body is dark above and white below, and its head has a broad band across the cheeks and eyes, rather like the Lone Ranger's mask. Once endangered by pesticides but now common in the Chesapeake region, ospreys build big nests of sticks, sometimes in trees but more often on almost any elevated surface surrounded by water, including shooting blinds, navigational markers, and nesting platforms provided by people. There are several nests at the Merkle refuge, including one atop the silo.

Ospreys are the only hawks that fish by plunging into the water — as opposed to eagles, which scavenge dead fish and sometimes catch live ones by swooping close to the surface and snatching them out with their talons. Circling at a height of 50 to 150 feet, an osprey hovers with beating wings when it sees a fish near the surface, then drops feet first into the water, from which it immediately emerges and takes off, for ospreys are not swimmers. As it gains altitude, the osprey interrupts its wing beats for a moment to shudder in mid-air like a dog shaking itself, and then — if it has not caught a fish — resume its circling. It is a dramatic performance, and one that is repeated again and again until a fish is caught and the osprey flies to its nest with its gleaming prey clamped in its talons.

≈   ≈   ≈   ≈

AUTOMOBILE DIRECTIONS: The Jug Bay Natural Area and the adjacent **Merkle Wildlife Sanctuary** are located in Maryland 20 miles southeast of Washington, not far from the interchange between Route 4 and Route 301. (See the top panel of **Map 58** on page 460, and also the lower-left corner of **Map 59** on page 469.) Directions to both the Jug Bay and Merkle areas are provided below. There are trails for walking at both places, but motorists interested in the Chesapeake Bay Critical Area Driving Tour must start at Jug Bay.

From Interstate 495 (the Capital Beltway): Leave the Beltway at Exit 11A for Route 4 (Pennsylvania Avenue)

South/East. Follow Route 4 for 7.7 miles to the exit for Route 301 South, which occurs shortly after the exit for Upper Marlboro. From the bottom of the exit ramp, follow Route 301 South 3.5 miles to an intersection at a traffic light for Route 382 (Croom Road). Turn left onto Route 382 and follow it 2.9 miles to an intersection with Croom Airport Road on the left. For Jug Bay and the Critical Area Driving Tour, turn left and continue as described in the next paragraph. To drive directly to the Merkle Wildlife Sanctuary, continue as described in the second paragraph below.

For Jug Bay and the Critical Area Driving Tour: Follow Croom Airport Road 0.7 to the Patuxent River Park entrance. For the Jug Bay Natural Area, turn left and go 1.6 miles to the end of the road at the visitor center and observation tower. For the Driving Tour, however, continue straight 0.9 mile, then turn left and follow the tour route past Selby's Landing, across Mattaponi Creek, and into the Merkle Wildlife Sanctuary, as shown by the bold line on Map 59. Occasionally the tour route passes small parking areas where trails lead to an observation tower, a boardwalk, and other vantage points. When you reach the end of the tour road, be sure to stop by the outstanding Merkle Visitor Center.

To drive directly to the Merkle Wildlife Sanctuary: Continue straight on Route 382 (Croom Road) past the intersection with Croom Airport Road. Go 1.1 miles, then turn left onto St. Thomas Church Road and go 2.9 miles to the entrance of the Merkle Wildlife Sanctuary on the left.

≈   ≈   ≈   ≈

WALKING and BICYCLING: Trails at the Jug Bay Natural Area and the Merkle Wildlife Sanctuary are shown on **Map 59** opposite.

The Chesapeake Bay Critical Area Driving Tour provides good walking and bicycling on Saturdays, May through mid-September, from 10 A.M. to 4 P.M. The tour route is shown by the bold line on Map 59. Hikers and cyclists may start at either end and go back and forth. Within the Merkle area, the tour route occasionally passes small parking areas where trails (not open to cyclists) lead to an observation tower, a boardwalk, and other vantage points.

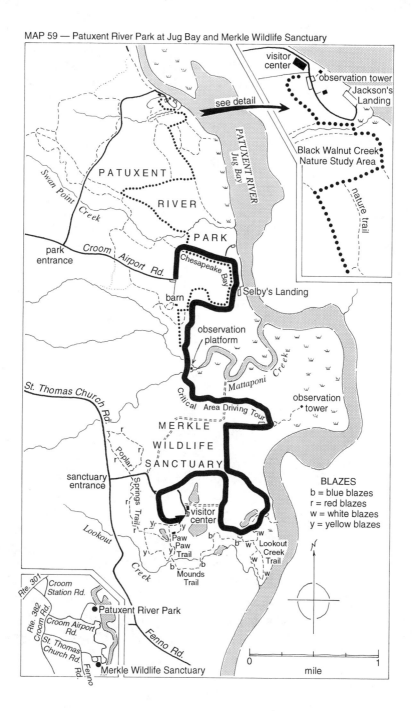

MAP 59 — Patuxent River Park at Jug Bay and Merkle Wildlife Sanctuary

visitor center

observation tower

Jackson's Landing

see detail

Black Walnut Creek
Nature Study Area

nature trail

PATUXENT
RIVER
PARK

PATUXENT RIVER
Jug Bay

Swan Point Creek

park entrance

Croom Airport Rd.

Chesapeake Bay

barn

Selby's Landing

observation platform

Mattaponi Creek

Critical Area Driving Tour

observation tower

St. Thomas Church Rd.

MERKLE
WILDLIFE
SANCTUARY

sanctuary entrance

Poplar

Springs Trail

Lookout

visitor center

Paw Paw Trail

Mounds Trail

Lookout Creek Trail

Creek

BLAZES
b = blue blazes
r = red blazes
w = white blazes
y = yellow blazes

N

Rte. 301
Croom Station Rd.
Rte. 382
Croom Rd.
Croom Airport Rd.
St. Thomas Church Rd.

Patuxent River Park

Fenno Rd.

Merkle Wildlife Sanctuary

0   mile   1

469

The dotted line on Map 59 shows an **8-mile walk** (round-trip) that starts at Jug Bay and goes south to the bridge and observation deck at Mattaponi Creek. If you go on a Saturday when the Chesapeake Bay Critical Area tour road is open to hikers, you can continue into the Merkle Wildlife Sanctuary. Directions are as follows:

From the parking area at the Jug Bay office and observation tower, follow a wood-chip path away from the river and downhill past a sign for the Black Walnut Creek Nature Study Area, as shown on the detail at the upper-right corner of Map 59. Follow the bottom of a ravine for a few dozen yards, then fork left. At a fence, bear right across Black Walnut Creek on a boardwalk, then fork left and continue with the broad Patuxent River on the left. A dozen yards after the end of the boardwalk, fork right uphill toward the "hiking trails" (as declared by a sign). Go 230 yards to a T-intersection (in the process passing a "nature trail" on the left). At the T-intersection, turn left and go several hundred yards, with the Patuxent River sometimes discernible through the trees on the left. At the first trail junction, turn right. Pass a trail intersecting from the right and eventually climb to a T-intersection. Turn left and follow the wide path, almost immediately passing a trail intersecting from the right.

Eventually, the wide path passes through a ravine, then emerges from the woods at a road. Cross the road and continue 5 yards to a T-intersection. Turn left and go 50 yards to the corner of a large field (old Croom Airport). Continue clockwise around the field on a trail that more or less parallels the road. Pass Selby's Landing and continue clockwise around the field. After swerving right away from the road to go around some woods, the trail again borders the road briefly, with a barn visible in the distance to the right. (As of 1996 there was a sign about bluebirds here.) Turn right through a gate and follow the edge of the woods away from the road and toward the barn. About 70 yards before the barn, turn left into the woods on a dirt road and follow it straight past trails intersecting from either side. Rejoin the paved tour road and follow it right downhill to the long wooden bridge at Mattaponi Creek, where there is an observation platform about half way across.

From Mattaponi Creek return by the way you came, or use Map 59 to devise another route.

39

CEDARVILLE STATE FOREST AND PARK

Walking and ski touring — 6 miles (9.7 kilometers). The route shown on **Map 60** on page 477 follows dirt roads and trails through the best part of this 4,000-acre demonstration forest, passing through old woods and occasionally skirting areas that have been cut recently and replanted. As shown on the map, other trails — including the 6-mile orange trail — provide the opportunity for still more hiking.

Cedarville State Forest and Park is open daily from 8 A.M. until sunset. Dogs must be leashed. Because **hunting** is allowed in season, you may prefer to walk on Sunday, when hunting is prohibited — or you can call for specific information on the hunting schedule.

Cedarville is managed by the Maryland State Forest and Park Service and is administered from the Merkle Wildlife Sanctuary office; telephone (301) 888-1410.

YOU MAY HAVE HEARD of cruises to nowhere: a voyage without destination or ports of call, purely for the pleasure of being out on the open ocean. Here is the sylvan equivalent: a woodland walk to nowhere. This excursion follows footpaths and dirt roads through an extensive forest, without particular highlights along the way, but thoroughly pleasant nonetheless.

As part of the Coastal Plain physiographic province, the Cedarville area is flat but not altogether without topographic variety. To some extent the level terrain, which stands at an elevation of about two hundred feet in the vicinity of Cedarville, has been dissected by the headwaters of the Wicomico River, an arm of the Potomac estuary. The streams have low volumes, low gradients, and correspondingly low erosive power, resulting is a branching system of shallow ravines. Zekiah Swamp Run, the Wicomico's main tributary, crosses Forest Road within the state property at an elevation of about 150 feet; thus its average gradient for the seventeen miles downstream to tidewater is merely seventeen hundredths of 1 percent — or that is, less than nine feet of descent per mile. The swamp itself starts about a mile below the southern boundary of the state forest and extends uninterrupted to saltwater in a belt about half a mile wide, making it the largest freshwater swamp in Maryland.

According to a geologic map of Maryland prepared by the Maryland Geological Survey, the Cedarville Area — indeed, much of southern Maryland — is a vast sand and gravel flat. These materials are thought to be fluvial deposits and remnants of deltas left by ancient streams, including ancestors of the Potomac, Patuxent, and Susquehanna rivers, that meandered across the plain in ever-shifting courses between five million and two million years ago. More recently, during periods of low sea level caused by the amassment of water in continental glaciers, these rivers entrenched themselves in their present courses, which have now become partly flooded by the resurgence of the sea as the ice has, in large part, melted. The widespread deposits of sand and gravel may also be associated with former shorelines that existed when the ocean, which inundated southern Maryland between twenty-four and five million years ago, slowly receded across the region. The picture is further complicated by relatively recent intervals of high sea level between periods of continental glaciation, but it is thought that the ocean rose no more than a hundred feet above its present level during these episodes. Finally, some sand formations appear to be remnants of ancient wind-blown dunes. In any case, covered by a veneer of meager topsoil, the sand and gravel near Cedarville are sufficiently free of silt and clay to be mined commercially. On the state land, small borrow pits are visible where sand and gravel were dug for the forest roads.

The state's acquisition of land to demonstrate good forestry techniques began at Cedarville in 1930, after a long period of agricultural decline and farm abandonment in southern Maryland. A vegetation map of Maryland prepared in 1976 by the Department of Geography and Environmental Engineering at Johns Hopkins University indicates that, where not cut and replanted in pines, the upland within the state forest is dominated by chestnut oak, post oak, and blackjack oak — all species that are tolerant of dry, impoverished, gravelly soil. In ravines red maple, tulip poplar, river birch, and sycamore are common. Throughout the forest other common trees in decreasing order of frequency are black gum, white oak, sassafras, American holly, Virginia pine, black oak, beech, flowering dogwood, sweet gum, and various other species of oak and also hickory. This ranking, of course, is a generalization that may not accurately reflect conditions at any specific spot. As for the name "Cedarville," it was

taken from a nearby post office. Eastern redcedars may once have been common during the shift from exhausted tobacco farms to forest, but if so, they have long since been overshadowed by the dominant hardwoods and by stands of Virginia and loblolly pine.

As a state forest, Cedarville is half park, half business. The area is managed for recreation (including hiking, hunting, and youth group camping) and the production of timber and other natural resources. For the most part, the cutting of timber is confined to plantations of Virginia and loblolly pine, sold as pulpwood to paper mills as far away as Pennsylvania and West Virginia. The walk outlined on Map 60 and described at the end of this chapter passes a few areas that have been cut or thinned at different times in the last three decades and that show various stages of forest resurgence. Some tracts have been cut clear and left to themselves. Because many deciduous species (but not pines) can sprout back from stumps, this technique favors resurgence by hardwoods, which often are seen to have two or three trunks that once were shoots growing from a single stump. Other areas have been replanted with seedlings of loblolly pine, favored as a pulpwood because it grows faster and is more resistant to disease and to windstorms than is Virginia pine. When stands of loblolly pine are harvested, a common practice is to leave a few mature trees — about ten per acre — to repropagate the area. After a few years, when the seedlings are established, the seed trees are cut also. To supplement natural repropagation, seedlings are also planted by hand. Another harvesting technique seen in different areas of the state forest is to cut parallel swaths through stands of pines. These areas are then reseeded in part by the trees left standing in the adjacent strips, which eventually are harvested in turn.

It is possible that in the future some of these timber operations will occur along the route described below (just as they have occurred in the past), altering appearances for short stretches, but the location of the trails and roads should remain unchanged.

≈   ≈   ≈   ≈

AUTOMOBILE DIRECTIONS: Cedarville State Forest and Park is located about 25 miles southeast of Washington. (See the corner panel on **Map 60** opposite.)

To Cedarville State Forest and Park from Interstate 495 (the Capital Beltway): Leave the Beltway at Exit 7A for Route 5 South (Branch Avenue) toward Waldorf. This exit occurs about two thirds of the way between the interchange with Route 50 and the Wilson Bridge across the Potomac River.

MAP 60 — Cedarville State Park and Forest

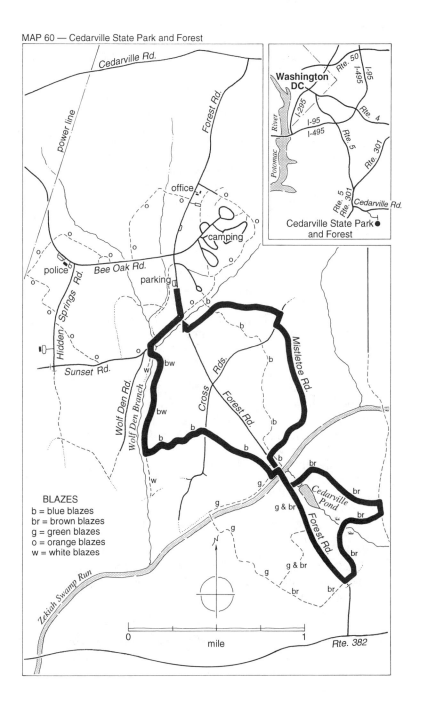

BLAZES
b = blue blazes
br = brown blazes
g = green blazes
o = orange blazes
w = white blazes

477

From the Beltway, follow Route 5 South more than 11 miles to a crossroads at a traffic light where McKendree Road intersects from the right and Cedarville Road from the left. Turn left onto Cedarville Road and go 2.3 miles to the entrance to Cedarville State Forest at Bee Oak Road. Turn right onto Bee Oak Road and follow it 1.7 miles, in the process passing the office of the Natural Resources Police. At a crossroads, turn right and follow a gravel road (Forest Road) 0.3 mile to a parking area on the right, just beyond a concrete-block charcoal kiln. Occasionally, this section of Forest Road is closed to automobiles, in which case you may have to turn left toward the maintenance area and go to the first parking lot by the side of the road.

≈   ≈   ≈   ≈

WALKING: The 6-mile route described below is shown by the bold line on **Map 60** on page 477.

From the parking lot by the charcoal kiln, follow Forest Road downhill. (Here and at other times when the route follows roads that are open to automobiles, walk on the far left and step off the road as cars approach.) Follow Forest Road about 140 yards, then turn right past a gate onto Sunset Road. After crossing a small bridge over Wolf Den Branch, go 25 yards, then turn left onto a footpath marked with blue and white blazes. Go 60 yards, then bear left on the blue-blazed trail across a footbridge. Follow the trail (which occasionally is marked with white as well as blue blazes) through the woods. Eventually, turn left on the blue-blazed trail where the white-blazed trail continues straight. Follow the blue trail as it zigzags through the woods, crosses a dirt road, and continues through the woods. At a T-intersection in front of Zekiah Swamp Run, turn left and follow the streambank 60 yards to Forest Road.

Turn right onto Forest Road and follow it straight 200 yards. When the main road curves left to a parking area, continue straight past a gate on Forest Road. Follow the road as it gradually climbs past Cedarville Pond, located downhill to the left. Continue straight past an area on the right where the trees, now 20 or 30 feet tall, were cut in 1983 and 1984.

Eventually, turn left at a gate at the edge of the state forest, within sight of some houses. Follow a brown-blazed woods road 125 yards, then bear left on the main track. Continue as the trail winds through the woods. Cross a swampy area where a stream has been dammed by beavers. Follow the trail uphill and through the woods, then turn left at a T-intersection. Go only 175 yards, then turn left again adjacent to an area where the trees were harvested in strips in 1990. Follow the trail through the woods and downhill below an earth dam at Cedarville Pond. Pass through the parking lot, then turn right onto Forest Road.

Follow Forest Road 300 yards, then turn right onto Mistletoe Road. Continue past a gate and then past an area on the left that was cut in 1991. Eventually, at an intersection with another woods road (Cross Road), turn right. Go 50 yards, then turn left onto a narrow, rough path though young, dense woods. Before long, the path widens as it enters older forest. Follow the path to a T-intersection with Forest Road. Turn right and follow Forest Road to the parking lot by the charcoal kiln.

IF YOU HAVE ENJOYED this book, you or your friends may also like some of the other guidebooks listed below. All follow the same format. These guides are widely available at bookstores, nature stores, and outfitters, or you can write to Rambler Books, 1430 Park Avenue, Baltimore, MD 21217, for current prices and ordering information.

DAY TRIPS IN DELMARVA

This book explores the Delmarva Peninsula, consisting of southern Delaware and the Eastern Shore of Maryland and Virginia. Emphasis is on the region's scenic back roads, historic towns, wildlife refuges, parks, undeveloped beaches, and trails for hiking and bicycling. *Day Trips in Delmarva* includes commentary, detailed directions, and forty-four maps showing car tours, walks, and bicycle trips.

"Few realize the wealth of sights the Delmarva Peninsula holds, which is why *Day Trips in Delmarva* is such an infinitely enjoyable book."—*Baltimore Magazine* • "The best organized, best written, most comprehensive and practical guide to daytrips on the Delmarva Peninsula."—*The Easton Star Democrat*

COUNTRY WALKS NEAR BALTIMORE

Like *Country Walks Near Washington*, this book includes directions, maps, and substantive essays, all of which have been updated for the third edition. Some of the trails are suitable for bicycling, including the Northern Central Railroad Trail, one of the best rails-to-trails conversions in the mid-Atlantic region.

"Fisher's books, with his own photos illustrating them, are models of pith and practicality. . . . The maps for '*Country Walks*' excel."—*Baltimore Sun*

COUNTRY WALKS & BIKEWAYS IN THE PHILADELPHIA REGION

This guidebook explores the Delaware Valley's parks, wildlife refuges, and trail networks from Wilmington in the south to Easton in the north, including eighty-five miles of canal trails along the Delaware River.

COUNTRY WALKS NEAR BOSTON

"An invaluable paperback."—*Boston Sunday Globe.* • "This is my favorite trail guide. . . . Unlike the others, it features a lot of social, cultural, and natural history."—*Boston Phoenix*

COUNTRY WALKS NEAR CHICAGO

"A handy guide. . . . The general information sections—which, if combined, constitute three-fourths of the book—are excellent."—*Chicago Tribune*